Cognitive Approaches to Lexical Semantics

W DE G

Cognitive Linguistics Research
23

Editors
René Dirven
Ronald W. Langacker
John R. Taylor

Mouton de Gruyter
Berlin · New York

Cognitive Approaches to Lexical Semantics

Edited by
Hubert Cuyckens
René Dirven
John R. Taylor

Mouton de Gruyter
Berlin · New York 2003

Mouton de Gruyter (formerly Mouton, The Hague)
is a Division of Walter de Gruyter GmbH & Co. KG, Berlin

∞ Printed on acid-free paper
which falls within
the guidelines of the ANSI
to ensure permanence and durability.

ISBN 3 11 017709 9

Bibliographic information published by Die Deutsche Bibliothek

Die Deutsche Bibliothek lists this publication in the Deutsche Nationalbibliografie;
detailed bibliographic data is available in the Internet at <http://dnb.ddb.de>.

Preface

The papers in the present volume offer new perspectives on cognitive lexical semantic research. Some were first presented at the "Workshop on Cognitive Approaches to Lexical Semantics", organized by Hubert Cuyckens (University of Leuven) and Dominiek Sandra (University of Antwerp) during the 16th Scandinavian Linguistics Conference held at the University of Turku, Finland, 15 November 1996. These are the papers by Stefan Grondelaers and Dirk Geeraerts, Hanna Lehti-Eklund, Sally Rice, Satoshi Uehara, Christof Vanden Eynde, and Jordan Zlatev. The other contributions (by Jens Allwood, Theo Janssen, Laura Michaelis, Kurt Queller, Augusto Soares da Silva, David Tuggy, Claude Vandeloise) were specially solicited for this volume. While most of the papers have matured over the past few years, all have been updated and revised, some of them several times, and most recently within the last twelve months.

The volume was made possible with the help of a great many people. First of all, we would like to express our thanks to all the authors for their contributions, for their speediness at every stage of the reviewing and editorial process, and for their patience. We would also like to thank all the linguists who acted as anonymous referees. We would like to acknowledge the work of Dominiek Sandra, who acted as co-editor of this volume during its initial stages, but who, unfortunately, had to leave the project. Thanks also goes to Jörg Behrndt for his invaluable work in formatting this volume, and to Anke Beck and Birgit Sievert of Mouton de Gruyter for seeing this project through.

Finally, the first editor would very much like to express his thanks to his co-editors, John Taylor and René Dirven, for their assistance in bringing the volume to fruition.

Hubert Cuyckens (University of Leuven)
René Dirven (University of Duisburg)
John Taylor (University of Otago)
May 2003

Contents

Preface v

Introduction:
New directions in cognitive lexical semantic research 1
John Taylor, Hubert Cuyckens and René Dirven

Meaning potentials and context:
Some consequences for the analysis of variation in meaning 29
Jens Allwood

Towards a pragmatic model of cognitive onomasiology 67
Stefan Grondelaers and Dirk Geeraerts

Monosemy versus polysemy 93
Theo A.J.M. Janssen

The grammaticalization of *alltså* and *således*:
Two Swedish conjuncts revisited 123
Hanna Lehti-Eklund

Word meaning, sentence meaning, and syntactic meaning 163
Laura A. Michaelis

Metonymic sense shift:
Its origins in hearers' abductive construal of usage in context 211
Kurt Queller

Growth of a lexical network:
Nine English prepositions in acquisition 243
Sally Rice

Image schemas and category coherence:
The case of the Portuguese verb *deixar* 281
Augusto Soares da Silva

The Nawatl verb *kīsa*: A case study in polysemy 323
David Tuggy

A diachronic perspective on prototypicality:
The case of nominal adjectives in Japanese 363
Satoshi Uehara

Containment, support, and linguistic relativity 393
Claude Vandeloise

The Dutch hedges *echt* and *gewoon*:
Markers of prototypicality? 427
Christof Vanden Eynde

Polysemy or generality? Mu. 447
Jordan Zlatev

List of contributors 495

Index 499

Introduction: New directions in cognitive lexical semantic research

John Taylor, Hubert Cuyckens and René Dirven

A central concern of Cognitive Linguistics is that lexical items, as well as word classes and grammatical constructions, are conceptual categories that have to be studied and investigated with respect to their cognitive function (rather than as reflecting purely formal linguistic principles), whereby "*cognitive* refers to the crucial role of intermediate informational structures in our encounters with the world" (Geeraerts 1995: 112–113). As such, lexical as well as grammatical categories constitute a "repository of world knowledge, a structured collection of meaningful categories that help us deal with new experiences and store information about old ones" (1995: 112–113). Importantly, Cognitive Linguistics holds that there is in fact no clear distinction between lexical and grammatical categories. As Langacker puts it, "Lexicon and grammar form a continuum, structures at any point along it being fully and properly described as symbolic in nature … the difference [between lexicon and grammar] is clearly one of degree, and any particular line of demarcation would be arbitrary" (2000: 18).

In spite of the unification of lexicon and grammar, Cognitive Lexical Semantics has always remained a vibrant field of research in its own right. It became a full-fledged field of cognitive linguistic research in the early eighties, when it was able to successfully transfer important research results in cognitive psychology on the internal structure of categories (prototype structure and family resemblance structure) onto the structure of lexical categories. Prototypically structured lexical categories offered a promising alternative to the "classical" description of word meaning (i.e., in terms of a set of necessary and sufficient features) and were at the same time able to account for the ever-present polysemy in word meaning. In the past two decades, then, research interests in cognitive lexical semantics have directed attention to (i) the internal structure of lexical categories (prototype structure, family resemblance structure, radial network structure); (ii) the polysemous nature of lexical items and the cognitive principles (e.g., metaphor, metonymy, image-schema transformations) motivating the relations between the different senses of lexical items; (iii) larger conceptual structures (e.g., metaphor research, frame semantics). Results in these research areas can be regarded as making up the "common core" of cognitive lexical semantic research. As such, they have also informed the papers in the present volume (Tuggy, Janssen, Allwood, and Zlatev on polysemy; Vanden Eynde, Uehara, and Rice on prototype structure; Queller and Lehti-Eklund on conceptual metonymy; Soares da Silva on image-schema transformation).

While these research interests still generate considerable interest, the contributions to this volume give unmistakable evidence of new directions emerging in cognitive lexical semantic research. For one, the widely held view in Cognitive Linguistics that polysemy is the norm for lexical items, especially for those that occur with any frequency, has re-ignited the debate concerning the polysemous vs. monosemous representations of word meaning. The papers by Allwood, Janssen, Tuggy, and Zlatev testify to the fact that "polysemy" is currently a much more contested issue than it was in the 1980s and 1990s. Second, the mechanisms that account for the relations between synchronic senses of a lexical item (e.g., metaphor, metonymy) are now also shown to account for the diachronic development of grammaticalized meanings (see the contributions by Lehti-Eklund and Uehara). Third, as evidenced by Rice's and Vandeloise's papers, acquisition data are brought to bear on the description of word meaning. Fourth, insights on prototypicality are undergoing further refinement; thus, Uehara applies the notion of prototype to parts of speech such as "Nominal Adjective" in Japanese, while Vanden Eynde goes into the relationship between prototypical category structure and hedging. Finally, Cognitive Lexical Semantics is looking into the relationship between lexical and constructional meaning (Michaelis) and between the meaning of words and the contexts in which they are encountered (Queller, Grondelaers and Geeraerts, Lehti-Eklund, Allwood, Vanden Eynde).

Interestingly, these new topics fall out from more general issues in cognitive lexical semantic analyses. These include: (i) the nature of word meanings; (ii) the interplay between the conventionalized resources of a language and the specifics of a communicative situation; and (iii) the relation between word meanings and the meanings of complex linguistic expressions in which they are used. These more general concerns, which have actually given a new impetus to the field of Cognitive Lexical Semantics, are due at least in part to the fact that a number of traditional and well-entrenched views about the lexicon have turned out to be inadequate. One can readily accept – at a pre-theoretical level – that words have meanings, and that these meanings are implicated, in some way or other, in the meanings of the complex expressions in which the words occur. Matters become more complex, however, when we inquire into the nature of word meanings. How are word meanings to be stated? Is the meaning of a word a fixed and determinate entity? In the case of words presumed to be polysemous, just how many different meanings do the words have? What is the relation between word meanings (however we decide to characterize them) and the meanings of the utterances in which the words are used? What is the relation between words and situations in the world which they can be used to denote?

The papers in the present volume assemble a number of current perspectives on these controversial, and largely unsolved issues. In order to appreciate the problematic nature of these questions, however, it is necessary to step back a little, and to enquire more deeply into traditional views of word meanings, and the assumptions on which they are based.

1. A traditional view of word meaning

According to a common view of the matter, knowledge of a language can be partitioned into two major components – knowledge of the lexicon and knowledge of the syntax. The lexicon lists the words of the language and states, for each word, its phonological properties, its syntactic category, and its meaning. The syntax comprises the rules whereby elements belonging to certain syntactic categories can be combined into larger configurations. The phonological properties of the complex expressions thus formed can be computed from the phonological properties of the constituent words and the way in which they are combined. Likewise, the semantic properties of the complex expressions can be worked out on the basis of the semantic properties of the contributing words and the manner of their combination. The way sentences are pronounced, and the way they are interpreted, thus depend, ultimately, on the properties of words.

The above paragraph has sketched out what we might call the "standard" view of the lexicon and its role within a broader linguistic theory (cf. Taylor, in press c). The view informs not only the dominant "Chomskyan", and many other formalist and modular views of linguistic knowledge, it is also reflected in popular conceptions of language. Thus, according to a popular conception, the essential reference tools of the foreign language learner are the dictionary and the grammar book.

Many of the papers in this volume challenge the basic assumptions behind the standard view of the lexicon and its role within a broader theory of semantics; others highlight problems and shortcomings associated with the standard view. In the discussion of these shortcomings, some earlier cognitive linguistic approaches to word meaning – in particular, the treatment of polysemous items in terms of the well-known and widely employed radial network model – also come under critical scrutiny.

One aspect, in particular, of the standard view should be highlighted from the outset. This is the assumption that the words of a language are associated with fixed and determinate meanings – more than one meaning, of course, in the case of words presumed to be polysemous. The very possibility of a dictionary (lexicon) is based on this assumption. A dictionary lists the existing words in a language, and is supposed to state, for each word, its meaning. In the case of words presumed to be polysemous, the dictionary lists for each word its different meanings and attempts a characterization of them. It is these discrete "chunks" of meaning which words are supposed to contribute to the complex expressions in which they occur.

That words have the above properties – i.e., that they have determinate meanings, and that these meanings are contributed to complex expressions – would appear to be self-evident, even axiomatic. It seems a matter of common sense that the words *cat*, *steal*, and *hat* have meanings, and that these meaning are implicated, in a fairly transparent way, in the fact that *The cat stole the hat* means what it does. As Sweetser put it:

> Linguists all agree, and so does the average lay person, that the reason *The cat stole the hat* means something different from *The cat ate the hat* is that *stole* and *ate* make different contributions to the interpretation of the whole, and that those contributions are systematically related to the usual conventional ranges of interpretations of *eat* and *steal* in other possible uses by English speakers. (Sweetser 1999: 132–133)

In spite of its apparent obviousness, the standard view brings with it a number of problems and paradoxes.[1] Consider, for example, the fact that users of a language are rarely required to confront the issue of word meanings. If asked to state the meanings even of very ordinary words in their language, most speakers find it hard to give satisfactory answers (Johnson-Laird 1987). From one point of view, this

1. We might note that Sweetser's example of the cat stealing the hat is not quite as unproblematic as she suggests. In the "usual conventional" uses of *steal*, as when we say that someone "stole my car radio", we attribute criminal intent to the thief – a person takes something which they know does not rightly belong to them. But do we want to attribute criminal intent to a cat? Does a cat have knowledge of which things rightly belong to which individuals? Presumably not. The possibility of predicating "steal the hat" of a cat – and the fact that hearers are easily able to give an interpretation to a statement that "the cat stole the hat" – is just a small example of the problems of word meaning alluded to here.

may not be at all surprising. Language users encounter meaning primarily as a property of utterances, not of decontextualized words. On the other hand, most utterances are unique occurrences. The question then arises, how is it possible for language users to "work out" the meanings of complex expressions if they are unable to state the meanings of the parts from which the expressions are composed. One might, to be sure, respond that language knowledge may well be, for the most part, unconscious, and not easily accessible to introspection. The fact that a lay person may not be able to state the meaning of a word does not entail that the word does not have a meaning, nor that speakers of a language do not have a mental representation of that meaning. Yet it is noteworthy that it is not only lay people who have difficulties stating the meanings of words. Determining the meanings of words is in fact a perennial issue in lexical semantics. In the case of words presumed to be polysemous, there is the additional issue of determining just how many distinct meanings the words are supposed to have. In order to appreciate that these are very real issues, even for professional linguists, we need look no further than to the literature on the lexical item *over*. Brugman's pioneering work (Brugman 1981) spawned a veritable cottage industry of *over*-studies (Lakoff, 1987; Vandeloise, 1990; Deane, 1993; Dewell, 1994; Kreitzer, 1997; Queller 2001; Tyler & Evans 2001, to mention just a few[2]). Recurring themes in this, by now very substantial literature have been, first, the question of how many distinct meanings of *over* need to be postulated, and, second, how these meanings, once identified, should be characterized. The issues are by no means settled, even after more than two decades of discussion.

In the following sections, we suggest that a good many problems in lexical semantics may be traced back to the very conceptualization of word and sentence meanings which frame the standard view.[3] Se-

2. Brugman (1981) also inspired a number of studies of the translation equivalents of *over* in other languages. See Bellavia (1996) and Dewell (1996) on German *über*, Geeraerts (1992) on Dutch *over*, and Taylor (1988) on Italian *su* and *sopra*.
3. On the role of 'cognitive models' in the framing of semantic theories, see Taylor (in press a, in press b).

mantic theories, whether traditional or more recent, are often based in metaphors of the nature of language, its use, and its structure. These metaphors have been taken over, mostly, from folk conceptions of language. It is therefore not a coincidence that expert and folk views on the role of the lexicon (or dictionary) and the syntax (grammar book) should correspond so closely. Since the metaphors are so deeply engrained, their entailments are rarely questioned. On the contrary, the entailments have been taken to be self-evident facts, almost with the status of theorems. Yet, as many contributions to this volume demonstrate, the metaphors may be ultimately misleading, or, at best, unhelpful.

We draw attention to two metaphors which have been particularly influential in shaping semantic theories. One of these is the conduit metaphor, according to which linguistic expressions are "containers" which allow their "contents" (that is, their meanings) to be "conveyed" from speaker to hearer. The second is the building block metaphor, according to which word meanings are semantic "building blocks" which are put together in the construction of more complex meanings. First, however, we give some brief remarks on the cognitive linguistic approach to metaphor in general.

2. Metaphor in Cognitive Linguistics

The study of metaphor has been a central topic in Cognitive Linguistics. The basic insight has been that metaphor is not just a manner of speaking. Metaphor cannot therefore be regarded simply as a rhetorical embellishment of an otherwise predominately "literal" mode of expression, and which is restricted in the main to the creations of poets and orators. On the contrary, metaphor is an important means whereby more abstract, intangible domains of experience can be conceptualized in terms of what is more concrete and more immediate. Symptomatic of its role in conceptualization is the fact that metaphor is ubiquitous, both in everyday language and in expert scientific discourse. In our informal day-to-day talk, we need to make reference to such abstract concepts as time, personal relations, and life itself, and we do so, mostly, in metaphorical terms. Scientific research, by its very nature, needs to go beyond observed phenomena and to theorize about underlying essences, processes, and causes. Very often, expert discourse elaborates the very same metaphors as those which permeate everyday talk. On the other hand, theoretical breakthroughs may consist in the subverting of folk metaphors, and replacing them with metaphors that are perceived to be more insightful to a study of the domain in question. The relation between metaphor and experience is therefore a dynamic one. While metaphor may facilitate the conceptualization of a domain, the "logic" of a metaphor might bring with it entailments which are difficult to reconcile with our experience. If applied uncritically, the metaphor might even inhibit the scientific investigation of the domain. In such circumstances, a reconceptualization of the domain, possibly in terms of alternative metaphors, may be called for.

One of the most intangible, yet ever-present aspects of our life is the phenomenon of language itself, and its role in our mental life and in our interpersonal relations. Perhaps the most mysterious, yet most distinctive aspect of language is its "meaningfulness". We readily attribute "meanings" to linguistic expressions, yet it is by no means obvious what meanings are, nor how it is that complex expressions, newly created by a speaker, come to have the meanings that they do. Meaning, as a property of language and of linguistic expressions, is one of those abstract phenomena which demands an understanding in terms of metaphor.

Some well-known and well-researched examples of metaphorical construals concern the conceptualization of time, life, theories, and arguments (in the sense of "disputes"). Thus, time is commonly conceptualized (and hence spoken about) in spatial terms; life is construed as a journey and difficult episodes in one's life are spoken of as obstacles along the journey; intellectual theories are construed as buildings, and like buildings, they may have secure (or, as the case may be, insecure) foundations; participants in an argument attack each other, they withdraw, and defend positions, just like they were opponents in a military conflict, and so on (Lakoff & Johnson 1980, 1999). As the above remarks will have suggested, the focus of attention in metaphor studies is not primarily on the actual metaphorical expressions themselves, but rather on the "conceptual metaphors" which make possible, or sanction, the specific expressions. It is the conceptual metaphor which construes life as a journey which sanctions specific expressions such as *My life isn't going anywhere*, *You've come a long way*, *He's still got a long way to go*, *We're going round in circles*, and countless more.

A conceptual metaphor maps elements from a source domain onto elements of a target domain. Most times, the correspondences between the two domains are not perfect. Consequently, it may not be possible to map every element of the source domain onto some element of the target domain, neither can every element of the target domain be put into correspondence with some element of the source domain. Moreover, the "logic" of the source domain – the entailments which it gives rise to, for example – do not always carry over to the target domain. The points can be illustrated on the example of the conceptual metaphor which construes time in spatial terms. In terms of the metaphor, time is construed as linear and directional, the present being a point on the time line, the future lying in front, and the past being behind. The present moment ("now") moves forward along the time line (or, according to a slightly different version of the metaphor, future events come towards a static "now", they pass by, and then recede into the past).[4] It will be evident that not all aspects of the spatial domain are mapped onto time. Most obviously, space is three-dimensional, whereas time is one-dimensional. Moreover, people can (within obvious limits) select their location in space, and they can re-occupy a spatial location. On the other hand, my present location on the time line is established by the properties of the time domain itself; I am not free to choose when "now" is, nor can I re-occupy, or return to, a location on the time-line. In other respects, too, the "logic" of the spatial domain does not quite map onto the time domain. As mentioned, the future is construed as lying ahead,

4. That the spatial metaphors of time are not just manners of speaking, but influence speakers' conceptualization of time, has been elegantly demonstrated by Boroditsky (2000) and Boroditsky, Ramscar and Frank (2002).

the past as behind. Thus, we "look forward to" the future, we "go into" the future, we "look back" on the past, we put things "behind us", and so on. It will be apparent that this way of talking about time conflicts with our experience of directed motion. We can see what is in front of us, but we cannot see what is behind us. Yet the future is unknown, while the past can be remembered. A strict application of the "logic" of the source domain to the target domain would lead to the absurd inference that we can readily "see into" the future, but only by making a special effort to turn our heads can we "see" (that is, have knowledge of) the past. In this case, to be sure, the incompatibilities between the source and target domains are so crass, that no one is likely to believe the metaphorical entailment that one can "see into" the future simply by looking ahead! Sometimes, however, the power of a metaphor is such that it can indeed induce a false understanding of the target domain. This is the case, we suggest, with some of the metaphors which we use to talk about language.

3. The conduit metaphor

One of the earliest studies of conceptual metaphor – and it is interesting to note that its first publication (1979) predated the appearance of Lakoff and Johnson's *Metaphors We Live By* (1980) – was Michael Reddy's paper, "The conduit metaphor" (Reddy 1979 [1993]). In his paper, Reddy drew attention to a cluster of metaphors which motivate a substantial amount of our talk about language and about the role of language in communication. In terms of the conduit metaphor, linguistic expressions are containers, meaning is their content, expressing oneself involves putting contents (i.e., meanings) into containers, communication is the sending of the containers, together with their contents, along a conduit to a hearer, understanding is the receiving of the containers and the retrieving of their contents. Thus, we speak of "putting ideas into words", of "getting ideas across" to an audience, we "extract ideas" from a piece of prose, and words which do not "convey" much meaning to us are said to be "empty". Reddy (1993: 189–197) cites well over 100 common expressions and expression types which, he claims, elaborate at least some facets of the conduit metaphor. These expressions far outnumber those which are based on other conceptual metaphors of language and linguistic communication, or which are, at best, "neutral" with respect to their metaphorical allegiance.[5]

The conduit metaphor maps elements from a source domain (in this case, our experience of putting goods into containers, sending the packaged goods to a recipient, who then unpacks the containers and retrieves the goods) onto a target domain (the act of verbal communication). While the conceptual metaphor may appear to give us a handle on some aspects of the target domain, it will be apparent that the correspondences between the two domains are at best imperfect. For example, if I send an object to someone, that person ends up having the object while I lose possession of it. But if I "give someone an idea", that person may end up "having" the idea, as per the metaphor, but I do not thereby "lose" the idea. Here, the clash between the source and target domains is so evident that, as with the time-line example mentioned above, no one is likely to be misled by it.

Other aspects of the metaphor are likely to impede or, at best, defer a clear understanding of the communication process. Consider, for example, our talk about "putting ideas into words". The image here is of a person putting objects, such as small gifts, into containers, such as boxes. According to the metaphor, this is just about all there is to the speech production process. Yet how, precisely, are we to understand this crucial step in the process of verbal communication? Should we infer that the containers (i.e., words, phrases, etc.) are initially empty (i.e., that they lack meaning), but can be filled by any contents of the speaker's choosing? On this view, a linguistic expression could mean just about anything that a speaker wanted it to mean – which is manifestly not the case. Are the ideas which speakers put into words to be taken as well-defined, pre-existing objects, each of which is inserted into the appropriate container? The

5. The question naturally arises, whether the metaphors discussed by Reddy are of universal validity, or whether they are peculiar to English and to other Western (and Westernized) languages. For hints that Japanese may employ different metaphors of verbal communication, see Ikegami (2003).

speaker's task, then, would be to select the containers appropriate to the intended contents. Should we take the metaphor to be referring to "word-sized" ideas and their individual containers, or to the fitting of more complex thoughts to more complex linguistic expressions? The conduit metaphor is silent on these questions. The metaphor also closes off discussion of the relation between the speaker's intended meaning and the meaning "contained" in the language that (s)he uses. What does a speaker do if the concept (s)he wishes to symbolize happens not to coincide with any of the pre-assigned word-contents?

With respect to the conduit metaphor, then, there is therefore a certain tension, even incompatibility, between the details of the source domain and nature of the target domain; as remarked, this situation is probably the norm with conceptual metaphors. The thrust of Reddy's paper, however, was not so much to point out the inadequacies of the metaphor, as to highlight its pernicious effects. The metaphor is pernicious because it can easily seduce us into a false and misleading understanding of the nature of verbal communication – all the more so, Reddy claims, since there are so few ways of talking about verbal communication which do not elaborate some aspects of the metaphor. Observe, first of all, that the metaphor entails the reification of meaning – meanings are objects, with fixed and determinate properties, which are assigned to linguistic expressions (Gibbs 1994: 151). Moreover, the metaphor entails that the meanings that the listener retrieves from a linguistic expression are identical (in ideal circumstances) to the meanings that the speaker intended should be there. Anything less would count as faulty, or imperfect communication. The metaphor therefore construes communication as a process of "telementation", that is, the transfer of thoughts from one mind to another (Harris 1981: 9). But since the contents of a person's mind are invisible to public scrutiny, we would be unable to ascertain, in any particular case, whether the telementation has taken place. Moreover, by presenting verbal communication as a (relatively straightforward) process of thought transfer between minds, the conduit metaphor marginalizes other and perhaps more fruitful avenues of research. It ignores the possibility that a linguistic expression may not, in principle, be able to symbolize all facets of a conceptualization entertained by a speaker. Inevitably, certain details must be omitted or represented only schematically, the full array of background assumptions can never be fully explicated (Searle 1983), and the conventional value of linguistic forms is rarely exactly suited to the specific needs of a speaker on a particular occasion (Langacker 1987). At best, what a speaker says are mere hints at what is intended. By exploiting the conventional linguistic resources available, a speaker (to use an alternative metaphor, one favored by Reddy 1993: 171ff.) is giving instructions to a hearer to do the best he can to construct a plausible meaning, given the circumstances of the speech event, the hearer's accumulated knowledge of the language, and his recollection of previous linguistic encounters. The conduit metaphor, however, attributes very little of the work of verbal communication to the hearer. All the hearer has to do is to unpack the containers – and nothing could be simpler than that. The listener in the communication process is reduced to a passive retriever of an intended message. Communication failure must lie with the speaker, who did not put the right contents, or indeed any contents, into the containers (though what that means, in terms of the metaphor, is not at all clear), or he did not select the right containers (again, something which the metaphor does not really explain).

In spite of these evident inadequacies, the conduit metaphor has profoundly influenced expert views of communication. Reddy cites as an example certain (mis-)understandings of Shannon and Weaver's (1949) mathematical model of communication, according to which a "message" is "encoded", by the "sender", into a "signal", which is "transmitted", through a "channel", to a "receiver", who, upon "decoding" the signal, retrieves the original message. Another example is provided by the well-known diagram in Saussure's *Cours* (1916 [1964]). This depicts the "speech circuit" ("*le circuit de la parole*", 1964: 27), whereby an idea, or concept, originating in the brain of Speaker A, gets transferred to the brain of speaker B. The process of thought transfer begins with a concept in the brain of speaker A triggering an associated linguistic form (or "acoustic image"). The linguistic form undergoes a series of transformations – into neuromuscular innervations, articulatory gestures, movements of air particles, vibrations of the listener's ear drum, processing in the hearer's auditory apparatus, etc. – on its journey from Speaker A to Speaker B. The result is that Speaker B receives the linguistic form and retrieves the associated concept. Observe that Saussure's model rests on the assumption that there is a fixed and determinate association between concepts and phonological forms, that speakers and hearers have a shared knowledge of these associations, and that speakers only verbalize concepts which have been conventionally associated with a phonological form. As per the conduit metaphor, the model entails (in the case of successful communication) that speaker B comes to have exactly the same concept that was entertained by speaker A.[6]

4. The building block metaphor: the hypostasization of fixed meanings

The importance of Reddy's essay lies in the fact that it exposed a pervasive, but ultimately misleading conceptualization of language, one which imbues not just folk theories of language, but expert theories as well. The second conceptual metaphor about language that we want to discuss is one which at first sight seems to be rather less harmful than the conduit metaphor, but whose entailments, we suggest, might be equally misleading – more so, in fact, since the source and target domains appear to be in such close correspondence. We are referring to the building block metaphor of syntagmatic composition (Gundersen 2001). In terms of the metaphor, complex linguistic expressions are formed by assembling smaller units according to certain principles. The smallest units – the building blocks – are commonly identified as words (or morphemes), while the principles whereby they are combined are the province of the syntax. It follows that the properties of the whole can be worked out on the basis of the properties of the parts, and the manner in which they are combined.

6. Harris (1987) presents a critique of the Saussurian "circuit de la parole" in the form of an imaginary dialogue between "A" and "B".

At first blush, the building block metaphor might not seem to be a metaphor at all; rather, it represents a self-evident fact about human language. Whereas animal communication systems are defined by a small and fixed repertoire of meaningful signals, human languages have the distinctive property of generativity, or creativity. That is to say, speakers are able to create a potentially infinite number of utterances, most of them unique, on the basis of their knowledge of a finite set of linguistic units and rules for their combination. From one point of view, therefore, it has to be a self-evident fact that speakers do create composite expressions by assembling their component parts in accordance with certain principles. Moreover, given that the composite expressions are (by and large) understood in the manner that the speaker (probably) intended, it should also be a self-evident fact that complex expressions have semantic properties which can be computed from the properties of the parts in association with the principles whereby the parts are combined. As already remarked, *The cat stole the hat* means what it does in virtue of the fact that *cat*, *stole*, and *hat* mean what they do, and are assembled in accordance with the syntactic rules of English. One might therefore see no reason to question the validity of the metaphor, which, as Langacker put it,

> sees the meaning of a composite expression as being constructed out of the meanings of its parts simply by stacking them together in some appropriate fashion. (Langacker 1987: 452)

If it were not for this property of human languages, no speaker would ever be able to extend his/her linguistic repertoire beyond a fixed set of preformed expressions.

The building block metaphor has been imported into semantic theory in the form of compositionality principle (Cann 1993). According to the compositionality principle, the meaning of the whole is fully determined (i) by the meanings of its component parts, in conjunction with (ii) the way in which the parts are combined. The compositionality principle can be broken down into the following more specific propositions (Taylor 2002: 98):

(1) a. Each component part of a complex expression has a fixed and determinate meaning within the language system;
b. The manner in which simpler items combine to form complex expressions makes a fixed and determinate contribution to the meaning of a complex expression;
c. The semantic properties of the parts of an expression are fully maintained in the complex expression;
d. There is no "surplus" meaning accruing to a complex expression that is not attributable to its parts and the manner of their combination.

Just as the conduit metaphor offers a less than fully satisfactory account of verbal communication, so too the building block metaphor – although it seems to capture some self-evident facts about language, and for this reason, perhaps, may not even be perceived to be a metaphor – turns out to be less than fully adequate as the basis for a study of semantics. There is no shortage of counterevidence for each of the propositions in (1) (Taylor 2002: chap. 6). The existence of polysemy – and the difficulties we encounter in determining, for a given word, just how many different meanings it has – cast doubt on the validity of (1a). The problematic status of (1b) becomes apparent in light of certain constructions whose semantic contribution seems to vary from case to case – nominal compounding is a well-known example. (Compare the different kinds of semantic relation between the components in *water tower, water fowl, water pistol*, etc.) "Privative" expressions, such as *fake gun* and *stone lion*, show that (1c) may not always apply. (Certain attributes which are presumably inherent to the concept "lion", such as that lions are living creatures, made of flesh, blood, and bones, are canceled when *lion* combines with *stone*.) Proposition (1d) is called into question by the widespread existence of "enriched" interpretations (Jackendoff 1997: chap. 3) – the phenomenon whereby complex expressions typically have semantic attributes which cannot be traced back to any of the component parts, nor to their manner of combination. The specific vs. nonspecific readings of *I want to marry a millionaire* (does the millionaire exist in reality, or only in the imagination of the speaker?) is a case in point.

5. Three clusters of issues

The issues raised by the conduit and by the building block metaphor come together in three major clusters:

(a) *The nature of word meanings.* In order for compositionality to go through, we need to be able to state the meanings of the building blocks (pre-eminently: words). Likewise, for "telementation" to be successful, meanings need to be taken to be well-defined objects with fixed and determinate properties. However, it is by no means obvious what word meanings are, nor how they are to be stated, nor, in the case of words presumed to be polysemous, just how many different meanings need to be postulated.

(b) *The interplay between the conventionalized resources of a language and the specifics of a communicative situation.* At issue here are: (i) whether there might be factors other than the words and the manner in which they are combined that contribute to the meaning of a complex expression, for example, the textual, contextual, and conceptual embedding of an expression; and (ii) whether the hearer does more than simply unpack the conventionalized meanings assigned to linguistic expressions (whether words or more complex expressions).

(c) *The relation between word meanings and the meanings of complex linguistic expressions in which they are used.* At issue here is the possibility that complex expressions might have "emergent" properties that are not derivable from the meanings (however characterized) of the constituent words. For example, the constructions in which words are used may be able to enrich, or to override, the meanings of their component parts.

The various contributions to this volume address, in one way or another, the issues that have been outlined above.

5.1. Characterizing word meanings

The characterization of word meanings raises a host of well-known problems. One concerns the level of generality at which word meanings are to be identified. It is evident that words can be used to designate a range of different situations. If we predicate *crawl* of different kinds of entities, as in the following examples, it is evident that we are dealing with different manners of motion. The examples are taken from Allwood's paper, who cites them from Fillmore and Atkins (2000).[7]

(2) a. *A small baby crawled out on its hands and knees.*
 b. *The two hedgehogs crawled from the nest.*
 c. *A beetle began to crawl up his leg.*
 d. *She felt his hand crawling up her thigh.*
 e. *A cloud of steam crawled slowly upwards from the chimney.*
 f. *I crawled into my sleeping bag.*

Faced with examples such as these, the question arises whether we should associate *crawl* with six distinct meanings, one for each of six different processes exemplified in (2), or whether we should postulate a single, general meaning, which somehow gets elaborated in different ways in the different contexts.

Our answer to this question impinges the vexed topic of polysemy vs. monosemy. Suppose we insist on strict compositionality, and require that the meanings of the parts fully determine the meaning of the whole, with no "surplus" meaning accruing to the whole which is not derivable from its parts. On this approach we should have to recognize six distinct senses of *crawl*. Only in this way can we compute

7. Note that the examples all pertain to the spatial domain. Non-spatial uses of *crawl* (as in *The weeks crawled by*) are also possible.

the specific readings of each of the sentences in (2) from the meanings of their parts. But since the number of entities of which *crawl* can be predicated is indefinite, we should have to suppose that *crawl* (and many other words in the lexicon) is indefinitely polysemous, and indefinite polysemy is something which Searle (1983: 146), for one, finds "absurd". The alternative would be to recognize a single, rather vague and general meaning of *crawl*, which somehow gets elaborated in different ways in the contexts in which it occurs. This approach also has its problems. Rather obviously, the approach means that we must give up on strict compositionality. It also implies that the speaker cannot offer the hearer a container with a well-defined content (i.e., a fixed meaning) that would simply need to be unpacked, with little interpretation work needed on the part of the hearer. Second, we shall need to state, preferably by appeal to general principles of interpretation, how the single meaning gets elaborated in each particular case. Third, it may turn out to be tantalizingly difficult to characterize this single general meaning, abstracted away from its specific instances. (The reader might like to try!) Moreover, the general meaning will need to meet two additional requirements. It must be stated with a sufficient degree of detail so as delimit the range of permissible elaborations (it is evident that *crawl* cannot be predicted of any and every entity that moves); the meaning must also be differentiated from the meanings of semantically similar words, such as *creep*.

The question of exactly how many meanings should be associated with a word form is still largely unresolved. Some contributors (e.g., Tuggy) argue strongly for the polysemy approach, on the grounds that a single general meaning (such as 'emerge' in the case of the Orizaba Nawatl verb *kīsa) does not allow us to* predict the range of specific, conventionalized uses of a word. Others, such as Allwood, tend to favor more abstract meanings. As Allwood notes, there is probably something wrong with the claim that the English word *nature* has over sixty different meanings. Janssen argues that the general meaning approach (monosemy) is complementary to a polysemy approach. Zlatev, on the other hand, pointedly notes that the question "Generality or Polysemy?" does not permit a coherent answer. But to recognize that it might be impossible, in principle, to decide between the options of polysemy vs. generality does not sit well with the assumptions of the building block and the conduit metaphors.

A further issue concerns the relationship between the syntactic function of a word and its meaning. It is evident that the noun vs. verb uses of *drink* correlate with different semantic values, and that these semantic values are intimately associated with the syntactic category of the word – a topic explored by Allwood. For accounts in terms of compositionality, the syntactic category of a word is of crucial importance, since it is this property of a word which determines its combinatorial possibilities. But are word classes clearly defined entities? Uehara argues that they may not be. He notes that the category of Nominal Adjective, in modern Japanese, has a prototype structure, with some of the more peripheral members of the category exhibiting noun-like properties, others exhibiting more adjective-like properties. Drawing on diachronic evidence, he offers a semantics-based account of how the present-day situation arose. A special problem is presented by discourse markers, discussed by Lehti-Eklund. These, more often than not, do not fit neatly into any of the major lexical categories, such as noun, verb, adverb, etc.

Concerning word meanings themselves, the question arises whether we should pursue a componential approach, whereby the meaning of a word can be analyzed into more primitive elements. If so, what is the nature of these more primitive elements? Are they universal? Are they abstract conceptual elements, or are they grounded in experience? These issues are addressed by Vandeloise, who explores the relevance of the experientially grounded (but prelinguistic) notions of control, containment, and support in the semantics of English *in*, and of its (near and not so near) equivalents in other languages. Like Vandeloise, Soares da Silva, in his study of the Portuguese verb *deixar* 'to leave, to let', also emphasizes the role of experientially-grounded notions of force dynamics in his account of the many uses of the verb in the modern language, and also their role in the historical development of the word from its Latin progenitor, *laxare*.

5.2. *Words and their textual, contextual, and conceptual embedding*

Both the building block and the conduit metaphor promote the idea of word meanings as reified objects, which can be characterized *independently* of the contexts in which they are encountered. Several contributors challenge this view (Allwood, Queller, Vanden Eynde, Lehti-Eklund, Rice, Grondelaers and Geeraerts). In his discussion of the item *crawl* (cf. supra), Allwood points out that lexical items can be used to designate different situations (e.g. *crawl up one's leg* vs. *crawl from the nest*); in other words, they are elaborated in different ways in different contexts. In this regard, Allwood introduces the notion of a word's "meaning potential"; a word provides access to a conceptual complex, only some aspects of which may be highlighted in a certain context. Queller, discussing a well-known example of semantic change in Middle English, argues that it was not the case that individual speakers extended the meaning of the word *bedes* from 'prayer' to 'bead', rather it was the expression *tell the beads* that was interpreted differently by speaker and hearer. The focus, in other words, shifts from words as building blocks to usage events, in all their contextual detail. Vanden Eynde, on the other hand, cites the evidence of the Dutch hedging expressions *echt* 'real' and *gewoon* 'ordinary, common' to argue (i) that the hedges are not used to denote invariant, prototypical members of the lexical category they combine with, but rather central members whose identity may differ in different contexts. In other words, the composite meaning of a complex expression *echt/gewoon + noun* may shift with context; the expressions may even acquire a nonce interpretation. Lehti-Eklund, then, in her discussion of the grammaticalization of the Swedish adverbials *alltså* and *således*, illustrates that the items' (metatextual and interpersonal) discourse marker usages could only arise through pragmatic enrichment (cf. Traugott & Dasher 2002) – a type of conceptual metonymy – in contexts of communication and rhetorical strategizing (and in which Levinson's Principle of Informativeness (1983: 146) seems ubiquitous).

Evidence that words do not acquire meanings out of context also comes from acquisition research. Rice specifically addresses the acquisition of the English prepositions. It is evident that speakers (mostly) do not learn words as such, they learn words in the context(s) of their use. The meanings of the composite expressions, as encountered, are therefore in a sense more basic than the meanings of the parts of which they are composed. Rice presents evidence that children do not acquire the English prepositions by starting out from what have often been presumed to be the prototypical, or central senses of the prepositions, gradually extending their uses according to the structure of a radial network. Rather, it seems that children might initially acquire uses which, in terms of the radial network model, are somewhat peripheral. As will be apparent, these findings call into question the psychological reality of radial network representations of polysemy.

Finally, Grondelaers and Geeraerts bring the onomasiological perspective to the study of word meaning (in addition to the semasiological perspective). This concerns the relation between words and their referents, and the choices that speakers have in relating word and referent. The onomasiological (or "naming") perspective, considers, for a given kind of entity, the various linguistics expressions which may be used to designate it. They see three factors determining the choice of a lexical item as a name for a referent (e.g., factors which might cause a speaker to refer to an entity with a non-basic level term, such as, in the case of the referent "cancer" the term *illness*). These factors are: (i) the degree of prototypicality of the referent with regard to the semasiological structure of the category, (ii) the onomasiological entrenchment of the category represented by the name, and (iii) the contextual features which interact with these principles. In their view, it is especially the contextual, sociolinguistic factors that need to be given more attention in an integrated model of lexical studies.

5.3. *Word meaning and constructions*

Michaelis argues that the meaning of the whole is in many cases not a compositional function of the meanings of its parts. It is not just that some additional meaning might accrue to the whole, which cannot be traced back to its parts. Rather, grammatical constructions themselves have meanings, no less than lexical items. Moreover, constructions may have priority, in that the construction may "coerce" the meanings if its constituents.

6. Alternative metaphors?

We have argued above that many of the current issues in Cognitive Linguistic approaches to semantics can be viewed against the background of assumptions and entailments of conceptual metaphors which have framed both popular and scientific conceptions of language. Since both the conduit metaphor and the building block metaphor turn out to be, at best, inadequate for a proper understanding of word meaning, phrase meaning, and utterance meaning, the question inevitably arises whether other metaphors, or cognitive models, might be more adequate to the task. We touch briefly on this question in this final section.

A good starting point in a search for an alternative model is the folk conception of what is needed to learn a language. We stated earlier that, according to a popular view, the essential tools for the language learner are the dictionary and grammar book. There is, however, a third learning tool, which we omitted to mention – and that is the phrase book, or book of idioms. The phrase book is necessary, precisely because the dictionary and the grammar book alone do not provide the language learner with the means for creating the full range of acceptable expressions in the language. Idioms cannot be created in accordance with the building block metaphor. They have to be learned as such.

It is interesting to note that linguists of several theoretical persuasions have been devoting increased attention to the role of the idiomatic in a language (e.g., Fillmore, Kay and O'Connor 1988; Nunberg, Sag and Wasow 1994; Jackendoff 1997; Culicover 1999). Indeed, recognition of the scope of the idiomatic was a major impetus for the development of construction grammars (Taylor, in press c). A construction grammar does not contain a set of rules for combining simpler elements according to their syntactic category, but rather consists of an inventory of patterns which sanction individual expressions. The patterns are specified with respect to both their formal and their semantic aspects (Michaelis). As such, constructions can vary along a number of dimensions. One dimension concerns their degree of "abstractness", or "schematicity". Thus, some constructions are lexically fully specified (such as *by and large*, an expression which exemplifies a syntactic pattern found nowhere else in English), others are partially specified, and permit only a limited number of items to fill their various "slots" (such as the construction exemplified by *day in day out*; cf. Taylor 1995: 201); others are akin to major phrase-structure patterns (such as the English ditransitive construction). Another dimension concerns their degree of internal complexity. According to some varieties of construction grammar, even individual lexical items count as constructions (Goldberg 1995). Construction grammar thus inverts the traditional view of the idiomatic as something peripheral to the regular, non-idiomatic "core" of the language. In a sense, everything turns out to be idiomatic, to a greater or lesser degree.

How are constructions learned? If constructions are idiomatic, their properties cannot be derived from general (e.g., innate) principles, they have to be acquired through exposure to their instances. Inevitably, therefore, construction grammars are usage-based. Constructions emerge as generalizations over encountered instances. Words are acquired in terms of their availability to slot into constructions. In some cases, words might be acquired in a range of specific collocations (and collocations are also constructions, of a kind), a possibility explored by Queller and Rice. The "meaning potential" (Allwood) of a word would then result from the stored knowledge of how that word has been used in previous linguistic encounters.

Clearly, the building block metaphor is incompatible with a usage-based construction grammar. What might be an alternative? How might the study of words, their meanings, and their role in complex expressions be re-conceptualized? What is to replace the notion of the "dictionary", with its listing of well-defined meanings, and its counterpart, the "grammar book"? One possibility, we suggest, is the notion of the "mental corpus". The corpus comprises memory traces of previous encounters with the language, specified in both their formal and semantic aspects, as well as generalizations over these memory traces. (To this extent, the mental corpus is not entirely comparable to real-world language corpora). Words are accessed with respect to their potential to contribute to constructions. Word meaning, and constructional meaning, generalizes over encountered instances.

The entailments of the metaphor still need to be explored. But that is the topic of a further volume ...

References

Bellavia, Elena
1996 The German *über*. In: Martin Pütz and René Dirven (eds.), *The Construal of Space in Language and Thought*, 73–107. Berlin: Mouton de Gruyter.

Bododitsky, Lera
2000 Metaphoric structuring: Understanding time through spatial metaphors. *Cognition* 75: 1–28.

Boroditsky, Lera, Michael Ramscar and Michael Frank
2000 The roles of body and mind in abstract thought. *Psychological Science* 13: 185–188.

Brugman, Claudia
1981 [1988] Story of *over*. M.A. thesis, University of California, Berkeley. (Reprinted as *The Story of Over: Polysemy, Semantics, and the Structure of the Lexicon*. New York: Garland.)

Cann, Ronnie
1993 *Formal Semantics: An Introduction*. Cambridge: Cambridge University Press.

Culicover, Peter
1999 *Syntactic Nuts: Hard Cases, Syntactic Theory, and Language Acquisition*. Oxford: Oxford University Press.

Deane, Paul
1993 Multimodal spatial representations: On the semantic unity of 'over' and other polysemous prepositions. Duisburg: LAUD (= Linguistic Agency, University of Duisburg).

Dewell, Robert B.
1994 *Over* again: Image-schematic transformations in semantic analysis. *Cognitive Linguistics* 5: 351–380.
1996 The separability of German *über*: A cognitive approach. In: Martin Pütz and René Dirven (eds.), *The Construal of Space in Language and Thought*, 109–133. Berlin: Mouton de Gruyter.
Fillmore, Charles J. and Beryl T.S. Atkins
2000 Describing polysemy: The case of 'crawl'. In: Yael Ravin and Claudia Leacock (eds.), *Polysemy: Theoretical and Computational Approaches*, 91–110. Oxford: Oxford University Press.
Fillmore, Charles J., Paul Kay and Mary C. O'Connor
1988 Regularity and idiomaticity in grammatical constructions: The case of *Let alone*. *Language* 64: 501–538.
Geeraerts, Dirk
1992 The semantic structure of Dutch *over*. *Leuvense Bijdragen* 81: 205–230.
1995 Cognitive Linguistics. In: Jef Verschueren, Jan-Ola Östman and Jan Blommaert (eds.), *Handbook of Pragmatics*, 111–116. Amsterdam: John Benjamins.
Gibbs, Raymond
1994 *The Poetics of Mind: Figurative Thought, Language, and Understanding*. Cambridge: Cambridge University Press.
Goldberg, Adele
1995 *Constructions: A Construction Grammar Approach to Argument Structure*. Chicago: The University of Chicago Press.
Gundersen, Helge
2001 Building blocks or network relations: Problems of morphological segmentation. In: Hanne Gram Simonsen and Rolf Theil Endresen (eds.), *A Cognitive Approach to the Verb: Morphological and Constructional Perspectives*, 95–127. Berlin: Mouton de Gruyter.
Harris, Roy
1981 *The Language Myth*. London: Duckworth.
1987 Saying nothing. In: *The Language Machine*, 163–174. Ithaca, NY: Cornell University Press.
Ikegami, Yoshihiko
2003 How language is conceptualized and metaphorized in Japanese. In: Hubert Cuyckens, Thomas Berg, René Dirven and Klaus-Uwe Panther (eds.), *Motivation in Language: Studies in Honor of Günter Radden*, 259–271. Amsterdam: John Benjamins.

Jackendoff, Ray
1997 *The Architecture of the Language Faculty*. Cambridge, MA: The MIT Press.

Johnson-Laird, Philip
1987 The mental representation of the meaning of words. *Cognition* 25: 189–211.

Kreitzer, Anatol
1997 Multiple levels of schematization: A study in the conceptualization of space. *Cognitive Linguistics* 8: 291–325.

Lakoff, George
1987 *Women, Fire, and Dangerous Things: What Categories Reveal about the Mind*. Chicago: The University of Chicago Press.

Lakoff, George and Mark Johnson
1980 *Metaphors We Live By*. Chicago: The University of Chicago Press.
1999 *Philosophy in the Flesh*. New York: Basic Books.

Langacker, Ronald W.
1987 *Foundations of Cognitive Linguistics*, Volume 1: *Theoretical Prerequisites*. Stanford: Stanford University Press.
2000 *Grammar and Conceptualization*. Berlin: Mouton de Gruyter.

Levinson, Stephen
1983 *Pragmatics*. Cambridge: Cambridge University Press.

Nunberg, Geoffrey, Ivan Sag and Thomas Wasow
1994 Idioms. *Language* 70: 491–538

Queller, Kurt
2001 A usage-based approach to modeling and teaching the phrasal lexicon. In: Martin Pütz, Suzanne Niemeier and René Dirven (eds.), *Applied Cognitive Linguistics*, Volume 2, 55–83. Berlin: Mouton de Gruyter.

Reddy, Michael
1979 [1993] The conduit metaphor: A case of frame conflict in our talk about language. In: Andrew Ortony (ed.), *Metaphor and Thought*, 2nd edition, 164–201. Cambridge: Cambridge University Press.

Saussure, Ferdinand de
1916 [1964] *Cours de linguistique générale*. Paris: Payot.

Searle, John
1983 *Intentionality: An Essay in the Philosophy of Mind*. Cambridge: Cambridge University Press.

Shannon, Claude and William Weaver
1949 *The Mathematical Theory of Communication*. Urbana, IL: University of Illinois Press.

Sweetser, Eve
1999 Compositionality and blending: Semantic composition in a cognitive realistic framework. In: Theo Janssen and Gisela Redeker (eds.), *Cognitive Linguistics: Foundations, Scope, and Methodology*, 129–162. Berlin: Mouton de Gruyter.

Taylor, John R.
1988 Contrasting prepositional categories: English and Italian. In: Brygida Rudzka-Ostyn (ed.), *Topics in Cognitive Linguistics*, 299–326. Amsterdam: John Benjamins,
1995 *Linguistic Categorization: Prototypes in Linguistic Theory*. Oxford: Clarendon Press.
2002 *Cognitive Grammar*. Oxford: Oxford University Press.
in press a Cognitive models of polysemy. To appear in Brigitte Nerlich, L. Todd, V. Herman and David D. Clarke (eds.), *Polysemy: Flexible Patterns of Meaning in Mind and Language*. Berlin: Mouton de Gruyter.
in press b Polysemy's paradoxes. To appear in *Language Sciences*.
in press c Why construction grammar is radical. To appear in *Cognitive Linguistics*.

Traugott, Elizabet C. and Richard B. Dasher
2002 *Regularity in Semantic Change*. Cambridge: Cambridge University Press.

Tyler, Andrea and Vyvyan Evans
2001 Reconsidering prepositional polysemy networks: The case of *over*. *Language* 77: 724–765.

Vandeloise, Claude
1990 Representation, prototypes, and centrality. In: Savas Tsohatzidis (ed.), *Meanings and Prototypes*, 403–437. London: Routledge.

Meaning potentials and context: Some consequences for the analysis of variation in meaning

Jens Allwood

Abstract

The purpose of this paper is to suggest a view of word meaning on the type level which is based on "meaning potentials" rather than on reified type meanings founded on either of the two traditional approaches of abstract generalization (*Gesamtbedeutung*) and typical or basic meaning (*Grundbedeutung*). It is suggested that actual meaning on the occurrence level is produced by context-sensitive operations of meaning activation and meaning determination which combine meaning potentials with each other and with contextually given information rather than by some simple compositionality operations yielding phrase and sentence meaning from simple type meanings of one of the two traditional kinds. To establish this goal, I first present the traditional notions and discuss some problems which arise when trying to handle variation in meaning. I then specifically discuss the relation of homonymy and polysemy to the traditional notions. In section 3, I introduce the notion of "meaning potentials" as an alternative to the traditional notions and then discuss in section 4 how this notion might be used to handle problems of meaning variation, focusing especially on homonymy and polysemy.

Keywords: determination of meaning, *Gesamtbedeutung* 'common meaning', *Grundbedeutung* 'basic meaning', homonymy, meaning activation, meaning potential, meaning variation, monosemy, polysemy, meaning reification.

1. Background

1.1. Approaches to lexical meaning

The nature of word meanings has been discussed since antiquity. The classical answers of realism, conceptualism, and nominalism (cf. Quine 1953a) derive from the ancient and medieval debate on the nature of universals. Realism is traditionally associated with the view that universals, and by extension word meanings, are abstract, independently existing essences which can be captured by stating the necessary and sufficient conditions for something to be what it is. Nominalism is a reaction to this view which instead claims that universals (word meanings) should be viewed purely extensionally as the set of things denoted by a particular word. On this view, there is no such entity as "redness", but only a multitude of things that are called "red". Conceptualism, proposed by Abelard (cf. Gilby 1967) building on Aristotle [1938], is a reaction to both of the preceding ideas, and claims that universals (word meanings) are concepts – mental or cognitive constructs created in confrontation with experience. Most linguists, if not philosophers, have since the days of Abelard probably been conceptualists in the sense that they have believed that word meanings are mental or cognitive constructs. The precise nature of the mental constructs corresponding to word meanings has, however, been controversial. Generally speaking, the following two positions can be discerned:

(a) *The* ***Gesamtbedeutung*** *or "intersection" approach.* The meaning of a word is the largest common semantic denominator for all uses of the word (or for all the things denoted by the word). This approach, in fact, is often equivalent to essentialism, which characterizes the essence or common denominator of a word's uses in terms of the necessary and sufficient conditions for whatever the word denotes. This is the view most often assumed in formal semantics and, if combined with conceptual realism, it is the classical view of Plato.

(b) *The **Grundbedeutung** or "basic example" approach.* The meaning of a word is associated with some concrete instance of its meaning; mostly, this instance is chosen because it is special in some sense. It could, for example, be the first instance of a meaning that a person encounters: this was the position of John Locke (1690). It could also be somehow functionally or biologically primary; this is the position of the proponents of "prototype" theory (Rosch 1977; Lakoff 1987). It could also be the product of an idealization intended to bring out a particular theoretical perspective; this is the idea behind the "ideal types" of Max Weber (Weber 1951; Runciman 1972). Finally, it could be the instance of meaning that is most commonly associated with the word, which could be called the "stereotype" (cf. Putnam 1975). In this chapter, I will use the term *Grundbedeutung* for all approaches that regard "basic" or "typical" examples as the most important ingredient in their account of word meaning, irrespective of whether these "basic" examples are historically primary or whether they number more than one.

1.2. The problem of variation in meaning

Let us now see how the different approaches briefly described above deal with the problem of variation in word meaning. In order to do this, we will consider a few examples of variation in word meaning.

1.2.1. Nature and democracy

In philosophy, conceptual analysis has often been based on an attempt to define "concepts" (in effect "meaning" in the sense of *Gesamtbedeutung)* through the use of necessary and sufficient conditions. An example can be found in the work of the American philosopher Arthur Lovejoy (1936), who distinguished sixty or more meanings of the word *nature*. Similarly, political philosophers have distinguished ten or more meanings of the word *democracy*. We may well ask whether this is a reasonable analysis from the perspective of a general approach to word meaning.

Whether or not we think the analysis is reasonable depends very much on our view of lexical meaning. Given an approach in which meanings are identified with necessary and sufficient conditions, results like the ones proposed by Lovejoy are more or less inevitable if the words and concepts which are studied are to retain a substantial empirical content and still be sharply distinguishable from other words and concepts. It may, however, be questioned whether these goals, taken one by one or in conjunction, are reasonable. If we abandon the goals and try to derive a common meaning for all uses, we instead face the problem of very abstract or almost empty meanings for words such as *nature* and *democracy*.

What the *Grundbedeutung* approach would lead to in this case is a little unclear since it depends on what type of *Grundbedeutung* is assumed. The kind of democracy which is ontogenetically or historically primary might not be the prototypical democracy, ideal democracy, or even stereotypical democracy. Whichever kind of democracy is chosen as the *Grundbedeutung,* it is clear that some types of democracy will have to be left out if only one *Grundbedeutung* is assumed. The next step would therefore be to assume several *Grundbedeutung*s. A problem here is that the notion *Grundbedeutung* implies more strongly that there exists one single basic meaning than do the notions *prototype*, *ideal type*, and *stereotype*. It might therefore be easier to use one of the latter three notions (cf. Lakoff 1987). The question is, however, how many meanings should be allowed and on what grounds? It is likely that if this question is pursued vigorously enough, the final answer will not be very different from that provided by those who believe in necessary and sufficient conditions. There will be many prototypical, ideal, and stereotypical democracies.

1.2.2. Intention and result

Most action verbs can be associated with an intention and a result and, very often, only one of the two need be present to justify the use of an action verb to describe a particular action (Allwood 1980). Consider the following examples:

(1) a. *I warned him but he did not hear me.* (intentional warning; 'to notify')
b. *I warned him without intending to do so.* (resultative warning; 'to make someone aware of, e.g., by doing something')

(2) a. *I flattered him but he did not notice.* (intentional flattery)
b. *I flattered him unintentionally.* (resultative flattery; e.g., *It flattered him that we still knew him*)

We may now ask whether intentional warnings and resultative warnings, or intentional flattery and resultative flattery, constitute two different meanings of the verbs *to warn* and *to flatter*? Our answer will probably again depend on our view of meaning. If our criterion is necessary and sufficient conditions (i.e., *Gesamtbedeutung*), our answer will probably be "yes", since it seems difficult if not impossible to define warnings without taking either intention or result into account; it is equally clear that the appropriate intention and result are not always present. Again, having only one meaning for *warn* or *flatter* runs the risk of being too abstract, even vacuous.

If we instead believe in *Grundbedeutung*s, we may choose one of the two cases or a combination of both as the basic meaning and then try to derive the other cases in some principled manner from the basic meaning. Another option would be to say that we have two *Grundbedeutung*s, which would diminish the difference between the *Gesamtbedeutung* and the *Grundbedeutung* approaches.

1.2.3. The meanings of the verb *gå* in Swedish

As a third example, we will consider the Swedish verb *gå,* 'to walk, to go'. Here are some of the very many uses of the verb (cf. Voionmaa 1993):

(3) a. *Pelle går till skolan.*
'Pelle walks to the school.'
b. *Pelle går i skolan.*
'Pelle goes to (attends) school.'
c. *Bilen går bra.*
'The car runs smoothly.'
d. *Motorn går inte.*
'The motor does not function.'
e. *Motorn går att laga.*
'The motor can be mended.'
f. *Det går inte att röka här.*
'It's not possible to smoke here.'
g. *Det går inte an att röka här.*
'It's not socially acceptable to smoke here.'
h. *Han går ofta på nitar.*
'He often runs into problems.'
i. *Han går ofta på bluffar.*
'He is often fooled.'
j. *Han går på alla så där.*
'He attacks everyone that way.'
k. *Vägen går från Göteborg till Borås.*
'The road leads from Göteborg to Borås.'
l. *Han går på bussen.*
'He enters the bus.'
m. *Det går bra.*
'That will be OK.'
n. *Det går jag inte med på.*
'I don't accept that.'
o. *Han går ut med henne.*
'He dates her.'
p. *Inget går upp mot sol.*
'Nothing is better than sun.'
q. *När går du upp på morgonen?*
'When do you get up in the morning?'
r. *Vad går det ut på?*
'What is it about?'

How many meanings of *gå* should we assume? Is the word homonymous or polysemous? Even if the problem can be somewhat reduced in complexity by regarding some phrases as separate verb-particle constructions, the question arises as to whether there are in fact a finite number of meanings for *gå* or whether, as seems more likely, we can expect the number to vary with new meanings being continuously added, which would imply that any approach based on a fixed set of meanings, whether it be based on generalizations or basic examples, would be inadequate.

1.2.4. Words that can function as several parts of speech

Yet another problem concerns words that can be assigned to several parts of speech.

In English, it is very common for some words to be used both as verbs and nouns, e.g., *to run* (verb) and *a run* (noun), or *a book* (noun) and *to book* (verb). Other words can have verbal (*be singing*), adjectival (*a singing child*), and nominal uses (*this singing*). In Swedish, there is a similar variation between adjectival and nominal functions, e.g., *unga plantor* 'young plants' (adjective) and *de unga* 'the young ones' (noun). Are we to say that words such as *book, singing*, or *unga* are homonymous or polysemous, i.e., are they different words which just happen to coincide in form, or are we dealing with one word with several meanings associated with different parts of speech? If we want neither homonymy nor polysemy for such words, what would be involved in claiming that they are monosemous?

1.3. Meanings of different types of linguistic expression

Linguistic expressions are not all of the same semantic type. Some, like nouns, pronouns, adjectives, and verbs, can be associated with denotations. Some, like verbs, pronouns, and some adverbs, help to deictically anchor what is said in the speech situation. Some, like other adverbs, prepositions, conjunctions, and quantifiers, are more difficult to associate with denotations and are more functional in character. Still others, like interjections, feedback words, and "own communication management words" (hesitation sounds, etc.), are functional but expressive rather than denotative. In addition, several types of expression such as *you know* are multifunctional, in that they can have more than one of the above mentioned functions.

It is not clear that the two approaches to meaning discussed above fit these different types of expression equally well. For instance, which of the following alternatives, then, would be the best characterization of the meaning of the preposition *in*? (See also Vandeloise, this volume.)

(a) An abstract relation of inclusion (*Gesamtbedeutung*): this characterization would be neutral as to whether we are talking about inclusion in a mathematical proof or inclusion in a bottle.
(b) A concrete spatial relation of inclusion (*Grundbedeutung*): this characterization would claim that inclusion in a bottle is more basic than inclusion in a mathematical proof, and would perhaps try to derive the latter from the former.

Whatever solution we adopt for *in*, it is not clear that we necessarily want to adopt the same solution for all other types of expression.

2. Monosemy, polysemy, and homonymy

2.1. *Criteria for polysemy and homonymy*

Linguists have long distinguished between polysemy and homonymy (e.g., Lyons 1977: 22, 235). Usually, an account like the following is given. Homonymy obtains when two words accidentally have the same form, such as *bank* 'land bordering on a river' and *bank* 'financial institution'. Polysemy obtains where one word has several similar meanings, such as *may* indicating 'permission' (e.g., *May I go now?*) and *may* indicating possibility (e.g., *It may never happen*).

Since it is not easy to say when two meanings are totally different or unrelated (as in homonymy) or when they are just a little different or related (as in polysemy), it has been customary to adduce additional, more easily decidable criteria such as one or more of the following:

(a) If two linguistically distinct forms have historically coalesced, we have homonymy, otherwise polysemy.
(b) If the meanings can be associated with two different parts of speech, we have homonymy, otherwise polysemy. This would mean that many, if not most, English concrete nouns are homonymous since by the process of conversion they can usually also be verbs, e.g., *a chair – to chair, a table – to table, a fork – to fork, a telephone – to telephone*, etc. Since most of these cases do not derive from different historical origins, we must either adopt a wider notion of homonymy and reject the historical criterion, or reject the part of speech criterion and say that part of speech variation is a case of polysemy.
(c) If the meanings, although associated with the same part of speech, can be associated with two different inflectional paradigms, we have homonymy, otherwise polysemy, as with the French-based Swedish loanword *en våg – flera vågor* ('a wave – many waves'), and the Germanic word *en våg – flera vågar* ('a scale – many scales').

The trouble is that, although helpful, these criteria are not totally compatible and do not go all the way. There are cases where we may think that the meanings are clearly distinct and that we therefore have homonymy, but which cannot be distinguished by the given linguistic formal criteria, e.g., *charm* may denote 'a kind of interpersonal attraction' and may also be used in physics denoting 'a kind of physical energy'. Not even the word *bank,* usually given in most textbooks as the archetypical example of homonymy, is clear-cut. Both the 'financial bank' and the 'river bank' meanings derive by a process of metonomy and metaphor, respectively from old French *banc* 'bench.' Since *bank* in its two meanings belongs to the same part of speech and is not associated with two inflectional paragdigms, the meanings of *bank* are not a case of homonymy by any of the above criteria. Conversely, the criteria also separate many meanings we perhaps feel are not so distinct, such as Swedish *en öl* 'a glass, a bottle of beer' and *ett öl* 'a kind of beer', or the already discussed switch between verbs and nouns in English. It seems that, in the last analysis, we have to rely on our intuition that clearly distinct meanings should be classified as homonyms and that less clearly distinct meanings should be classified as polysemy. Traditional linguistic criteria for distinguishing homonymy from polysemy, although no doubt helpful, in the end turn out to be insufficient.

Let us now consider whether the examples given above of *nature, democracy, warn, flatter*, and the Swedish verb *gå* are to be considered as cases of homonymy or polysemy. Guided by formal criteria such as the ones above, most linguists would probably say they should all be seen as cases of polysemy. But if we are to be guided by intuitions of distinctness of meaning, perhaps reinforced by an analysis of necessary and sufficient conditions for distinct meanings, the answer is less clear. What does the meaning of *nature* in *the nature of this equation is unclear* have in common with the meaning of the word in *our family enjoys life in nature*, and what does a *democracy* which is a dictatorship for the "good of the people" (as in the people's democracies of the former Soviet Union or China) have in common with so-called "direct democracy"? Concerning Swedish *gå,* we may ask what the meaning of 'possibility' has in common with the meaning of 'walking'. Perhaps, after all, these words should be regarded as homonymous …

2.2. *Monosemous accounts related to* Gesamtbedeutung *and* Grundbedeutung

We may now more explicitly relate the three notions of monosemy, homonymy, and polysemy to the two classical conceptualist approaches to word meaning discussed above. We will first be concerned with what would be involved in giving a monosemous account using the *Gesamtbedeutung* and *Grundbedeutung* approaches, and then consider homonymous and polysemous accounts.

On the *Gesamtbedeutung* approach, a monosemous account would involve trying to find the largest common denominator for all the meaning variants of a word. This might result in the following characterizations: (i) after having excluded 'government by the people', because of the above mentioned "people's democracies", *democracy* would equal 'some form of leadership involving people' (which, of course, would not distinguish democracy from any other form of leadership), (ii) *nature* would equal 'something existing' (which would not distinguish nature very well from anything else), (iii) *warning* would equal 'behavior with causal potential to intentionally alert another person' (which really includes most behaviors), and (iv) *gå* would equal 'possible process' (which actually would characterize any process). These semantic characterizations are clearly too abstract and general. The attendant loss of information would be so great that one would probably feel dissatisfied with a *Gesamtbedeutung* approach and suggest instead that the words are homonymous or polysemous.

On the *Grundbedeutung* approach, one might try to determine a prototypical sense of *democracy, nature, warning*, and *gå*. However, as already pointed out, it is not entirely clear how this would be achieved. It is especially not clear that the same criteria for prototypicality could be used in order to determine a prototype in all four cases. It also remains unclear whether any of the examples need more than one prototype (i.e., whether they are homonymous and/or polysemous) to do justice to the conceptual material involved. If we turn from prototypes to the other possible types of *Grundbedeutung,* e.g., "the original case", "the ideal case", or "the most popular case", it remains an open question whether any of these would actually in all cases correspond to what one might feel should be the basic meaning of a word.

2.3. Monosemous accounts and context

I will now turn to the problem of relating word meaning to context. In a sense, most of the problems of meaning variation disappear if context is taken into account. The problems are to a large extent artificial, in the sense that they exist on an abstract type level but not, for the most part, on the level of concrete tokens and occurrences in context. It is when we attempt to give a general account of the meaning of a word that the problem of how to harmonize very different shades of meaning (or different senses) arises; it is then that we have to decide whether to abandon monosemy and opt for homonymy or polysemy.

Let us now consider how the two approaches, given a monosemous account in principle, can be adapted to handle variation in meaning and contextual determination of meaning.

(a) *Gesamtbedeutung*. If we believe in word meanings as common semantic denominators, these will almost always turn out to be more abstract and general than meanings in context. What will therefore be needed is some process of "information addition". For example, if we analyze the meaning of the word *I* 'ego' as 'the current speaker', we need procedures for supplying information about the identity of this person. Such procedures, in ordinary talk, are available through processing a combination of linguistic and non-linguistic information given by hearing and sight.

(b) *Grundbedeutung*. If we believe in word meanings as basic meanings, we will instead need procedures of "information change" or transformation. For example, if the basic meaning of *friend* includes such components as "a personal relationship", "feelings of affection", "mutual obligations", and "common interest", in order to account for a sentence like *Churchill and Stalin were friends during the war*, we might have to make use of an operator of metaphorical extension which would delete most of the above given requirements on friendship.

Neither of the two described procedures is unproblematic. "Information addition" brings the problem of where the additional information comes from, and the criteria by which it is identified. In the case of deictic words like *I*, mentioned above, there is a fairly clear answer to these questions: the information can be obtained by direct perception in the speech situation. But the answer is not equally clear for words like *nature* or *democracy*.

To some extent, "information change" involves the same problems as "information addition", since some types of change entail addition of information. Very often, however, what is involved is the opposite, i.e., information loss. This is, for example, one of the essential ingredients of metaphorical extension, which operates on the basis of similarity abstraction, i.e., the selection of one or more properties which are similar to or compatible with other elements in the linguistic or extralinguistic context, while leaving out those properties which are not similar or compatible.

2.4. Homonymous and polysemous accounts

As we have seen, it is very likely that attempts to give a monosemous account of word meaning on a *Gesamtbedeutung* or *Grundbedeutung* approach will not be possible in all cases. Instead, in addition, the notions of homonymy and/or polysemy will have to be introduced. On the *Gesamtbedeutung* approach, homonymous or polysemous words will be associated with a more or less structured set of necessary and sufficient conditions, and on the *Grundbedeutung* approach with a more or less structured set of prototypes. However, the introduction of several reified meanings does not really provide a solution for handling meaning variation and contextual determination, since it introduces the problem of "information selection", i.e., the problem of how to select the contextually appropriate meaning variant in a particular circumstance.

"Information selection" is a process which, on the basis of context, selects the relevant meaning of a homonymous or polysemous word. In addition to the problem of how and on what basis to determine the multiple meanings, "information selection" involves providing criteria of selectional relevance. A popular suggestion is to analyze selectional relevance in a way similar to metaphorical extensions, i.e., in terms of compatibility of semantic features. Each of a word's meanings will thus have to be analyzed in terms of features, and that meaning is chosen which is most compatible with features of the preceding or possibly succeeding words. Some problems with this approach are that it is not clear that all meanings can be successfully decomposed into features and that, even if such decomposition were possible, it is often too coarse a procedure for describing the resulting contextual meaning. Another problem is that a word's meaning must often be compatible with more than just with features of the words in the local context.

In addition, it would probably not be correct to assume that the problem of "selection" would entirely replace the problems of "addition" and "change". It is more likely that however many meaning variants are chosen, they will remain contextually insufficient (see the discussion of *gå*), and that a *Gesamtbedeutung* approach will have to cope with both "information addition" and "selection", while a *Grundbedeutung* approach will have to cope with both "information change" and "selection".

3. Word meanings as meaning potentials

To attempt to remedy, or at least provide a new perspective on the problems discussed above, I would now like to suggest a slightly different approach to the problem of word meaning. In addition to the two alternatives discussed above, i.e., (i) intersection (*Gesamtbedeutung* or common meaning) and (ii) basic examples (*Grundbedeutung* or basic meaning), a third approach is proposed, namely (iii) the union or "meaning potential" approach. The inspiration for this way of viewing lexical meaning comes from Wittgenstein's ideas of "meaning as use" and "family resemblance" (Wittgenstein 1952), as well as from Rommetveit's observations on the role of context for meaning (Rommetveit 1974) and the ideas of Naess on "intentional depth" (Naess 1966). The notion is also very close to that of "meaning potential" as used by Halliday (1976) and in some ways to the notion of "polysemy" employed by Bréal (1897) (cf. Nerlich & Clarke 1997).

In brief, I would like to suggest that the basic unit of word meaning is the "meaning potential" of the word. The meaning potential is all the information that the word has been used to convey either by a single individual or, on the social level, by the language community. The meaning potential, then, does not result from trying to find a generally valid type meaning for a word; rather, it is the union of individually or collectively remembered uses. This union of uses may serve as a basis for attempting to find a common meaning in terms of necessary and sufficient conditions, or a basic meaning in terms of some criterion of typicality. The meaning potential is a unit on a more basic level than the *Gesamtbedeutung* and *Grundbedeutung* approaches to word meaning and is therefore potentially compatible with both.

A consequence of this approach is that no attempt is made to distinguish between lexical and encyclopedic information in terms of the kind of information that is contained in the meaning potential. Meaning potentials contain both kinds of information – information deriving from use of language and information deriving from other experience with the world. (For arguments concerning the arbitrariness and difficulties of drawing a line between lexicon and encyclopedia, see Quine 1953b; Haiman 1980; Allwood 1981, 1989; Langacker 1987; and Geeraerts 1993.)

Meaning potentials are activated through various cognitive operations. Some of these are triggered through language use; others can be activated independently of language. Whether or not linguistically triggered, the activation of a meaning potential always takes place in a context which creates certain conditions for its activation, with these conditions determining the way in which the potential is activated. The result of an activation is normally a structured partial activation of the potential, which I will refer to as a "determination of meaning". The various kinds of typification discussed in connection with *Grundbedeutung* above are all examples of activation operations. From the meaning potential of *horse,* we can, through different kinds of typification operations, produce a "prototypical horse", an "ideal horse", or a "stereotypical horse". The three cases of typification are all examples of operations that can be triggered by a single word. Another example of such an operation might be what we could call "abstraction of essence", which would activate the necessary and sufficient criteria for being a horse.

Normally, however, we are not concerned with activation of information through the use of single words but through the use of words constrained by other words and by extralinguistic context in such a way that the expression as a whole must make relevant sense in the situation at hand. A *heavy question* is, thus, a question which requires cognitive effort to understand and answer, while a *heavy stone* is a stone which requires physical effort to lift. The meaning potentials of *heavy* and *question* are activated more or less simultaneously in such a way that the head word of the constituent (*question*) sets up criteria for what parts of the meaning potential for *heavy* can be activated if *heavy* is to serve as a meaningful and relevant property of *question*. The same kind of conditions on the activation of the meaning of *heavy* would come into play if the word were to be uttered as an elliptical comment on the difficulty of a previously posed question, as in the philosophical dialog in (4):

(4) A: *What is the being of being?*
B: *Heavy.*

Another factor which comes into play is the memory of past activations. Once activated in a particular situation to meet certain contextual requirements, a meaning potential is probably much easier to activate again in the same or a similar way.

The notion of meaning potential provides a way of handling what has been called the "underspecificity of meaning", i.e., the fact that the full lexical and structural potential of a linguistic expression is normally not made actual use of; in other words, only what is necessary and/or sufficient for the needs of a particular communicative situation is activated. For example, language users probably activate less information about "carburetors" when they interpret (5) than (6).

(5) *A carburetor is a part of a car.*
(6) *A car need not have a carburetor since gasoline can be directly injected.*

In order to understand (5), the meaning of *carburetor* needs to be less specified than in order to understand (6). It follows that the activation of meaning potentials needs to be related to individual communicators, since different individuals do not share the same elaboration of all meaning potentials and therefore cannot always activate the same information. The same kind of reasoning would apply to the interpretation of so called PP attachments, a case of which is (7):

(7) *The boy saw the girl on the street.*

Here a particular speaker or listener might not need to know whether both the girl and the boy, or only one of them, was on the street. For yet another person, this might be essential.

Thus, the notion of meaning potential provides a way of conceptualizing "underspecificity of meaning", as well as other related notions such as the Norwegian philosopher Arne Naess's notion of "intentional depth" (Naess 1966) and the notion of "depth of understanding" discussed in Allwood (1976, 1986).

4. Meaning potentials and the problems of word meaning

Let us now consider how the proposal of contextually determined cognitive activation of meaning potentials can deal with the examples and problems previously discussed.

4.1. *Democracy* and *nature*

On a meaning potential approach, *democracy* and *nature* would each be assigned only one meaning potential. In principle, then, they could be viewed as monosemous items. Operations of essence abstraction or typification (yielding prototypes, ideal types, or stereotypes) could then in particular contexts be applied to the meaning potential to give less rich but more structured and determinate meanings.

A consequence of having only one meaning potential is that the two words would not be homonymous. The question whether they would be polysemous requires somewhat more careful consideration. One answer is that they would not be, since each word has only one meaning potential. Another answer is that they potentially would be, since it would be possible to partially activate the meaning potential in such a way that the activated information would correspond to each of the distinct meanings postulated by a reifying polysemy approach. However, one difference between a reifying polysemy approach and the meaning potential approach would be that in the latter the different meanings are not seen as a constant feature of a particular word. The fact that Arthur Lovejoy could identify sixty meanings of *nature*, while a lexicographer might distinguish only five or six, is not a cause for concern. It simply means that each has activated the meaning potential in different ways. In due course, someone else will probably activate the potential in a different way and find a different number of meanings. Another difference, which follows from the first, is that there is no assumption that the different meanings are disjoint. Activation differences may be very gradual in response to different contextual requirements.

A third difference emerges in relation to the determination of meaning in context. On the *Gesamtbedeutung* or common meaning approach, this has to be accomplished by combining the addition and selection of information. On the *Grundbedeutung* or basic meaning approach, it has to be accomplished through a combination of change and selection. In the present approach, addition and change are not needed (except in the case of activation and determination of the meaning of "deictic" words) since the meaning constructs that necessitate these operations are not viewed as fundamental but are themselves merely examples of ways in which information in a meaning potential can be activated.

When it comes to the question of whether selection operations are needed in the meaning potential approach, one answer would be that there is no selection since there is no set of reified meanings to select from. Another answer would be that, even if there is no selection, there is a process of activation which functionally resembles selection, in that it only highlights certain parts of the information that is available in the meaning potential. (For other suggestions, using the "floodlight metaphor" of activation, see Geeraerts 1993 and Tuggy 1993, and for the related "aspect metaphor", see Allwood 1980.) However, what differentiates activation from selection (of reified meanings) is that activation is not merely seen as a passive selection of already available meanings or semantic features but also as an active construal or shaping of the activated information. We will see below how this construal or shaping is very often triggered by so-called syncategorematic features.

4.2. Intention and result

Warn and *flatter*, like *democracy* and *nature*, would be associated with only one meaning potential. The differences between intentional and resultative warnings or intentional and resultative acts of flattery would be seen as differences in activation triggered by differing contextual requirements on sense making. If a person does not hear a warning, aspects of the meaning potential of *warn* which are connected with results cannot be activated. Likewise, if an action of warning is explicitly stated to be unintentional, the aspects connected with intention cannot be activated.

There is therefore no assumption of reified polysemy either on the type level or on the contextual token level. The type level is characterized only as meaning potential, i.e., as unactivated potential information which, as a consequence, is not polysemous. The token level will be characterized only by actualized activated information which normally will be non-ambiguous, i.e., non-polysemous. It should, however, be pointed out that the above observations do not exclude the possibility that meaning potentials can be structured by habitual uses of set phrases or collocations or by encyclopedic facts. For example, the contrast between intention and result can, in appropriate circumstances, become a potential or more permanent structuring feature of many verbs.

4.3. The verb gå

As in the previous examples, *gå* would only be assigned one meaning potential. It would thus be neither polysemous nor homonymous. The different determinations of its meaning would be triggered by the requirement that the information which is activated is capable of constituting a relevant and meaningful unit in association with information activated by the other linguistic expressions with which it is constructed and by the extralinguistic context.

Consider some of the expressions involving *gå*. *Bilen går* 'the car runs' cannot be construed in terms of walking since cars, as we know, cannot walk; consequently, that part of the meaning potential of *gå* related to walking is not activated. Instead the notion of "functioning activity", which originally was probably derived from "walking" by abstraction and implication, is activated, giving the meaning 'the car functions' or 'the car is working'. Note that the present approach does not entail that abstraction and implication take place *ab novo* each time language users hear an expression like *bilen går*. Since, most likely, they have experienced similar uses many times before, the readiness for this kind of abstraction is part of the meaning potential. Note also that we are not covertly assuming polysemy here since, even if the meaning potential contains a readiness for uses which could be seen as fixed and established meanings, it is assumed that these meanings could also be produced *ab novo*, if the need arises.

Let us consider one more use of *gå*, in the expression *gå ut* '*gå* + out'. A possible way of looking at an expression like this is to treat it as a separate lexical item, since in Germanic languages like Swedish, verb + particle expressions often replace what in other languages (e.g., Romance) is lexicalized by a single word. The following examples make clear that the situation is not so simple:

(8) *Pelle går ut genom dörren.*
'Pelle walks out through the door.'
(9) *Pelle går ut med a trevlig flicka.*
'Pelle dates a nice girl.'
(10) *Pelles prenumeration går ut.*
'Pelle's subscription expires.'
(11) *Pelle går ut med ett meddelande om konkurs.*
'Pelle sends out a notice of bankruptcy.'

The examples show that the meaning of *går ut* shifts between 'walks out', 'dates', 'expires', and 'sends out' as a function of the lexical and grammatical context of the phrase. Each time, the meaning potentials of *gå* (first anchored temporally by the present tense ending *-r*) and *ut* are activated and determined in such a way that the resulting meaning makes sense, given the grammatical construction and the meaning potentials of subject, particle, preposition, and object. The cognitive operations which produce this result can be used *ab novo* but they can also be facilitated by the fact that the meaning potential contains traces of past activations of a similar type.

It might here be worth pointing out another feature of the notion of meaning potential, which involves both expression and meaning and is therefore not a purely semantic notion. It is the word *gå* which has a meaning potential rather than any of its possible determinations of meaning. The verb *promenera* 'to walk, to take a walk' has a meaning potential which overlaps with that of *gå*. Both can mean 'to walk' but the other possible determinations of meaning for *gå* are normally not available for *promenera*. For example, an expression like *motorn promenerar* would, if comprehensible, receive as its primary interpretation 'the motor walks' rather than 'the motor is running/working', which would be the primary interpretation of *motorn går*. This shows that *gå* is conventionally associated with a set of meaning determinations which are not normally available for *promenera*. However, it would be possible to contextually force *promenera* to acquire such a meaning determination by assuming that *motorn promenerar* was uttered by a person who did not fully know the language. Meaning potentials are thus a result of conventionalizations of semantic operations meeting contextual requirements.

4.4. Parts of speech

In classical linguistic approaches, the question whether two meanings of a word can be associated with different parts of speech has often been taken as a decisive criterion for determining whether a word is homonymous or polysemous. In the present approach, this criterion does not have a privileged status. The view can again best be discussed in relation to an example. Let us compare cases like *a house – to house, a bike – to bike*. Rather than postulating two different words, a noun and a verb, it is assumed that there is one root form (*house* and *bike*) with one meaning potential. This root meaning potential has some structure and among other things contains the factual information that houses and bikes are independent material entities which can be used in certain ways. In the first case, the meaning potential is activated through the indefinite article *a* (which semantically is an entity operator), producing the entity expressions (or nominals) *a house* and *a bike*; in the second case, it is through the use of the infinitival *to*, a process abstraction operator which produces the non-temporally anchored process expressions (or verbs) *to house* and *to bike*. Since *houses* and *bikes* denote independent material entities, the process abstraction activated by use of the infinitival *to* takes "house" or "bike" as arguments, in this case as instruments, yielding *to house* 'process which uses house as instrument' and *to bike* 'process which uses bike as instrument'. If we instead consider the root meaning of a process oriented root like *run*, its meaning potential would contain no information that *run* is an independent material object, but rather that it can be "a process of intentional quick leg movement". An entity expression like *a run* must therefore derive an entity from this process. One way of doing this is by "holistic process reification", i.e., by regarding the process as a whole as a reified entity. Another way is by resultative reification, e.g., *a wash* for the result of washing some particular entity.

Returning to process abstraction, another role than instrument might be preferred depending on the nature of the process and of the entities involved, but the most common role in process abstraction from entity is that of instrument. In some cases, history and social convention have given the activated meanings a special status. For example, *to book* is not just instrumental in the sense of 'to use a book', but also locative in the sense of 'to record something in a book, often to record a commitment to participation in a future event'. Over time, as the media have changed, this recording no longer has to be in a book. So today, *to book* has a meaning which is close to that of *to order*. The special sense of *to book* which, in this case and in many similar cases, is compatible with the effects of the original infinitival abstraction, are part of the meaning potential. However, it seems likely that even though we retain the ability to derive *to book* (in the sense of 'to use a book') by use of the infinitival *to* on the root *book,* we also store a kind of phrasal meaning potential for *to book.*

The need to assume meaning potentials not only for roots but also for derived forms and phrases can be seen when comparing English with Swedish, where the definite article and infinitival form are marked as suffixes on the root. The example just discussed would, in Swedish, be as follows: root form *bok* 'book', *bok-en* 'the book', *att bok-a* 'to book', where only the *a*-suffix is needed to show the infinitival form. In Swedish, there would therefore be a meaning potential for *bok* which could be operated on through use of the definite and infinitival suffixes. Besides this basic pattern, there would also be derived complex meaning potentials for *boken* 'the book' and *boka* 'to book'. The extent to which such derived complex meaning potentials are mentally stored will probably depend on how often they are used and how irregular the meaning of the complex is in relation to its constituents.

4.5. Meanings of different types of linguistic expressions

As has been noted above, different types of linguistic expressions, such as different parts of speech, often have different functions. The consequence for the present approach is that meaning potentials must be able to contain many types of semantic-pragmatic information. For nouns, verbs, adjectives, prepositions, and conjunctions, there must be information about entities, properties, processes, and relations as well as about states, events, and courses of events. There must also be information about emotions and attitudes and about ways of managing communication. The latter type of information is especially important for interjections, feedback words, and hesitation words. The information must further clarify whether use of the word is to "express", as in the normal use of the interjection *wow* or hesitation word *eh*, to "denote", as in the normal use of words such as *car* and *red*, or to "anchor in the speech situation", as in the normal use of pronouns, tense affixes, and definite articles.

4.6. Contextual determination

Contextual determination of meaning is a crucial feature of the present proposal. Indeed, activated actual meaning only exists in context, and outside of context, there is only potential meaning. Contextually determined meaning is normally fairly unambiguous, even if there are exceptions. Ambiguities are mostly unactualized potentials which are allowed by the linguistic structure and can be observed by not taking all contextually given restrictions into account.

In accordance with what has been suggested above, all linguistic expressions (morphemes, words, idioms, phrases, etc.) are associated with meaning potentials. Meaning potentials connect an expression both to encyclopedic information and to more specifically linguistic information concerning its use. When used, a linguistic expression activates its meaning potential through cognitive operations whose function is to achieve compatibility between the meaning potential of a particular expression, the meaning potentials of other expressions, and the extralinguistic context. Contextually determined meanings thus result from partial activation of the meaning potentials of the expressions guided by cognitive operations. A subset of these operations can be characterized as semantic-epistemic operations (Allwood 1989, 1999); the operations are connected with a linguistic expression or structural configuration and with a conceptual-epistemic effect. The basis for the operations are general cognitive operations like discrimination, similarity abstraction, typification, and reification, which exist independently of language but are expanded and elaborated by being connected with language.

Given this outlook, a crucial task is to show how different contextual requirements together contribute to activating linguistic meaning. Since this is a fairly complex task, all the present paper allows is a brief consideration of some of the main linguistic and extralinguistic requirements.

4.6.1. Linguistic requirements

One way to approach the linguistic requirements on meaning activation is to divide the vocabulary into "categorematic" and "syncategorematic" expressions. Syncategorematic expressions consist of conjunctions, prepositions, pronouns, quantifiers, some adverbs, some interjections, and derivational and inflectional suffixes, as well as "construction types" like predication, attribution, etc. The use of these expressions, as an important part of their meaning potentials, allows activation of the semantic-epistemic operations mentioned above. Another part of the vocabulary is made up of "categorematic" roots and stems, i.e., roots and stems which normally are used as nouns, verbs, and adjectives (as well as, in some cases, adverbs and interjections). The meaning potentials of such roots are claimed to be subject to both syncategorematic and categorematic contextual determination yielding actual, more complex contextually determined meanings. Thus, the categorematic root *run* combined with the syncategorematic determiner *a* and the construction type "determiner–head" yields as a result the nominal *a run* with a reified process meaning. Another example is given by the compound *glass house,* which requires a slightly different kind of activation than *house glass*, since in the former case, *glass* has to be activated as a property of the head *house* and, in the latter case, *house* has to be activated as a property of the head *glass*. Thus, syncategorematic requirements often determine the way categorematic terms should be related, i.e., the two ways of relating *glass* and *house* discussed above are syncategorematically different. The categorematic restrictions are given by the encyclopedic information connected with the meaning potentials of the root forms *glass* and *house* themselves.

Syncategorematic restrictions operate through the semantic requirements of different grammatical constructions like modifier-head or subject-predicate. This idea is similar to the concepts of "tagmeme" (Pike 1967) and "constructional meaning" (Goldberg 1995). They also operate, in general, through the use of inflectional and derivational morphology as well as through the use of syncategorematic or functional parts of speech like prepositions, conjunctions, some adverbs, numerals, interjections, feedback words, and "own communication management" words. The combination of categorematic and syncategorematic requirements constitutes the most important part of the linguistic requirements on the activation of a word meaning.

4.6.2. Extralinguistic requirements

Meaning is also determined through extralinguistic contextual conditions and requirements. The most important of these are: (i) perceptually available information in the speech situation, (ii) requirements imposed by whatever activity the speaker and listener are pursuing, and (iii) other activated information.

Perceptually available information in the speech situation is required to help determine the meaning of deictically used pronouns and adverbs. For example, it is used to spatially and temporally anchor what is being talked about, by the use of tense markers and adverbs. Information concerning the activity is needed, for example, to help determine the function of what is being said. The function of the word *ice cream* will, for example, vary depending on whether it is uttered by an ice cream sales person offering ice cream or uttered by a child as a response to a question like *What do I have in the bag?* or *What would you like for dessert?* In the first case, it would be a guess rather than an offer and, in the second, an assertion of a desire. Activity may also determine denotative meaning. For instance, *morphology* means one thing when doing linguistics and another when doing cellular biology; *force* means one thing in physics and many other things in everyday life. Finally, "other activated information" includes other types of activated information which perhaps extend outside of the immediate situation or the current activity. If I say *Everyone came*, the universe of quantification must be implicitly available if a meaningful predication is to result. If I say *He is small*, the universe of comparison must be implicitly available for a meaningful predication to be made. This type of information is necessary but does not need to be given by perception of the speech situation or a joint activity.

4.7. Homonymy and polysemy

What conclusions can be drawn with regard to the problems of homonymy and polysemy? As we have seen, the approach suggested tries to make use of "reified polysemy" as little as possible. Words on the type level have meaning potentials which, depending on context, allow for many different determinations. Some of these might occur frequently, and traces of their activation can be stored as part of the meaning potential. They can, however, always be constructed again if they are products of regular processes for determining lexical meaning. In the case where such processes have been combined with idiosyncratic conventional features, as in the case of *to book*, the determinations of meaning are separately stored. The present approach predicts that there is potentially a continuum of meanings (determinations of meaning) rather than a small set of meanings. It also leads to an expectation of and a readiness for ever new shades of meaning.

The meanings which are actually constructed are always the products of memory activation and the application of contextually sensitive cognitive and/or linguistic operations on meaning potentials.

The approach, thus, does not assume that language users either only store or only generate new meanings, but rather that they often do both, as is also claimed by Langacker (1987). Language users have mechanisms for partially activating meaning potentials in a context-sensitive way which can always be used *ab novo* but, once an activation has taken place, they can store a trace of the activation and are, therefore, in a position to activate many meanings both productively and as a result of reactivation of a stored trace. Since the trigger for a particular activation of a meaning potential is a contextually given requirement of sense making, mostly involving compatibility with the meaning potential of other words constrained semantically by a particular grammatical construction as well as by extralinguistic context, the traces of activation often involve storage of collocational relationships to other morphemes or words as well as to stored information about extralinguistic context. It is the complex of all this information which constitutes the meaning potential of a word.

Returning to the notions of homonymy and polysemy, we have seen that traditional linguistic criteria are not in the end sufficient to distinguish the two notions. Let us now try to push the analysis further by considering whether reification of variation in meaning should in some sense be allowed for. The most radical approach answers this negatively and points out that, since very little actual ambiguity (except, perhaps, in jokes and word play) exists in word use on the occurrence level, homonymy and polysemy in a reified sense on the type level really only come into existence through the work of lexicographers or other linguistic analysts who try to summarize the actual uses of a word.

A less radical and perhaps more reasonable approach allows for reification of meaning variation also in ways which are more directly dependent on ordinary language users. We may here distinguish reification on an individual and a collective level. On the individual level, we could talk of variation in type meaning which is reified in the sense of being stored in memory, because of:

(a) being so different that separate meaning potentials have developed,
(b) irregularity in derivation,
(c) habitual occurrence in a specific collocation,
(d) the study of dictionaries, or
(e) remembered explicit stipulations.

For example, we might stipulate the polysemy of *crawling* by abstracting over and reifying its meanings in examples such as the following (cf. Fillmore & Atkins 2000, from whom the examples are taken):

(12) a. *A small baby crawled out on its hands and knees.*
b. *The two hedgehogs crawled from the nest.*
c. *A beetle began to crawl up his leg.*
d. *She felt his hand crawling up her thigh.*
e. *A cloud of steam crawled slowly upwards from the chimney.*
f. *I crawled into my sleeping bag.*

On the collective level, reification can be manifested in at least three ways:

(f) similarities between language users with regard to criteria (a)–(e) above – the greater the degrees of similarity in terms of individual reification, the more collective reification will be established;
(g) the existence of norms and normative sanctions supporting the similarities between users;
(h) the existence of artifacts (like dictionaries) externally reifying and supporting certain patterns of meaning differentiation.

These five individual and three collective criteria of reification can be used to define more or less restrictive notions of polysemy and homonymy. In fact, we are faced with what is basically a terminological choice, whereby different authors may want to define polysemy in different ways depending on their theoretical interests or goals. It should be noted, however, that if we want to make use of both the terms *homonymy* and *polysemy*, a restrictive use of polysemy will force us to make an even more restrictive use of homonymy. Since this might be inconvenient, it is preferable to give both terms a clear domain of application and allow a fairly clear way of distinguishing them. A suggestion in this direction using the first three criteria on the individual level is the following. *Homonymy* could be used when actual variation in meaning is felt to necessitate the assumption of two or more disjoint meaning potentials on the type level. A somewhat broader notion of homonymy would also include cases when a particular determination of meaning cannot be produced by regular context-sensitive meaning activation operations from a meaning potential. When it can be produced in a regular way, we speak of "polysemy". This suggestion would make polysemy the general case for word meaning on the type level and thus, perhaps, come close to Bréal's (1897) conception of polysemy (Nerlich & Clarke 1997). The fact that *bike* has a potential for both an object and a process determination is not sufficient to say that the root is homonymous, since both processes are regular. The expression *to bike* is regularly derived as a process involving a bike as an instrument or object and, following this suggestion, both the object and process determination could be regarded as part of the regular polysemy of *bike*.

A different case would be the expression *to book* since here the derivation is not regular. *To book* does not normally mean a process involving a book as an instrument or object; rather, for historical reasons, a very specific use was conventionalized whose function is such that it requires no books at all today (cf. above). In this case, it would, therefore, be possible to speak of homonymy. The discontinuity between the two meaning determinations is also strengthened by the fact that they are associated with different parts of speech, but this is an auxiliary rather than a decisive criterion.

The suggestion is therefore to associate polysemy with regular variation in meaning and homonymy with disjoint meaning potentials as well as with the lack of existence of regular processes of context-sensitive activation. This leads to the question what a regular activation is. I will first give a few examples of polysemy here (for further examples, see Allwood 1989, 1999; Pustejovsky 1991).

(13) The relation between instance and type in Swedish

a. instance	*Där kommer en bil* 'A car is coming'
b. type	*Volvo är en bil jag gillar* 'Volvo is a car I like'

(14) Activity dependent focus shifts

a. object → process	*a bike → to bike*
b. process → object	*John is washing → Take your washing*
c. object → event	*The film → During the film*
d. event → object	*During dinner → Eat your dinner*
e. intention	*I warned him but he did not hear me*
f. result	*I warned him without intending to*

(15) The relation between individual and substance in Swedish

a. individual	*Där kommer en bil* 'A car is coming'
b. substance	*Här får du inte mycket bil för pengarna* 'Here you don't get much car for the money'

Homonymy is involved when no regular derivation of this type can be found or when there are a number of special restrictions on the derivation. This treatment of homonymy assumes a fairly broad notion, whereby the meanings covered by a single word form, in fact, can be more or less disjoint. If a word has two meanings that are very different, like the two meanings of *bank*, a joint integrated meaning potential could hardly exist. Even if a child misled by the similarity tried to build one up, it would sooner or later probably develop into two different potentials. In other cases like *book*, the historical connection is more recent, so that for some historically oriented language users the variation in meaning would tend toward *polysemy* rather than *homonymy*.

The linguistic criteria of homonymy also play a role in the present approach. If two meanings are really disjoint, the fact that different syncategorematic operations can be applied to them tends to reinforce the impression that there are several meaning potentials rather than one. Differences in inflectional paradigms are therefore, also in this approach, a reason to declare homonymy. But they do not constitute a foolproof reason. If two meanings have much in common, as in the case of *a bike* and *to bike*, the differences might be attributable to a set of regular meaning determining syncategorematic operations which have activated the difference, rather than to irregularity and an inherent disjoint structure in the meaning potential itself.

The suggestion is thus to use "polysemy", on the type level, for all variation of meaning supported by regular derivational processes. Some parts of this variation will be reified in the sense of being stored in memory supported by often used collocations. It might also be reified by individual stipulations or by being recorded by lexicographers. "Homonymy" is reserved for variation in meaning which is connected with disjoint meaning potentials or which cannot be produced by regular processes. This is, however, a terminological choice and nothing much in the arguments presented above for meaning potentials and contextual determination would depend on it.

5. Summary and conclusion

In this paper, I have attempted to show that traditional theories of word meaning often lead to a very large number of reified meanings combined with procedures for selecting the contextually appropriate meaning. If, instead, only one or a small number of meanings is assumed, these theories are forced also to assume a number of meaning-adding and meaning-changing operations which are difficult to justify. Sometimes these two difficulties are combined, as when each word becomes associated with a multiplicity of reified meanings, which forces the assumption of selection mechanisms as well as of operations of addition or change in order to produce contextually appropriate meanings.

As an alternative to these approaches, I have suggested that words on the occurrence level should be seen as, in general, monosemous. On the type level, these words should also, as often as possible, be seen as monosemous and associated with a meaning potential. The meaning potential is an activation potential for all the information (linguistic and encyclopedic) connected with a word. It can be structured in various ways, for example by being connected with a basic epistemic or ontological orientation such as entity, process, or property. So, for example, *bike* has an entity orientation while *wash* has a process orientation. The meaning potential also contains traces of meaning determinations through coactivation with other linguistic expressions. These traces can be freshly produced if the process of meaning determination is of a regular type. If a regular type occurs frequently, it can be stored and need merely be reactivated rather than freshly produced. If it is of an irregular type, as in the case of deriving *to book* from *book*, the collocation probably acquires a permanent meaning potential of its own with new information which can be more or less connected with the regularly activated information. If the processes of activation are regular and based on a common underlying meaning potential, it is suggested that the term *polysemy* be used. If they are irregular, leading to disjoint meaning potentials, the term *homonymy* can be used.

The contextually determined meaning of words on the occurrence level is also usually monosemous and is the result of an imposition of a number of linguistically and situationally given requirements on the activation of a meaning potential. Ambiguity and polysemy are seen as non-actual structural possibilities which exist only when we, as analysts or speakers, ignore some of the contextual restrictions on meaning. Since the degree to which a meaning potential needs to be activated also varies with context, the phenomenon of underspecificity turns out to be an expectable feature of the contextual determination of meaning. The approach thus allows for homonymy when meanings are conceptually disjoint, but appeals to this notion as seldom as possible. Homonymy is involved, only when an explanation in terms of a linguistically and extralinguistically conditioned activation of two or more meanings from a joint meaning potential fails. I have also pointed to the continuum which exists from regular context-sensitive activation of a meaning potential to polysemy and homonymy. This continuum, to be sure, still leaves open the question, how to delimit polysemy in relation to variation in word meaning on a type and occurrence level. If a greater degree of specification is desired, this could be obtained by talking of "type polysemy" and "occurrence polysemy".

Finally, it is worth pointing out that the meaning potential approach in relation to traditional approaches is, in a sense, a case of trying to have your cake and eat it. This is so because the meaning potential approach allows both generalizations (*Gesamtbedeutung*s) and typical examples (*Grundbedeutung*s) to be produced from the meaning potential, when needed. However, both approaches are seen as making use of processes available for the contextual determination of meaning rather than as descriptions of the ultimate nature of meaning.

References

Allwood, Jens

1976 *Communication as Action and Cooperation.* (Gothenburg Monographs in Linguistics 2). Göteborg University, Department of Linguistics.

1980 On the analysis of communicative action. In: Michael Brenner (ed.), *The Structure of Action*, 168–191. Oxford: Basil Blackwell.

1981 On the distinctions between semantics and pragmatics. In: Wolfgang Klein and Willem Levelt (eds.), *Crossing the Boundaries in Linguistics*, 177–189. Dordrecht: Reidel,.

1986 Some perspectives on understanding in spoken interaction. (Special issue *Logic and Abstraction*, Guest eds. Mats Furberg, Tomas Wetterström and Claes Åberg). *Acta Philosophica Gothoburgensia* 1: 13–59.

1989 Om begrepp – deras bestämning, analys och konstruktion [On concepts – their determination, analysis, and construction]. Ms. Göteborg University, Department of Linguistics.

1999 Semantics as meaning determination with semantic-epistemic operations. In: Jens Allwood and Peter Gärdenfors (eds.), *Cognitive Semantics*, 1–17. Amsterdam: John Benjamins,.

Aristotle
[1938] *Categories: On Interpretation and Prior Analytics*. (Translated by Harold P. Cooke and Hugh Tredennick.) London and Cambridge, MA: Loeb Classical Library, Harvard University Press and W. Heineman Ltd.

Bréal
1897 *Essai de sémantique: Science des significations*. Paris: Hachette. (English translation: *Semantics: Studies in the Science of Meaning*. Translated by Mrs. Henry Cust, with a preface by J.P. Postgate. London: Heinemann, 1900. Reprinted, with a new introduction by J. Whatmough. New York: Dover, 1964.)

Fillmore, Charles J. and Beryl T.S. Atkins
2000 Describing polysemy: The case of 'crawl'. In: Yael Ravin and Claudia Leacock (eds.), *Polysemy: Theoretical and Computational Approaches*, 91–110. Oxford: Oxford University Press.

Geeraerts, Dirk
1993 Vagueness's, puzzles, polysemy's vagaries. *Cognitive Linguistics* 4: 223–272.

Gilby, Thomas
1967 Peter Abelard. In: Paul Edwards (ed.), *Encyclopedia of Philosophy*, 3–6. Concon: Collier MacMillan Publishers.

Goldberg, Adele E.
1995 *A Construction Grammar Approach to Argument Structure*. Chicago: The University of Chicago Press.

Haiman, John
1980 Dictionaries and encyclopedias. *Lingua* 50: 329–357.

Halliday, M.A.K.
1976 The form of a functional grammar. In: Gunther Kress and M.A.K. Halliday (eds.), *System and Function in Language*, 7–25. Oxford: Oxford University Press.

Lakoff, George
1987 *Women, Fire, and Dangerous Things: Wht Categories Reveal about the Mind*. Chicago: The University of Chicago Press.

Langacker, Ronald W.
1987 *Foundations of Cognitive Grammar*, Volume 1: *Theoretical Prerequisites*. Stanford: Stanford University Press.

Locke, John
1690 [1960] *An Essay Concerning Human Understanding*. Gateways editions. (Fifth printing, 1969. Chicago: Henry Regnery Company.)

Lovejoy, Arthur O.
1936 [1960] *The Great Chain of Being: A Study of the History of an Idea*, 2nd edition. New York: Harper & Row.

Lyons, John
1977 *Semantics*. Cambridge: Cambridge University Press.

Nerlich, Brigitte and David D. Clarke
1997 Polysemy patterns of meaning and patterns of history. *Historiographia Linguistica* XXIV: 349–385.

Naess, Arne
1966 *Communication and Argument*. Oslo: Universitetsforlaget.

Pike, Kenneth L.
1967 *Language in Relation to a Unified Theory of the Structure of Human Behavior*. The Hague: Mouton.

Pustejovsky, James
1991 The generative lexicon. *Computational Linguistics* 17: 409–441.

Putnam, Hilary
1975 The meaning of meaning. In: Hilary Putnam, *Mind, Language and Reality. Philosophical Papers*, Volume 2, 215–271. Cambridge: Cambridge University Press.

Quine, Willard V.O.
1953 a On what there is. In: Willard V.O. Quine, *From a Logical Point of View*, 1–19. Cambridge, MA: Harvard University Press.
1953 b Two dogmas of empiricism. In: Willard V.O. Quine, *From a Logical Point of View*, 20–46. Cambridge, MA: Harvard University Press.

Rosch, Eleanor
1977 Human categorization. In: Neil Warren (ed.), *Studies in Cross.-Cultural Psychology*, Volume 1, 1–49. London: Academic Press.

Rosch, Eleanor and Carolyn B. Mervis
1975 Family resemblances. *Cognitive Psychology* 7: 573–605.

Rommetveit, Ragnar
1974 *On Message Structure*. London: John Wiley & Sons.

Runciman, W.G.
1972 *A Critique of Max Weber's Philosophy of Social Science*. Cambridge: Cambridge University Press.

Tuggy, David
1993 Ambiguity, polysemy, and vagueness. *Cognitive Linguistics* 4: 273–290.

Vandeloise, Claude
this volume Containment, support, and linguistic relativity.

Voinonmaa, Kaarlo
1993 *On the Semantics of Adult Verb Acquisition*. (Gothenburg Monographs in Linguistics 12). Göteborg University, Department of Linguistics.

Weber, Max
1951 *Gesammelte Aufsätze zur Wissenschaftslehre*, 2nd edition. Mohr: Tübingen.
Wittgenstein, Ludwig
1952 *Philosophical Investigations*. Oxford: Basil Blackwell.

Towards a pragmatic model of cognitive onomasiology

Stefan Grondelaers and Dirk Geeraerts

Abstract

We argue for an onomasiological reorientation of cognitive lexical semantics: the existing focus on semasiological phenomena like prototypicality should be supplemented with a focus on lexical selection and the factors governing the same. We show what kind of methodology may be used to effectuate such a shift, and we present a conceptual framework for distinguishing between the relevant phenomena. We further argue that the onomasiological perspective inevitably encompasses pragmatic and sociolinguistic variation: the proper development of cognitive onomasiology implies the elaboration of a full-fledged sociolexicological theory and methodology.

Keywords: lexical selection, lexicology, onomasiology, pragmatics, salience, semasiology, sociolexicology, sociolinguistics, variation.

1. Introduction

Cognitive Linguistics (as it is associated with the ideas of Ron Langacker, George Lakoff, Len Talmy, and others) is to a large extent characterized by a research strategy that extrapolates findings from lexical semantics to grammar at large: grammatical constructions are assumed to exhibit the same semantic features (such as prototypical structuring) as lexical items. This shift from the lexicon to the grammar of constructions does not imply, however, that the cognitive linguistic theory of the lexicon has in any way reached a final stage. In this paper, we would like to present one specific way of taking cognitively inspired lexicology one step further, viz., by extending it into the field of onomasiological research.

Our aim is twofold: on the empirical level, we will present the distinction between a *static*, *structural*, and a *dynamic*, *pragmatic* interpretation of onomasiology, and we will define the basic factors at work in a dynamic conception of onomasiology. It will be shown that the choice of a term for a referent in a given context is determined simultaneously by (i) the semasiological salience of that term, (ii) its onomasiological salience, and (iii) contextual factors of a sociolinguistic nature. On the methodological level – which is predominant in this paper – we will demonstrate that the actual implementation of a dynamic model of onomasiology (or of lexical choice) requires a more integrated type of lexical studies. A major impediment to the latter is the fact that, due to a lack of corpus-based research, (i) the onomasiological perspective in Cognitive Linguistics is underdeveloped, and (ii) contextual factors have so far received little theoretical attention in cognitively inspired work. Research into variational phenomena of a contextual kind is mostly restricted to sociolinguistics, traditionally a field with its own methodology and quantitative techniques. We will, however, demonstrate with a selected number of case studies that a true quantitative sociolinguistics of the lexicon, or sociolexicology, is indispensable in order to obtain a reasonably comprehensive model of lexical selection. We believe, in addition, that this goal can never be achieved without thorough empirical substantiation. It is our intention to demonstrate that the three components of the model (semasiological salience, onomasiological salience, contextual factors) – and not just the first one – are amenable to the same type of quantitative analysis, viz., observation of non-elicited language use. A unified methodology, we will also show, is a pivotal step in bridging the traditional gap between lexicology and sociolinguistics.

This paper is organized as follows. The second section presents the basic principles of pragmatic onomasiology. Sections 3 and 4 focus on empirical data substantiating the import of semasiological salience and onomasiological salience, respectively. Section 5 introduces the contextual perspective and sociolexicology, and sections 6 and 7 discuss sample studies which illustrate contextual influence on conceptual onomasiological variation and formal onomasiological variation. Section 8, finally, is devoted to conclusions and theoretical consequences.

2. Towards the basic principles of cognitive onomasiology

The distinction between onomasiology and semasiology is a traditional one in Continental structural semantics, but it has hardly found its way into the canonical English terminology of linguistics; it does not appear, for instance, in most standard textbooks of linguistics. The following quotation from the Swiss Romanist Kurt Baldinger provides a good definition of this distinction: "Semasiology ... considers the isolated word and the way its meanings are manifested, while onomasiology looks at the designations of a particular concept, that is, at a multiplicity of expressions which form a whole" (1980: 278). The distinction between semasiology and onomasiology, then, equals the distinction between meaning and naming: semasiology takes its starting-point in the word as a form, and charts the meanings that the word can occur with; onomasiology takes its starting-point in a concept, and investigates by which different expressions the concept can be designated, or named.

While Baldinger's definition of onomasiology suggests that "the designations of a particular concept" and "a multiplicity of expressions which form a whole" are equivalent, we submit that they point to two different onomasiological subfields. On the one hand, studying "a multiplicity of expressions which form a whole" is the domain of the traditional, structuralist conception of onomasiology, i.e., the study of semantically related expressions (as in lexical field theory, or the study of the lexicon as a relational network of words interconnected by links of hyponymy, antonymy, synonymy, etc.). On the other hand, studying "the designations of a particular concept" paves the way for a contextualized, pragmatic conception of onomasiology, which focuses on the actual choices made for a particular name as a designation of a particular referent.

This distinction between a structural and a pragmatic interpretation of onomasiology can be defined even more precisely by equating it with a distinction between an investigation of *structure* and an investigation of *use*. On the structural interpretation, onomasiology deals with sets of related expressions, and basically asks the question: What are the relations among the alternative expressions? On the pragmatic interpretation, onomasiology examines the actual choices made from among a set of related expressions, and basically asks the question: What factors determine the choice for one or the other alternative? It is precisely with the latter issue that this paper will be concerned.

A systematic treatment of pragmatic onomasiology, however, presupposes one more distinction, namely that between what may roughly be described as the *qualitative* versus the *quantitative* aspects of linguistic semantic structure. Let us first consider how this distinction operates in semasiology. The qualitative study of semasiological structure looks at the following questions: What meanings does a word have, and how are they semantically related? The outcome is an investigation into polysemy, and the relationships of metonymy, metaphor, etc. that hold between the various readings of an item. A quantitative study of semasiological structure, on the other hand, involves the question whether all the readings of an item carry the same structural weight. The outcome, obviously, is an investigation into prototypicality effects of various kinds. Obviously, the qualitative perspective is much more traditional in semasiological lexicology than the quantitative one, which has been taken up systematically only recently, with the development of prototype theory.

The distinction between qualitative and quantitative aspects of semasiological structure has an onomasiological counterpart. The qualitative question then takes the following form: What kinds of (semantic) relations hold between the lexical items in a lexicon (or a subset of the lexicon)? The outcome, clearly, is an investigation into various kinds of lexical structuring: field relationships, taxonomies, and lexical relations like antonymy, hyponymy, etc. Research into the quantitative aspects of onomasiology revolves around the following questions: Are some lexical categories cognitively more salient than others, that is, are there any differences in the probability that one category rather than another will be chosen for designating things out there in the world? Are certain lexical categories more obvious names than others? Again, this type of quantitative research is fairly new, and does as yet only exist in an embryonic form. The best-known model to date is Berlin and Kay's basic level model (1969), which claims that the generic level in a taxonomy constitutes the default "basic level" for categorization. (This hypothesis will be nuanced below.)

The overall picture of the field of lexicology that emerges from the foregoing is presented in Table 1. This table serves as a background for the next important step in our discussion, where we will make clear that the quantitative aspects of semasiological structure and onomasiological structure are among the crucial factors determining lexical selection.[1]

Table 1. The field of lexicology.

	Semasiology	Structural onomasiology	Pragmatic onomasiology
Qualitative aspects: elements & relations	senses + semantic links (metaphor, metonymy, etc.)	lexical items + lexical relations (fields, taxonomy, etc.)	factors determining lexical selection
Quantitative aspects: differential weights	salience phenomena, core vs. periphery	cognitive salience of categories	

The factors determining the selection of a name for a referent, or more generally, the principles of a pragmatic onomasiology, are in fact the following:

1. The overall sketch of the field of lexicology that is presented in Table 1 is elaborated in Geeraerts (2002a). The historical evolution of lexicology (which may be seen as a gradual expansion of the field as charted in Table 1) is discussed in Geeraerts (2002b).

(a) the degree of prototypicality of the referent with regard to the semasiological structure of the category (*semasiological salience*);
(b) the onomasiological entrenchment of the category labeled by the name (*onomasiological salience*);
(c) contextual features of a classical sociolinguistic (geographical, stylistic, etc.) nature.

In what follows, empirical results pertaining to (a)–(c) will be presented. Just like the model of lexicology presented here, these results are treated in more detail in Geeraerts, Grondelaers and Bakema (1994), Grondelaers and Geeraerts (1998), and Geeraerts, Grondelaers and Speelman (1999).

3. The influence of semasiological salience on naming

Semasiological salience, or prototypicality, in a lexical category can be determined in a rather straightforward manner. Indeed, prototypical status is usually assigned to that category member whose configuration of defining features is not only attested the most (i.e., has the highest frequency) in a sufficiently large database, but also whose feature configuration combines the highest number of dominant features. As such, prototypicality shows a correlation between the intensional and the extensional aspects of semasiological structure. This is, to be sure, a classical conception of prototypicality, as it was first introduced by Eleanor Rosch. Its impact may be established by examples such as Figure 1.

Figure 1 charts the semasiological range of the Dutch clothing term *colbert* 'formal jacket', such as it is used in a number of fashion magazines and women's magazines. The database on which the analysis is based consists of 9,000 records in which an attested clothing term is coupled with a componential description of its referent. These featural descriptions are set up on the basis of the pictures

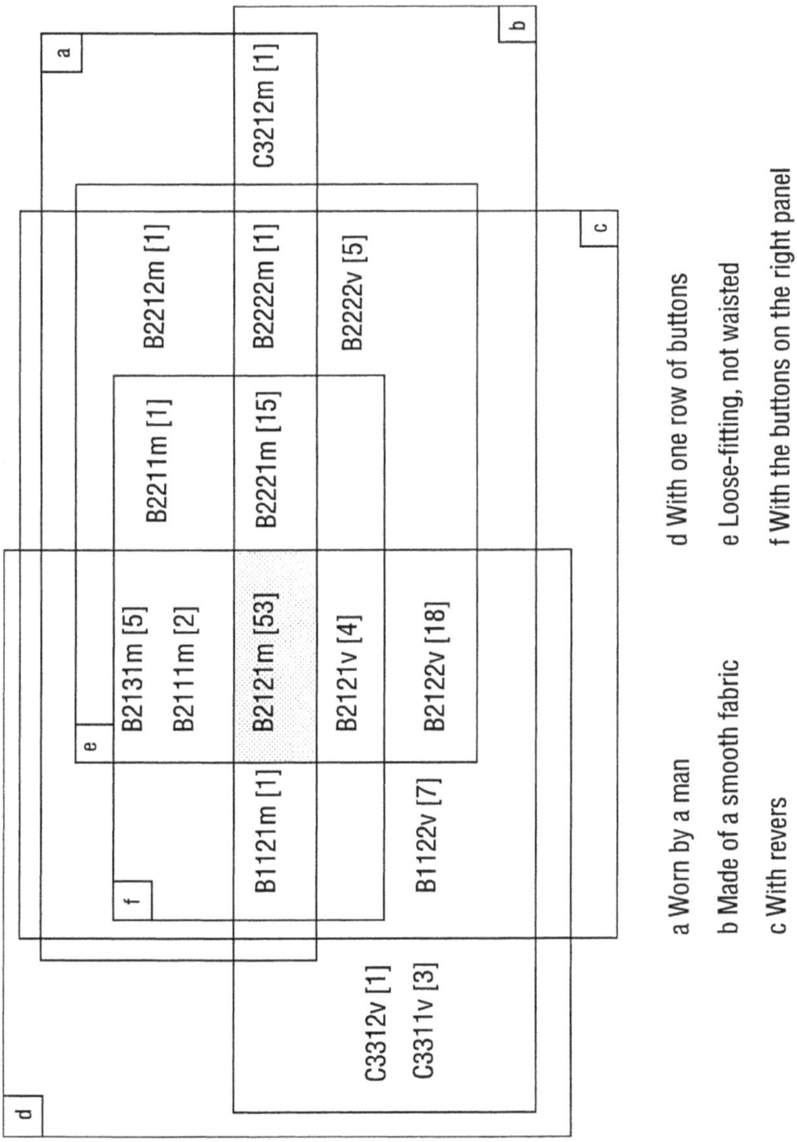

Figure 1. The semasiological range of the Dutch clothing term *colbert.*

and drawings the clothing terms occur with in the magazines, whereby each feature configuration denotes a distinct type of garment. Figure 1 shows various feature configurations (such as

B2121m) which are each labeled *colbert*. The capitals "B" and "C" in the configurations respectively refer to formal jackets with revers and knitted cardigan-like jackets, while "m" and "v" indicate the sex of the wearer. The feature breakup is as follows: the first digit after the capital indicates the jacket's width, with values "1" (waisted) and "2" (loose-fitting); the second digit specifies whether the jacket has a single-breasted ("1") or a double-breasted ("2") button fastening; the third digit identifies the fabric the jacket is made of: thin ("1"), thick but smooth ("2"), or thick and coarse ("3"); the last digit indicates whether the buttons are located on the right ("1") or left front panel ("2").

The numbers between square brackets following the feature configurations indicate the absolute frequency with which *colbert* occurs in the corpus as the name for the type of garment represented by that particular feature configuration. Now, the various configurations in the structure of *colbert* may be divided into subsets on the basis of the features that they share. The feature configurations in Figure 1 allow a classification in terms of subsets "a" to "f"; each of these subsets shares a specific value on the features discussed in the previous paragraph. Prototypicality shows up in that the type of referent with the highest frequency (B2121m, n = 53) is at the same time the type of referent that combines all the dominant features "a"–"f", whereas the less frequently attested referents lack one or more of these features. Graphically, this highest frequency referent is situated in the area where all of the subsets "a"–"f" overlap (indicated by shading).

The kind of prototypicality structure of lexical items such as illustrated in Figure 1 will have an influence on the selection of lexical items if the following hypothesis holds:

> *A referent is more readily named by a lexical item if it is a salient member of the category denoted by that item.*

That is to say, there is a positive correlation between the prototypical referent of a word (i.e., a referent's centrality in the semasiological structure of a word), and the probability of that word being selected –

rather than alternative words – to name/label the referent. The latter may be expressed by an *onomasiological cue validity* measure: a referent (or a set of referents) in the extension of a lexical category has a high cue validity with regard to that category if the category is readily chosen as a name for designating the referent. Onomasiological cue validity, then, can be measured by computing the ratio between the number of times that a lexical item is chosen as a name for a particular (set of) referent(s), and the total corpus frequency of that (set of) referent(s).

Table 2. Correlation between prototypicality (in terms of frequency) and onomasiological cue validity for the item *colbert.*

Set of configurations	Cumulative semasiological frequency per set	Cumulative onomasiological cue validity per set
B2121m	53	72.60
B2121v, B2122v, B2131m, B2111m	82	33.60
B2121m, B2121v, B2122v, B2131m, B2111m, B1121m, B1122v, B2212m, B2211m, B2221m, B2222m, B2222v	113	29.89
B2121m, B2121v, B2122v, B2131m, B2111m, B1121m, B1122v, B2212m, B2211m, B2221m, B2222m, B2222v, C3312v, C3311v, C3212m	118	24.48

Table 2 presents four central subsets of the category COLBERT in Figure 1; these subsets were singled out by starting from the maximally overlapping area in Figure 1 (B2121m) (the most prototypical case), and gradually enlarging this core area towards less central cases. The more the semasiological core of the category is enlarged, the fewer features the items in the subsets have in common, and the more their relative frequency diminishes. It is crucial for a correct understanding of Table 2 that the semasiological frequencies in the second column and the cue validities in the third relate to cumulated sets of configurations. The cue validity value 33.6, for instance, relates to the set constituted by the configurations B2121m, B2121v, B2122v, B2131m, and B2111m. The rightmost column in Table 2 shows that our hypothesis concerning the correlation of semasiological salience and onomasiological cue validity is indeed correct for the category COLBERT as charted in Figure 1: the cue validity diminishes (from 72.6 to 24.48) as the subset under consideration is extended towards the periphery of the category (for more examples, see Geeraerts, Grondelaers & Bakema 1994: 156 ff.).

4. The influence of onomasiological salience on naming

Let us now turn our attention to the onomasiological domain. If a particular category A (named by A) is more firmly anchored in the user's knowledge than category B, i.e., if the members of a category A are more readily identified as members of A than as members of B, then category A can be said to be more *entrenched* (or onomasiologically salient) than category B. In a corpus-based approach, categorial entrenchment can be operationalized by computing the ratio between the corpus frequency of a category name (and its synonyms) and the corpus frequency of the members of the category. This is, to be sure, a cue validity measure just like the onomasiological cue validity measure computed above. At this point, however, it is applied to a lexical category as a whole (within a corpus), rather than to individual members or subsets (within a category): a lexical category is highly entrenched if its extension as a whole has a high cue validity with regard to the name(s) of the category.

Note that Berlin and Kay's basic level hypothesis mentioned earlier (cf. section 2) stipulates that the entrenchment of individual categories is determined by their taxonomical level: all categories belonging to the basic level should roughly have the same (high) entrenchment, if the basic level does indeed embody naming preferences. The empirical results in Geeraerts, Grondelaers and Bakema

(1994), however, indicate that this is not the complete story. Major differences of entrenchment among co-hyponyms establish that entrenchment is a matter of individual categories rather than taxonomical levels.

The onomasiological hypothesis involving entrenchment may now be formulated as follows:

> *A referent is more readily named by a lexical item if that item denotes a highly entrenched lexical category.*

As such, if in a particular corpus of language use, a particular referent is named by two lexical items, A and B, then there is a positive correlation between the respective entrenchment of the two categories A and B and the choice for either A or B as a name for the referents. Consider, by way of example, the clothing terms *topje* 'top' and *blouse* 'blouse'; the referential ranges of these terms overlap because informal, sleeveless blouses may be called *blouse* as well as *topje.* The absolute frequency with which *topje* is used for referents that lie in the intersection of both categories (i.e., that could be called either *topje* or *blouse*) is 11, whereas 26 of the garments in the intersection of both categories are actually called *blouse.* Now, the entrenchment of *topje* is 29.62; that of *blouse* is 61.52. As predicted by the hypothesis, the actual selection of either *topje* or *blouse* for referents in the overlapping area correlates highly with the entrenchment values of these categories, in that the item with the highest entrenchment is indeed more readily chosen as a name for the referents in the intersection of both items. Mathematically, the ratio of, on the one hand, the ratio of absolute frequencies (11/26 = 0.423) and, on the other hand, the ratio of entrenchment values (29.62/61.52 = 0.481) is as high as 0.879 (for more examples, see Geeraerts, Grondelaers & Bakema 1994: 169 ff.).

5. Introducing the contextual perspective

Whether a lexical category is chosen as a name for a referent is not only determined by the degree of prototypicality of the referent with respect to the semasiological structure of the category or the onomasiological entrenchment of that category: semasiological and onomasiological factors themselves correlate with numerous types of contextual factors, such as the sociological and geographical properties of the participants in the communicative interaction, or characteristics of the speech situation itself. In integrating contextual values, we have in fact ventured from lexicology into sociolinguistics, a discipline traditionally considered to have its own subject matter and empirical methodology. We will demonstrate by means of two sample studies that this orientation to the field of sociolinguistics is a necessary one as far as lexical selection is concerned, viz., that a true *sociolexicology* is indispensable in order to obtain a workable model of lexical selection.

The fact that lexicology and sociolinguistics are not evident partners is due, we feel, to two factors. First and foremost, sociolinguistics rarely concerns itself with lexical variation. Sociolinguists who examine the relationship between social factors and language preferably select linguistic factors they can measure in a reliable way; as a result, they predominantly focus on easily quantifiable phonological or morphological variables such as "absence or presence of post-vocalic /r/" (which features prominently in, e.g., Labov's classic (1966) investigation into the stratification of English in New York and Trudgill's (1974) study on the social differentiation of English in Norwich). Since the sociolinguistic study of lexical variation is hindered by the collective interference of several types of – fairly unmanageable – semantic variation, lexical variables are but occasionally included in traditional sociolinguistic research.

An indispensable tool for any linguist – whether sociolinguist or lexicologist – who wishes to undertake the hazardous enterprise of studying contextual differentiation in lexical variation is a theoretical framework in which distinct types of semantic and non-semantic variation are minutely identified, distinguished, and disentangled. In

Geeraerts, Grondelaers and Bakema (1994), the preliminaries to such a model are presented, and considerable attention is devoted to a distinction which is central to the appreciation of pragmatic onomasiology, viz., the distinction between "conceptual" (or "semantic") and "formal" (non-semantic) onomasiological variation. Whereas conceptual onomasiological variation involves the choice of different conceptual categories for a referent, formal onomasiological variation merely involves the use of different names for the same conceptual category. The names *jeans* and *trousers* for denim leisure wear trousers – to give an example – constitute an instance of conceptual name variation, for they represent different categories; *jeans* and *blue jeans*, however, represent no more than different (but synonymous) names for the same category.[2]

If sociolinguists are interested in lexical variation, they invariably – and unsurprisingly – focus on non-semantic variation of the formal onomasiological type (as illustrated in section 7). In Geeraerts, Grondelaers and Bakema (1994), however, we have established that all the types of semantic variation we have hitherto identified are also – and to a large extent – influenced by contextual factors. For a well-known example of geographical variation in the semasiological realm, consider the case of *vest* (1994: 105 ff.). In Netherlandic Dutch, *vest* is

2. Although Cognitive Linguistics upholds the idea that different words designate different categories, we assume that categories can be isolated from the words which are used to designate them. In this paper, the concept "category" basically receives a referential definition: if words have the same referential range, they designate identical categories in our view. To this procedure, one could object that referential identity need not imply conceptual identity, since denotationally synonymous words may have different stylistic or sociolinguistic values. Rather, however, than a priori demanding that the sociolinguistic and stylistic value of denotationally synonymous words be identical, we exclusively rely on denotational synonymy as far as establishing categories is concerned, because in the model of lexical selection we advocate, stylistic variation – of the type discussed in section 6 – and sociolinguistic variation – as in section 7 – have to be determined empirically on the basis of text corpora. Stylistic and sociolinguistic values of categories, in other words, are dependent variables in our investigation, rather than pre-empirically assumed categorial features (cf. also Geeraerts, Grondelaers & Bakema 1994: 178 ff.).

used exclusively to denote knitted, cardigan-like garments, whereas in Belgian Dutch, *vest* also refers to formal jackets (in substandard Belgian Dutch, *vest* is in fact the principal term to refer to formal jackets). Contextual differences also determine the relative preference of groups of speakers for a certain taxonomical level, in the sense that an expert is more likely to use specific, technical terms than the layman (1994: 146 ff.; a more elaborate example of contextual influence on conceptual onomasiological variation is presented in the following section). Sociolexicology is the practical consequence of the idea that all semantic and non-semantic components of our model of lexical selection – and not just one – require sociolinguistic attention, if we want the model to work.

Second, lexicology and sociolinguistics differ not only with respect to subject matter, but also with respect to empirical methodology. Labov (1972) lists three major kinds of linguistic method: linguistic analysis may be based on introspection, on the elicitation of data with questionnaires and experiments, and on the observation of non-elicited language use. Although the bulk of the sociolinguistic research into lexical variation in Dutch is based on elicitation rather than observation (cf. Geeraerts, Grondelaers & Speelman 1999: 32, 52–53, for an overview and exceptions), it is our intention in the remainder of this paper to demonstrate with two case studies that sociolinguistic variation in the lexical domain can be studied just as efficiently and rigorously as semasiological or onomasiological variation by concentrating on non-elicited written language data. As such, our methodology is in line with the Anglo-American sociolinguistic tradition, where observation of non-elicited language material is customary – notable cases in point are, again, Labov (1966) and Trudgill (1974). This possibility of a common method constitutes a major bond between the two linguistic disciplines sociolinguistics and lexicology, which are traditionally thought to be very different.

Before we embark on the case studies, two points need to be addressed. First, it should be noted that the concept of sociolexicology is not entirely new (although the term "sociolexicology" may be new). By insisting on a quantitative sociolinguistics of the lexicon, we are in fact resuming the thread of lexicological work by William

Labov (1973, 1978). The second point relates to the choice of independent and dependent variables in quantitative sociolexicology. With respect to the selection of *independent* variables, it should be pointed out that our corpus-based method and sociolinguistic elicitation differ greatly concerning the basis on which contextual factors are identified. When elicitation is involved, sociolinguistic factors (geography, social stratification, expertise, etc.) can be defined in terms of the characteristics of the speakers in the samples that are compared. In sociolexicology, on the other hand, the comparanda are (necessarily) identified in terms of intended audience, the underlying rationale being that authors of texts intended for a regional or professional subgroup will tailor their word use to that subgroup. The *dependent* variable in sociolexicological corpus-based research differs as to the type of onomasiological variation concerned. When the choice of different conceptual categories – i.e., conceptual variation – is studied, contextual variation is measured in terms of entrenchment values; when different names for the same category are at stake – i.e., formal variation – the dependent variable of the sociolexicological investigation will be defined as the onomasiological profile of a concept, viz., the set of synonyms designating the concept, differentiated by their relative frequency.

In what follows, we will first present an example of contextual influence on conceptual onomasiological variation. Our account of how euphemistic considerations structure the designation of the disease cancer will also focus on how one can identify and disentangle competing contextual factors. The second case study not only concentrates on formal onomasiological variation, it also introduces the diachronic perspective. The investigation of onomasiological change in Netherlandic Dutch and Belgian Dutch presented in section 7 demonstrates that lexical choice is subject to significant change, even when no semantic change is involved.

6. Contextual influence on conceptual onomasiological variation

In this section, we deal with the contextual values of different lexical categories used to designate the disease cancer. The basic question here is how avoidance strategies influence the choice of cancer designations (an elaborate answer to this question is found in Grondelaers & Geeraerts 1998). More particularly, we are interested in finding out how the emotive value of, on the one hand, generic or specific cancer terms such as *cancer* or *breast cancer* and, on the other, vague terms such as *disease* or *illness* influence lexical choice; it is indeed to be expected that in some contexts the vaguer terms will be preferred for euphemistic reasons. To that effect, we have investigated a CD-ROM text corpus – which consists of the 1991–1994 volumes of the Belgian weekly *Knack*, and the 1994 edition of the Dutch quality newspaper *De Volkskrant*. In particular, we looked for quantitative support for the hypothesis that vague terms for cancer are favored in (i) non-scientific contexts, viz., articles which do not or not primarily report on medical topics, and in (ii) personalized contexts, i.e., contexts in which the effects of cancer on individual victims are portrayed (vs. "generic" contexts, in which cancer is referred to in general). The dependent variable in this study is lexical specificity in the naming of cancer, and is quantified as the ratio between the frequency of hyperonymous designations for cancer (such as *disease* or *illness*), and the overall frequency with which the disease cancer is mentioned (by means of various lexical items) in the sources. Again, this is a sort of entrenchment measure, albeit one that is applied to taxonomical level rather than to referents or to individual lexical categories.

Table 3 contains the hyperonym ratios in the naming of cancer in the Belgian weekly *Knack* and the Dutch newspaper *De Volkskrant*. This table distinguishes, vertically, between personalized contexts and generic contexts, and horizontally between medical and non-medical texts. As predicted, average hyperonym ratios are indeed significantly higher in non-medical contexts (0.647 > 0.126) and personalized contexts (0.837 > 0.147), which seems to confirm the hypothesis outlined in the previous paragraph.

Table 3. Hyperonym ratios in the naming of cancer in *Knack* 1991–1994 and *De Volkskrant* 1994.

	-medical	+medical	Total
+personal	0.878 (36/41)	0 (0/2)	0.837 (36/43)
-personal	0.296 (8/27)	0.127 (26/204)	0.147 (34/231)
Total	0.647 (44/68)	0.126 (26/206)	0.255 (70/274)

A methodological problem which complicates the identification of avoidance factors – and contextual factors in general – is the fact that the same variational pattern may be caused by more than one factor. In our cancer-example, the predominance of vague designations in non-medical contexts could just as well be due to an upward shift of the taxonomical basic level as a result of the irrelevance of medical detail in articles which are not primarily concerned with scientific progress (cf. Dougherty 1978: 77, but see also Cruse 1977: 163).

Table 4. Absolute and relative frequency of different taxonomical ranks in the naming of specific types of cancer in *Knack* 1991–1994 and *De Volkskrant* 1994.

	-medical	+medical
Unique beginner	22 (61.12%)	23 (13.45%)
Generic	2 (5.5%)	16 (9.36%)
Specific	12 (33.33%)	132 (77.19%)

Table 4, however, constitutes additional evidence in favor of a taboo-related explanation of the asymmetrical distribution of hyperonymy in Table 3. Table 4 charts absolute and relative frequencies of different taxonomical ranks in the designation of specific types of cancer such as breast cancer or lung cancer. On the vertical axis, unique beginners such as *disease* or *disorder* are contrasted with the generic item *cancer* and specific terms like *breast cancer* or *lung cancer*. Now, if the absence of technicality engendered an increased use of hyperonymy in non-medical contexts, this increase would affect both the generic level and the unique beginner level in roughly the same way; in other words, unlike the medical context, the non-medical context would show an increase of hyperonymy, but this increase would be comparable on both the generic and the unique beginner level. Table 4, however, shows that the generic level and the unique beginner level are affected differently, in that increased hyperonymy almost exclusively affects the unique beginner level; there is, in other words, a tendency to "jump over" the generic level. This avoidance of the generic term can best be explained in light of the fact that the generic term *cancer* is still specific enough to cause offense; it would be difficult to explain as the result of decreased technicality alone.

7. Contextual influence on formal onomasiological variation

This section contains some results from a systematic study of geographical variation between Netherlandic and Belgian Dutch which was undertaken at the University of Leuven (a more detailed report can be found in Geeraerts, Grondelaers & Speelman 1999). The reader who is not familiar with the linguistic situation in the Dutch speaking region, which comprises Belgian Flanders in the south and The Netherlands in the north, should keep in mind that in the Renaissance, linguistic standardization was well on its way in many European countries. In Flanders, however, the ongoing standardization was blocked as a result of the political separation of Flanders from the Netherlands. Instead of developing its own linguistic standard, Flanders increasingly used French as a supraregional standard language. In the nineteenth century, this frenchification was at its height in all public domains. Although Dutch was reinstated as the official language in Flanders during the reunification of the Southern and the Northern Netherlands (1814–1830), and standard Dutch emerged as the supraregional Flemish language in the 1930s, the standardization of Belgian Dutch is not completely finished up to this day. An issue which occupies students of Dutch in this respect concerns the question whether – and to what extent – Belgian Dutch orients itself to Netherlandic Dutch in its development. Is there convergence between Belgian and Netherlandic Dutch in the sense that Belgian Dutch takes Netherlandic Dutch as a norm, or is there divergence, in the sense that Belgian Dutch is developing its own separate standard?

The existing literature lists conflicting tendencies (see Geeraerts, Grondelaers & Speelman 1999, for an overview). On the one hand, there is the traditional expectation of convergence, due to a growing standardization in Belgian Dutch along with a normative orientation towards Netherlandic Dutch. On the other hand, research into the development of pronunciation differences clearly shows actual divergence (Van de Velde 1996).

To settle matters in the lexical domain, we have embarked on a study which is innovative in regard to its empirical basis and its analytical methodology. Empirically, our study is based on a 40,000-record database of lexical items by means of which 30 concepts from two lexical fields – 15 concepts from the field of clothing and 15 concepts from the field of football – are designated. This corpus is structured to accommodate geographical variation – Belgian and Netherlandic sources are compared – as well as diachronic variation. The diachronic variable is implemented by comparing data from 1950, 1970, and 1990. Recall that in this investigation of formal onomasiological variation, the starting-point is the onomasiological profile of a concept in a language sample, i.e., the set of alternative terms (each with its individual frequency) for a concept attested in a source or in a collection of sources (for instance, the Belgian magazines). Recall also that semantic variation is factored out by restricting the analysis to synonymous designations of the same conceptual category. For instance, only the synonyms *legging*, *leggings*, and *caleçon* 'legging' are included in the onomasiological profile of the category LEGGING, but not the hyperonym *broek* 'trousers' or the hyponym *stretchlegging* 'legging made of elastic fabric'.

Analytically, convergence has been quantified in terms of the degree of uniformity between the onomasiological profiles in two language samples, whereby convergence equates with increasing uniformity, and divergence equates with decreasing uniformity. Maximal uniformity between two samples obtains when the distribution of synonyms in the onomasiological profiles in the two samples is identical, either because only one name is used for a concept in the two varieties (as in Table 5), or because several names are used with identical relative frequencies (as in Table 6).

Table 5. Identical onomasiological profiles with 1 item.

CONCEPT X	Var A	Var B
item 1	56 = 100%	20 = 100%

Operationally defined as the sum of the minimal frequency per item over the compared varieties, this uniformity measure (to be called MIN*item*) yields maximal uniformity for the examples in Tables 5 and 6: since the frequency per item over varieties is identical in these examples, the sum cannot be anything but 100% in Table 5 and MIN*item1*(50;50)+MIN*item2*(35;35)+MIN*item3*(15;15) = 100% in Table 6.

Table 6. Identical onomasiological profiles with 3 items.

CONCEPT X	Var A	Var B
item 1	100 = 50 %	20 = 50 %
item 2	70 = 35 %	14 = 35 %
item 3	30 = 15 %	6 = 15 %

Table 7. Differing onomasiological profiles.

CONCEPT X	**Var A**	**Var B**
item 1	56 = 80 %	20 = 50 %
item 2	7 = 10 %	14 = 35 %
item 3	7 = 10 %	6 = 15 %

In the – more realistic – situation illustrated in Table 7, the uniformity between Var A and Var B is the sum of MIN*item1*(80;50), MIN*item2*(10;35) and MIN*item3*(10;15), which is 70%.

The degree of uniformity between varieties A and B as a whole is quantified as the average uniformity of the concepts on which the comparison between A and B is based. In this type of global uniformity measure, the 15 concepts in the fields of clothing and football carry the same weight. Should we wish, however, to take into account the real frequency with which a concept appears in our material, we do not average the uniformity per concept, but sum the degrees of uniformity per concept weighted with the relative frequency of the concept within the total set of concepts. This weighted procedure is preferable from the pragmatic point of view that significantly different onomasiological profiles may cause communicative inconvenience where high frequency concepts are concerned, whereas a low degree of uniformity will not normally lead to communicative difficulties when low frequency concepts are involved.

Let us apply this weighted procedure to the field of clothing in Figure 2, and the field of football in Figure 3. In these diagrams, B stands for Belgian Dutch, N for Netherlandic Dutch, and 50, 70, and 90 for respectively the 1950, 1970, and 1990 material. The figure on the left vertical axis of the diagrams reflects the evolution of uniformity in the Belgian material, whereas the figure on the right vertical axis represents the same evolution in the Netherlandic material. The figures on the horizontal axes denote the evolution from 1950 to 1990 of the uniformity between Belgian and Netherlandic Dutch.

The data in Figures 2 and 3 exhibit a gradual – albeit modest – increase of uniformity – and hence convergence – between Belgian and Netherlandic Dutch, as represented by the lexical fields of football (69.84 < 74.59 < 81.70) and clothing (66.22 < 72.04 < 77.08). In addition, the lower figures on the left vertical axis (56.95 < 63.54 and 69.54 < 75.20) indicate that linguistic change is more significant in Belgian Dutch, which is indicative – in the context of convergence – of a normative orientation of Belgian Dutch towards Netherlandic Dutch.

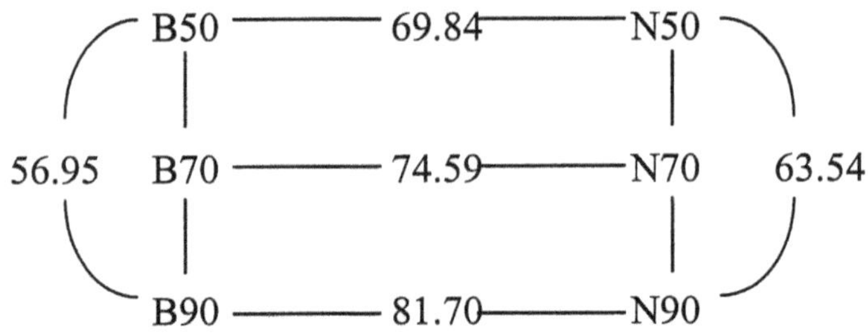

Figure 2. Uniformity in the field of clothing terms.

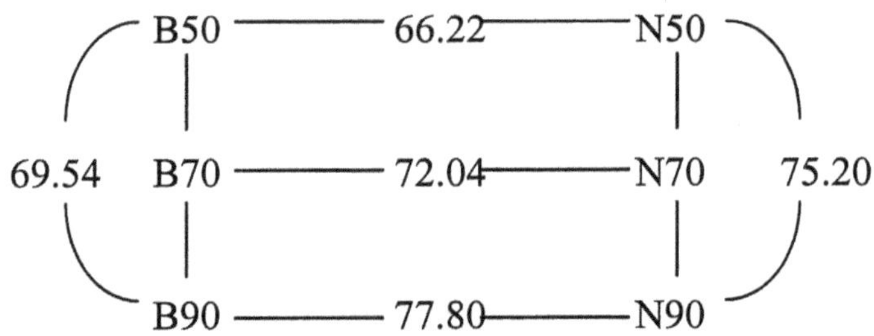

Figure 3. Uniformity in the field of football terms.

There is a lot more, of course, to the linguistic situation in Belgium and The Netherlands than this limited case study could possibly show (again, see Geeraerts, Grondelaers & Speelman 1999, for a more elaborate overview). Rather, however, than showing definite results, it was our intention in this sample study to demonstrate that sociolinguistic and especially language-geographical diversity manifests itself at its best where variation cannot be reduced to semantic differences.

8. Conclusion

Let us briefly go over the observations in this paper. As far as lexical choice is concerned, we have established that the choice of a lexical item as the name for a particular referent is determined by the degree of prototypicality of the referent with regard to the semasiological structure of the category, by the onomasiological entrenchment of the category represented by the name, and by contextual features which interact with these principles. Of these three components, only semasiological salience has enjoyed some theoretical attention in mainstream Cognitive Linguistics, though predominantly in the shape of prototypicality effects, never in the context of lexical selection. The importance of the onomasiological perspective has mostly been neglected, and interfering contextual factors are – incorrectly – assumed to be outside the scope of Cognitive Linguistics.

In order to give these components the attention they deserve, Cognitive Linguistics is in need of a more integrated conception of lexical analysis. This entails, first and foremost, a theoretical framework in which distinct types of semantic and non-semantic variation are minutely identified, distinguished, and disentangled. In earlier work, we have provided the preliminaries to such a model. This paper contains an example of semasiological and onomasiological variation, but it concentrates chiefly on the treatment of contextual, sociolinguistic variation; in this respect, it advocates the integration into Cognitive Lexicology of a genuine sociolinguistics of the lexicon, or sociolexicology. An integrated model of lexical studies presupposes, second, a unified methodological framework. We have demonstrated with a number of case studies that all the varieties of semantic, non-semantic, and contextual variation discussed in this paper are amenable to the same type of quantitative analysis, viz., the observation of non-elicited language data. The demonstration, surely, has been based on a single example in each case, but more examples may be found in Geeraerts, Grondelaers and Bakema (1994), Geeraerts (1997), Grondelaers and Geeraerts (1998), and Geeraerts, Grondelaers and Speelman (1999).[3] It was our special intention in this

3. Further refinements of the approach described here may be found in the following articles: Geeraerts (2001a, 2001b), Geeraerts and Grondelaers (2000), Grondelaers, Speelman and Geeraerts (2002), Grondelaers, Geeraerts, Speelman and Tummers (2001). In all of these papers, specific attention is paid to the formal onomasiological type of lexical variation and to the quantitative methods that may be used to study it. Geeraerts (2000) offers a typology of the different types of lexical salience that issue from the variational approach pre-

paper to show that contextual, sociolinguistic factors can fruitfully be studied with non-elicited corpus data. This possibility of a common quantitative approach constitutes a major link between two linguistic disciplines traditionally thought to be so different as sociolinguistics and lexicology.

The importance of the extrapolation of lexicology towards a use-oriented conception of onomasiology, as suggested here, lies in yet another field: the extrapolation from lexicology to grammar that is typical of Cognitive Linguistics might be effectuated here as well. The focus then shifts from lexical selection to the choice of a grammatical construction. The key concept is that of motivation: just like lexical items, constructions can be both semasiologically and onomasiologically motivated. Semasiologically, a construction is motivated if the idea to be expressed fits in the semantic range of the construction. Onomasiologically, the choice of a particular construction is motivated if it is plausible, given the joint effect of prototypicality and entrenchment. The next step to take, obviously, will be to put this model of constructional motivation to the test: can the determination of constructional selection by prototypicality effects and entrenchment be established with the same kind of quantitative methods that we illustrated here for the lexicon?

References

Baldinger, Kurt
1980 *Semantic Theory*. Oxford: Basil Blackwell.

Berlin, Brent and Paul Kay
1969 *Basic Color Terms: Their Universality and Evolution*. Berkeley and Los Angeles: University of California Press.

Cruse, D. Alan
1977 The pragmatics of lexical specificity. *Journal of Linguistics* 13: 153–164.

---

sented here. An elaboration in a slightly different direction is Geeraerts (1999), where our preference for an empirical, data-based approach is defended in contrast with an introspection-based conception of lexical studies.

Dougherty, Janet
1978 Salience and relativity in classification. *American Ethnologist* 5: 66–80.

Geeraerts, Dirk
1997 *Diachronic Prototype Semantics. A Contribution to Historical Lexicology*. Oxford: Clarendon Press.
1999 Idealist and empiricist tendencies in Cognitive Linguistics. In: Theo Janssen and Gisela Redeker (eds.), *Cognitive Linguistics: Foundations, Scope, and Methodology*, 163–194. Berlin: Mouton de Gruyter.
2000 Salience phenomena in the lexicon. In: Liliana Albertazzi (ed.), *Meaning and Cognition*, 125–136. Amsterdam: John Benjamins.
2001 a Everyday language in the media: The case of Belgian Dutch soap series. In: Matthias Kammerer, Klaus-Peter Konerding, Andrea Lehr, Angelika Storrer, Caja Thimm and Werner Wolski (eds.), *Sprache im Alltag: Beiträge zu neuen Perspektiven in der Linguistik*, 281–291. Berlin: Mouton de Gruyter.
2001 b On measuring lexical convergence. In: Augusto Soares da Silva (ed.), *Linguagem e Cognição: A Perspectiva da Linguística Cognitiva*, 51–61. Braga: Associação Portuguesa de Linguística.
2002 a The scope of diachronic onomasiology. In: Vilmos Ágel, Andreas Gardt, Ulrike Hass-Zumkehr and Thorsten Roelcke (eds.), *Das Wort: Seine strukturelle und kulturelle Dimension*, 29–44. Tübingen: Max Niemeyer.
2002 b The theoretical and descriptive development of lexical semantics. In: Leila Behrens and Dietmar Zaefferer (eds.), *The Lexicon in Focus: Competition and Convergence in Current Lexicology*, 23–42. Frankfurt: Peter Lang.

Geeraerts, Dirk and Stefan Grondelaers
2000 Purism and fashion: French influence on Belgian and Netherlandic Dutch. *Belgian Journal of Linguistics* 13 (1999): 53–68.

Geeraerts, Dirk, Stefan Grondelaers and Peter Bakema
1994 *The Structure of Lexical Variation: Meaning, Naming, and Context*. (Cognitive Linguistics Research 5.) Berlin: Mouton de Gruyter.

Geeraerts, Dirk, Stefan Grondelaers and Dirk Speelman
1999 *Convergentie en divergentie in de Nederlandse woordenschat: Een onderzoek naar kleding- en voetbaltermen*. Amsterdam: P.J. Meertensinstituut.

Grondelaers, Stefan and Dirk Geeraerts
1998 Vagueness as a euphemistic strategy. In: Angeliki Athanasiadou and Elzbieta Tabakowska (eds.), *Speaking of Emotions: Conceptualization and Expression* (Cognitive Linguistics Research 10), 357–374. Berlin: Mouton de Gruyter.

Grondelaers, Stefan, Dirk Speelman and Dirk Geeraerts
2002 Regressing on 'er': Statistical analysis of texts and language variation. In: Anne Morin and Pascale Sébillot (eds.), *6ièmes Journées internationales d'Analyse statistique des Données Textuelles - 6th International Conference on Textual Data Statistical Analysis*, 335–346. Rennes: Institut National de Recherche en Informatique et en Automatique.

Grondelaers, Stefan, Dirk Geeraerts, Dirk Speelman and José Tummers
2001 Lexical standardisation in internet conversations: Comparing Belgium and The Netherlands. In: Josep M. Fontana, Louise McNally, M. Teresa Turell and Enric Vallduví (eds.), *Proceedings of the First International Conference on Language Variation in Europe*, 90–100. Barcelona: Universitat Pompeu Fabra, Institut Universitari de Lingüística Aplicada, Unitat de Investigació de Variació Lingüística.

Labov, William
1966 *The Social Stratification of English in New York City*. Washington, DC: Center for Applied Linguistics.
1972 Some principles of linguistic methodology. *Language in Society* 1: 97–120.
1973 The boundaries of words and their meanings. In: Charles-James Bailey and Roger Shuy (eds.), *New Ways of Analyzing Variation in English*, 340–373. Washington, DC: Georgetown University Press.
1978 Denotational structure. In: Donka Farkas, Wesley Jacobsen and Karol Todrys (eds.), *Papers from the Parasession on the Lexicon*, 220–260. Chicago: Chicago Linguistics Society.

Trudgill, Peter
1974 *The Social Differentiation of English in Norwich*. Cambridge: Cambridge University Press.

Van de Velde, Hans
1996 *Variatie en Verandering in het Gesproken Standaard-Nederlands (1935–1993)*. Ph.D. dissertation, Katholieke Universiteit Nijmegen.

Monosemy versus polysemy

Theo A.J.M. Janssen

Abstract

This paper argues that polysemous and monosemous analyses of word meanings are not necessarily mutually exclusive but that they can effectively complement one another. In particular, the polysemous approach to word meanings should be replaced as much as possible by a monosemous approach based on conceptualization principles which account for the diversity of a word's usages.

First, the paper discusses the following issues: Is it necessary to assume that each concept corresponds with a sense? Can one concept correspond with a combination of two words which clearly do not constitute a compound or lexical phrase, and, if so, should a polysemous explanation be postulated? Is it necessary to assume different senses if a word participates in different word classes? In all three cases, it is suggested that a monosemous approach is possible albeit that in some cases complementary principles are needed.

Subsequently, a cognitive-pragmatic approach is suggested to reference-point constituents, i.e., explicitly possessive structures (possessive pronouns, the genitive, the *of*-construction) and implicitly possessive structures (metonymic usages of personal pronouns). It is argued that the speaker's choice of a possessive structure is based on a prelinguistic process of "thinking for speaking", in which a relationship is conceptualized in order to select the right wording. The speaker selects the morpheme which is best suited to signal the so-called possessive relationship. The relationship signaled by means of a possessive morpheme must be compatible with what can be integrated into the conceptualization of the frame of reference that is kept updated on the basis of one or more previous utterances (or on the basis of the context of situation and knowledge of the world). The current frame of reference is held to be partly based on how the interlocutors expect to conceptualize their world. Therefore, lexical meanings serve as cues which guide the hearer in his or her process of thinking for understanding the utterance.

Keywords: compatibility principle, genitive, heterosemy, metonymy, monosemy, part-whole relationship, polysemy, possessive pronoun, posture verb, preposition, reference-point relationship.

1. Introduction

The general aim of this paper is to explore whether and, if so, to what extent polysemous analyses of words can be replaced by a monosemous approach which takes into account what interlocutors minimally need for mutual understanding, and particularly what their conceptualization of the current frame of reference can contribute to this process.[1] The goal of both the monosemous approach and the polysemous approach is to explain how one single word (or lexeme) can be used in a wide variety of situations while generally each particular actual usage of that word can be understood effortlessly.

Can a monosemous approach offer a type of explanation that is more insightful than a polysemous approach?[2] In his *Foundations of Cognitive Grammar*, Langacker (1987: 28) warns against the "exclusionary fallacy", by saying, "The gist of this fallacy is that one analysis, motivation, categorization, cause, function, or explanation for a linguistic phenomenon necessarily precludes another." I interpret this important postmodern methodological caveat as a sound justification for an attempt to row against the mainstream of Cognitive Semantics, which assumes "that a frequently-used morpheme or lexical item has a variety of interrelated senses" (Langacker 1991a: 35; see also Lakoff 1987: 416).

As Kirsner (1996) shows, a monosemous approach raises a number of questions: In what way are specific usage types of a word related to the general meaning of the word? Can this relationship be

1. I am very grateful to René Dirven, Robert Kirsner, John Taylor and the anonymous referees for valuable suggestions.
2. See Taylor (1995) for a valuable comparison of Bierwisch's monosemous and Langacker's polysemous approach.

conceived of as being mediated or served by extralinguistic[3] concepts? And what is the status of these extralinguistic concepts in a cognitive linguistic theory? Are they pre-established in the relevant ontology or can they result instantaneously and creatively from more or less fixed procedures in the process of interpreting utterances? What clues does the interpreter have at his/her disposal to determine which usage type or which type of concept is at issue in the case of a concrete utterance? Are there any interesting cognitive relationships among the mediating concepts themselves?

My comparison of the polysemous and the monosemous approach will mainly concentrate on the uses of so-called possessive expressions. Section 2 considers some assumptions and objectives held by linguists when describing the semantics of words, and section 3 suggests a descriptive approach in which the monosemous and the polysemous types of analysis are united into a cognitive-pragmatic approach. Section 4 concludes this paper.

2. Meaning and senses

The question of what is communicated by a particular utterance is a vital linguistic issue for the language user. Answering this type of question in a principled way is, in my opinion, the fundamental objective of linguistics. Presumably, all linguistic theories share as their basic assumption the idea that utterances can be conceived of as a string of one or more words (morphemes or lexemes) on which the understanding of the message involved hinges. However, as soon as issues on the semantics of utterances are at play that go beyond this assumption, linguistic theories diverge widely. For instance, there is a lack of consensus on what semantic value should be assigned to the words of an utterance, to their combination, and to the way in which they are ordered. Linguistic theories differ even in their views on what exactly constitutes word meanings, and also on what words

3. By the word *extralinguistic*, I mean "outside of the particular language but not necessarily outside of the purview of linguistics".

contribute to the semantics of utterances. This latter point can be seen as the source of all other divergences in the field of semantics.

Several modern linguistic approaches to the semantics of lexical items distinguish three factors determining the meaning of words: (i) the innate cognitive or linguistic faculty, (ii) conventionally established linguistic information, and (iii) knowledge of the world. This type of approach can be called modular. In Cognitive Semantics, however, the innate cognitive faculty, conventionally established information, and knowledge of the world are seen as contributing to the understanding of words in an integrative way, so that this approach can be called holistic. Not only language and cognition are seen as unitary but meanings and concepts as well. The meaning of a word is assumed to consist of a variety of interrelated senses. Both the meaning and senses of a word are assumed to be conventionally established. The interrelated senses form a network which can be related to other networks by mental schemas (e.g., Langacker 1988, 1991a). These schemas embody the generalizations extracted from an array of specific senses. The networks of senses and mental schemas are conceived of as representing categorized knowledge of the world.

If Cognitive Grammar and, by implication, Cognitive Semantics aim at giving a full account of conventional uses, and if not only meanings but also senses must be seen as conventionally established, it is obvious that Cognitive Semantics must deal with both meanings and senses. If, subsequently, meanings and senses must be seen as embodying knowledge of the world, Cognitive Semantics must develop a principled view on this type of knowledge.

If both meanings and senses incorporate knowledge of the world, the question arises what the functional relevance is of the idea that a word can have (or should be ascribed to) both a meaning and a set of senses. Let us assume that a sense is more specific than a word's meaning in a monosemous view or, put differently, that a sense incorporates knowledge of the world which is more specific than the word's meaning in a monosemous view. Should we, then, assume that a sense enables the hearer to determine what the speaker refers to more precisely than a word's meaning in a monosemous view?

I would like to ask a number of preliminary questions: How do we determine what the meaning of a word is and what its senses are? Due to the very existence of a word, we must assume that its meaning is conventionally established. But how do we know what the senses of a word are and that they are conventionally established as well (at least to a certain extent)? Furthermore, how does the hearer know which of a word's senses applies that allows him/her to find or imagine the actual entity or state of affairs referred to? In other words, what is it that activates the selection of the relevant sense? Which guiding principles does the hearer have to take a decision? Would it be possible that the basis for his/her decision is found in the hearer's knowledge of the real-world relationships between the entities referred to in the current situation and that the words involved allow the assumption of a certain relationship?[4]

If the "conventional meaning of a lexical item" is defined by the network of interrelated senses (Langacker 1991a: 3), all we have to do in order to find the meaning of a word is to determine its senses and their relatedness. Let us then examine how to determine these senses. In doing so we meet several problems. I will concentrate on three of them. First, to what extent may we identify concepts with senses? Second, how should we deal with cases in which a single concept is represented by a combination of words? And third, should a word that participates in more than one word class be ascribed at least as many senses as the number of word classes in which it participates?

4. Allwood's (this volume) assumption that "words on the type level have meaning potentials which, depending on context, allow for many different determinations" seems akin to the present view. However, in his view, a meaning potential *contains* "information deriving from use of language and information deriving from other experience with the world" and is "the union of individually or collectively remembered uses". I agree that word meanings are based on experiential practices (in which language users acquire unconscious knowledge of which word might fit best in a given situation and which words would not), but I reject the idea that words (or meaning potentials) are containers – see Reddy's (1979) criticism of this idea – of "individually or collectively remembered uses". Usually, language users do not remember occurrences of a word, and certainly not collectively.

2.1. Different concepts, different senses

In the framework of Cognitive Semantics, different senses necessarily imply different concepts. But is this one-to-one correspondence between senses and concepts also in line with the spirit of Cognitive Semantics? In other words, is there a one-to-one correspondence between concepts and senses?

I would like to shed light on this question with an analysis of the Dutch preposition *op* 'on, at'. A cognitive semantic analysis of its spatial usages has been presented by Cuyckens (1994). In his view, the common characteristic of *op*'s spatial usages is that the trajector has a coincidence relationship with the landmark. With regard to three of *op*'s senses, the landmarks are assumed to feature different types of dimensionality. Let us consider Cuyckens's examples.

(1) *Ik woon al jaren op het vasteland.*
'I have lived on the continent for years now.'

(2) *Dit dorp ligt op de grens.*
'This village is located on the border.'

(3) *Er is een ongeval gebeurd op het kruispunt.*
'An accident happened at the intersection.'

With regard to example (1), Cuyckens sees the relevant dimensionality of the landmark *het vasteland* 'the continent' as two-dimensional, that is, he views it as a surface; in (2), he regards the landmark *de grens* 'the border' as one-dimensional, namely as a line; in (3), he views the landmark *het kruispunt* 'the intersection' as zero-dimensional, namely as a point. On the basis of these three conceptual differences, Cuyckens concludes that there are different senses for the preposition *op*. Thus, his differential lexical characterization is based on "physical" (topological) concepts.

However, when Cuyckens explains why one and the same preposition may apply to the different types of dimensionality, he argues that "a line can be seen as a surface which does not extend in two dimensions, but only in one" (1994: 189) and that "a point can be seen as some sort of a mini-surface" (1994: 191); in Cuyckens's words, "this justifies the use of *op*" (1994: 191). It appears, then, that if the landmark is conceivable as a surface, the preposition *op* can be used in a coincidence relationship.

Now, one wonders what it is that determines the use of the preposition *op* in examples (2) and (3). Is it the concepts one- and zero-dimensionality with which the landmark is associated that are decisive? Or is it the fact that a line and a point can also be conceived of as a surface? One should really ask: Can a border and an intersection (metonymically) be conceived of as surfaces? If the answer is yes, the notion of surface seems far more crucial to the use of the preposition *op* than the concepts of two, one, and zero-dimensionality.

If the concepts of one and zero-dimensionality are not relevant for the semantics of *op*, we have reason to doubt that linguistic knowledge (senses) and knowledge of the world (concepts) are related in a one-to-one correspondence. Of course, one could argue that our world knowledge contains the information that, in certain circumstances, a line (or a border) and a point (or an intersection) may (metonymically) be conceived of as surfaces; and one could suggest that the possibility of conceiving of a line or a point in this way should be made part of the preposition's meaning. However, I would say that what is relevant for *op*'s usages is that the landmark can be seen as a surface. If we can agree on this, an inferential conceptualization has to be assumed in cases where the landmark "is" a line or point. Such a rule can be provisionally formulated, as in the addendum to (4).

(4) *The landmark of the preposition* ***op*** *is a surface.*
If the landmark of the preposition ***op*** *is normally not conceptualized as a surface, the entity involved must be conceivable as a surface and must be conceived of as such.*

A conceptualization such as in (4) may be considered accidental or occasional. However, the very fact that speakers and hearers realize such a conceptualization can be assumed to be due to a cognitive principle, which could be called the Compatibility Principle.[5]

2.2. *One concept, two words*

Can one concept be represented by a combination of words? In order to describe complex idiomatic expressions, Langacker (1987: 93–94) proposes a twofold structure consisting of a sanctioning and a target structure. However, the question I will raise here is: How should productive composite expressions be analyzed when regarded as conveying one concept? Let us consider sentences (5)–(13).[6]

		preposition	verb of posture
(5)	*In de ontvangsthal ligt een marmeren vloer.* 'The reception hall has a marble floor.'	*in* 'in'	+ *ligt* 'lies'
(6)	*Over deze schaal ligt een gouden glans.* 'This plate has a golden gleam.'	*over* 'over'	+ *ligt* 'lies'
(7)	*Op dit huis staat een hoge schoorsteen.* 'This house has a high chimney-stack.'	*op* 'on'	+ *staat* 'stands'
(8)	*Boven het artikel staat een onbegrijpe-lijke titel.* 'The article has an incomprehensible title.'	*boven* 'abo-ve'	+ *staat* 'stands'
(9)	*In de deur zit een ruitvormig raam.* 'The door has a diamond-shaped pane in it.'	*in* 'in'	+ *zit* 'sits'
(10)	*Om deze ton zitten vier hoepels.* 'This barrel has four hoops.'	*om* 'round'	+ *zitten* 'sit'
(11)	*Onder deze kast zitten balpoten.* 'This cabinet has ball legs.'	*onder* 'under'	+ *zitten* 'sit'

5. See Janssen (1986), Boogaart (1995, 1999), and Allwood (1999, this volume).
6. For a more elaborated discussion of sentences such as (5)–(13), see Janssen (1994).

(12)	*Op deze kist zit een slot.* 'This chest has a lock on it.'	*op* 'on'	+ *zit* 'sits'
(13)	*Aan de wandelstok zit een ijzeren punt.* 'The walking stick has an iron spike.'	*aan* 'on'	+ *zit* 'sits'

These sentences can be interpreted as indicating the concept of a part-whole relationship between the trajector and the landmark. However, each sentence can also indicate a spatial and a posture relationship between the trajector and the landmark.[7] How can these two valid, simultaneously present interpretations and their interrelatedness be accounted for?

Importantly, this twofold interpretability is not an intrinsic semantic property of sentences indicating a spatial and a posture relationship between the trajector and the landmark. In this respect, consider a sentence such as (14),[8] which lacks the interpretation of a part-whole relationship.

(14) *Aan de wandelstok zit wat modder.*
'There is some mud on the walking stick.'

One way to account for the cognitive discrepancy between sentences such as (13) and (14) would be to assign one sense (complex) to the combination of the verb *zit* and the preposition *aan* in (14), i.e., a spatial + posture relationship, and two senses (or sense complexes) to their combination in (13), i.e., a part-whole relationship and a spatial

7. Asher and Sablayrolles (1995: 170) give a different definition of the concept "posture". They define the concept by means of the relations between the parts of the entity involved.
8. Cases such as the following are strongly related to sentences such as (5)–(13):
(i) *Op dit bureau staat een telefoon.* 'This desk has a telephone.'
(ii) *Achter dit huis ligt een prachtige tuin.* 'This house has a beautiful garden.'
(iii) *Voor het landhuis ligt een brede oprijlaan.* 'This cottage has a broad drive way.'
Here, one can assume an "appurtenance relationship" between (i) the desk and the telephone, (ii) the house and the garden, (iii) the cottage and the drive way. Possibly, this relationship can unite the semantics of cases such as (i)–(iii) and (5)–(13).

+ posture relationship. In the latter case, the following questions arise: What is the relationship between the two interpretations in sentences such as (13)? How do the senses of the spatial and posture relationships and the sense of the part-whole relationship cooperate in such sentences? Are the spatial and posture relationships suppressed?

The cognitive discrepancy between sentences (13) and (14) can be explained in an alternative fashion. Given that it is our knowledge of the world that states that a part-whole relationship is possible between the entities referred to in sentences (5)–(13) and that a part-whole relationship between mud and a walking stick in (14) is implausible, the question arises whether there is any need to analyze sentences (5)–(13) as signaling a part-whole relationship. I suggest analyzing sentences (5)–(13) as merely describing a spatial and a posture relationship between the trajector and the landmark, just as sentence (14) does. The reason why sentences such as (5)–(13) are readily understood as indicating a part-whole relationship is that the very combination of the spatial and posture relationships between trajector and landmark is characteristic of the situation in which these entities are assumed to be in a part-whole relationship.

Thus, it seems that the semantics of sentences (5)–(13) can be determined on the basis of the meaning of the prepositions and verbs involved and that it is our knowledge of the world which subsequently says – by way of an implicature – that the combination of the spatial and posture relationships between the entities involved allows us to conceptualize a part-whole relationship between these entities. Admittedly, from a speaker's point of view, such a detour seems questionable, since generally sentences such as (5)–(13) are first and foremost used to bring the part-whole relationship to the fore and not the various topological preconditions involved. Furthermore, one may wonder how *have* in the English translations of (5)–(13) should be interpreted: should *have* in these sentences be analyzed as being used to signal a part-whole relationship,[9] or should it be assumed that the part-whole relationship in these cases is conceivable due to some type of inference?

2.3. *One word, different word classes*

Let us now consider the situation in which a word can participate in different word classes. I will concentrate on Dutch *maar*, which can serve as a conjunction ('but'), a focus particle ('only', 'just'), or a modal particle ('only', 'just'). The word *maar* is analyzed by Foolen (1993) as being heterosemous.[10] This means that a different sense is ascribed to *maar* in its participation in three word classes. However, in contrast with Foolen's heterosemous characterization of *maar*, I assume one meaning (Janssen 1995), which is described in (15).

(15) By using Dutch *maar* the speaker signals a restriction on what, in the speaker's view, one might expect in the given or similar circumstances.
[The role of the speaker (more generally, the conceptualizer) includes the role of the subject of consciousness or the reflector character (Fludernik 1993: 198–199)]

Maar serving as a conjunction is traditionally subdivided into three types of use: it may indicate (i) restrictive adversitivity ('denial of expectation') as in sentence (16), (ii) pure adversitivity ('opposition')

9. And, additionally, should we analyze *have* in these sentences as being used to signal a spatial relationship between the subject's referent and the direct object's referent?
10. The notion of heterosemy is defined by Persson (1990: 160) as "the relationship between phonologically identical but semantically contrastive lexemes separately derived from the same lexeme". Lichtenberk (1991: 476) applies the notion of heterosemy particularly to a relation between lexical items that can function cross-categorically, such as verb, particle, preposition, adjunct, or suffix. This use of the notion is adopted by Foolen (1993: 97).

as in sentence (17), and (iii) substitutive adversitivity ('correction') as in sentence (18).

(16) *Jan is klein maar dapper.*
'Jan is short but brave.'
(17) *Jan is groot, maar Piet is klein.*
'Jan is tall, but Piet is short.'
(18) *Jan is niet rijk maar arm.*
'Jan is not rich but poor.'

Foolen presents a unified semantic characterization of *maar*, as exemplified in sentences (16)–(18). The key element in his account is that *maar* signals a cancellation of an expectation rather than a restriction on an expectation, as suggested in (15). But the notion of restriction can be assumed to be more, or at least equally, applicable to the usages of *maar*, because cancellation can be seen as a case of restriction.

In his analysis of *maar* serving as a focus particle, Foolen observes that *maar* signals a restriction on a quantitative or, broadly formulated, a sociocultural hierarchy, as in sentences (19) and (20).

(19) *Jan heeft maar één broer.*
'Jan has only one brother.'
(20) *Jan is maar gewoon soldaat.*
'Jan is just an ordinary common soldier.'

Although the notion of restriction is part of Foolen's characterization of *maar* as a focus particle, he assumes that it has to be combined with the notion of scalarity. Stipulating the latter notion is redundant, however. If a speaker uses *maar* in sentences such as (19) and (20), he signals that the gradation to which he/she implicitly refers reaches no higher than the position (on the implied scale consisting of the possible number of brothers, or of military ranks) to which he actually refers. In other words, the actual degree is restricted to the point on the implied scale. The implied scale is based on the type of entity mentioned in the scope of *maar*. The implication itself is triggered by *maar* in its combination with the qualifications *één* 'one' and *gewoon* 'ordinary'. This means that the scalarity implied does not need to be separately stipulated. It naturally follows from characterization (15).

Subsequently, Foolen considers *maar* serving as a modal particle in, for instance, sentences (21)–(23).

(21) *Ik ga maar naar huis.*
'I might just go home now/I think I'll go home now.'

(22) *Kom maar.*
'Do come.'

(23) *Was ik maar thuis!*
'If only I were at home!'

Here, the use of *maar* implies that there exist various alternatives to the situation at issue. The fact that the situation mentioned is considered (21), suggested (22), or wished for (23) can be seen as a restriction on what, in the speaker's view, is possible in the given or in similar circumstances. For instance, by using *maar* in (21), the speaker indicates that he/she has hardly any other choice than to go home, although he/she could possibly imagine a range of alternatives in the given circumstances, such as having another drink or lighting up one last cigarette before leaving. Foolen (1993: 174) argues that the modal use of *maar* originates from its use as a focus particle, losing the semantic feature of scalarity. Thus, in his view, restriction is the key notion in the semantic characterization of this particular use of *maar*. This corroborates my hypothesis that restriction is the key notion for characterizing all of *maar*'s uses.

If the semantic characterization of *maar* is the same for the three functions of conjunction, focus particle, and modal particle, we are faced with the theoretical problem of how to motivate semantic distinctions between word classes. We have the following dilemma: if a word has one meaning and if it can participate in different word classes, word classes cannot have different semantic profiles. If word classes have different semantic profiles, it is then impossible for a word to have one integral meaning with which it participates in various word classes.

However, it is a natural linguistic phenomenon that, for instance, a so-called noun can surface as a so-called verb (Clark & Clark 1979), and the other way around.[11] Therefore, we may question whether the notion of word class is a well-motivated linguistic category. Of course, nobody would deny that in a number of languages certain lexemes are used only to refer to things, that certain lexemes are used only to refer to processes, and that other lexemes are neither used to refer to things nor to processes. However, it is rather difficult to predict that a lexeme cannot be used nominally or verbally. The lexeme *maar*, for instance, can be used nominally in expressions like (24), verbally in (25), and as the verbal basis of the nominal derivation *gemaar* meaning 'raising ifs and buts'.

(24) *Er is één maar aan verbonden.*
'There is one but in the matter.'

(25) *Niets te maren.*
'Don't 'but' me.'

We can solve our quandary by reinterpreting the notion of word class as a linguistic category of use. This means assuming the linguistic rule that if a lexeme is used nominally, the entity at issue can be seen as a *thing*; if, for instance, the lexeme is used verbally, the entity at issue can be seen as a *process*. I use the terms *thing* and *process* in accordance with Langacker's (1987: 183, 214) schematization of the nominal and verbal categories. I suggest that the nominal use of a lexeme implies that a thing is concerned. Thus, a lexeme used nominally does not lose its meaning as a result of the item's apparent conversion to the word class of nouns.[12]

The fact that a word is actually interpreted as indicating a thing is, in my view, the result of its syntactic use. When we use a word nominally or verbally, its use is not a priori based on the word's dif-

11. See also, e.g., de Vries (1975: 162–163) and Dirven (1999).

12. In many languages featuring more than one gender it is rather unpredictable which gender is taken by the morphemes used nominally. This suggests that in some degree the nominal use of morphemes must be assumed to be conventional.

ferential semantic potential. In my view, a word's possibility of being used nominally in one case and verbally in another is based on its undivided, highly abstract meaning and the language user's creative use of the linguistic Principle of Compatibility. This does not detract from the primary linguistic convention which is constitutive of the pairing of a word's form and meaning, reconfirmed again and again in every usage of the word. What this primary convention implies directly is that speakers can use the word in utterances, which, as a matter of fact, is its only *raison d'être*.

3. A cognitive-pragmatic approach

What could be the advantage of a polysemous over a monosemous approach to the semantics of lexemes? One possible answer is that a polysemous characterization of lexemes is less abstract than a monosemous characterization. But even so, a polysemous analysis of a word's meaning is also very abstract, as anyone knows who has tried to circumscribe a word's various senses as precisely as possible (e.g., in order to help a second-language learner to use the word correctly). Can a polysemous approach to word meanings be replaced, then, by a monosemous approach based on conceptualization principles which account for the relationship between word meanings in the monosemous view and the diversity of their usages? In other words, can a monosemous approach to lexemes offer a type of explanation which is more insightful than a polysemous approach, at least in some respects?

Monosemous approaches raise various questions (see Kirsner 1996, 2002). In what way is the meaning of a word related to specific types of usage? Can the relationship between the meaning of a word and specific types of use be conceived of as being dependent on extralinguistic concepts (Janssen 1994)? What is the status of such extralinguistic concepts in a cognitive linguistic theory? Are they preestablished in the relevant ontology or are they products of instantaneous creative procedures in the process of producing and interpreting utterances? What clues does the interpreter have at his/her disposal to determine which type of use or which type of concept is at issue in the case of an utterance?

By examining explicitly and implicitly possessive structures, I will compare polysemous and monosemous approaches to elements with possessive functions.

3.1. Explicitly possessive structures

In Cognitive Semantics, possessive structures have been thoroughly investigated by Taylor (1989, 1994, 1996), Nikiforidou (1991), and Langacker (1991b, 1992, 1993). Taylor (1989, 1994) and Nikiforidou view the genitive as a polysemous morpheme. Langacker (1993: 7), however, proposes "to account in a unified way for the extraordinary variety of relationships coded by possessive determiners". In his – and Taylor's (1996) – view, the entity referred to by means of the genitive noun phrase "is invoked as a reference point for purposes of establishing mental contact" with the entity determined by means of the genitive noun phrase. For instance, by using the construction *Carla's friend*, a speaker relates a person to the individual Carla.

Langacker (1993: 8) assumes that the reference-point relationship, which is intrinsically asymmetric (de Groot 1956; Janssen 1980), can incorporate "conceptual archetypes" such as "ownership, kinship, and part-whole relations involving physical objects". However, he rejects explicitly "that any one concept (like ownership) necessarily constitutes a unique, clear-cut prototype and basis for metaphorical extension" (Langacker 1993: 8). Although he does not comment explicitly on the issue of whether the archetypes involved are related to senses in a one-to-one correspondence, such a correspondence seems to be implied when he says, "At the most schematic level, the possessive morpheme [...] invokes as its base nothing more than the reference-point relationship" (Langacker 1993: 11). The senses may surface at the less schematic levels, I assume.

In English, the reference-point relationship can be lexicalized by means of the genitive, possessive pronouns, and the preposition *of*. Each of these lexicalizations can be used in structures in which the entities involved can be taken as featuring an ownership, kinship, or part-whole relationship, as is illustrated by the examples in (26).

(26)

		1. poss. pron.	2. nom. + genitive	3. *of* + nominal
a.	ownership	*his car*	*John's car*	*the car of that man*
b.	kinship	*his son*	*John's son*	*the son of that man*
c.	part-whole	*his nose*	*John's nose*	*the nose of that man*

In Dutch, the ownership, kinship, and part-whole relationships can be lexicalized by four types of possessive expression with type 2 (nominal + genitive) mainly being restricted to proper names and type 4 (nominal + possessive pronoun) being informal. Consider (27) (*auto* 'car', *zoon* 'son', *neus* 'nose', *man* 'man').

(27)

		1. poss. pron.	2. nominal + genitive	3. *van* + nominal	4. nominal + poss. pron.
a.	ownership	*zijn auto*	*Jans auto*	*de auto van die man*	*die man z'n auto*
b.	kinship	*zijn zoon*	*Jans zoon*	*de zoon van die man*	*die man z'n zoon*
c.	part-whole	*zijn neus*	*Jans neus*	*de neus van die man*	*die man z'n neus*

If all these types of expression share the senses (a)–(c), how, then, can we explain that the polysemy of each of these types is highly comparable, if not the same? Furthermore, they share many other types of relationship; witness the rather arbitrary list of relationships in the case of, for instance, types 1 and 2, which are provisionally characterized in (28).

(28)

		1. possessive pronoun	2. nom. + genitive
a.	factual usership	*his rook*	*John's rook*
b.	habitual/planned usership	*his train*	*John's train*
c.	private life relationship	*his friend*	*John's friend*
d.	professional relationship	*his colleague*	*John's colleague*
e.	civil relationship	*his king*	*John's king*
f.	element-set	*his group*	*John's group*
h.	physical property	*his stature*	*John's stature*
i.	mental property	*his intelligence*	*John's intelligence*
j.	accidental physical state	*his fever*	*John's fever*
k.	accidental mental state	*his anger*	*John's anger*
l.	physical attribute	*his smell*	*John's smell*
m.	nonphysical attribute	*his charisma*	*John's charisma*
n.	housing conditions	*his street*	*John's street*
o.	working conditions	*his office*	*John's office*
q.	agent-process/result	*his decision*	*John's decision*
r.	patient-performance	*his funeral*	*John's funeral*
s.	creator-physical product	*his sculpture*	*John's sculpture*
t.	creator-mental product	*his idea*	*John's idea*
u.	experiencer-happening	*his accident*	*John's accident*
v.	profession	*his lectureship*	*John's lectureship*
w.	function	*his chairmanship*	*John's chairmanship*
x.	task	*his work*	*John's work*
y.	way of life	*his conduct*	*John's conduct*
z.	legal position	*his privacy*	*John's privacy*

As a matter of fact, this list is far from exhaustive. For instance, it does not mention that possessive structures can be used to indicate the desired or favorite entity to work with, to play with, to go to, to read, to watch, to listen to, to talk about, etc. Nor does it indicate how the relationships involved in *his/John's life*, *his/John's future*, *his/John's prospects*, *his/John's value* should be characterized? Furthermore, list (28) disregards all kinds of relationships in which the possessor is inanimate, such as in *Amsterdam's/its canals* and *yester-*

day's lectures. In sum, I believe that it is impossible to complete the list of relationships that can be involved in possessive pronouns and genitives.[13] If this is correct, we are faced with an endless number of senses. Assuming that each sense is based on convention, one wonders how any linguistic theory can explain that a language user is able to learn an infinite set of conventions in order to interpret possessive constituents adequately.

Since language users are able to understand possessives in various circumstances, we have to look for an explanation which is different from polysemous analyses which seem to accept an infinite number of senses. My explanation (cf. Janssen 1975) is based on Bendix's (1966) study of possessive expressions in various languages. Bendix observes that possessive structures can be used when very casual relationships are at issue, as in (29):

(29) a. *A bull chased me and a bull chased John.*
b. *My bull was fiercer than John's bull.*

In (29a), the bulls and the persons are in a chaser-chased relationship. Now, the question is: Is there also a chaser-chased relationship signaled by means of the possessive pronoun and the genitive in the second utterance? If the relationship between the bulls and their antagonists as signaled in the second utterance is taken as a chaser-chased relationship, it is an entirely accidental relationship, which cannot be known independently of the previous utterance. Therefore, the chaser-chased relationship cannot qualify as a conventionally established sense of the possessive pronoun and the genitive. Doing so would be the start of a never ending task, since the origins of relationships such as the chaser-chased relationship are innumerable and unmistakably ad hoc. A satisfactory characterization of the semantics of the possessive structures as in (29b) can be found by comparing them with the use of the definite article in the utterance in (30b).

---

13. See, e.g., de Groot (1956), Bendix (1966), Uhlenbeck (1967), Weydt (1972), Seiler (1973), Janssen (1975), Aronoff (1980), Kay and Zimmer (1990).

(30) a. *A bull chased me.*
b. *The bull was fierce.*

By using *the bull*, the speaker refers to "the bull which chased me" (30a), which is, of course, not the meaning or sense of *the bull*. In using the definite article in (30b), the speaker sets up a frame of reference to which the bull can be related and in which it is unique. Similarly, the function of the possessives in (29b) is to indicate a reference relationship,[14] whereby the speaker needs a frame of reference to which the entity at issue can be related and in which it is unique (Janssen 1975).[15] In (29b), the speaker conceptualizes two subframes of reference, each comprising one bull and some person. When using *my bull* and *John's bull*, the speaker indicates that in one frame, the bull is unique and related to the speaker, and that in the other frame, the bull is unique and related to John.

One could object, correctly, that the relationship between the entities involved is not always explicitly established in a previous utterance. When this is the case, all the hearer needs to know is that the entity to be determined can be related, in the speaker's view, to another entity's frame of reference in which it is unique in the relevant situation. This resembles what one has to do when encountering the sign *Beware of the dog!* at the gate of a house. Finding the relevant frame of reference is all that one can do; everything else must be taken on trust from the speaker (Hawkins 1984: 656). Of course,

---

14. Three remarks are in order here. First, so-called possessive structures do not always signal a reference relationship. In, *My dear, dear little child!*, for instance, the use of *my* does not give rise to the child being singled out. Second, in using a structure such as *I would like to meet a colleague of John*, the speaker does not relate *a colleague* as a unique element to John in the relevant frame of reference. Third, the structure *X of Y* can be used to indicate a partitive relationship such as in *Nine of them were lost.*

15. In *Does your finger hurt?*, for instance, where one finger is singled out although the addressee has nine more, the relevant frame of reference is conceived of as being confined to the frame highlighted by the salience of the finger at issue due to the fact that, e.g., it is the addressee's only finger which is bandaged (Janssen 1975). See also Epstein (2001, 2002), who rightly modifies the referential view of the use of definite articles.

knowledge of the world tells the viewer that he/she has to watch out for the dog related to the house with the sign outside it. But nobody, I guess, would assume that the article *the* has a sense signaling this particular relationship.

In the present analysis, speakers and hearers are not assumed to search a list of senses of possessive morphemes in order to decide which one is applicable in the situation at issue. They are assumed to conceptualize a frame of reference on the basis of the information which appears to be relevant at the current stage of the developing discourse (Janssen, in prep.). For instance, with regard to the utterance in (29b), the information about the chaser-chased relationship which is cognizable on the basis of the first utterance, is reconceptualized in function of the indication (or determination) under construction. The speaker selects the morpheme which is fit to signal the possessive relationship, without specifying what already is cognizable. Morphemes such as the possessive pronouns and the genitive qualify for this task. However, although these morphemes are compatible with a wide range of cognizable relationships, the question could be raised as to why it is odd to combine relationships of list (28). Consider examples (31) and (32).

(31) *I see his car, son, and nose.*
(32) *I see John's car, son, and nose.*

The oddity of (31) and (32) suggests that the relationships involved are incompatible. At first glance, it seems that this incompatibility can be accounted for by assuming polysemy of the possessive pronoun and the genitive. However, what is the value of this explanation if in other contexts such relationships appear to be compatible and their combination produces plausible sentences? Consider sentences (33) and (34).

(33) *John likes to talk about his family, work, vacations, way of life, irritations, recent decisions, ideas, plans, and prospects.*
(34) *Can you tell me who are John's colleagues, neighbors, friends, teammates, and closest relatives?*

The entities involved in each series in sentences (33) and (34) are, in the light of list (28), rather diverse but do combine very well. They share a – perhaps entirely accidental – feature which enables them to be united into one category. This accidental feature may be such that the words it applies to cannot be assumed to have it as an aspect of their meaning. It is the way we conceptualize the entities in the current frame of reference that allows us to categorize them as comparable.

In my view, the speaker's choice of a possessive structure is based on a prelinguistic process of 'thinking for speaking' (Slobin 1987; Levinson 1997; Nuyts 2001), in which a relationship is conceptualized in order for the speaker to select the right wording. The speaker selects the morpheme which is fit to signal the so-called possessive relationship. The relationship signaled by means of a possessive morpheme must be compatible with what can be integrated into the conceptualization of the frame of reference which is updated on the basis of one or more previous utterances (or on the basis of the context of situation and knowledge of the world).

It is due to the conceptualization of the current frame of reference that it is superfluous for the speaker and the hearer to seek a morpheme featuring the appropriate sense by searching a list of a morpheme's senses, or of a morpheme's possibly emergent senses. In this view, the issue is finding a morpheme meaning – a semantic superschema (Langacker 1988: 135), i.e. a morpheme's highest schematic characterization (Langacker 1993: 7) – which can cover the conceptualization at issue. I do not exclude that conceptual archetypes such as ownership, kinship, and part-whole relationship can be active in the prelinguistic process of "thinking for speaking". However, I assume that they have to be activated in a way similar to the activation of the conceptual relationship defined creatively in the current context of situation, including the preceding text, such as in (29), where the utterance *A bull chased me and a bull chased John* can be the basis of the relationship in the light of which both *my bull* and *John's bull* in the next utterance *My bull was fiercer than John's bull* are used.

3.2. Implicitly possessive structures

A great variety of reference-point constituents lack a possessive pronoun or genitive; for a survey, I refer to Langacker (1993).[16] Here, I will concentrate on metonymic usages of personal pronouns as in examples (35)[17] and (36).

(35) *Are you parked over there?*
(36) *You're on top of this pile.*

Because of the word *parked* in sentence (35), the speaker can be assumed to refer with *you* to the addressee's car. Sentence (36) offers less obvious indications of how to interpret the reference of *you*. It is possible that the speaker uses *you* to refer to a book, a request, or a report his/her addressee has written. The referent of *you* could also be a book the addressee has ordered at the bookshop or library, or it could be a report on the addressee's conduct, or still a photo taken of the addressee, etc. Obviously, the referent must be an element of a set of similar entities which constitute the pile involved. Other indications for determining the reference of *you* must be derived from the current situation, particularly from the roles the speaker and the addressee play in this situation.[18]

Let us now consider the types of metonymic relationship between the addressee and the entity actually referred to by means of *you* in both examples. In sentence (35), where the actual referent of *you* is your car, the relationship of ownership or usership can be assumed. In sentence (36), the interpretation that the book was ordered by the addressee at the bookshop or library might allow us to infer the relationship of a projected ownership or usership. Where the referent of *you* can be interpreted as a book, request, or report the addressee has

16. A wide variety of similar relationships are documented in Janssen (1986: 28).
17. See also Nunberg (1979, 1995).
18. In Janssen (1986), I suggested that this type of metonymic referencing is based on the inferability of a close relationship between the entity mentioned directly and the entity actually referred to, albeit indirectly. This type of metonymic relationship was related to a genitival relationship.

written, the producer-product relationship can be assumed. When the referent of *you* can be interpreted as the addressee's picture or as a report on his/her conduct, we may assume a relationship between the object of production and the product.[19]

Whatever the interpretation may be in sentences (35) and (36), in each case our knowledge of the current situation is crucial for determining the referent (Langacker 1987: 271–274). In particular, it requires that the addressee recognize that the entity referred to is seen as a unique element in his or her current dominion (Langacker 1993: 6; Newman 1993: 459–60; Taylor 1996: 236–237). In determining the referent, it is questionable that the addressee has previously learned the types of relationships he or she can have with the actual referent of the pronoun *you*, in which case these types of relationships would have to be part of the meaning of the pronoun *you*. Rather than assuming that the pronoun *you* has as many senses as types of relationships that can be distinguished in sentences like (35) and (36), I would like to argue that the relationships vary with the current functions of the entities involved? In order to account for the great variety of relationships, I would suggest that the linguistic convention in (37) should be assumed (cf. Nunberg 1995; Langacker 1993: 32).

(37) *Metonymic use of personal pronouns*
A personal pronoun can be used to refer to an entity which is conceivable as a unique and prominent ("noteworthy") element in the current dominion of the person on which the pronoun's use is based.

Rule (37) characterizes the general aspect of the linguistic convention at issue; however, the rule's precise scope has to be defined in more detail, while taking into account differences between language users' current ontologies. And, apart from the merely referential aspect, it should be clarified why a metonymy is used and what its effects are.

---

19. Nunberg (1995: 109) suggests that "the derived property should be a 'noteworthy' feature of its bearer".

4. Conclusion

The main criticism of the polysemous analyses discussed may seem that the expressions concerned are assigned more semantic information than can be justified and, therefore, that this surplus or overcapacity should be removed by Occam's razor.[20] However, there are two more interesting points of theoretical criticism than this methodological issue that detract from a polysemous approach to word meaning. First, language users can safely be assumed to be more creative in determining the role of expressions in real-life utterances than they are purported to be on the polysemous approach, which seems to neglect Reddy's (1979) warning (in his discussion of the CONDUIT metaphor) that linguistic signs may not be assumed to yield ready-made information. Language users benefit instantaneously from various kinds of both linguistic and non-linguistic knowledge when communicating through their language. Second, the speaker's choice of linguistic elements can be assumed to be made in the process of "thinking for speaking", which cannot but interact with the conceptualization of the current frame of reference. The current frame of reference must be assumed to be partly based on how the interlocutors expect to conceptualize their world. Therefore, lexical meanings should be viewed "not as little semantic building blocks or atoms of description which the language user stacks up to communicate a complete message, but rather as mere clues, hints, messages, the details of which the hearer is held to fill in by a process of intelligent inference" (Kirsner 2002: 340) as part of the process of thinking for understanding the utterance.

Do polysemous and monosemous analyses of word meanings necessarily exclude one another or can they effectively complement one another? Monosemous analyses tend to concentrate on regularities (based on inferential rules currently made), whereas polysemous analyses tend to concentrate on the great variety of usages (based on conceptualizations made in the history of a particular language; see, e.g., Kirsner 1996: 97). If it is the linguist's task to determine the

20. Compare Nuyts's (2001) critical view of the overcapacity of grammars.

linguistic conventions in order to explain actual usages, then monosemous analyses should integrate the qualities of the detailed cognitive semantic analyses in order to establish prelinguistic and linguistic processes based on well-defined general principles,[21] which take into account the great variety of the actual linguistic usages on the basis of language users' current conceptualization and (emergent) ontology.

References

Allwood, Jens
1999 Semantics as meaning determination with semantic-epistemic operations. In: Jens Allwood and Peter Gärdenfors (eds.), *Cognitive Semantics; Meaning and Cognition*, 1–17. Amsterdam: John Benjamins.
this volume Meaning potentials and context: Some consequences for the analysis of variation in meaning.
Aronoff, Mark
1980 Contextuals. *Language* 56: 744–758.
Asher, Nicholas and Pierre Sablayrolles
1995 A typology and discourse semantics for motion verbs and spatial PPs in French. *Journal of Semantics* 12: 163–209.
Bendix, Edward H.
1966 *Componential Analysis of General Vocabulary: The Semantic Structure of a Set of Verbs in English, Hindi, and Japanese*. The Hague: Mouton.
Boogaart, Ronny
1995 Towards a theory of discourse aspectuality. In: Pier Marco Bertinetto, Valentina Bianchi, James Higginbotham and Mario Squartini (eds.), *Temporal Reference, Aspect and Actionality*, Volume 1: *Semantics and Syntactic Perspectives*, 221–236. Torino: Rosenberg & Sellier.
1999 *Aspect and Temporal Ordering: A Contrastive Analysis of Dutch and English*. The Hague: Holland Academic Graphics.
Clark, Eve V. and Herbert H. Clark
1979 When nouns surface as verbs. *Language* 55: 767–811.

21. See, e.g., Pustejovsky and Bouillon (1995).

Cuyckens, Hubert
1994 Family resemblance in the Dutch spatial preposition *op*. In: Monika Schwarz (ed.), *Kognitive Semantik/Cognitive Semantics: Ergebnisse, Probleme, Perspektiven*, 179–195. Tübingen: Gunter Narr.

de Groot, A.W.
1956 Classification of the uses of a case illustrated on the genitive in Latin. *Lingua* 6: 8–66.

de Vries, Jan W.
1975 *Lexicale morfologie van het werkwoord in modern Nedelands* [Lexical morphology of the verb in modern Dutch]. Leiden: Universitaire Pers.

Dirven, René
1999 Conversion as a conceptual metonymy of event schemata. In: Klaus-Uwe Panther and Günter Radden (eds.) *Metonymy in Language and Thought*, 275–287. Amsterdam: John Benjamins.

Epstein, Richard
2001 The definite article, accessibility, and the construction of discourse referents. *Cognitive Linguistics* 12: 333–378.
2002 Grounding, subjectivity and definite descriptions. In: Frank Brisard (ed.), *Grounding: The Epistemic Footing of Deixis and Reference*, 41–82. Berlin: Mouton de Gruyter.

Fludernik, Monika
1993 *The Fictions of Language and the Language of Fiction: The Linguistic Representation of Speech and Consciousness*. London: Routledge.

Foolen, Ad P.
1993 *De betekenis van partikels: Een dokumentatie van de stand van het onderzoek met bijzondere aandacht voor* maar [The meaning of particles: A research survey focusing on *maar*]. Ph.D. dissertation, Catholic University of Nijmegen.

Hawkins, John A.
1984 A note on referent identifiability and co-presence. *Journal of Pragmatics* 8: 649–659.

Janssen, Theo A.J.M.
1975 Possessieve konstrukties [Possessive constructions]. *De Nieuwe Taalgids* 68: 1–13.
1980 Coreference and interreference in anaphoric relations: Grammatical semantics or pragmatics? In: Johan van der Auwera (ed.), *The Semantics of Determiners*, 67–80. London: Croom Helm.

1986 *De betekenis van het Nederlands* [The meaning of Dutch]. Amsterdam: VU University Press. (Reissued in: *Forum der Letteren* 28 [1987]: 1–23).

1994 Betekenis en interpretatie, of hoe taal en wereldbeeld elkaar aanvullen [Meaning and interpretation, or how language and world view complement each other]. In: Tieme van Dijk and Roel Zemel (eds.), *Het is kermis hier*, 5–18. Amsterdam: Stichting Neerlandistiek VU / Münster: Nodus Publikationen.

1995 Heterosemy or polyfunctionality? The case of Dutch *maar* 'but, only, just'. In: Thomas F. Shannon and Johan P. Snapper (eds.), *The Berkeley Conference on Dutch Linguistics 1993*, 71–85. Lanham, MD: University Press of America.

in prep. *Indeterminacy: Lexical and Grammatical Meanings in the Controversy between Monosemy and Polysemy.*

Kay, Paul and Karl Zimmer

1990 On the semantics of compounds and genitives in English. In: Savas L. Tsohatzidis (ed.), *Meanings and Prototypes: Studies in Linguistic Categorization*, 239–246. London: Routledge.

Kirsner, Robert S.

1996 The human factor and the insufficiency of invariant meaning. In: Edna Andrews and Yishai Tobin (eds.), *Toward a Calculus of Meaning*, 83–106, Amsterdam: John Benjamins.

2002 The future of a minimalist linguistics in a maximalist world. In: Wallis Reid, Ricardo Otheguy and Nancy Stern (eds.), *Signal, Meaning, and Message: Perspectives on Sign-Based Linguistics*, 339–371. Amsterdam: John Benjamins,.

Lakoff, George

1987 *Women, Fire, and Dangerous Things*. Chicago: The University of Chicago Press.

Langacker, Ronald W.

1987 *Foundations of Cognitive Grammar*, Volume 1: *Theoretical Prerequisites*. Stanford: Stanford University Press.

1988 A usage-based model. In: Brygida Rudzka-Ostyn (ed.), *Topics in Cognitive Linguistics*, 127–161. Amsterdam: John Benjamins.

1991 a *Concept, Image, and Symbol: The Cognitive Basis of Grammar.* Berlin: Mouton de Gruyter.

1991 b *Foundations of Cognitive Grammar*, Volume 2: *Descriptive Application*. Stanford: Stanford University Press.

1992 The symbolic nature of Cognitive Grammar: The meaning of *of* and *of*-periphrasis. In: Martin Pütz (ed.), *Thirty Years of Linguistic Evolution*, 483–502. Amsterdam: John Benjamins. (Reissued

as: The meaning of *of*. In: Ronald W. Langacker, *Grammar and Conceptualization*, 73–90. Berlin: Mouton de Gruyter, 2000.)
1993 Reference-point constructions, *Cognitive Linguistics* 4: 1–38.

Levinson, Stephen C.
1997 From outer to inner space: Linguistic categories and non-linguistic thinking. In: Jan Nuyts and Eric Pederson (eds.), *Language and Conceptualization*, 13–45. Cambridge: Cambridge University Press.

Lichtenberk, Frantisek
1991 Semantic change and heterosemy in grammaticalization, *Language* 67: 475–509.

Newman, John
1993 The semantics of giving in Mandarin. In: Richard A. Geiger and Brygida Rudzka-Ostyn (eds.) *Conceptualisations and Mental Processing in Language*, 433–486. Berlin: Mouton de Gruyter.

Nikiforidou, Kiki
1991 The meaning of the genitive: A case study in semantic structure and semantic change. *Cognitive Linguistics* 2: 149–205.

Nunberg, Geoffrey
1979 The non-uniqueness of semantic solutions: Polysemy. *Linguistics and Philosophy* 3: 143–184.
1995 Transfers of meaning. *Journal of Semantics* 12: 109–132.

Nuyts, Jan
2001 *Epistemic Modality, Language, and Conceptualization: A Cognitive-Pragmatic Perspective*. Amsterdam: John Benjamins.

Persson, Gunnar
1990 *Meanings, Models and Metaphors: A Study in Lexical Semantics in English*. Stockholm: Almqvist & Wiksell.

Pustejovsky, James and Pierette Bouillon
1995 Aspectual coercion and logical polysemy. *Journal of Semantics* 12: 133–162.

Reddy, Michael J.
1979 The conduit metaphor: A case of frame conflict in our language about language. In: Andrew Ortony (ed.), *Metaphor and Thought*, 284–324. Cambridge: Cambridge University Press.

Seiler, Hans-Jakob
1973 Zum Problem der sprachlichen Possessivität. *Folia Linguistica* 6: 231–250.

Slobin, Dan I.
1987 Thinking for speaking. In: Jon Aske, Natasha Beery, Laura Michaelis, Hana Filip (eds.), *Proceedings of the Thirteenth Annual*

Meeting of the Berkeley Linguistics Society, 435–445. Berkeley: Berkeley Linguistics Society.

Taylor, John R.

1989 *Linguistic Categorization: Prototypes in Linguistic Theory*. Oxford: Clarendon Press.

1994 "Subjective" and "objective" readings of possessor nominals. *Cognitive Linguistics* 5: 201–242.

1995 Models of word meaning in comparison: The two-level model (Manfred Bierwisch) and the network model (Ronald Langacker). In: René Dirven and Johan Vanparys (eds.), *Current Approaches to the Lexicon*, 3–26, Frankfurt: Peter Lang. (Reissued with *Afterword* in: Bert Peeters (ed.), *The Lexicon-Encyclopedia Interface*, 115–141. Oxford: Elsevier, 2000).

1996 *Possessives in English: An Exploration in Cognitive Grammar*. Oxford: Clarendon Press.

Uhlenbeck, Eugène M.

1967 Some further remarks on transformational grammar. *Lingua* 17: 263–316.

Weydt, Harald

1972 Le concept d'ambiguïté en grammaire transformationelle-générative et en linguistique fonctionelle. *La Linguistique* 8: 41–72.

The grammaticalization of *alltså* and *således*: Two Swedish conjuncts revisited

Hanna Lehti-Eklund

Abstract

In sixteenth-century Swedish, two adverbs of manner, *alltså* and *således,* appear as synonyms with the meaning 'in such a way', 'in such a manner'. This paper addresses the semantic development of these two words, with special reference to their grammaticalization. After a summary of their development up to the nineteenth century, the focus is on the uses of *alltså* and *således* in twentieth-century Swedish. The main trends are then discussed in reference to grammaticalization. The main hypothesis is that both *alltså* and *således* have changed semantically and grammaticalized from the meanings and functions they had at the end of the nineteenth century. Two questions are addressed: (i) do *alltså* and *således* show any semantic-functional changes compared with the situation of a hundred years ago; (ii) do the semantic-functional changes, if any, correlate with changes in the structural behavior of the words, e.g., their word class, position in an utterance, or other characteristics suggested to be typical of further grammaticalization of adverbs?

Keywords: conjuncts, discourse markers, discourse particles, grammaticalization, semantic-functional change, subjectification.

1. *Alltså* and *således*: developments up to 1900

In sixteenth-century Swedish, two adverbs of manner, *alltså* and *således,* appear as synonyms with the meaning 'in such a way', 'in such a manner'. This paper addresses the semantic development of these two adverbs. First, I will review the developments up to the end of the nineteenth century; this review is largely based on Lehti-Eklund (1990).

1.1. The main development: from adverb of manner to consecutive conjunct

In the sixteenth century, *alltså* was borrowed into Swedish from German in its original meaning as an adverb of manner. The other adverb, *således,* is of Swedish origin: it goes back to the Old Swedish adverbial phrase *svaleþis*, originally meaning 'on such a road' (*sva* 'such' + *leþis* = genitive of **leþe* 'road, way') (Lehti-Eklund 1990: 105, 129–136).

In a period of three hundred years, from the seventeenth to the nineteenth century, *alltså* and *således* underwent several semantic and functional changes. As has been shown in Lehti-Eklund (1990), the most important development is that from adverbs of manner to consecutive conjuncts meaning 'consequently', which took place for *alltså* during the seventeenth century and for *således* a hundred years later. In (1), from a letter of 1652 where Johan Ekeblad is telling his brother about gossip at the court, *alltså* is already a consecutive conjunct:

(1) *Sedan som nu then*[*n*]*a Stratagem wppenbar wardt låter iagh eder att Judicera huru mannen måtte wara till mods som sigh sielff för kuplare haffuer bruka låtte åth sin egen hustru, och* ***altså*** *sielff orsak till sitt hederliga hanreysstånd.*
'As the husband's strategy now had become obvious, I'll let you judge what the husband must have felt, because he had let himself be used as a pimp for his own wife, and *consequently* was himself the cause of having become a cuckold.' (Allén 1965: 57)

In this paper, consecutive conjuncts (Swedish *konsekutiva konjunktionella adverb*) are defined as adverbs signifying conclusion between two clauses or sentences (Thorell 1987: 602 f.). As a word class, consecutive conjuncts in Swedish semantically resemble consecutive conjunctions (e.g., *så* 'so'), but behave syntactically as sentential adverbs. They can be placed initially or in the middle field after an initial constituent and the finite verb, whereas conjunctions are only found in initial position (Thorell 1987: 228).

The semantic change of *alltså* and *således* from manner adverb to consecutive conjunct seems to have started in cases where the manner adverb summed up what had been happening previously, but in which this summary of previous discourse could, at the same time, be interpreted (or reanalyzed) as a result or conclusion based on that previous discourse. In other words, the change occurred in contexts where a summarizing proposition (usually containing textually given information) invited the inference of a conclusive or resulting proposition (containing new information). The pragmatic inference inducing the conclusive interpretation could be based on Levinson's (1987: 66, 74) Principle of Informativeness, according to which the receiver would interpret the proposition including *alltså* and *således* as strongly and informatively as possible. Pragmatic strengthening as a typical feature of early stages of grammaticalization has been put forward by Traugott (1988, 1995; see also Traugott & König 1991).

In the following example (from a letter from Magnus Stenbock to his wife, 1703), *således* is probably still an adverb of manner, but it could also be interpreted as 'consequently':

(2) *Han [kungen] är eij heller otaksam i dätt han mig eij allenast skienkt 10000 riksd. uthan och anförtrott att värfva ett Regement Dragoner, och* ***således*** *åther förökt min lön på 70 riksd. om månaden.*
'Neither is he [the king] ungrateful in that he has not only given me 10,000 rix-dollars but also trusted me to hire a whole regiment of dragoons and *in such a manner/consequently* [he has] again increased my pay by 70 rix-dollars a month.' (Stenbock 1913: 37)

In this paper, *alltså* and *således* signaling 'conclusion' will be called *alltså*$_{1a}$ and *således*$_{1a}$. The semantic change of *alltså* and *således* was accompanied by a change of syntactic category, from adverbs of manner to conjuncts. As conjuncts, their position in the clause also changed: they no longer stood as arguments of the verb among the adverbials at the end of the clause, but as sentential adverbs either initially or after an initial constituent and the finite verb in the middle of the clause. The number of syntactic categories where they appeared narrowed down so that, between 1800–1900, they all but disappeared from, e.g., infinitives and participles and appeared mostly in main and subordinate clauses.

During the same period (1600–1900), the Swedish vocabulary was enriched with at least five other conjuncts (*emellertid, eljest, annars, dessutom*, and *dessutan)* which underwent a process similar to *alltså* and *således.* All having propositional meanings to start with, they developed new textual meanings and ended up syntactically as conjuncts (Lehti-Eklund 1990; see also Haskå 1988).

1.2. Other semantic changes

1.2.1. Explanative conjuncts: *alltså*$_{2a}$ and *således*$_{2a}$

Besides the change from manner adverb to consecutive conjunct, both *alltså* and *således* later also underwent other semantic changes.

During the nineteenth century, *alltså* appeared in a new textual function, as an explanative conjunct with the meaning 'that is'. The explanative meaning seems to have developed from the consecutive onc in contexts where the proposition preceded by *alltså,* instead of presenting new information and a conclusion, can be analyzed as containing less important, parenthetical or specifying information. In German, *also* was both a manner adverb and an explanative conjunct at the time when *alltså* was borrowed into Swedish. The explanative meaning, however, was not observed in Swedish until the nineteenth century. In its explanative meaning, *alltså* mostly precedes parenthetical phrases marking an explanation. This function is illustrated in (3), from 1866, where Fredrika Runeberg states in a letter to her son:

(3) *och sjelf skrifver du att du fick 2200,* ***altså*** *2.000 utöfver det begärda.*
'and you yourself are writing that you got 2,200, *that is* 2,000 more than you had asked for.' (Runeberg 1971: 172)

Explanative *alltså* and *således* will be called *alltså*$_{2a}$ and *således*$_{2a}$. The adverb *således,* however, did not appear with explanative meaning before 1900.

1.2.2. Metatextual markers: *alltså*$_{1b}$ and *således*$_{1b}$

In addition to the conjunctive and explanative meanings, the period from 1600 to 1900 already saw a few instances of *alltså* (17 out of a total of 330) in a new function, which would become more common after 1900 and which will be discussed in detail in section 3.1. In this function, *alltså* and *således* behave as metatextual markers referring to and taking up a theme which has been discussed earlier. In English, *alltså* and *således* used in this function could be translated with 'as I wrote earlier', 'as I have said', 'as has been mentioned'. In this function, *alltså* and *således* will be called *alltså*$_{1b}$ and *således*$_{1b}$. The function is illustrated in (4), from a letter of 1829 from Esaias Tegnér to his wife, where Tegnér suspects that she has been ill. Having received a letter from his wife confirming this, he takes up the topic with *alltså*:

(4) *Jag hade* ***alltså*** *beklagligtvis ej orätt då jag till följe af ditt bref misstänkte att du var sjuk.*
'*As I mentioned*, I was not wrong in suspecting because of your letter that you were ill.' (Palmborg 1956: 199)

In comparison to *alltså*'s consecutive use, I consider this use to be more grammaticalized and semantically weakened. In employing *alltså*, the writer no longer presents a conclusion, but merely makes a non-local connection in the text (Linell & Gustavsson 1987: 152). Similar observations hold for *således,* which also appears in a few instances (4 out of 273) as a metatextual marker taking up previously mentioned information.

1.2.3. *Alltså* as a discourse marker from 1500 to 1900

The first possible instances of *alltså* as a discourse marker can be observed towards the end of the period under consideration, in the nineteenth century.

The term "discourse marker" is reserved both by Fraser (1990) and Traugott (1995) for specific kinds of pragmatic markers or discourse particles. They can be defined as "a class of expressions, each of which signals how the speaker intends the basic message that follows to relate to the prior discourse" (Fraser 1990: 387). Discourse markers do not create meaning in discourse but orient the hearer and signal "the speaker's view of how the following relates to the preceding" (Fraser 1990: 390–391; Traugott 1995). According to Schiffrin (1987), discourse markers can be further characterized as a subcategory of discourse particles, a set of devices with which speakers situate their "communicative intentions ... within an integrated framework of interactionally emergent structures, meanings and actions" (1987: 22; see also Gumperz 1982: 131). Discourse particles have such functions as to connect turns to each other, giving cues to the discourse situation or the speech activity one is engaged in (Hakulinen 1989: 116–117; Hakulinen & Saari 1995: 482–483; Saari 1995: 91). Further characteristics of discourse markers will be discussed in sections 4.2 and 4.2.4.

Written texts are to some extent problematic for the study of grammaticalization and discourse markers; as Brinton (1990: 59) suggests, "oral features function in written discourse in a similar but not identical way". As one of the goals in Lehti-Eklund (1990) was to study grammaticalization in action, the written texts were collected with a view to maximum spontaneity and closeness to or imitation of spoken language, as in letters to family members, diaries, and plays. But even if the appearance of *alltså* as a discourse marker during the nineteenth century is in accordance with grammaticalization theory (cf. section 1.3; Traugott 1986: 540; Traugott 1995, 1999b), it is difficult to say when *alltså* was first used in spoken Swedish as a discourse marker. Given the conservatism of the written language, it is fairly certain that at the time *alltså* as a discourse marker first appeared in written texts, it had been established in spoken language for some time.

In a letter of 1852, Tullberg writes just before leaving Rome and Florence:

(5) *Rom och Florens skulle jag gärna velat återse... men jag blir min föresats trogen och tar i mitt sinne afsked äfven af dessa kära ställen, som jag ej heller mera får återse: Farväl* ***alltså,*** *du sköna land!*
'I would have liked to have seen Rome and Florence again, … but I will remain true to my intentions bidding in my mind farewell to these dear places that I no longer will be able to see again: Farewell, *then*, you beautiful country!' (Beskow Tainsh 1972: 115)

Here, *alltså* could be regarded as a discourse marker, or very close to one (as such, it is similar to $alltså_{1c}$ discussed in 4.2.1). It is not a conjunct drawing a conclusion from the preceding text; instead, *alltså* puts the writer's farewell in connection with his decision to leave, his knowledge of never being able to return (he is an old man), and his presentation of this in the preceding text.

Således, the other conjunct studied in this paper, is not known to have been used as a discourse marker between 1500 and 1900.

1.3. The grammaticalization of alltså *and* således *from 1500 to 1900*

The developments shown by *alltså* and *således* in the period from 1500 to 1900 can be represented as follows (*alltså* as a discourse marker is shown in brackets as it is only observed in a few cases; as documented in section 4, *alltså* develops into a full discourse marker only during the twentieth century):

adverb of manner *således*	>	consecutive conjunct *således*$_{1a}$	>	metatextual marker *således*$_{1b}$		
adverb of manner *alltså*	>	consecutive conjunct *alltså*$_{1a}$	>	metatextual marker *alltså*$_{1b}$	>	(discourse marker for reference *alltså*$_{1c}$)
	>	explanative conjunct *alltså*$_{2a}$				

The changes found in *alltså* and *således* at this stage meet long-attested and more recently established characteristics of grammaticalization (cf. Traugott 1995). According to Traugott's (2001: 1) definition, "grammaticalization is a hypothesis about a robust tendency" where "lexical … or grammatical items develop new grammatical functions". In their development up to 1900, *alltså* and *således* exhibit the following long-attested characteristics:

(a) *Generalization of meaning*. The meaning of *alltså* and *således* becomes generalized in the sense that as conjuncts they can refer to a wider range of units on different textual levels, varying from clauses to larger chunks of text, e.g., stories. Adverbs of manner often refer to a proposition in the immediate syntactic vicinity (cf. Traugott 1995). The reduction in the type of clauses that conjuncts bind together could be associated with the widening reference and regarded as a consequence of the generalization of meaning: when moving away from reference to a concrete referent and a close association with the main verb towards showing that the proposition of the clause is a consequence from the previous discourse, it is natural for *alltså* and *således* to appear in the main clause of the sentence in which the main information is embedded.

(b) *Decategorialization. Alltså* and *således* can be said to decategorialize, in that by losing their characteristics as adverbs of manner, they move "down the scale from more major to more minor word class membership" (Brinton 1996: 273); see also Hopper (1991: 30–31) and Traugott (1995).

(c) *Persistence* (Hopper 1991). The summarizing meanings which *alltså* and *således* had when they were adverbs of manner persist in consecutive $alltså_{1a}$ and $således_{1a}$.[1]

Alltså and *således* also illustrate more recently established semantic-functional features, especially pragmatic strengthening and increased subjectivity (i.e., increased association with speaker attitude). The semantic changes of *alltså* and *således* arise with the help of strengthened pragmatic inferences (Lehti-Eklund 1990: 30; Levinson 1987: 74; Traugott 1989, 1990; Traugott & König 1991: 190–192). The semantic change into $alltså_{1a}$ and $således_{1a}$, and further into $alltså_{1b}$ and $således_{1b}$ is evidence of a shift towards greater subjectivity: from things done in a certain way, to drawing a conclusion from the previous discourse, to making a connection with the previous discourse (Traugott 1982: 253, 256; 1989, 1990, 1995; Traugott & König 1991: 189). Depending on one's view of semantic change, pragmatic strengthening and subjectification could be characterized as a metonymical or as a metaphorical transfer from one cognitive domain to another (Traugott & König 1991: 210–211; Heine, Claudi & Hünnemeyer 1991: 31) and is thus consonant with motivations for semantic change in cognitive semantics. As "the most pervasive tendency in semantic change", subjectification is "an activity that draws on cognitive principles but takes place in the context of communication and rhetorical strategizing" (Traugott 1999a: 189).

By the beginning of the twentieth century, *alltså* and *således* had also been recruited into a new syntactic position. More specifically, they had moved from clause-final position, which in Swedish is re-

1. Other characteristics associated with early grammaticalization, such as bonding within the phrase or phonological reduction (Traugott 1995), are not met with *alltså* and *således* but can be observed in the grammaticalization of the other five conjuncts studied in Lehti-Eklund (1990).

served for adverbial arguments, to the position after the finite verb or to initial position, both neutral positions for conjuncts in seventeenth- to nineteenth-century Swedish.

In view of these developments, both *alltså* and *således* can certainly be said to have proceeded as far as to sentence adverbials on the cline proposed by Traugott (1995) for the grammaticalization of adverbials: Clause-internal adverbial > Sentence adverbial > Discourse particle. As Traugott (1995) has shown for English, it seems to be typical of propositional adverbs that they develop into sentential adverbs and further into discourse particles or discourse markers. The first shift is attested in *alltså* and *således* before the beginning of the twentieth century, but the latter is only just starting; the cases shown in 1.2.2 and 1.2.3, for instance, suggest that the development will go further on the cline during the twentieth century (cf. section 4).

A comparison with the six parameters that Lehmann (1982: 123) proposes for grammaticalization shows that *alltså* and *således* only partially meet his criteria of grammaticalization: the criteria paradigmatic integrity, paradigmacity, and syntagmatic variability are satisfied (Lehti-Eklund 1990: 52–59); however, the syntagmatic bondedness of the conjuncts does not increase as it should do in grammaticalization according to Lehmann (1982: 147). Furthermore, the parameters of paradigmatic variability and scope are not met. In this respect, Traugott (1995) argues that a decrease in syntactic freedom and scope should not be considered as typical of grammaticalization (cf. Onodera 1995: 428).

In the light of the first instances of the discourse marker *alltså*$_{1c}$ at the beginning of this century, *alltså* can be considered as having been grammaticalized a little further than *således* and it also has a wider spectrum of functions than *således.*

2. *Alltså* and *således* in present-day Swedish

Using written and spoken Swedish from the 1980s, I will examine whether *alltså* and *således* have developed further semantically and functionally since 1900 – which is where the investigation carried out in Lehti-Eklund (1990) ended. The use of both written and spoken language enables us to capture the changes in the usage of these conjuncts more accurately.

It is to be expected that both *alltså* and *således* have grammaticalized further and have developed increasingly subjectified and intersubjectified meanings (Traugott 1999a, 1999b); indeed, *alltså* seems to have developed further into a discourse marker, at least in spoken language.

When looking at modern dictionaries today, one finds that the main meaning given for *alltså* and *således* is the one I have marked as 1a: 'consequently'. As regards *alltså,* dictionaries also mention a weakened meaning in spoken language and the following example is given: *du är ju knäpp alltså* (*Svensk ordbok* 1988: s.v. *alltså*). The English equivalent of this would be: 'you must be mad'. The use of *alltså* together with the particle *ju* here signals a context to which the speaker reacts with a strong statement. Both *alltså* and *ju* seem to suggest the following unexplicated inference: *Since you are behaving like that/doing that, you must be mad* (for the use of *ju,* see Saari 1995: 97–102). As for *således,* the dictionary (*Svensk ordbok* 1988: s.v. *således*) also mentions that the word is very rarely used as an adverb of manner. The actual usage of both words in contemporary material is, however, much more complex than the dictionaries attest and shows a variety of meanings not codified in writing.

The written material excerpted for this study consists of a Swedish newspaper corpus, *Dagens Nyheter* (4,132,784 words) from 1987. The spoken material consists of two everyday conversations and one radio conversation among Finland Swedes in Helsinki and six dialogues by Swedes in Gothenburg, Sweden.[2]

2. The Helsinki conversations were recorded for the project *Svenska samtal i Helsingfors* (Conversations in Swedish in Helsinki) at the Department of Nordic Languages and Nordic Literature, Helsinki University. The director of the project is Anne-Marie Londen and the conversations were recorded in 1990. Two of them are everyday conversations: SAM:V1 between five men in their thirties (length 45 minutes), SAM:V2 between four women in their sixties (length 90 minutes). SAM:RS4 is a live radio conversation between two studio

Table 1 shows the occurrence of *alltså* and *således* in written and spoken language. It can be observed that *alltså* is much more frequent than *således* in written language. In the conversations there is not a single occurrence of *således*, whereas *alltså* is used frequently. As such, then, *således* no longer seems to be a word used in spoken language. However, in the archives of the Finnish Research Center for Finnish and Swedish languages, I have found indications that *således* is still used in the Finland Swedish dialects as an adverb of manner with the meaning 'thus', 'in such a manner'. This kind of usage is very archaic, resembling the way *således* was used in Sweden in the seventeenth and eighteenth centuries.

Table 1. *Således*, *alltså*: frequencies in written and spoken language.

	således	*alltså*	Frequency per minute
Dagens Nyheter 1987	196	2834	
Helsinki SAM:V1	-	48	1.060
Helsinki SAM:V2	-	3	0.033
Helsinki SAM:RS4	-	51	1.020
Gothenburg M1-6	-	35	0.190
N	196	2971	

The frequency of *alltså* per minute gives a rough picture of its popularity. It could be inferred that *alltså* is more frequent in Swedish in Finland than in Sweden, but the material is too limited for any definite conclusions. For example, Swedish adolescents could be a group using *alltså* very frequently (cf. Eriksson 1997: 74, 277; Kotsinas 1994), but this age category is not included in my material. The fre-

hosts and four studio guests (two men and two women) (length 50 minutes). The Gothenburg dialogues were recorded for the project *Språksociala studier i en talspråklig databas* (Social language studies in a database consisting of speech) at Språkdata in Gothenburg. The project was directed by Sture Allén and the recordings were made in 1979. The recordings are each 30 minutes long; in M1 and M3 it is two women that are having a conversation, in M2 and M4 it is a man and a woman, and in M5 and M6 it is two men.

quencies shown by Allwood (1996: 1) for the phonetically reduced version *asså* as being more frequent (268 instances) in comparison with the less reduced *allså* (236) and *alltså* (214 instances) also point towards *alltså* being frequent in Sweden as well. The difference between the Helsinki conversations could be explained by age: in SAM:V2, the participants are elderly women, whereas the participants in the other two conversations are between 30 and 50.

3. *Alltså* and *således* in written present-day Swedish

3.1. *The consecutive conjuncts* alltså_{1a}, således_{1a} *and the metatextual markers* alltså_{1b} *and* således_{1b}

In written present-day Swedish, both *alltså* and *således* are still used extensively as consecutive conjuncts; at the same time, we find that they are increasingly used in the other functions mentioned in section 1. More specifically, (i) we now find occurrences of explanative $\textit{således}_{2a}$ modeled after explanative $\textit{alltså}_{2a}$; (ii) the use of both *alltså* and *således* as metatextual markers taking up given information has increased. Table 2 shows the frequencies of the different meanings (note that with regard to *alltså*, only the first 200 instances of the total number of occurrences have been analyzed). Clearly, both words have undergone semantic development since the beginning of

Table 2. *Således, alltså*: meaning and function in written material.

	således	%	*alltså*	%
consecutive 1a	95	48.4	82	41.0
metatextual marker 1b	91	46.4	78	39.0
discourse marker 1c	-	-	3	1.5
explanative 2a	4	2.0	19	9.5
Other/do not know	6	3.0	18	9.0
N	196	99.8	200	100.0

this century, with the consecutive meaning losing importance and the weaker, more grammaticalized function as a metatextual marker gaining ground.

The following examples (6a) and (6b) show *alltså*$_{1a}$ and *således*$_{1a}$ as consecutive conjuncts in clauses presenting a conclusion and new information:

(6) a. *Och jag ska fråga mig vad mina fötter behöver. Skor! Har jag i min oskuld tänkt. Dom gamla är slut,* ***alltså*** *behöver jag nya.*
'I'll ask myself what my feet need. Shoes! I've naïvely thought. The old ones are worn out; *consequently*, I'll need new ones.'
b. *Elefanter med lite dressyruppfostran har ett eget språk, som är en blandning av tyska, franska, hindi och lite av varje. De vet* ***således*** *att till exempel 'Fuss allez' betyder att de ska lyfta ett framben.*
'Elephants that have had a little training have a language of their own, which is a mixture of German, French, Hindi, and a little of this and that. *Consequently*, an elephant knows that for example 'Fuss allez' means that it ought to lift one of its forelegs.'

In (7a, b, and c) *alltså* as well as *således* appear in the metatextual function 1b making a non-local connection (cf. section 1). This meaning could be translated into English with 'as you've already seen', 'as you already know', 'as has been mentioned'.

(7) a. *Skagersjö, chef för tekniska kontoret hävdar att det ska bli lika bra städat med den nya städmetoden. Bakgrunden till förslaget är att Svensk hemservice ville privatisera städningen och spara in 2,7 miljoner.*
Stort jobb [*rubrik*]
[2 meningar] Han [Skagersjö] hävdar ***alltså*** *att städningen ska hålla samma kvalitet som i dag fast till en så mycket lägre kostnad.*

'Skagersjö, Director of the Technical Office, claims that everything will be cleaned equally well as before with the new cleaning method. The reason for the proposition is that Svensk hemservice (a cleaning company) wanted private companies to do the cleaning and save 2.7 million.
A big job [a headline]
[2 sentences] He [Skagersjö] is claiming *as mentioned* that the cleaning will maintain the same standard as today but at a lower price.'

b. *Mensätra och Oxelvägen i Ålta ska i vinter få isbanor som kommunen spolar. Sammanlagt spolar kommunen 17 isbanor med start i januari. [2 meningar] I stället spolar kommunen* ***således*** *banorna på Mensätra gärde och Oxelvägen i Ålta.*
'This winter Mensätra and Oxelvägen in Ålta will get an ice rink that the municipality will freeze. Altogether the municipality will freeze 17 ice rinks beginning in January. [2 sentences] *As mentioned*, the municipality will freeze the ice rinks at Mensätra gärde and Oxelvägen in Ålta, instead.'

c. *Hälsoskyddskontoret och tekniska nämnden har gått emot deras planer på en småbåtshamn intill strandpromenaden i Kallhäll. I DN Järfällas artikel förra veckan stod det att tjänstemännen ansåg promenadvägen viktig för Kallhällsborna. Folk brukar bada vid en liten sandstrand strax söder om badberget. Stranden var särskilt lämplig för småbarn. Tjänstemännen framhöll vidare att blandskogen längs stranden var mycket artrik. Många olika sorters fåglar trivs där. Tjänstemännen ansåg* ***alltså*** *att det var olämpligt att lägga en ny båthamn vid strandpromenaden och föreslog i stället att Kallhälls båtklubb skulle kunna hysa fler båtar.*
'The health board and the technical board have decided against their plans to build a boat harbor near the strand promenade in Kallhäll. DN's Järfälla article last week stated that the officials considered the promenade to be important for the people in Kallhäll. They are accustomed to swim-

> ming on a little sand beach right to the south of the bathing cliff. The beach was regarded as especially suitable for children. The officials also said that the mixed forest along the beach had an abundance of species. Many different sorts of birds live there. *As mentioned*, the officials were of the opinion that the place near the strand promenade was unsuitable for a boat harbor and suggested instead that the boat club in Kallhäll could take in more boats.'

It is my contention that *alltså*'s and *således*'s use as a metatextual marker has developed from its consecutive use. In its metatextual meaning, *alltså* and *således* no longer precede new information, i.e., the conclusion drawn from previous discourse, but mark information as given, either in the text or with respect to encyclopedic world knowledge. Whereas conclusive *alltså*$_{1a}$ and *således*$_{1a}$ refer to the immediate context, metatextual *alltså*$_{1b}$ and *således*$_{1b}$ refer further back. Reintroducing old topics or subtopics, they work on different textual levels. As they are relics of manner adverbs, they typically appear in a summarizing context.

Alltså$_{1b}$ and *således*$_{1b}$ show a higher degree of grammaticalization than *alltså*$_{1a}$ and *således*$_{1a}$. In line with Traugott's (1995) cline from evidential > metatextual reference, they can be considered as semantically weakened or bleached because the 'conclusive' sense has disappeared from them. They also represent a shift towards a more subjectified and intersubjectified meaning: whereas a writer uses *alltså*$_{1a}$/*således*$_{1a}$ to mark proposition *b* as a conclusion from the previous proposition *a*, he/she uses *alltså*$_{1b}$/*således*$_{1b}$ to signal to him-/herself and the reader how the text ought to be read in connection with what is known. Traugott (1999b: 1) defines subjectification as a process "whereby meanings come ... to encode the [speaker's] perspectives and attitudes". In intersubjectification, according to Traugott (1999b: 3), meanings "become more centered on the addressee". This semantic-functional change does not (yet) correspond with a change in structural behavior. As Table 3 shows, no great differences can be observed in the syntactic behavior of the conjuncts *således*$_{1a}$/*alltså*$_{1a}$ and the metatextual markers *således*$_{1b}$/*alltså*$_{1b}$, in that both categories tend to be placed after the finite verb (which, as has been pointed out earlier, is a possible position of sentential adverbs in Swedish). With regard, then, to *alltså*$_{Ib}$'s and *således*$_{Ib}$'s status on the cline Clause-internal adverbial > Sentence adverbial > Discourse marker, they still ought to be regarded as sentential adverbs. Since subordinate clauses are not included, the numbers differ to some extent from those in Table 2. X stands for any initial constituent.

Table 3. *Således*$_{Ia}$/*således*$_{Ib}$ and *alltså*$_{Ia}$/*alltså*$_{Ib}$: syntactic position in main clauses.

Syntactic position	Initial	Subject+verb+ *således/alltså*	X+verb+subject +*således/alltså*	X+verb+*således/ alltså*+subject	N
således$_{Ia}$	6.0	58.0	5.0	3.0	72.0
%	8.3	80.5	6.9	4.1	99.8
således$_{Ib}$	4.0	50.0	15.0	9.0	78.0
%	5.1	64.1	19.2	11.5	99.9
alltså$_{Ia}$	12	45.0	11.0	7.0	75.0
%	16.0	60.0	14.6	9.3	99.9
alltså$_{Ib}$	-	41.0	17.0	13.0	71.0
%	-	57.7	23.9	18.3	99.9

One cause for the tendency of the sentential adverbs in Swedish not to be placed in initial position can be traced to the development towards a stricter syntactic position of constituents, a development which has been underway ever since Swedish lost its cases in the fifteenth century and started changing into an analytic language (Lehti-Eklund 1985). During this development, the subject together with some temporal and conditional adverbials have slowly emerged as prototypical initial constituents, with the result that sentential adverbs prefer a position after the finite verb.

Finally, it should be mentioned that in the twentieth century, the syntactic contexts in which *alltså* and *således* occurred have reduced even further to subordinate and main clause (cf. section 1.1); gradually, *således*$_{Ia}$ and *således*$_{Ib}$ are being narrowed down as a main clause phenomenon. The same sort of syntactic development applies to *alltså*. Today, *alltså*$_{1a}$ and *alltså*$_{1b}$ are restricted to main clauses. This gradual change seems to be connected with the generalization of meaning where both *alltså*$_{1a/1b}$ and *således*$_{1a/1b}$ connect the main information in the main clause with the earlier discourse rather than embedded information in subordinate clauses.

3.2. *The explanative conjuncts* alltså$_{2a}$ *and* således$_{2a}$

Explanative *alltså*$_{2a}$ and *således*$_{2a}$, translated into English as 'that is', often appear in the written material together with parenthetical phrases, not with whole clauses. As I mentioned, *alltså*$_{2a}$ first appeared in the nineteenth century, but there are no occurrences of *således*$_{2a}$ in the period 1600–1900; it acquired its explanative meaning during the twentieth century. The explanative meaning is illustrated in (8a) and (8b):

(8) a. *Det är särskilt svårt att undgå de upprepade och mycket fnissiga samtalen. Bästisarnas,* ***alltså***.
'It is especially difficult to avoid the repeated telephone calls full of chuckle; *that is*, calls between best friends.'

b. *Ett genomgående drag, påpekar Lönnroth, är att de äldsta kungarna –* ***således*** *de svenska, senare blir de norska och ädlare – ofta skildras förklenande.*
'A dominating trait, Lönnroth points out, is that the oldest kings – *that is*, the Swedish ones, later on they become Norwegian and more noble – are often described with contempt.'

Syntactically, *således*$_{2a}$ and *alltså*$_{2a}$ mostly mark adverbial or nominal phrases and thus differ syntactically from the consecutive conjunct *alltså*$_{1a}$/*således*$_{1a}$ and the metatextual marker *alltså*$_{1b}$/*således*$_{1b}$ (cf. section 3.1).

4. *Alltså* and *således* in spoken language

Alltså's semantic range in written language differs considerably from that in spoken language. While its main meaning in the written material is consecutive, there is not a single instance of *alltså* as a consecutive conjunct in the spoken material. Furthermore, there are only a few instances in the spoken material where *alltså* behaves as a metatextual marker. *Således,* then, which has become a conjunct and a metatextual marker belonging mainly to written language, does not appear in my spoken material at all.

4.1. Similarities with the written material

4.1.1. Metatextual marker *alltså*$_{1b}$

There are a few instances where *alltså* behaves as a metatextual marker with the meaning 'as has been mentioned'. An example is provided in (9), where the participants discuss the repair of a welding machine and A as the foreman must decide what to do. A refers with *alltså*$_{1b}$ to what B has just said about car batteries exploding. Here *alltså*$_{1b}$ seems to have the meaning 'as you said', and it still stands after the finite verb, behaving syntactically as a sentential adverb:

(9) B: *ja just detta men det är väl samma fenomen detta som med bilbatterier också att det finns möjlighet om dom är gamla så kan dom explodera också när man gör en sån strömöverföring*
'yes exactly but I suppose it's the same thing as with car batteries that there is a possibility if they are old they can explode even when you make such a power transfer'
[five utterances]
A: *hm man får väl jag får väl jag får väl antagligen komplettera bilden med det att det är det finns* ***alltså*** *kan finnas vissa risker i det här om man inte om man gör det slarvigt*

'hm one must I suppose I must I suppose I'll have to add that that it is there is *as you said* can be certain risks in this if one is not if one is sloppy' (Gothenburg 521)

4.1.2. Explanative conjunct/repair marker

Alltså$_{2a}$ is found several times with the explanative meaning 'that is' and in similar surroundings as in the written material, i.e., it often appears together with phrases. In example (10), BS specifies the adjective *tekniska* 'technical' with another adjectival phrase *direktivbetonade* 'like directives', whereby *alltså*$_{2a}$ marks the beginning of the specification. Explanative *alltså*$_{2a}$ can also be used to make an addition to an utterance, as in (11).

(10) BS: *de e klart om man räknar laganas antal så kommer en massa av dem att fa- att fattas i Bryssel just genom att di e (.) di e rent tekniska* ***alltså*** *direktivbetonade*
'it is clear if you count the number of laws that a lot of them will be made in Brussels precisely because they are purely technical *I mean* like directives' (SAM:RS4)

(11) BE: *de sto i tidningen* ***alltså*** *ida att Erkki Tuomioja ha bytt från sin gamla (0.6) förening*
'it was in the paper *that is* today that Erkki Tuomioja has left his old club' (SAM:RS4)

In (12), AR rephrases the contents of the first sentence. The meaning of *alltså*$_{2a}$ here is quite similar to that in examples (10) and (11). Syntactically, *alltså*$_{2a}$ has scope over a whole clause, even if it does not stand initially but comes after the subject *man* 'one' and the predicate *va* 'was'.

(12) AR: *utan mitt intryck blev väl nog att de kanske snarare va fråga om en rädsla för framtiden man va* ***alltså*** *rädd för att när den (.hh) när den sovjetiska armén (0.8) förr eller*

senare (.nff) lämnar Estland så (.) så blir den här ryska minoriteten då (.nff) då #m# i ett utsatt läge
'but I got the impression I think that it probably was a question of being afraid for the future *I mean* one was afraid that when (.hh) when the Soviet army (0.8) sooner or later (.nff) leaves Estonia the position of the Russian minority becomes #m# exposed' (SAM:RS4)

I submit that the explanative, parenthetical conjunct *alltså*$_{2a}$ has developed in spoken language into the discourse marker *alltså*$_{2b}$ marking repair, either self- or other-initiated (Fox, Hayashi & Jasperson 1996: 185–189). It is likely that this repair marking function has come about through instances such as example (12), where the speaker rephrases his/her words. Actually, the instances of *alltså*$_{2a}$ as an explanative conjunct (10), a conjunct preceding an addition (11), and a repair marker (13) should be viewed on a continuum, i.e., they do not make up discrete categories. As such, it might be difficult to know when, for instance, an explanative conjunct changes into a discourse marker used for repair.[3] In addition, in all three functions, *alltså* behaves syntactically in the same way.

The difficulty of deciding which category *alltså* belongs to is shown in the following three examples. When B in (13) rephrases *smålänning* 'a person living in Småland' as *acklimatiserad smålänning* 'an acclimatized Smålander', he not only uses a more specific phrase but also repairs the phrase A had used.

(13) A: *ja men han har ju tydligen han han blivit riktig smålänning vet du*
'yes but he has obviously become a real Smålander, you know'

3. The difficulty of knowing when an explanative conjunct changes into a discourse marker used for repair only becomes apparent when studying spoken material. In written language there is no need for the repair function, where explanative *alltså*$_{2a}$ precedes a parenthetical commentary or a specification of what has been said earlier.

B: *ja **alltså** acklimatiserad smålänning då*
'yes *you mean* an acclimatized Smålander, then' (Gothenburg 521)

In (13)–(15), *alltså* probably already functions as a discourse marker *alltså*$_{2b}$. In (14), A chooses another verb, *göra* 'make' instead of *få* 'get', and marks the change with *alltså.* Here, *alltså* can be translated with 'you mean', as in (13).

(14) B: *du för resten kan man få kan man få kopia på dian*
'hey by the way is it possible is it possible to get a copy of the slide'
A: *kopia **alltså** göra dia- diakopior*
'copy *you mean* to make slide- slide copies' (Gothenburg 507)

In (15), BS corrects himself and changes *europeiska* 'the European' into *EG* 'EC'. Here *alltså* could be translated with 'I mean':

(15) BS: *nå de fin- de (.) finns ren nu en en modell för europeiska gemenskapen (.h) den som: existerar ida. (.h) å dä har vi tisempel (.) den öh europeiska e- (.) **alltså** EG (0.6) öh parlamentarismen så den ha man ju liksom: (.hh) FLINAT åt för den har ju ingen haft nån funktion*
'well there i- there (.) is already now a model for the European community (.h) that that exists today (.h) and we have there for example (.) the eh European E- (.) *I mean* EC (0.6) eh parliamentarism and that we have so to speak (.hh) been LAUGHING at because it doesn't have hasn't had any function'(SAM:RS4)

In the examples shown above, the use of *alltså* still resembles its functions in written language to a great extent.

In addition to these, *alltså* has a great variety of functions as a discourse marker. Here, we trace a path of grammaticalization that leads further away from the sentential adverb. A few of these functions are presented in the following section.

4.2. *Alltså as a discourse marker*

In addition to its functions as a metatextual marker and an explanative conjunct, *alltså* shows in spoken Swedish a wide range of functions as a discourse marker, a number of which will be presented in this section. With *alltså*'s semantic-functional development into a discourse marker corresponds a structural development that leads further away from the sentential adverb.

The main functions of *alltså* as a discourse marker can be divided into three main categories. First, *alltså* is used when referring to different contexts or activities either in the conversation or outside it. Second, it is used to structure one's utterance on different levels. These two partially overlapping functions will be referred to as *alltså*$_{1c}$. In its third function, *alltså*$_{2b}$, it is used in speech planning as a hesitation and repair marker. There are also some additional minor functions.

Typically, *alltså*$_{1c}$ and *alltså*$_{2b}$ are used in contexts or turns which constitute a reaction to something said before. In this reactive function, *alltså* almost always shows traces of the earlier consecutive or explanative meanings. In its most 'bleached' function, where the trace of earlier meanings is almost non-existent, *alltså* marks hesitation – a usage which can hardly be said to constitute a reaction to what has been said before. It is in this function that *alltså* has probably been grammaticalized further than in its other functions.

As instances of grammaticalization, discourse markers have been argued to show the following characteristics: functional change with pragmatic strengthening, subjectification and intersubjectification followed by movement to an initial position, and different intonation (Traugott 1995, 1999b; Ferrara 1997). I regard the discourse marker *alltså*$_{1c}$ as the result of further grammaticalization from the consecutive conjunct *alltså*$_{1a}$ and the metatextual marker *alltså*$_{1b}$, and the repair and hesitation marker *alltså*$_{2b}$ as a further development from the explanative conjunct *alltså*$_{2a}$. *Alltså*'s functional changes will be outlined in sections 4.2.1, 4.2.2, and 4.2.3; other characteristics, such as its syntactic position as a discourse marker, will be discussed in section 4.2.4.

First I show how *alltså* is used in referring to different contexts or activities either in the conversation or outside it. The contexts and activities which are referred to can vary a great deal.

4.2.1. Reference to different contexts and activities

In control questions, *alltså*$_{1c}$ precedes the speaker's conclusion based on the previous utterance; its role is thus to refer back in a conversation. This kind of use is clearly connected with the consecutive conjunct *alltså*$_{1a}$; only the conclusion that is drawn is weaker and can no longer be paraphrased with 'consequently'. In (16), Olle is asking Erik if the building where Erik used to live is still standing and then goes on to check if he has correctly understood the location of the house. Erik's answer shows that Olle is completely mistaken. Here *alltså*$_{1c}$ could be translated with 'you mean' or 'then'.

(16) Olle: *aj de finns fortfarande kvar?*
'oh it's still there?'
Erik: *de finns [kvar*
'it's [there'
Olle: *[**alltså** där vi vi (.) Bolars va heter de Bolarskog*
'[*you mean* there near near (.) Bolars what's its name Bolarskog'
Erik: *ne ne int e de*
'no no it isn't' (SAM:V1)

Schiffrin (1987: 254 f.) describes similar requests with the discourse marker *then* in English as requests for confirmation. She defines these warranted requests as requests (i) that are based on shared background knowledge, and (ii) that focus sequentially on a recent statement and receive confirmation with an agreement token. The conversational contexts in (16) as well as (17) show that a certain amount of background knowledge is shared by the participants, but as (16) shows, it is not detailed knowledge. Both Olle's and Mats' requests in (16) and (17) are syntactically similar to Schiffrin's requests for confirmation in that they are presented as declarative statements. In both cases, the first speaker interprets the statement as a request for confirmation and answers with a token of agreement/disagreement. In (17), Göran is telling about his relatives and Mats checks whether his conclusion that Göran's relatives were considered Germans, even though they originally came from the Baltic countries, is correct. In these cases, *alltså*$_{1c}$'s position is typically at the beginning of the utterance:

(17) Göran: *bodde där var precis var Träskbergs skola står nu men sen när (.) när dedär (1.2) när krige to slut så (0.6) så dedär beslagstos all (1.1) all dedär egendom som tyskar ägde i Finland å de övergick då ti (0.7) [ryssarna*
'lived there exactly where the Träskberg school is now but then when (.) when eh (1.2) when the war was over then (0.6) then eh all (1.1) all eh the property that Germans had in Finland was confiscated and it went over to (0.7) [Russians'
Mats: *[**alltså** dom räknades som tyskar*
'[*so* they were considered as Germans then'
Göran: *jå (.) dom va alltså dom va tyska medborgare*
'yes (.) they were they were German citizens' (SAM:V1)

In using *alltså*$_{1c}$, speakers may not only refer to what has been said in the ongoing conversation but also to the context outside the conversation. As such, they may refer to past contexts, e.g., their own knowledge of what has happened in the past or general knowledge assumed to be common to each participant, or to present contexts, e.g., the concrete, local context (for local sensitivity, see Bergmann 1990: 207), an abstract world, or their opinions and values.

In (18), B is telling a story of what she could see on ultrasound scans of the different stages of her (then) unborn child. The conversation clearly shows that *alltså,* refers to common ground, which is established with the particles *då* 'then' (Lehti-Eklund 1993: 43) and *ju* (Östman 1979); the participants are reminiscing, as B's answer "yes I remember" confirms:

(18) B: */.../ efter det här ultraljudet jag gick å inbillade mej allt möjligt först var det ju då **alltså** det första stadiet*
'after this ultrasound examination I imagined all sorts of things first there was like *you know* the first stage'
A: *ja det kommer jag ihåg*
'yes I remember' (Gothenburg 502)

Alltså may also refer to the local, physical context as a sort of attention marker 'look at this here' (see Bergmann 1990: 207). In (19), B is talking to a child about A's jumper and A is referring to her jumper with *alltså.* Here an adequate English translation could be either 'don't you think' or 'isn't this a funny jumper', a phrase with which the speaker both refers to the jumper and to the other participants. In the Swedish version the function of referring to the jumper dominates.

(19) B: *titta Musse Pigg*
'look Mickey Mouse'
A: *ja konstig tröja **alltså** det får jag säga en vuxen människa har en sån tröja med Musse Pigg på va*
'yes *don't you think* it's a funny jumper I must say a grown-up person with a jumper like that' (Gothenburg 502)

In (20), A is probably taking the magazine *Mad* into his hand and refers to this activity with *alltså*$_{lc}$. This is a conversation where two young men find it very difficult to sit and talk to each other in front of the microphone. A's utterance in (20) is preceded by a pause. The function of *alltså*$_{1c}$ could be described as a combination of reference to the activity in taking up the magazine and attention marker with the meaning 'look here's *Mad*'.

(20) A: *Mad* ***alltså*** *jävla sjukt*
'*Hey* Mad bloody sick'
B: *jag läste den i går vet du*
'I read it yesterday you know' (Gothenburg 518)

Example (21), then, shows how *alltså* can mark one's opinion. The men are arguing about different songs in the Eurovision Song Contest. Micke's utterance that a song was 'euroarranged' is followed by Mats' statement that the song was not 'euroarranged' but 'overarranged'. Mats' utterance serves two functions: it states his opinion and corrects Micke's statement. The English translation 'I don't think' shows even more clearly that it is his opinion that Mats is marking with *alltså*. This kind of multifunctionality is typical of discourse markers. As we have seen in sections 4.1.2 and 4.2.3, *alltså* is also used to mark repairs.

(21) Micke: *n: di e int rikit (1.5) så där euroarrangerade=*
'n: they are not really (1.5) sort of euroarranged='
Göran: =[[*så ha de (-)*
'=[[then they have (-)'
Lasse: =[[>*nå de kan ju* [*hända att*<
'=[[>well I suppose it can [happen that<'
Mats: [*int över (.)* ***alltså*** *de e int fråga om euroarrangemang de e fråga om överarrangemang*
'[not over (.) *I don't think* it's a question of euroarrangement, rather overarrangement' (SAM:V1)

In addition to referring to different contexts, *alltså*$_{1c}$ can be used in structuring the contents in an utterance. This function is discussed in section 4.2.2.

4.2.2. Structuring content in conversation

It is a typical feature of many discourse particles that they can be used to mark transitions between different contents or activities in conversation (for *nå* in Swedish, see Lehti-Eklund 1992: 182–183; for *förresten,* see Londen 1989: 194; for *anyway,* see Ferrara 1997; for *besides,* see Traugott 1995). With *alltså*$_{1c}$, the function of referring to a particular context and structuring different contents in a conversation seem to partially overlap. In some cases, it prototypically refers to a certain context (cf. above), and in others it is more a marker of a transition, e.g., to a quotation or a parenthetical comment. However, the structuring of contents or activities is mostly linked with a weak reference to a particular context.

An illustration of such an overlap is provided in (22): *alltså*$_{1c}$ refers outside the discourse to the speaker's mind, his/her opinions and values; at the same time, *alltså* marks a transition to these opinions and values from what is said earlier in the utterance. The speaker (KH=Klaus Hellberg) first makes a general statement about the negotiations with the EFTA countries (the conversation is from 1991) and then prefaces his opinion with *alltså*:

(22) KH: *men de här (.) de här beror no också? (.) också på de att hur nu Efta länderna [kommer*
'but this (.) this depends also (.) also on how the Efta countries [will take part'
BS: [Klaus Hellberg
KH: *i förhandlingar å hur hur går de me Sverige (.)* ***alltså*** *(0.5)* ***alltså*** *vi kan ju int bli (0.6) vi kan int vara de enda land som nu blir utanför de här*

'in the negotiations and what what happens with Sweden (.) *I mean* (0.5) *I mean* we can't (0.6) we can't be the only country that stays outside this' (SAM:RS 4)

The use of *alltså* here is very similar to *I mean* as a marker of speaker orientation to ideas: *I mean* in English can be used to "preface speaker key in general"; it "focuses on the **speaker's** modification of his/her **own** talk" and has a "tendency to preface propositions through which a speaker predicates something of him-/herself" (Schiffrin 1987: 299).

In (23), Asta structures an indirect quotation with *alltså.* When quoting the Finnish president, she makes a parenthetical comment revealing that she has actually forgotten what the quoted utterance was and marks her comment with *alltså* 'I mean':

(23) Asta: *Koivisto sa (0.8) å dedär m eh m* ***alltså*** *den va oerhört bra men nu ha ja den där (0.5) pointen så så ha ja sen glömt va de va*
'Koivisto said (0.8) and eh m eh m *I mean* it was very well said but now I've the point (0.5) I've forgotten what it was' (SAM:V2)

In (24), *alltså*$_{1c}$ also precedes a parenthetical comment. Here BS, who is hosting a radio discussion, asks one of the participants a question. After the question, BS comments on her question and explains more explicitly what she means. The beginning of the comment is marked with *alltså* and a higher speech tempo, but one could also say that *alltså* refers to knowledge outside the conversation that BS has of the delegations that have been sent to Estonia.

(24) BS: *viken viken roll hade du när du: reste nu di t >**alltså** vi ha ju< (.hh) (.) i sej ha ju Finland int skicka nå officiella (0.9) delegationer (.) till Estland (0.6) men du va*
'what was your role when you went there >*I mean* we haven't< (.hh) (.) as a matter of fact Finland hasn't sent any official (0.9) delegations (.) to Estonia but you were' (SAM:RS4)

4.2.3. *Alltså*$_{2b}$: marking hesitation and repair

This section deals with *alltså*$_{2b}$ as a marker of repair and hesitation. It is a further development from *alltså*'s use as an explanative marker, and forms the current end point of the grammaticalization path from *alltså*$_{2a}$ > *alltså*$_{2b}$. The function where *alltså* has developed the furthest from the explanative meaning is when the speaker uses it to mark hesitation.

In (25), Erik starts his utterance in overlap with the previous speaker, which might explain his use of several hesitation markers (*nå, men, alltså*, and *liksom*). Here *alltså,* together with the other markers, can be translated as *well*:

(25) Erik: [*nå men* ***alltså*** *liksom* <u>*poin*</u>*ten är ju den att de e int nån vit- eh skillna* <u>*va*</u> *vi snarvlar*
'*well* eh eh the point is that it makes no poin- no difference what we talk' (SAM:V1)

Another use of *alltså*$_{2b}$ as a hesititation marker occurs when one is searching for a word. In (26), *alltså* prefaces BS's utterance when she is searching for the word *anpassning* 'adjustment':

(26) BS: => *jå men de e i alla fall?<* ***alltså*** *de e en en anpassning*
'>yes but anyway?< *I mean* it is an an adjustment' (SAM:RS4)

The transition from explanative *alltså*$_{2a}$ to its use as a repair marker *alltså*$_{2b}$ was discussed in section 4.1.2. Here, I will illustrate one further example of a repair of the previous speaker's utterance, where *alltså* is the only indication that a repair has been made. In (27), the men are comparing their ages. Olle starts the conversation by asking Göran if he is already thirty. By replying *va e trettiett Erik* 'what is thirty-one Erik', Micke implies that he is already thirty-one and expects Erik also to be thirty-one. Erik's repair *alltså trettitvå* 'you mean thirty-two' shows that Micke is mistaken and that Erik is a year older. By repeating “thirty-two” Micke shows his understanding of and acceptance of Erik’s repair (Schiffrin 1987: 299):

(27) Olle: *ha du fyllt tretti också*
‘are you also thirty’
Micke: *va e trettiett Erik*
‘what is thirty-one Erik’
Erik: ***alltså*** *tretti<u>två</u>*
‘*you mean* thirty-two’
/…/
Micke: *va e tretti<u>två</u>*
‘what is thirty-two’ (SAM:V1)

4.2.4. The discourse marker *alltså* and grammaticalization

During the twentieth century, *alltså* moved to the end of the grammaticalization cline, Clause-internal adverbial > Sentence adverbial > Discourse particle (Traugott 1995). One of the characteristics of grammaticalization from adverbs to discourse markers is their shift to initial syntactic position (Onodera 1995; Traugott 1995; Ferrara 1997). Table 4 below shows that *alltså*$_{1c}$ and *alltså*$_{2b}$ as discourse markers prefer sentence-initial position; this is in contrast to the conclusive conjunct *alltså*$_{1a}$, the metatextual marker *alltså*$_{1b}$, and the explanative conjunct *alltså*$_{2a}$, whose position varies between post-verbal and initial; cf. Table 3. It should be added that a comparison with Table 3 is indicative only, since the numbers in Table 3 are drawn from written language and main clauses, whereas those in Table 4 are from conversations and comprise both clauses and phrases.

The grammaticalization of discourse markers has also been linked with a change in intonation (Ferrara 1997). The recordings on which the present analysis is based unfortunately do not meet the quality criteria that pitch-extraction programs like SWELL require. The study of intonation of *alltså* would have required studio tape-recorded separate voices, as Ferrara (1997: 355) has shown. It is difficult, therefore, to study the intonation of discourse markers in an authentic context, in authentic conversation. Intonation as a criterion for discourse markers may, however, be language dependent. The intonation of initial markers in Swedish and Finland Swedish does not resemble those in English (Elert 1989: 129, 132; Johansson 1976: 121); simply listening to different instances of *alltså* as a discourse marker does not support the suggestion of different intonation curves as Ferrara (1997) shows for *anyway* in English. However, the intonation of initial markers in spontaneous speech in Swedish is an important question that needs to be studied (cf. Bruce 1998: 192).

Table 4. *Alltså*$_{1c}$ and *alltså*$_{2b}$: syntactic positions.

Syntactic position	Initial	After finite verb	Final	Other	N
alltså$_{1c}$:					
- referring to different contexts	29	8	4	–	41
- structuring of utterance	10	–	-	–	10
alltså$_{2}$*b*:	29	3	2	2	36
- speech planning					
- repair	12	1	1	–	14
Other	8	–	–	–	8
N	88	12	7	2	109

Even if their intonation remains undocumented, the discourse markers *alltså*$_{1c}$ and *alltså*$_{2b}$ meet other criteria of grammaticalization, thus lending support to *alltså*'s move to the end of the grammaticalization cline, Clause-internal adverbial > Sentence adverbial > Discourse particle. In addition to its preference for initial position (Onodera 1995; Ferrara 1997), *alltså* as a discourse marker meets the following criteria of grammaticalization:

(a) *It shifts* from a propositional adverb via a sentential adverb to a discourse marker, thus demonstrating a change typical of grammaticalization from a lexical item through a grammatical item to a discourse marker (Traugott 1995; cf. *actually* in Traugott 1999b).

(b) *Generalization.* Especially in its development from *alltså*$_{1a}$ > *alltså*$_{1c}$, *alltså* applies to a wider range of contexts, from preceding discourse to shared knowledge, thoughts, and beliefs.

(c) *Subjectification and intersubjectification.* In the development *alltså*$_{1a}$ > *alltså*$_{1b}$ > *alltså*$_{1c}$, the meanings of conclusion (*alltså*$_{1a}$) and the function of marking information as known (*alltså*$_{1b}$) are semantically bleached. At the same time, *alltså*$_{1c}$ attests to an increase in subjectification, as it creates coherence by marking earlier utterances, thoughts, beliefs, or knowledge as relevant with reference to the current discourse. Marking one's utterance as relevant at a certain point in discourse is a central function of discourse particles (Brinton 1990: 55; Schiffrin 1987: 91). The change *alltså*$_{2a}$ > *alltså*$_{2b}$ also attests to an increase in pragmatic function and intersubjectification from an explanative conjunct on a textual level to a marker of repair (Traugott & König 1991: 208–209; Traugott 1999b).

(d) *Decategorialization.* As a discourse marker, *alltså* has moved from the category of adverbs down the scale to particles.

(e) *Phonological reduction.* Although not attested in my material, *alltså* as a discourse marker has become phonetically reduced to [asso] in Sweden (but not in Finland Swedish), especially in the speech of adolescents. This is shown in (28) in a discussion between five girls[4] where H is referring to her opinion about soft bananas with *asså*:

(28) H: *min pappa gillar eh han ÄLSKAR såna här bananer*
'my daddy likes eh he LOVES bananas like these'
/.../
B: *jag klarar inte [a:v de*
'I can't stand it'

4. Kerstin Nordenstam, Department of Swedish Language, University of Gothenburg, has kindly let me use this example. It has been recorded in her project *Samtalsstrategier hos kvinnor och män i vardagliga gruppsamtal* (Women's and men's conversation strategies in everyday group conversations), 1991–1994.

H: *[jag* *<u>ha:tar</u>* *de* ***asså*** *>eh så när< dom e mjuka (.) å* <u>FY FAAN</u> *vad äckliga*
'[*I mean* I hate it >eh when< they're soft (.) and OH HELL how disgusting' (GRUPPSAM: Petra, 1341–1346)

According to Allwood (1996: 1), who listed word frequencies of words in colloquial Swedish in Sweden, *asså* (116th) precedes both *allså* (236th) and *alltså* (139th). Allwood's list does not, however, say anything about the discourse functions of the different word forms.

5. Conclusions

Both *alltså* and *således* have developed since the beginning of the twentieth century, with *alltså* showing more substantial changes than *således*. In written language, *alltså* and *således* increasingly occur as metatextual markers. Furthermore, *således*'s usage as a conjunct is mostly restricted to written language. In spoken language, *alltså* has developed further and is no longer used as a conjunct, but only as a discourse marker with several different functions. The shifts in function and meaning follow the typical path of change from propositional adverbs to sentential adverbs, and for *alltså*, further on to discourse markers. This development meets several criteria associated with grammaticalization. Despite the semantic bleaching that *alltså* and *således* have undergone, the traces of the summary sense which they have had since their earliest use as adverbs of manner persist (Hopper 1991: 28 f.), also in some instances with *alltså*$_{1c}$ as a discourse marker.

The grammaticalization paths for *alltså* and *således* can be summarized as follows:

Således

adverb of manner	>	consecutive conjunct *således*$_{1a}$	>	metatextual marker *således*$_{1b}$
	>	explanative conjunct *således*$_{2a}$		

Alltså

adverb of manner	>	consecutive conjunct *alltså*$_{1a}$	>	metatextual marker *alltså*$_{1b}$	>	discourse marker *alltså*$_{1c}$
	>	explanative conjunct *alltså*$_{2a}$	>	discourse marker for repair and hesitation *alltså*$_{2a}$		

The semantic development of *således* has come to an end as it does not occur in the spoken language. The semantic change of *alltså* follows two paths, the first going from consecutive meaning to marking reference and structuring discourse, the second from marking explanation or parenthesis to marking repair or hesitation.

Transcription conventions

[	Overlap onset
[[	Overlap onset at the start of an utterance
=	There is no discernible silence between the line connected by two equal signs.
(-)	A word which the transcriber cannot understand
(.hh)	Inhalation
(.nff)	Sniffing
(0.5)	Numbers in parentheses indicate silence, represented in tenths of a second
(.)	A micropause, under 0.5 seconds
-	A hyphen after a word indicates a cut-off.
word	Underlining indicates some form of stress
WORD	Loud talk
#word#	A creaky voice
>word<	Rushed talk
word:	A lengthened sound
?	Rising intonation
.	Falling intonation

References

Allén, Sture (ed.)
1965 *Brev till brodern Claes Ekeblad* 1639-1655 [Letters to brother Claes Ekeblad]. (Acta Universitatis Gothoburgiensis, Nordistica Gothoburgiensia 2). Department of Swedish, University of Gothenburg.

Allwood, Jens (ed.)
1996 *Talspråksfrekvenser* [Spoken language frequencies]. (Gothenburg papers in theoretical linguistics S 20). Department of Linguistics, University of Gothenburg.

Bergmann, Jörg
1990 On the local sensitivity of conversation. In: Ivana Marková and Klaus Foppa (eds.), *The Dynamics of Dialogue,* 201–226. Hemel Hempstead: Harvester Wheatsheaf.

Beskow Tainsh, Karin (ed.)
1972 *På biblioteket – där har jag min största förnöjelse* [In the Library – There I Enjoy Myself]. Stockholm: Almqvist & Wiksell.

Brinton, Laurel J.
1990 The development of discourse markers in English. In: Jacek Fisiak (ed.), *Historical Linguistics and Philology,* 45–71. Berlin: Mouton de Gruyter.
1996 *Pragmatic Markers in English.* Berlin: Mouton de Gruyter.

Bruce, Gösta
1998 *Allmän och svensk prosodi* [General and Swedish Prosody]. (Praktisk lingvistik 16). Institute for Linguistics, University of Lund.

Elert, Claes-Christian
1989 *Allmän och svensk fonetik* [General and Swedish Phonetics]. Stockholm: Norstedts.

Eriksson, Mats
1997 *Ungdomars berättande: En studie i struktur och interaktion* [Storytelling in Adolescence]. Ph.D. dissertation, Institutionen för nordiska språk vid Uppsala universitet, University of Uppsala.

Ferrara, Kathleen W.
1997 The discourse marker *anyway*: Implications for discourse analysis. *Linguistics* 35: 343–378.

Fox, Barbara A., Hayashi, Makoto and Robert Jasperson
1996 Resources and repair: A cross-linguistic study of syntax and repair. In: Elinor Ochs, Emanuel A. Schegloff and Sandra A.

Thompson (eds.), *Interaction and Grammar,* 185–237. Cambridge: Cambridge University Press.

Fraser, Bruce
1990 An approach to discourse markers. *Journal of Pragmatics* 14: 383–395.

Gumperz, John
1982 *Discourse Strategies.* Cambridge: Cambridge University Press.

Hakulinen, Auli
1989 Partikkelit ja muut kiteymät vuoroissa [Particles and other clusters in turns]. In: Auli Hakulinen (ed.), *Kieli* 4, 115–146. Helsinki: Helsingin yliopiston suomen kielen laitos.

Hakulinen, Auli and Mirja Saari
1995 Temporaalisesta adverbista diskurssipartikkeliksi [From a temporal adverb to a discourse particle]. *Virittäjä* 4: 481–500.

Haskå, Inger
1988 Standardisering inom fornsvenskans bestånd av kausalmarkörer [Standardization among causal markers in Old Swedish]. In Gertrud Pettersson (ed.), *Studier i svensk språkhistoria* [Studies in Swedish Language History], 86–103. Lund: Lund University Press.

Heine, Bernd, Ulrike Claudi and Friedrike Hünnemeyer
1991 *Grammaticalization: A Conceptual Framework.* Chicago: The University of Chicago Press.

Hopper, Paul J.
1991 On some principles of grammaticization. In Elizabeth C. Traugott and Bernd Heine (eds.), *Approaches to Grammaticalization*, Volume I, 17–35. Amsterdam: John Benjamins.

Johansson, Stig
1976 *Kort lärobok i engelsk fonetik* [Short Textbook on English Phonetics]. Lund: Studentlitteratur.

Kotsinas, Ulla-Britt
1994 *Ungdomsspråk* [Young People's Language]. (Ord och stil 25). Uppsala.

Lehmann, Christian
1982 *Thoughts on Grammaticalization* I. (Arbeiten des Kölner Universalien-Projekts 48). Institut für Sprachwissenschaft, Universität Köln.

Lehti-Eklund, Hanna
1985 Topikaliseringen och dess funktioner i fem texttyper från äldre nysvensk tid [Topicalization and its functions in five texttypes from Early Modern Swedish period]. Unpublished licentiate thesis, Institutionen för nordiska språk, University of Helsinki.

1990 *Från adverb till markör i text* [From Adverb to Textual Marker]. (Skrifter utgivna av Svenska litteratursällskapet i Finland [Studies published by the Swedish Literature Society in Finland] 561). Helsinki: Svenska litteratursällskapet i Finland.

1992 Användningen av partikeln *nå* i helsingforssvenska samtal [The use of the particle *nå* in Swedish conversations in Helsinki]. In: Staffan Hellberg et al. (ed.) *Svenskans beskrivning* [Description of Swedish]19, 174–184. Lund: Lund University Press.

1993 Användningen av *då* i historiskt och nusvenskt perspektiv [The use of *då* in a historical and modern Swedish perspective]. In: Ann-Marie Ivars, Hanna Lehti-Eklund, Pirkko Lilius, Anne-Marie Londen and Helena Solstrand-Pipping (eds.), *Språk och social kontext* [Language and social context] (Meddelanden från institutionen för nordiska språk och nordisk litteratur vid Helsingfors universitet B: 15), 29–48. Helsingki: Universitets-förlaget.

Levinson, Stephen C.

1987 Minimization and conversational inference. In: Jef Verschueren and Marcella Bertucelli-Papi (eds.), *The Pragmatic Perspective,* 61–129. Amsterdam: John Benjamins.

Linell, Per and Lennart Gustavsson

1987 *Initiativ och respons* [Initiative and Response]. Tema Kommunikation. Universitetet i Linköping.

Londen, Anne-Marie

1989 *Litterärt talspråk* [Fictional speech]. (Skrifter utgivna av Svenska litteratursällskapet i Finland [Studies published by the Swedish Literature Society in Finland] 557). Helsinki: Svenska litteratursällskapet i Finland.

Nordenstam, Kerstin

1994 Korpus Gruppsam [The corpus Gruppsam]. (Meddelanden från Institutionen för svenska språket [Publications from the Department of Swedish language] 4). Department of Swedish, University of Gothenburg.

Onodera, Noriko Okada

1995 Diachronic analysis of Japanese discourse markers. In: Andreas Jucker, (ed.), *Historical Pragmatics,* 393–437. Amsterdam: John Benjamins.

Östman, Jan-Ola

1979 Om svenskans talarattitydsadverbial [On modal adverbials in Swedish]. In: Olle Josephson, Hans Strand and Margareta Westman (eds.), *Svenskans beskrivning* 11 [Description of

Swedish], 195–209. Institutionen för nordiska språk, University of Stockholm.

1981 "*You know": A Discourse Functional Approach*. Amsterdam: John Benjamins.

Palmborg, N. (ed.)

1956 *Esaias Tegnérs brev* V 1861–1879 [Letters from Esaias Tegnér]. (Skrifter utgivna av Svenska litteratursällskapet i Finland [Studies published by the Swedish Literature Society in Finland] 47). Helsinki: Svenska Litteratursällskapet i Finland.

Quirk, Randolph, Sidney Greenbaum, Geoffrey Leech and Jan Svartvik

1974 *A Grammar of Contemporary English*, Fourth impression. London: Longman.

Runeberg, Fredrika

1971 *Brev till sonen Walter 1861-1879 [Letters to the son Walter].* (Skrifter utgivna av Svenska litteratursällskapet i Finland [Studies published by the Swedish Literature Society in Finland] 47). Helsinki: Svenska litteratursällskapet i Finland.

Saari, Mirja

1995 Synpunkter på svenskt språkbruk i Sverige och Finland [On the use of Swedish language in Sweden and Finland]. *Folkmålsstudier* 36: 75-108.

Schiffrin, Deborah

1987 *Discourse Markers*. Cambridge: Cambridge University Press.

Stenbock, Carl Magnus

1913 *Magnus Stenbock och Eva Oxenstierna: En brefväxling* I [Magnus Stenbock and Eva Oxenstierna: A correspondence]. Stockholm: P. A. Norstedt & söner.

Svensk ordbok [Swedish lexicon]

1988 Gothenburg: Språkdata och Esselte Studium, University of Gothenburg.

Thorell, Olof

1987 *Svensk grammatik* [Swedish grammar]. Stockholm: Esselte.

Traugott, Elizabeth C.

1982 From propositional to textual and expressive meanings: Some semantic-pragmatic aspects of grammaticalization. In: Winfred P. Lehmann and Yakov Malkiel (eds.), *Perspectives on Historical Linguistics,* 245–271. Amsterdam: John Benjamins.

1986 From polysemy to internal semantic reconstruction. In: Vassiliki Nikiforidou, Mary Van Clay, Mary Niepokuj and Deborah Feder (eds.), *Proceedings of the Twelfth Annual Meeting of the Berkeley Linguistics Society*, 539–550. Berkeley, CA: Berkeley Linguistics Sociery.

1988 Pragmatic strengthening and grammaticalization. In: Shelley Axmaker, Annie Jaisser and Helen Singmaster (eds.), *Proceedings of the Fourteenth Annual Meeting of the Berkeley Linguistics Society,* 406–416. Berkeley, CA: Berkeley Linguistics Society.

1989 On the rise of epistemic meanings in English: An example of subjectification in semantic change. *Language* 65: 31–55.

1990 From less to more situated in language: The unidirectionality of semantic change. In: Sylvia Adamson, Vivien Law, Nigel Vincent & Susan Wright (eds.) *Papers from the Fifth International Conference on English Historical Linguistics,* 496–517. Amsterdam: John Benjamins.

1995 The role of discourse markers in a theory of grammaticalization. Paper presented at the 12th International Conference on Historical Linguistics Manchester, UK, August 1995. (http://www.stanford.edu/~traugott/traugott.html).

1999 a The rhetoric of counter-expectation in semantic change: A study in subjectification. In: Peter Koch and Andreas Blank (eds.), *Historical Semantics and Cognition* (Cognitive Linguistics Research, 13), 177–196. Berlin: Mouton de Gruyter.

1999 b From subjectification to intersubjectification. Paper presented at the Workshop on Historical Pragmatics, 14th International Conference on Historical Linguistics, Vancouver, Canada, July 1999. (http://www.stanford.edu/~traugott/traugott.html).

2001 Legitimate counterexamples to unidirectionality. Paper presented at Freiburg University, October 17, 2001. (http://www.stanford.edu/~traugott/traugott.html).

Traugott, Elizabeth C. and Ekkehard König

1991 The semantics-pragmatics of grammaticalization revisited. In: Elizabeth C. Traugott & Bernd Heine (eds.), *Approaches to Grammaticalization* I, 189–218. Amsterdam: John Benjamins.

Word meaning, sentence meaning, and syntactic meaning

Laura A. Michaelis

Abstract

The lexicon has long been assumed to be the source of all conceptual content expressed by sentences. Syntactic structures have correspondingly been seen only as providing instructions for the assembly of the concepts expressed by words. Under this view, sentences have meaning, but the syntactic structures which sentences instantiate do not. This paper challenges this view: it uses the phenomenon of implicit type-shifting to demonstrate that constructions have meanings distinct from those of words and that, in cases of conflict, construction meaning overrides word meaning. It further argues that such overrides are predictable by-products of the general mechanism of construction-word integration. This mechanism will be described with respect to three different kinds of constructions: argument-structure constructions, which specify linkings of thematic roles to grammatical functions; aspectual constructions, which encode the situation type denoted by the verb or verb phrase; and sentence types, which pair a discourse function with a clausal structure. On the basis of these three short case studies, I will argue that appeal to constructional meaning greatly enhances the descriptive power of a theory of sentence semantics.

Keywords: argument structure, aspect, concord construction, construction grammar, constructional meaning, implicit/explicit type-shifting, lexical projection, lexical semantics, sentence types, shift construction.

1. Introduction[1]

In this paper, I will offer a general framework for understanding the relationship between lexical and syntactic meaning. In merely stating this intention, however, I have presupposed something controversial – the existence of syntactic meaning. Words have long been assumed to be the sole contributors of the concepts expressed by sentences. Syntactic structures have correspondingly been seen only as providing instructions for the assembly of the concepts expressed by words. Accordingly, sentences have meaning, but the syntactic structures which sentences instantiate do not.

Strong challenges to this view, which is assumed either implicitly or explicitly by the majority of formal theorists, have been offered by cognitive-functional linguists. Section 2 will describe the nature of this challenge, and the alternative model which underlies it. In this model, grammatical constructions are viewed as the basis of syntax (Fillmore, Kay & O'Connor 1988; Pullum & Zwicky 1991; Zwicky 1994; Goldberg 1995, 1997; Michaelis & Lambrecht 1996; Kay & Fillmore 1999; Michaelis & Ruppenhofer 2001; Fillmore et al., to appear). Grammatical constructions are not arcane things; they are patterns of word combination that speakers use for specific communicative purposes – questioning, exclaiming, asserting, etc. – and the very idea that syntacticians could debate the existence of something so indispensable to language description and pedagogy must strike many scholars of language as absurd. Grammatical constructions have played a central role in linguistic description since ancient times (Harris & Taylor 1997), and for most of that history they have been treated no differently from words – forms with specific meanings and functions. However, with the advent of generative grammar, constructions came to be seen as something of an embarrassment. It is easy to understand why: the idea that principles of word combination could be intrinsically meaningful simply cannot be accommodated

1. I would like to thank Adele Goldberg, Knud Lambrecht, Leonard Talmy, Ron Langacker, Charles Fillmore, and Renaat Declerck for their many and significant contributions to my understanding of this topic. They are not responsible for any gaps thereof.

within the logical structure of the projection-based view. If, for example, we were to change the associations within an arithmetic sequence like *2 x (3 + 4)* so as to create the sequence *(2 x 3) + 4*, we would clearly change what the sequence denotes – from 14 to 10 – but we would not thereby change what the numbers denote. Still, a coherent worldview is not necessarily an accurate one, and we will see that the lexicalist model of sentential meaning fails as an account of both usage and interpretation. In what follows, we will review findings which suggest that words do not designate in the way that numbers do and that word meaning is in fact malleable – the kind of event, property, or entity a word denotes shifts according to sentential context. It is precisely this malleability of open-class words which provides the strongest support for the construction-based view of grammar.

In construction-based grammars, constructions mean what they mean in the same way that words do: they denote types of things and relations. And like words, grammatical constructions feature idiosyncratic constraints on meaning and use. Given two sources of meaning in a sentence – "bottom up" words and "top down" constructions – we would predict that the potential for conflict exists, and this prediction is borne out. The idiosyncratic constraints which define constructions have been shown to interact in specific ways with the semantics of open-class words with which they combine. Section 3 will describe this interaction with respect to three different kinds of constructions: *argument-structure constructions* (Goldberg 1995, 1997), which specify linkings of thematic roles to grammatical functions, *aspectual constructions*, which encode the situation type denoted by the verb and verb phrase (Michaelis 1998, to appear), and *sentence types*, which pair a discourse function with a clausal structure (Zwicky 1994; Lambrecht 1994; Michaelis & Lambrecht 1996).

On the basis of these three short case studies, I will argue that appeal to constructional meaning greatly enhances the descriptive power of a theory of sentence semantics. First, it allows us to describe interpretation at all levels of linguistic combination – from word morphology to phrase formation. Second, it makes possible an account of sentence meaning in which one general interpretive mechanism underlies both *elaboration* (in which lexical meaning and constructional meaning match) and *conversion*, in which semantic features intrinsic to a content expression conflict with semantic features intrinsic to the construction containing that expression. In the course of this exposition, I will demonstrate that the scope of the conversion phenomenon in grammar is very wide.

2. The challenge to lexical projection

Theories of sentence meaning are designed to describe the relationship between the meaning of a sentence and the meanings of the words of that sentence, both lexical and grammatical. Those who study this relationship have long focused on the connection between the semantic requirements of the content verb (i.e., its argument structure) and the event or state denoted by sentences in which that verb serves as a syntactic head. Theories of this connection, whether they are framed as models of phrase structure (Ritter & Rosen 1998), the syntax-semantics interface (Jackendoff 1990), or the mapping between syntactic and functional structure (Bresnan 1994, 2001), have been based upon some version of what has come to be called the *projection principle*. The projection principle holds that the basic scene denoted by a sentence (the set of participant roles expressed) derives from the argument structure of the head verb. Thus, for example, it appears clear that sentence (1)

(1) *We gave the account to her.*

denotes a scene of transfer involving an agent, a theme, and a goal because the semantic frame associated with the head verb *give* denotes a scene of transfer, and likewise requires the presence of these three participants. The projection principle is intrinsic to a compositional theory of semantics – a theory which has been deemed central to any account of syntax-semantics isomorphism, including cognitively oriented theories like that of Jackendoff, who states (1990: 9), "It is widely assumed, and I will take for granted, that the basic units out of which a sentential concept is constructed are the concepts expressed by the words in the sentence, that is, lexical concepts." A more recent version of this principle is stated by Jackendoff as the principle of syntactically transparent composition: "All elements of content in the meaning of a sentence are found in the lexical conceptual structures of the lexical items composing the sentence" (1997: 48).[2]

The projection principle has often been associated with a theory of syntax based on the autonomy of syntactic description. For example, in Government and Binding theory, the level at which thematic roles are represented (d-structure) represents those roles as grammatical functions, i.e., positions in syntactic structure. This syntacticization of semantic roles created the rationale for movement rules, by which, e.g., the passive linking is represented as the "movement" of an element from object to subject position. As Jackendoff (1997) has recently observed, the current consensus embraces *unification* rather than movement as the primary syntactic operation. However, whether or not the projection principle is regarded as a constraint on mapping between syntactic levels (e.g., d-structure and s-structure), it is cru-

2. This more recent compositional principle is framed within a model which allows for an enriched conception of composition. In the enriched conception, the principle of syntactically transparent composition is treated as a default. The extended conception of composition allows for cases in which material that is not expressed by lexical items of the sentence may nevertheless be part of the conceptual content of the sentence. These are cases of coercion, in which extra meaning is "added" in order to achieve well-formedness in conceptual structure and/or to "satisfy the pragmatics of the discourse or extralinguistic context" (1999: 49). For example, the "iteration" feature is added to a sentence like *I blinked for two minutes* because a single blink cannot plausibly be viewed as lasting two minutes. The problem with Jackendoff's analysis, as I see it, is that coercion does not seem to have anything to do with the meaning of the syntactic pattern employed; Jackendoff does not posit a locus of association between semantic properties and syntactic form, i.e., a construction. For this reason, it would seem that coercion phenomena described by Goldberg (1995) and discussed in this paper with respect to examples like (5)–(8) could not be easily handled by Jackendoff's coercion principle – the verb meaning is not modulated by particular co-occurring words or phrases, but by the particular linking configuration with which the verb integrates.

cial to a "rule-free" conception of universal grammar in which there are no category-specific phrase-structure rules. Under this conception, sentence structure is a result of the projection of the valence requirements of lexical heads *modulo* the constraints of X'-syntax.

Even among those syntacticians who, like Bresnan (1994, 2001), have laid out strong objections to accounts of typological variation based on constituent structure, the projection principle has remained central to the description of argument structure, since Lexical-Functional Grammar is also driven by the assumption that "argument roles are lexically underspecified for the possible surface syntactic functions they can assume" (Bresnan 1994: 91). Universal linking rules map these argument roles to grammatical and pragmatic functions, and these rules do not add to, subtract from, or alter the array of thematic roles associated with the verb. For example, in Bresnan (1994), locative inversion in English and Chichewa is represented as one linking possibility for verbs like *stand*, which subcategorize for locative and theme arguments. Such verbs are subject both to the linking rule which produces the configuration in (2) and to the linking rule which produces the configuration in (3):

(2) *Two women stood in the plaza.*
(3) *In the plaza stood two women.*

The syntactic structures of (2) and (3) are equivalent to subcategorization frames associated with the verb *stand*. However, assumption of lexical projection here makes it difficult for Bresnan to account for examples of locative inversion like the attested example in (4), which involves an interpretive phenomenon which we will refer to (following Talmy 1988) as *implicit conversion*:

(4) *Down at the harbor there is a teal-green clubhouse for socializing and parties. Beside it* ***sparkles*** *the community pool.* (*Vanity Fair*, August 2001)

Examples like (4) are problematic in Bresnan's framework because the verb *sparkle* does not assign either a locative role or a theme role

– it is a monovalent verb of light emission – and yet it can appear in the locative-inversion configuration. In examples like (4), Bresnan argues (1994: 91), a locative-theme argument structure imposed by the pragmatic requirement of presentational focus is "overlaid" on the argument structure of the base verb. The problem with this type of account is simply that it is not explicit. If argument structures are products of the linkings licensed by given verbs, and not independent form-meaning pairings, it is difficult to determine the source of the "overlay".

Adherence to the projection principle results not only in *ad hoc* devices like an "overlay theme" in cases like (4), but also, as Goldberg points out (1995, 1997), appeal to implausible verb senses. Goldberg discusses examples like the following:

(5) *Most likely they were fellow visitors, just* ***panting*** *up to the sky-high altar out of curiosity.* (Lindsey Davis, *Last Act in Palmyra*, p. 28)
(6) *As they had* ***waved*** *us along the raised causeway and into the rocky cleft...* (op. cit., p. 31)
(7) *If time is money, then* ***save*** *yourself rich at Snyder's!* (= Goldberg 1997, (3a))
(8) *They can't just* ***analyze*** *away our data.*

Goldberg points out that on the assumption that argument structure is determined exclusively by head verbs, we would need to assume the existence of a special verb sense for each of the usages exemplified in (5)–(8). Sentence (5) would require a special sense of *pant* equivalent to the formulation 'move while panting'; (6) would require a special sense of the verb *wave* whose definition would be 'signal permission to move to a place by waving'; (7) would require a sense of the verb *save* which might be captured by the formulation 'cause to be in a state by saving'; and, finally, sentence (8) would require one to view *analyze* as a verb which denotes (metaphorical) caused motion. Such word senses, as Goldberg points out, are not only *ad hoc* and unintuitive, but also compatible only with an assumption of radical and unconstrained polysemy.

Crucially, as Goldberg and Fauconnier and Turner (1996) have demonstrated, examples like (5)–(8) cannot easily be viewed as marginal or special cases. Sentence (5), for example, exemplifies a lexicalization pattern – conflation of manner and motion – which Talmy (1985) and Slobin (1997) have shown to be strongly entrenched in Germanic languages. Further, the examples in (5)–(8) cannot be regarded merely as violations of selectional restrictions associated with the verbal heads – or even as violations which might trigger manner-based implicata. If, for example, sentence (8) merely exemplified a violation of the selectional restrictions associated with the verb *analyze*, we would fail to predict its well-formedness – let alone the uniformity of its interpretation across speakers; sentence (8) is necessarily interpreted as denoting metaphorical caused motion.

In addition, as Michaelis and Ruppenhofer (2001) argue, linking accounts based exclusively on lexical projection cannot easily account for idiosyncratic semantic constraints associated with particular linking patterns. Such constraints go beyond those which require the input verb to license a certain theta frame. They include constraints on animacy or configuration of certain arguments. Michaelis and Ruppenhofer exemplify such constraints with respect to German *be*-prefixation, an applicative construction whose core semantics involves the thorough coverage of a location by a theme. They observe with regard to an alternation regarding the verb *wohnen* 'live' that one can express the assertion "Peter lives in an apartment" either through the use of the *be-* linking pattern *(Peter bewohnt ein Apartment in München)*, in which the location is linked to the direct object function, or through the use of the oblique-location pattern (*Peter wohnt in einem Apartment in München*). They notice, however, that if the denoted location is a large expanse of space relative to the denotatum of the theme argument, the *be*-pattern declines in felicity: the sentence *Peter bewohnt Schwabing* 'Peter occupies Schwabing' is odd. The oblique-location alternative is, by contrast, acceptable: *Peter wohnt in Schwabing*. In sum, they argue, if the location is large enough that thorough coverage by the theme argument is not possible, the *be-* linking pattern is not permissible. Such constraints are expected if linking patterns denote schematic scenes with specific properties (like thorough coverage); they are unexpected if linking patterns are transparent to verb meaning, and merely represent possibilities for the realization of a verb's arguments.

Cases like the German applicative alternation and the English examples in (4)–(8) give strong evidence that the projection principle, despite providing a parsimonious account of default cases like (1), is invalid. The alternative, construction-based model of argument structure outlined by Goldberg is founded on a body of work, of which Talmy (1988) is representative, which focuses on universal differences in the inventory of concepts expressed by open-class versus closed-class elements, and in particular on the nature of the semantic interaction between grammatical and lexical elements. Crucially, grammatical constructions are viewed as belonging to the general set of meaning-bearing grammatical elements, which includes prepositions and derivational markers, among others. An essential tenet of these works is expressed in (9) as the *override principle*:

(9) *Override principle.* If lexical and structural meanings conflict, the semantic specifications of the lexical element conform to those of the grammatical structure with which that lexical item is combined.

The operation of (9) can be illustrated with regard to nominal syntax in examples (10)–(12):

(10) *Give me* ***some pillow****!*
(11) *They have good* ***soups*** *there.*
(12) *Did you get* ***a pudding****?*

These examples are closely analogous to those in (5)–(8), in that the syntactic requirements of the lexical heads in (10)–(12) similarly fail to determine the syntax of the phrasal projection of the category. As in the case of verbal argument-structures, we find that it would be implausible to propose special senses for each of the nouns involved in cases like (10)–(12). We also find that we would fail to capture an important generalization about nominal syntax and semantics if we were to propose a special nominal construction for, e.g., (11), which would license the combination of a mass noun and plural suffix. Instead, in accordance with Talmy and others, we can presume that examples like (10)–(12) are licensed by the same constructions which license ordinary nominal constructs like *some water*, *cats*, and *a watch*. The accounts hinge on the presumption that nominal constructions have meaning independent of their nominal heads – they denote types of entities.

Thus, the nominal construction which licenses the combination of *some* and a nominal sister denotes a mass entity. It requires a nominal head which is also a mass. Although the noun *pillow* canonically denotes a count entity, it receives a mass construal in the context of (10) via (9). The nominal construction which licenses the combination of a noun and plural suffix *-s* requires that its nominal head denote a count entity. While soup, as a liquid, is prototypically viewed as a mass, the noun *soup*, when combined with the plural construction, as in (11), receives the individuated construal associated with count entities, and is thereby seen, via (9), as denoting a portion or type. Finally, (12) exemplifies an override involving that determination construction whose left daughter is the indefinite article. This construction requires a noun denoting a count entity as its right daughter. Via (9), the noun *pudding* receives the individuated construal associated with the class of count nouns.

In discussing the conceptual underpinnings of nominal syntax, Talmy (1988) introduces a distinction which has proven crucial to our understanding of linguistic overrides and how they are accomplished. Talmy classifies overrides into cases of implicit and explicit conversion. Cases of implicit conversion involve grammatical markers whose function is to signal a semantic feature intrinsic to the lexical item which serves as head. The marker and the head lexical element have the same specification for a given semantic feature. Let us call these constructions *concord constructions*. A nominal construction of this type is that which licenses indefinite NPs like *a jar*. This construction flags the uniplex feature of its head noun, in this case *jar*. As shown in (12), the uniplex feature associated with the indefinite article *a* can also be combined with a mass specification: *a* appears as the right sister of the mass noun *pudding*. As discussed, this situation creates conflict, which, via (9), is resolved in favor of the meaning of the closed-class element.

Cases of explicit conversion involve grammatical constructions in which the external semantics of the construction carries a value for a given feature (say, boundedness) that is distinct from the value associated with a lexical filler. Let us call these constructions *shift constructions*. Shift constructions do not signal concord between lexical and grammatical specifications, as do concord constructions like the indefinite article. The purpose of shift constructions is to alter the conventional designation of the lexical filler. Semantic shift is entailed by the semiotic function of the construction. The partitive construction in English (*a unit of x*) is an example of a shift construction. It is designed to shift the unbounded value of the (necessarily undetermined) lexical complement (say *pie*, as in *a piece of pie*) to the bounded value associated with the head (*piece*). An essential property of shift constructions is that they involve a distinction between internal and external semantics: the external semantics of the construction is the "output value", and the internal semantics is the "input value". The distinction between internal and external semantics can be manifested linguistically: shift constructions are often periphrastic, with the head of the construction representing the output value and the complement representing the input value. In the case of the partitive construction, for example, the head bears the count feature of the whole, while the complement (the *niece* of the head) denotes the mass feature called for as the internal semantics.

Because they have distinct internal and external semantics, shift constructions, which, as we have seen, conventionally signal explicit conversion, also perform implicit conversion. This is so because each shift construction specifies something about the nature of the "input" lexical item – the content word that occupies the conceptual slot which Langacker (1987, 1991) refers to as the *elaboration site* of a construction. For example, as we saw above, the English partitive construction requires that the nominal complement of the PP headed by *of* denote a mass entity. What happens when a count entity instead occupies the position reserved for a nominal complement denoting a mass? Implicit conversion results, as in (13):

(13) *Give me a shred of sheet.*

In (13), the noun *sheet*, which conventionally denotes a bounded entity, receives a mass construal. This is so because this mass construal is associated with the PP-complement slot of the partitive construction. Thus, shift constructions perform explicit conversion because the head of the construction (which in the case of the partitive construction denotes a *portion*) has semantic features distinct from those of the lexical complement; shift constructions perform implicit conversion because, just like concord constructions, they constrain the properties of the open-class words with which they combine.

Implicit and explicit conversion are concepts which both appeal to constructional semantics. Both concord and shift constructions designate something, e.g., an entity. Shift constructions have the functions they do because the entity designated by the construction is distinct from the entity designated by the item which occupies the elaboration site of the construction. It may be suggested that the existence of shift constructions does not provide a challenge to the projection principle, since the argument structure of a partitive construct[3] like *a piece of pie* can be attributed to the argument-structure requirements of the head noun denoting the portion (*pie*). A strong objection to this argument can be made by pointing to cases of implicit conversion involving the head-noun role of the partitive construction. Partitive constructs which exemplify this phenomenon are *a splash of coffee* and French *une larme de vin* (lit. 'a tear of wine'). While the words *splash* and *larme* (unlike, e.g., the words *slice* and *piece*) do not intrinsically designate units or portions, they do so in the context of the partitive construction. Hence, the argument structure of the NP *a splash of coffee* cannot be attributed to the valence

3. A *construct* is a linguistic expression which is licensed by a construction or combination of constructions (Kay & Fillmore 1999; Fillmore et al., to appear).

requirements of the word *splash*, but must instead be attributed to the semantic requirements of the partitive construction.

While shift constructions and concord constructions overlap in allowing instances of implicit conversion, shift constructions differ from concord constructions in that explicit conversion does not involve principle (9): explicit conversion does not hinge on the resolution of conflict between lexical and constructional specifications. Unlike shift constructions, concord constructions, which do involve conflict resolution of the type described in (9), are problematic for implementations of construction-based grammar based on *unification grammar* (Kay & Fillmore 1999). The reason for this is that in a unification-based grammar, the combination of lexical items and constructions, which can be understood as the superimposition of one set of specifications upon another, requires *lack of conflict* between those overlapping specifications. Thus, for example, the English determination construction whose left daughter is the indefinite article *a* requires a count noun as its right daughter. If a mass noun like *pudding* were to be combined with this NP construction, the result would be conflict, and therefore a *failure of unification*.

However, given the existence of well-formed NP constructs like *a pudding*, Fillmore and Kay (1993) must find a way to license such constructs. Their solution to this problem within the unification framework is to propose several *type-shifting* constructions. Type-shifting constructions resemble shift constructions in that they perform conversions in a compositional fashion, but they are distinct from shift constructions in that they do not have constituent structure (i.e., branching structure). Each type-shifting construction has an *external semantic value* which is distinct from that of its sole daughter node. For example, the construction which shifts a mass noun to a count noun unifies with a mass noun, e.g., *pudding*. Its external semantics is that of a count noun, which can of course unify with the construction that licenses indefinite NPs.

The use of type-shifting constructions appears to be motivated entirely by a theory-internal consideration – the need to circumvent positive exceptions to unification. Type-shifting constructions are not only *ad hoc* mechanisms but ones which conflict with the goal of parsimony. If we do not assume a strict model of unification, we need not resort to extra mechanisms to explain away well-formed constructs which represent failures of unification. In accordance with Talmy, Langacker, and Goldberg, we will assume that lexical specifications and constructional specifications *can* conflict, and that this conflict is resolved as per principle (9).

3. Case studies in conflict resolution

3.1. Argument-structure constructions

As described in the previous section, the constructional analysis of argument structure offered by Goldberg (1995, 1997) is founded on the assumption that linking patterns are "directly correlated with one or more semantic structures" (1997: 83). Among the linking patterns considered by Goldberg are the *ditransitive* pattern (whose core semantics she captures with the formula 'X CAUSES Y TO RECEIVE Z'), the *caused-motion* pattern ('X CAUSES Y TO MOVE WITH RESPECT TO Z') and the *resultative* pattern ('X CAUSES Y TO BECOME Z'). Examples of each of these patterns are given in (14)–(16):

(14) *We gave her the account.*
(15) *She put the checkbook on the counter.*
(16) *We painted the walls white.*

Goldberg uses the term *sentence type* to refer to these linking patterns. In accordance with Fillmore et al. (to appear), however, we will regard linking patterns not as sentence structures but as verb-level constructions, which unify with the lexical entries of verbs. The rationale for this terminological decision is twofold. First, we prefer to reserve the term *sentence type* for structural patterns like declarative, imperative, interrogative, with which speech-act functions are associated (see section 3.3). Second, if we were to view patterns like the ditransitive linking pattern as sentence types, we would lose a generalization regarding passive instances of those patterns, as in the sentence *She was given the account by us*. Since this sentence has the same semantics as its active counterpart *We gave her the account* (viz., 'X CAUSES Y TO RECEIVE Z'), we would not wish to regard ditransitive semantics as uniquely associated with the active-form pattern. Instead, as per the practice of Fillmore et al. (to appear), we will assume the existence of a "nominal oblique theme" linking construction, which will add to the minimal valence of an appropriate verb the specification that the theme argument is linked to an oblique role that is necessarily encoded by an NP (rather than a PP). Via instantiation constructions (see Fillmore et al., to appear: chap. 5), this role will be realized in postverbal position in the case of the passive sentence and in the position following the direct object in the case of the active sentence. This unification has the effect of augmenting what Fillmore et al. (to appear) refer to as the *minimal valence* of the verb (the repertoire of semantic roles inherent to the meaning of the verb). The *fully specified* verbal valence which results from unification of a verb's lexical entry with a linking construction is one in which each semantic role is assigned a *grammatical function*.

Crucial to Goldberg's account is the idea that the repertoire of thematic roles assigned by the linking construction may *properly include* the repertoire of thematic roles in the verb's minimal valence. Examples of this phenomenon are given for each of the linking patterns exemplified in (14)–(16) in (17)–(19):

(17) *We painted them a landscape.*
(18) *She blew the dust off the picture.*
(19) *We cried our throats ragged.*

The verb *paint*, a verb of creation, denotes a two-place relation, involving the creator and a created item. However, sentence (17), an instance of the ditransitive linking pattern, adds an additional participant to the making scenario – a potential recipient. This recipient is not intrinsic to the making scenario; it is instead intrinsic to the transfer scenario with which the ditransitive pattern is associated. Likewise, while the verb *blow* is a one-place relation, involving an agent, (18) adds two additional participants – a theme and a goal. These participants are intrinsic to the caused-motion construction which the sentence instantiates. Finally, in (19), the verb *cry* appears with two more participants than it ordinarily has – a patient and a resultant state. The additional participants are intrinsic to the resultant-state construction which licenses (19).[4]

The examples in (17)–(19) strongly resemble the examples in (5)–(8), which were used to undermine the validity of the projection principle. Both sets of examples involve implicit conversion. We can regard linking patterns like the ditransitive and caused-motion patterns as concord constructions. These patterns may, and indeed typically do, reflect the inherent semantics of the verbal head. Examples of concord, given in (14)–(16) are those which provide the motivation for the projection principle. Goldberg (1997) refers to these

---

4. Goldberg argues (1995: chap. 8) that the so-called fake objects found in the resultative and caused-motion constructions are in fact semantic arguments – of the construction. That the transitivity of the verbal head is irrelevant to the well-formedness of a resultative or caused-motion sentence becomes evident when one considers sentences like the following:
   (a) *I just can't seem to drink you off my mind.* (The Rolling Stones, "Honky Tonk Woman")
   Although the verb *drink* is transitive, the NP *you* is not of a semantic type which would generally allow it to serve as the object of *drink.* Instead, the sense of *drink* which is found in (a) is the same intransitive activity sense found in sentence (b):
   (b) *They drank all night.*
   Therefore *drink* in (a) denotes an activity which provides the means by which metaphorical motion occurs. The same point can be made for examples like that in (c), in which the object-denotatum is clearly not the theme argument of the verb *eat*:
   (c) *They ate themselves sick.*
   Instead, in (c), as in (a)–(b), the theme argument of the verb is null-instantiated and has a non-specific interpretation. The crucial role played by null instantiation emerges clearly when one compares sentences (d) and (e). The anomaly of (d) is a function of the anomaly of (e): as shown by (e), the verb *devour* does not permit null complementation; it accordingly lacks the intransitive activity sense necessary for its successful use with a reflexive object in the resultative construction, as shown in (d):
   (d) **They devoured themselves sick.*
   (e) **They devoured last night.*

kinds of examples as instances of *elaboration*, in which the verb codes a more specific instance of the action designated by the construction.

Examples of implicit conversion, given in (5)–(8) and (17)–(19), show, as Goldberg points out, that while the head verb typically does elaborate the meaning of the construction, there are other relations which the verb may bear to the construction. A prominent relation, both across constructions and languages, is *means*: the verb may code the means by which the action designated by the construction occurs. Examples of the means relation are given in (18)–(19), in which, respectively, blowing is the means by which the dust is moved from one location to another and crying is the means by which the hoarseness is effected.

Because the means by which an action is accomplished is intrinsic to the causal event denoted by the linking constructions we have looked at, the means relation and the elaboration relations may often be difficult to distinguish. This is evident when we look at the verbs which combine with the German *be*-construction (Michaelis & Ruppenhofer 2001). An example of a *be*-construct is given in (20):

(20) *Auch die Höhen um Fulda* ***bebauten*** *die Mönche des frühen Klosters mit Kapellen, Kirchen und Propsteien*. (Rudolf Pörtner, *Die Erben Roms*)
'The monks of the early period of the monastery also *be-built* the hills around Fulda with chapels, churches, and provosts' residences.'

It would be difficult to determine for (20) whether the verb denotes the means by which coverage is effected or an elaboration of the constructional meaning 'Theme covers location thoroughly', since erecting structures on a piece of land is a type of covering. Because both a means and an elaboration analysis would entail that the verb denotes an aspect of the causal sequence denoted by the construction, they are equivalent. In fact, it appears that the means and manner and elaboration relations are equally prototypical of verb-construction integration, despite the fact that the latter is compositional while the former is not. The prototypicality of the means relation is underscored by the fact that, as Goldberg (1997) observes, the interpretation of denominal verbs is frequently instrumental, as in (21) and (22):

(21) *She nailed the poster up.*

(22) Message-Id: <4lq28k$lsr@nz12.rz.uni-karlsruhe.de>
*Also *m.E.* regelt 41, wie ein Radweg zu* ***beschildern*** *ist und wer darauf was zu suchen hat und wer nicht...*
'Well, *in my opinion* [paragraph] 41 regulates how a bike path needs to be *be-trafficsigned* and who has any business on it and who doesn't.'

The examples in (21)–(22) again illustrate implicit conversion. In these cases, the construction does not merely augment the argument structure of the word which appears in the head-verb slot, but in fact creates an argument structure for that word. The creation of valence is strongly correlated with invocation of the means relation: the nail is understood to denote the means of causing motion, just as the traffic sign is understood to be the means by which coverage is effected. To account for the conceptual shift from noun to verb in contexts like (21)–(22), Goldberg (1997) proposes that denominal verbs like *hammer* metonymically stand for actions involving the source nouns. Notice, however, that it would be a mistake to claim, as Clark and Clark (1979) do, that denominal verbs *denote* a participant in the scene designated by the construction. According to this line of reasoning, for example, the denominal verb *beschildern* denotes the theme argument in the coverage scenario denoted by the construction. The theme argument, if present, would be denoted by a nominal expression, as we would expect, and the only reason that it is missing in (21)–(22) is that its type is recoverable from the syntactic context. If it were not, it would be expressed, as in the example *She nailed the poster up with antique brass nails*. Hence, there is a difference between identification of the theme argument, which is something that the verb can do, and expression of the theme argument, which is something that a verb cannot do.

The relationships that nouns and verbs may bear to constructional meanings are not as limited as the foregoing discussion has implied. Goldberg points out that verbs can designate *preconditions* for actions denoted by constructions. An example is found in (17): the act of creation denoted by *paint* represents a precondition to transfer. It is also evident that some of Goldberg's denominal examples can be viewed in terms of the precondition relation. A nominal example of this kind is found in (23) (= Goldberg 1997, (23a)):

(23) *They planned to vacation in Spain.*

In (23), the noun *vacation* metonymically denotes a precondition (having a vacation) for one's being located in Spain. As Goldberg argues, the concept of a precondition is intrinsic to the causal scenario – every causal sequence involves preconditions. Therefore, examples involving preconditions give support to Goldberg's contention, expressed in her (1997) paper, that verbs tend to denote aspects of the causal sequence denoted by a construction.

The various relationships (precondition, means, etc.) that constructions bear to verbs and nouns can be seen as distinct senses of the construction, with elaboration representing the core sense of each construction. Thus, 'Agent successfully causes Recipient to receive Patient' can be seen as the central sense of the ditransitive construction,[5] while the precondition reading exemplified in (17), which Goldberg (1995: chap. 2) represents by the formula 'Agent intends to cause Recipient to Receive Patient', can be seen as another sense of that construction. However, Goldberg (1995) maintains a distinction between (i) the set of relationships that verbs can bear to a given constructional meaning and (ii) the set of meanings that can be associated with that construction. She maintains this distinction because, for example, successful transfer is an entailment of both the means reading and the elaboration reading of ditransitive sentences. That is, the difference between a means reading (as in *She handed him the*

5. Goldberg demonstrates the basic-level status of the 'successful receipt' sense by reference to interpretation of nonce forms, among other diagnostics.

report) and an elaboration reading (as in *She gave him the report*) does not accord with a difference in constructional meaning. (By contrast, the precondition reading in (17), which does not entail transfer, does represent a distinct meaning of the ditransitive pattern.) Therefore, different constructional meanings may each license several verb-construction relationships. An additional example of this principle comes from Goldberg's analysis of the caused-motion construction. This construction, as Goldberg observes (1995: chap. 7), has an *enablement* sense, in which the agent does not cause but merely *permits* directed motion by the theme. This sense can license both an elaboration reading (*She allowed him onto the stage*) and a means reading (*She invited him backstage*).

Thus, the interpretive latitude which characterizes linking patterns in context stems from two sources: the set of verb-construction relationships and constructional polysemy. The claim that linking constructions may be polysemous accords with the general idea, advanced here, that syntactic structures represent Saussurean signs – form-meaning pairs – and therefore have meanings assigned by linguistic convention rather than computed via composition. Thus, the fact that constructions, like words, exhibit polysemy makes sense. As shown by Michaelis (1994) with respect to the Latin correlative conditional, constructions, like words, are subject to systematic semantic extension over time, and like words, may denote an array of concepts whose interrelationships seem opaque from the perspective of synchrony.

The linking constructions which we have looked at in this section represent concord constructions. Like the set of nominal constructions, the set of linking constructions also includes shift constructions. Those linking constructions which are shift constructions do not license an elaboration relationship; verb meaning and construction meaning never match. Instead, the verb frame must invariably accommodate to the construction's frame. One example of an override construction is the *Way*-construction, analyzed in detail by Jackendoff (1990), Goldberg (1995), and Israel (1996). This construction is exemplified in (24)–(25):

(24) *She chatted her way down the receiving line.*
(25) *He slashed his way through the brush.*

The meaning of the *Way*-construction, as described by the aforementioned authors, involves the notion of an agent creating a path by means of some activity – in the case of (24)–(25), chatting and slashing, respectively.[6] The verbal head, an intransitive, denotes an activity which does not involve directed motion (that is, neither chatting nor slashing intrinsically involves directed motion). The scene denoted by the construction as a whole denotes an act of motion along a path. As a shift construction, the *Way*-construction necessarily performs conversion. This is shown by the fact that verbs which *do* denote directed motion inherently are not welcomed by the construction, as shown in (26)–(27):

(26) ??*He walked his way into the meeting.*
(27) ??*She ran her way along the shore.*

As an override construction, the *Way*-construction also allows for implicit conversion. Since the verb which enters into the construction is necessarily construed as an activity (i.e., a process), verbs which do not otherwise have processual readings receive such readings in the context of the construction. Examples of implicit conversion involving the *Way*-construction are given in (28)–(29):

6. As Goldberg points out, the *Way*-construction is polysemous. In addition to a 'means' interpretation, the construction also has a 'manner' interpretation, exemplified in (a):
(a) *...anyone who has ever had the occasion to observe the average American family as they snack their way toward the departure gate...* (Fran Lebowitz, *Vanity Fair*, October 1997)
The interpretation of (a) is one in which eating activity attends movement along a path. Since the *Way*-construction is polysemous, instances of it may be ambiguous:
(b) *He shmoozed his way through the meeting.*
Sentence (b) is ambiguous as to whether shmoozing is the means or the manner of his getting through the meeting.

(28) *She blinked her way into the light.*
(29) *He dove his way into the hearts of millions of viewers* (??*with a single dive*).

While the verbs *blink* and *dive* have momentaneous (semelfactive or achievement) readings under ordinary circumstances, they are interpreted as iterated, and therefore processual events in the context of the *Way*-construction: the subject-denotatum in (28) is necessarily construed as having blinked numerous times; the subject-denotatum in (29) is necessarily understood as having performed a series of dives.

Thus, it can be shown that argument-structure constructions, like nominal constructions, are used to perform explicit and implicit conversion operations. And as is the case of nominal syntax, implicit conversion is achieved both through concord constructions and override constructions.

3.2. Aspectual constructions

The effects of grammatical context on the interpretation of verb semantics has long been of interest to investigators of aspectual meaning. Aspectologists have in fact often argued that aspectual categorization does not concern verbs by themselves, but instead verb-plus-argument combinations (Dowty 1979; Foley & Van Valin 1984; Van Valin & LaPolla 1997). In particular, it has been claimed, e.g. by Dowty (1986), that the Aktionsart classes originated by Vendler (1967) (activity, accomplishment, etc.) are classes of *situations* rather than of verbs. Dowty (1986), among others, assumes a distinction between the *lexical aspect* of the verb and the situation type denoted by the sentence as a whole, as well as a mechanism by which, e.g., the boundedness of an argument may impose a bounded construal on the verb. An alternative to a model based on feature passing is one based on conceptual gestalts. In accordance with Langacker (1991) and Smith (1986, 1991), Michaelis (1998) adopts the view that distinctions like telic-atelic, bounded-unbounded, and dynamic-static arise from scene construal, and are not lexical features. Thus, while (30)–(32) denote events without intrinsic stopping points (i.e., activities), (33)–(34) denote scenes which have inherent points of culmination (accomplishments and achievements):

(30) *He scrubbed dishes.*
(31) *She walked.*
(32) *Tourists entered the temple.*
(33) *He scrubbed the dishes.*
(34) *She walked home.*
(35) *A tourist entered the temple.*

While the examples in (30)–(35) concern the telicity distinction, the examples in (36) show that argument structure also influences a more fundamental distinction made in scene construal: the *event-state* (or, equivalently, *dynamic-static*) *distinction*:

(36) a. *She reminded me of my mother.*
b. *She reminded me of my dentist's appointment.*

Sentence (36a) denotes a state – a situation which does not involve change over time and which has no intrinsic endpoint. Sentence (36b) denotes an event – a situation which does involve change over time and which does have an inherent stopping point (in the case of (36b), a resultant state in which the speaker recalls the appointment). Stative situations can be said to obtain at a single moment alone, while events can only be said to be instantiated over a period of time (however small that period might be). In English, as observed by Langacker, Smith, and others, the (simple) present tense is understood, as a matter of linguistic convention, to denote full instantiation now.[7]

7. There is evidence to suggest that the prohibition on present-tense reporting of events does not, as claimed here, arise from the momentaneous conceptualization of the present tense per se, but instead more generally from a momentaneous conceptualization of the time of encoding, be it past or present. The evidence for this broader semantic analysis comes from the interpretation of

Therefore, only states can be reported by means of the simple present tense, as shown by the contrast between (37a) and (37b), where (37b) is assigned a star only on the 'ongoing right now' reading (and not, e.g., on a habitual reading):

(37) a. *She reminds me of my mother.*
b. **She reminds me of my dentist's appointment.*

The contrast in (37) can be explained by reference to the *subinterval* or *distributivity* property of states (Herweg 1991a, 1991b): any temporal subpart of a state is equivalent to the whole. An event is only instantiated over the course of time. Therefore, to report an event is to report its completion; events require past-tense reporting.[8] Further, when events are reported in the past, they are viewed as wholly contained within the relevant past interval, while states reported in the

---

clausal complements of *verba sentiendi ac declarandi*, in which those clausal complements exhibit secondary sequence of tense:
(a) *I said that she reminded me of my mother.*
(b) *I said that she reminded me of my dentist's appointment.*
In (a), the stative clause *She reminded me of my mother* can receive either a past-in-past or a present-in-past interpretation. That is, either the speaker is purported to have said "She reminds me of my mother" or "She reminded me of my mother". As Declerck (1995) observes, the eventive clause *She reminded me of my dentist's appointment* can receive only a past-in-past interpretation. That is, one cannot reconstruct the speaker's past speech act as either "She reminds me of my dentist's appointment" or "She is reminding me of my dentist's appointment", but only as "She reminded me of my dentist's appointment". This restriction on the interpretation of (b) parallels that restriction which is manifested as a well-formedness constraint in (37b). The parallel suggests that the time of encoding, whether past or present, has a punctual interpretation in English, and therefore cannot accommodate the temporal profile of an event.

8. In this discussion, I am focusing on default reporting contexts, and not such special-case reporting contexts as the so-called play-by-play context, the performative context, or historical-present narrative; see Langacker (1991) and Michaelis (1998), e.g., for discussion of these special-case reporting contexts. (I thank an anonymous referee for pointing out the need to circumscribe the class of cases I have in mind here.)

past are viewed as *including* that past point: since states are internally homogenous, a momentaneous "sample" is sufficient to verify the presence of a state.

Given the fundamental analogy between space and time (Talmy 1988), aspectologists have been inclined to exploit the parallels between entities, which occupy space, and situations, which obtain or occur over time. The postulation of parallels between mass entities and states, on the one hand, and count entities and events, on the other, has been fundamental to explanation in aspectology (Mourelatos 1978; Langacker 1991; Michaelis 1998). And since nominal syntax reflects the distinction between implicit and explicit conversion, it should come as no surprise that aspectual syntax does as well. In this section, we will briefly look at concord and shift constructions whose meanings hinge on the event-state distinction. Concord constructions are discussed in section 3.2.1, and shift constructions in section 3.2.2.

3.2.1. Aspectual concord constructions

In this section, we will look at two classes of aspectual concord constructions: adverbial constructions and tense constructions. The adverbial constructions which we will consider are VP-level constructions which pair a V' with an aspectually sensitive adjunct. We will examine two such constructions: the frame-adverb construction and the frequency-adverb construction. The tense constructions that we will consider are verb-level constructions which pair a verb with a suffix that expresses past tense. We will look at two such constructions: that past tense which selects for a state verb, the so-called *imperfective past*, and that past tense which selects for an event verb, the so-called *perfective past*. Examples of concord involving the two aspectually sensitive adjuncts at issue are given in (38)–(39):

(38) a. *She recognized him in a minute.*
b. *We fixed it in an hour.*

(39) *They went to France twice.*

As shown in (38), the frame adverbial can be paired with an achievement predicate like *recognize him*, in which case it has a reading in which the event occurred *after* the denoted period of time elapsed. This durative phrase can also be paired with an accomplishment predicate like *fix it*, in which case it has a reading in which the event denoted occupied the period, culminating at the end of it. Via the logic of containment, (38b) entails that the fixing event can fit within any interval larger than an hour, and (via quantity implicature) implies that this event cannot fit into an interval smaller than an hour.

Stative predications are not compatible with *in*-phrases of duration. The reason for this is that states, unlike events, have the subinterval property: any interval at which a state goes on might also be a subinterval of a larger interval at which that state goes on (see Herweg 1991a, 1991b). As Michaelis argues (1998: chap. 1), a sentence like *He was in London yesterday* can always be interpreted in such a way that the state of being in London is not circumscribed by (and in fact contains) the temporal boundaries denoted by *yesterday*. Since the *in*-phrase of duration (by the logic of containment) entails that the situation denoted is wholly circumscribed by the expressed interval, state predications are incompatible with *in*-phrases of duration.

The frequency adjunct exemplified in (39) can be viewed, in accordance with Herweg (1991a), as specifying the number of applications of the event-type predicate *We go- to France*. As Herweg argues, only events are countable. States are not countable because the application of a state-type predicate is infinite, owing to the subinterval property: every subinterval of the overall period for which a state obtains is also a period at which that state obtains. An event-type predicate applies only once to the interval of which it is predicated, and therefore counting events amounts to counting the intervals which are arguments of a given event-type predicate. The application of the spatial analogy is straightforward: individuated entities, like events, are countable because the application of a categorizing predicate (e.g., *Jar'*(x)) is not infinite; masses, like states, are not countable because the application of a categorizing predicate, e.g., *Pudding'* (x), is potentially infinite.

Both frame and frequency adjuncts represent concord constructions: in each construction, the head daughter (a V') and its sister (the adjunct) share a semantic feature: the *event*, or equivalently, *perfective*, feature. That is, any verb or verb projection which denotes an event can unify with the construction, and the adjunct has a valence member which calls for an event (see Michaelis 1998: chap. 5 for formal details of this unification). This general pattern of mutual invocation is of course identical to that found among nominal concord constructions like indefinite determination: the open-class daughter denotes a bounded type, be it a situation or an entity, and its sister is a grammatical expression which calls for that same type.

The examples in (40) illustrate implicit conversion involving the two adjunct constructions:

(40) a. *She was outside in three minutes.*
b. *We were in France twice.*

In (40a), we see that a stative situation, which can be represented by the tenseless proposition *She be- outside*, is construed as an event when combined with the frame adverbial *in three minutes*. Via (9), the event feature associated with the head of the construction overrides the stative feature of the input V'. This means that the predicate *She be- outside* receives an achievement interpretation, in which the event of her beginning to be outside occurs within the three-minute time span. This type shift is minimal in the sense that it merely adds an onset transition to the input state representation. The override which occurs in (40b) is similar, although in this case the enriched construal resulting from the override imposes both an offset and an onset transition on the state. That is, the event denoted by (40b) is not merely the onset of a state but instead a full state phase, with beginning and endpoints entailed. This episodic or 'closed' interpretation is required by the frequency-adverb construction: because a single state cannot begin more than once, enumeration entails that for every onset counted there must be an offset as well. Of course, the foregoing observation leads us to ask why the enriched representation associated with (40a) does not contain an offset transition as well. Certainly, the presence of an offset transition would not conflict with the semantics of the frame-adverbial construction. The answer appears to be simply that the offset transition is not entailed by the semantics of the frame-adverbial construction, and that override interpretations tend to be economical: they add no more structure than what is required to resolve conflict between lexical and constructional semantics (see Michaelis, to appear for a detailed exposition of this constraint on operations which add aspectual structure).

Herweg (1991a) sees the meanings of sentences like (40a–b) as *non-compositional*: they cannot be assigned a meaning under the ordinary combinatory constraints of the two adjuncts, since the theta frame for each adjunct presumably requires an event argument. In the constructional model, in which the pairing of predication and adjunct is licensed by a construction, we need not presume that the interpretation of these sentences is idiomatic. As discussed, the interpretation of these sentences is in fact compositional, via (9) (see Goldberg 1995: chap. 1 for arguments concerning the compositional nature of the constructional account of argument structure).

Like the adjunct constructions discussed, morphological constructions which license perfective and imperfective past-tense inflections in languages like French are concord constructions whose meanings are exploited for the purpose of implicit conversion. Examples of concord involving the two constructions are given in (41)–(42):

(41) *Elle préférait le vin blanc.*
'She preferred white wine.'
(42) *Elle est venue à deux heures.*
'She arrived at two.'

Sentence (41), whose verbal head is marked as imperfective, illustrates the concord usage of the construction which licenses the imperfective past tense. The predicate *préférer le vin blanc* canonically denotes a stative situation. The imperfective ending exhibits concord with this state feature; that is, this ending selects for a verb denoting the stative type. The verb *venir* in (42) canonically denotes an event.

Accordingly, the perfective past-tense inflection exhibits concord with this event feature.

Sentences (43)–(44) exemplify implicit conversions involving the two morphological constructions in French; the relevant verbs are in boldface.

(43) Raymonde: *Qu'est-ce qu'ils voulaient, les deux messieurs?*
Robert: *On s'**échangeait** nos adresses!*
'Raymonde: What did they want, those two men?
Robert: We *were exchanging* addresses.'
(Binet, *Les Bidochon* 2, p. 50)

(44) *Henri s'est **retourné**. Margot **a eu** l'air heureuse.*
'Henri *turned* around. Margot cheered up (lit. '*started to* look happy').'

The verb in (43), *échanger*, is one whose situation aspect is perfective, and yet this perfective verb is paired with a past-tense suffix which calls for a state verb. Via (9), this pairing results in an override whereby an otherwise perfective verb receives a stative interpretation: the address-exchanging situation is understood to include the past reference time evoked by Raymonde's question, rather than being included within it. In terms of Michaelis (to appear), this stative construal is a chained transition. First, the activity component of the causal chain denoted by the predicate *échanger nos adresses* is selected. This activity component is the series of transfer events which leads up to the state at which each participant has the other's address. Second, this series of grossly identical transfer events is construed at a level of granularity which renders its internal structure irrelevant, leading to the stative construal. In (44), by contrast, the situation aspect of the verb *avoir* is imperfective. In (44), *avoir* is paired with perfective past-tense inflection, which is otherwise compatible only with an event-type predicate. Via (9), an override occurs in which the verb receives an event construal: as reflected in the English translation, the event denoted is the *beginning* of the state in which Margot looks happy. This event occurs within a reference time just after the time of Henri's turning around; Margot's looking happy is accordingly understood not to obtain prior to the first-mentioned event.[9]

3.2.2. Aspectual shift constructions

The shift constructions which we will look at in this section are the English perfect and progressive constructions, exemplified in (45)–(46), respectively:

(45) *They have now visited us twice.*
(46) *The dog was digging a hole in the yard.*

Investigators of tense and aspect have long debated the appropriate characterization of these constructions: are they tense markers or aspect markers? Each exhibits semantic properties associated with tense markers. The progressive construction alternates with the simple present-tense in reporting contexts: as we have seen in the discussion of (35)–(36), the simple present is used to report states which overlap with the time of speaking, while the present progressive is used to report events which overlap with the present. The perfect construction denotes anteriority of an event or series of events with respect to the present. The present perfect in particular denotes anteriority with respect to speech time, a function associated with the past tense. Despite functional and semantic overlaps with tense markers, one can make a convincing case that these two constructions are aspectual, in that each performs a *stativizing* function. Perfect and progressive predications qualify as stative predications on a number of diagnostics. Both perfect and progressive predications can be used as simple present-tense reports – a property shown above to be unique to stative predications. Both perfect and progressive sentences pass the *when*-test for stativity: the situation which they denote can be

9. Notice that in English, by contrast, a sentence like (a) is vague as to whether Margot's looking happy started after Henri's turning around (and observed it) or obtained for some time prior to Henri's turning around:
(a) *Henri turned around. Margot looked happy.*

construed as holding prior to the event denoted by a subordinate clause introduced by *when*. This is shown for past progressive and perfect sentences in (47)–(48):

(47) *When we came in, they were playing cards.*
(47') *When we came in, they played cards.*
(48) *When we arrived, they had packed up everything.*
(48') *When we arrived, they packed up everything.*

The sentences in (47') and (48') are distinct from their non-prime counterparts in that (47') and (48') contain perfective main clauses. Since these sentences have perfective-form main clauses, they cannot be construed as denoting a situation in which the main-clause event was going on for some time prior to the event of the subordinate clause. Instead, the main-clause situation is necessarily understood to begin *after* the event denoted by the subordinate clause. By contrast, (47) and (48) are compatible with a construal in which the main-clause situations began *prior* to the event denoted by the subordinate clause. In allowing this construal, (47) and (48) are identical to stative sentences like (49):

(49) *When we got home, she was upset.*

A likely interpretation of (49) is one in which the situation of her being upset obtained prior to the event denoted by the subordinate clause. Given that perfect and progressive sentences class as stative sentences according to several diagnostics, we can conclude that perfect and progressive sentences denote stative situations. In accordance with Herweg (1991a, 1991b), we can view the perfect construction as denoting a state of aftermath following the culmination of one or more events, and the progressive as denoting a state that obtains during the time at which an event occurs. In other words, perfect and progressive predications denote a state defined with respect to a background event. The state is denoted by the auxiliary head; the background event (which Michaelis (1998) refers to as the *reference situation*) is denoted by the participial complement. While progressive and perfect constructions denote states defined relative to background events, other shift constructions, like the inceptive, may denote events defined relative to background states. An example of this usage of the inceptive is given in (50):

(50) *She began to look sad.*

The periphrastic structure of aspectual shift constructions like the perfect and inceptive mirrors that of shift constructions like the partitive in the domain of nominal syntax. Again, we see that the analogy between entities and situations is useful in thinking about aspectual meaning: just as the partitive construction denotes a count entity defined with respect to a backgrounded mass entity, so constructions like the inceptive can denote a bounded situation (an event of inception) defined with respect to an unbounded situation (a state like looking sad).

By thinking of the progressive as a shift construction, we find an answer to a question frequently asked not only by aspectologists but also by native English-speaking learners of Romance languages like French: what is the difference between the progressive construction in English and the imperfective in a language like French? Clearly, the two constructions overlap in many contexts, including that in (43), where a French imperfective sentence is translated by an English progressive. However, they are not functionally identical, as one can see from the impossibility of translating an imperfective sentence like (41) by means of an English progressive sentence like the anomalous sentence **She was preferring white wine*.

The simple answer to the puzzle relics on a distinction which we have already made: the English progressive is a shift construction, while the French imperfective is a concord construction, in particular a past-tense construction which selects for a particular aspectual class, that of states. The lexical complement of a progressive sentence must be eventive, since the purpose of the construction is to derive, so to speak, a state predication from an eventive predication. Therefore, a stative predicate like *prefer- white wine* cannot unify with the progressive construction, while its French equivalent can unify with the imperfective construction.

As it stands, however, this explanation overlooks the fact that, as pointed out by Langacker (1991) and others, stative predicates certainly are sometimes compatible with the progressive construction, as shown in sentences (51)–(52):

(51) *I am really liking your explanation.*
(52) *We are living in Boulder.*

Speakers report that (51) has an interpretation in which the state of liking is developing toward some point of culmination, and that (52) has an interpretation in which living in Boulder is a temporary state. These observations indicate that progressive-form statives are construed as events. It is easy to see that development toward a point of culmination is an eventive property; eventive (activity) predicates like *grow* exemplify this property. It is somewhat more difficult to see temporality as an eventive property. After all, living in Boulder, however short its duration, is a situation that is internally homogeneous. However, as Langacker (1991) shows, there are a number of internally homogeneous situations, like wearing a sweater and sleeping, which qualify as events with regard to the present-tense reporting diagnostic (**The baby sleeps!* **He wears a red sweater.*). In terms of their Aktionsart classification, such situations are most closely aligned with activities, since they are bounded in time but lack an inherent point of culmination. Therefore, it seems reasonable to conclude that progressive-form statives are construed as activities. The fact that state predicates which appear as complements in the progressive construction are construed as events makes sense in light of what we now know about shift constructions: such constructions, in addition to performing explicit conversion, are also used for implicit conversion. The examples in (51)–(52) illustrate the use of the progressive construction to signal implicit conversion: each denotes a state which holds during the time at which an event occurs. The participial complement is one which otherwise denotes a state, but receives an activity reading by virtue of its constructional context.

An example of implicit conversion involving the perfect construction is given in (53):

(53) *I've been rich and I've been poor.*

There is a straightforward shift interpretation of *I've been rich* in which *I be- rich* is a state phase whose terminus is the present (this is the so-called continuative reading of the perfect). Michaelis (1998: chap. 5) argues that this reading is licensed by the continuative construction, whose participial complement denotes a state phase and has a stative head (see Herweg 1991a for arguments that state phases qualify as events). There is another reading of (53), sometimes referred to as an existential reading, in which *I've been rich* asserts the occurrence of one or more episodes of being rich prior to now. This is the reading associated with (53), which invokes an alternation between rich and poor episodes in the past. The existential reading of (53) involves implicit conversion: a stative complement receives an episodic reading in the context of a construction (the existential-perfect construction) whose participial complement denotes an event. Although this event is a state phase on either the continuative or existential reading, it is only on the existential reading that this state phase has an episodic interpretation, in which its duration is not foregrounded. This is the reading associated with inherently perfective complements like *visit*, which unify with the existential-perfect construction in straightforward cases like (45).

3.3. *Sentence types*

A sentence type is a conventional pairing of form and discourse function. Traditionally recognized sentence types are declaratives, imperatives, and questions. Beyond those types targeted by speech-act theory, we find expressive types like exclamations and focus constructions like presentationals. Descriptive grammar is largely based on sentence types, but the relationship of form to function is not a straightforward one. As Michaelis and Lambrecht (1996) argue with respect to English exclamations, the relationship between form and discourse function is many-to-one, both within and across languages. Further, as Levinson (1983) points out, there is a good deal of formal overlap among sentence types. The purpose of this brief section is not, however, to defend a particular theory of sentence types. Instead, it is to examine the way in which sentence types are relevant to a theory of conversion.

There are two aspects of the conversion phenomenon that I wish to consider here. Both involve accommodation to constructional pragmatics. The first involves the manner in which sentence-type constructions override the function of sentence types with which they unify. The second involves the way in which sentence types override inherent semantic specifications of open-class items within them, including argument structure. Exploration of the second phenomenon will return us to a consideration of problems which stem from the assumption of lexical projection.

3.3.1. Function override

Function override is illustrated in English by the use of *wh*-question complements in factive contexts. A main-clause usage of a *wh*-question form is given in (54):

(54) *Who spoke up?*

The *wh*-question construction, when used in a main-clause context, presupposes the speaker's ignorance of the identity of the element coded by the question word or phrase. For example, sentence (54) presupposes that the speaker does not know the identity of the person or persons who spoke up. *Wh*-questions also presuppose a *propositional function* in which the element represented by the question word or phrase appears as an unbound variable. For example, (54) presupposes a propositional function of the form *X spoke up*. As Lambrecht and Michaelis (1998) argue, *wh*-questions assert the speaker's desire to know the identity of this variable.[10] When used as complements, the semantic properties of *wh*-questions change. Sentences (55)–(56) illustrate two contexts in which *wh*-questions appear as complements:

(55) *I realize who spoke up.*
(56) *I can't believe who spoke up!*

Both (55) and (56) presuppose that someone spoke up. Sentence (55) asserts that the speaker is aware of this proposition, while (56) asserts that the speaker is surprised by some aspect of this proposition. Both (55) and (56) presuppose that the speaker knows the identity of the person who spoke up. Hence, the use of *wh*-questions as complements in factive contexts not only changes what the form is taken to assert, but also overrides the presupposition of speaker ignorance associated with matrix *wh*-questions. The semantic content preserved across factive and question contexts is the presupposed open proposition; factives, by definition, presuppose the truth of their complements. Factive constructions call for complements which express a proposition known to both speaker and hearer; this proposition may be coded by a *that*-clause, but, as we have observed, it may also be coded by a *wh*-complement whose question word has a denotation known to the speaker. The presuppositional shift undergone by the question-form complement is a result of the semantics imposed by the factive construction via (9).

Another aspect of functional override is evident when we look closely at exclamations like (56). Such sentences do not simply assert the speaker's surprise at the proposition "Someone spoke up". Instead, (56) is taken to assert something relative to a pragmatic scale. Sentence (56) presupposes, or rather creates the presupposition that

10. *Assert* here is not to be taken as synonymous with the speech-act function of declaratives. Instead, assertion is used to describe the effect of an utterance on the addressee's knowledge state. E.g., as a result of hearing (54), the hearer knows the speaker's desire to learn the identity of the person who spoke up. On this understanding, it is not only declaratives that assert, but also questions (see Lambrecht & Michaelis 1998 for further discussion of this point).

the individual in question is ranked on a scale of, e.g., speakers with regard to their reticence. Why should this be? Exclamations, as argued by Michaelis and Lambrecht (1996), are used to express surprise at the high degree to which a given property has been manifested on some occasion, as in (57):

(57) *I can't believe how smart she is!*

In accordance with Fillmore, Kay and O'Connor (1988), we assume that individuals are assigned positions on a given property scale. The purpose of (56) is to invoke a high point on the relevant property scale (a point associated with the individual in question), and express surprise that this point has been reached. The interpretation in which the question word *who* denotes a degree on a property scale is not a fact about *wh*-question forms, but instead a fact about the interpretation of these forms in the context of an exclamative construction.

As observed by an anonymous reviewer, the override phenomenon at issue is difficult to describe by means of (9), as that principle is stated. *Wh*-question complements are not lexical items, and therefore the semantic conversion which they undergo when embedded as complements in exclamative constructions cannot be described as the result of an interaction of lexical and grammatical semantics. I will leave open the question of how (9) should be broadened in order to embrace the types of conversion which occur when sentence types combine. However, it is appropriate to observe that the example at hand is one in which a sentence type (the *wh*-question complement construction) is *embedded* in another. Insofar as this embedded construction serves as a complement, it occupies a role (that of argument) that is canonically filled by a lexical item.

But what sort of argument relation does the embedded-question complement bear to the construction as a whole? As Michaelis (2001) has argued, exclamations are double predications. That is, they not only predicate a scalar property (e.g., smartness in (57)) of a referent (e.g., the denotatum of *she* in (57)), but also predicate an epistemic property (that of inducing disbelief, etc.) of a *degree*. Insofar as this degree is the argument of a predication, the complement of an indirect exclamative may be a noun phrase denoting a degree, either directly or metonymically (see the discussion of (65) below and other examples discussed by Michaelis and Lambrecht (1996), including predications like *It's amazing the* DIFFERENCE*!*). The alternation between *wh*-clause complements and NP-form complements in indirect exclamations – initially observed by Grimshaw (1979), among others – is explicable insofar as degrees are entities. The entity status of degrees is evidenced by the fact that languages may index them by means of anaphoric words (as in, e.g., *He's that tall*). If degrees are entities, it stands to reason that they may be referred to by means of noun phrases, which canonically denote entities (Croft 1990: 64–154). If we view degrees as arguments of exclamative predications, we have some basis for treating complements of indirect exclamatives like (56) as analogous to lexical items, in particular nouns.

3.3.2. Sentence types and lexical projection

Zwicky (1994) suggests that a theory of sentence types might explain exceptions to a principle which he refers to as *strictly categorial determination*, i.e., the assumption that the syntactic category of a given maximal projection is entirely determined by the syntactic category of the head. An example of an exception involving a sentence type is given in (58):

(58) ***As smart as she is**, she is having difficulty getting a job.*

The phrase in boldface receives the interpretation associated with a concessive clause like *Although she is smart* or *Despite the fact that she is smart.* This phrase is not inherently a clause – let alone a concessive one. Its head is an adjective, and it functions as an AP in contexts like (59):

(59) *We are as smart as she is.*

The interpretation of (58) as a clause, with a factive interpretation, is a function of its embedding in a concessive construction. It is this construction which imposes the concessive interpretation upon what is in other contexts merely an AP.

Examples like the foregoing clearly illustrate exceptions to the principle of lexical projection at the syntactic level. Exceptions at the semantic level, which may involve either the inherent semantics of a lexical head or the semantic requirements (valence) of a lexical head, also reveal themselves when we look at sentence types. One such exception was discussed in section 2 with regard to Bresnan's (1994) analysis of locative inversion. That sentence, sentence (4), is repeated here as (60):

(60) *Down at the harbor there is a teal-green clubhouse for socializing and parties. Beside it* ***sparkles*** *the community pool.* (*Vanity Fair*, August 2001)

As discussed in section 2, Bresnan's model has some difficulty accounting for this type of example under the assumption that locative inversion is an alternative linking possibility for some set of unaccusative verbs. If, however, we abandon this assumption in favor of the assumption that locative inversion is a sentence type, accounting for examples like (60) is straightforward. Locative inversion can be considered an instance of a presentational sentence type referred to by Lambrecht (1994) as the *sentence-focus* type. Sentence-focus constructions, also known a *thetic* sentences, report events and states, and in so doing introduce the referents which serves as arguments in the predication. Lambrecht (1995) argues that while sentence-focus sentences *tend* to contain unaccusative verbs and stative verbs of location, this tendency comes from the semantic-pragmatic properties of presentational constructions, whose function is not to predicate something of an entity under discussion, but to introduce an entity into a conversation or narrative, making it available for predications subsequently. Hence, as Bresnan herself observes, the semantic role that an entity would ordinarily play with respect to a verb like *sparkle* is in a context like (60) overlaid by another role – in Lambrecht's terms, this role is not the role of theme, but rather the role of *focus*. The focus role is more salient in the presentational context than the semantic role assigned by the lexical head. Accordingly, as Lambrecht (1995) points out, the agency of the caller role vis-à-vis the verb *call* is backgrounded relative to its focal status in the English prosodic construction in (61). Similar interpretive effects can be observed for the pragmatic equivalent of this construction in French (a cleft construction) and Italian (an inversion construction):

(61) *Bob called.*
(62) *Il y a Bob qui a téléphoné.*
(63) *Ha telefonato Bob.*

Presentational constructions like those in (61)–(63) give us evidence for implicit conversion involving the presentational sentence type, and against an account like Bresnan's, which reduces presentational constructions to lexical linking rules.

Conversion phenomena involving modulation of the meanings of epistemic adjectives give evidence against another account in which sentence types are derived from the subcategorization possibilities of lexical items: Grimshaw's (1979) account of exclamations. In Grimshaw's account, exclamations are complements which are called for by a specific class of lexical verbs and adjectives, including the negated verb *believe* and the adjective *amazing*. However, an important point about adjectives which denote the property of causing disbelief is that they do not form a circumscribed set. Adjectives which do not intrinsically denote the property of causing disbelief may nevertheless appear as matrix predicators in exclamatives which take the form of extraposition structures. When this occurs, the semantics of the adjective is modified in such a way that it is compatible with the semantics of the construction. Examples of this phenomenon are given in the boldfaced portions of (64)–(65):

(64) *Allen served just two years there and it was a transforming experience.* ***'It was frightening, that whole time, how much***

anger I had.' (*Time*, 12 December 1994) (= Michaelis and Lambrecht 1996, (32a))

(65) *'The cops? Are they friends of yours?' 'Hardly', I said, but I sat there smiling.* ***It was terrible, really, the joy I took at the notion of skunking Pigeyes.*** *I already had a few ideas.* (Scott Turow, *Pleading Guilty*) (= Michaelis and Lambrecht 1996, (1e))

The adjectives *frightening* and *terrible* do not denote the property of inducing disbelief. Instead, *frightening* denotes the property of inducing fear and *terrible* the general property of inducing a negative response (censure, disgust, etc.). In the context of an exclamative construction, however, the fearful and censorious responses invoked by these adjectives are understood as entailed by a judgement about the degrees of anger and joy, respectively. E.g., the degree of anger is high enough to induce fear. In other words, the extraposed exclamative construction – whose semantic-pragmatic properties are those of the exclamative sentence type – appears to impose its meaning on the matrix adjectives with which it combines. The existence of conversion examples like (64)–(65) suggests that the source of exclamative meaning is an exclamative construction, rather than the argument structure of a set of psychological adjectives which commonly combine with this construction.

In concluding this section, we should observe that although we have focused on sentence types which are concord constructions, and therefore on instances of implicit conversion – examples in which sentence types modulate the semantic or pragmatic features of their parts – there are also straightforward examples of sentence types which perform explicit conversion. Examples are found, e.g., in Vietnamese, in which sentence-final particles are used to override the illocutionary force of the clauses to which they are attached. For example, the sentence-final particles *di* (lit. 'go') and *không* (a negative marker) function to impose, respectively, an imperative reading and a yes-no interrogative reading on a clause which would otherwise have declarative force.

4. Conclusion

We have seen that appeal to constructional meaning provides a unified treatment of two very different kinds of semantic interactions: the "unmarked" type, in which lexical items match the meanings of the constructions with which they are combined, and the "marked" type, in which the meanings of lexical elements conflict with constructional meanings. On the constructional account, the "marked" combinations, far from being unexpected or exceptional, behave in accordance with the override principle, and serve a function identical to that of demonstrably compositional constructions like the partitive and progressive, i.e., type-shifting. In fact, as we have seen, describing the semantics of nominal constructions, linking constructions, aspectual constructions, and sentence types requires reference to both explicit type-shifting (as performed by shift constructions) and implicit type-shifting (as performed by both shift and concord constructions).

Our exploration of shift and concord constructions at several morphosyntactic levels has shown that an understanding of sentence meaning relies on the study of syntactic meaning. The study of syntactic meaning relies in turn on an understanding of concepts and distinctions that are fundamental to construal (entity types, the event-state distinction, causation, plexity, boundedness). In addition, it requires an elaborated model of the functions served by syntactic forms like exclamatory and presentational constructions – a model which includes discourse-pragmatic roles like focus and discourse-theoretic properties like presupposition. Since constructions, like words, freely combine semantic features (like image schemas) with pragmatic features (like use conditions), the study of constructional meaning entails the integration of cognitive and discourse-functional explanation. This integrated approach to the study of meaning and use is already widely precedented in the cognitive sciences: studies of language acquisition, language breakdown due to focal brain injury, and sentence processing place increasingly strong emphasis on the role of usage factors, in particular the frequency of words and morphosyntactic patterns. Such studies have shown, for example, that the onset of verb over-regularization errors in early language is triggered by a marked increase in the proportion of regular to irregular verbs in the child's vocabulary (Marchman & Bates 1994), that sentence interpretation becomes harder for both Broca's aphasics and normal adults when there is conflict between the preferred syntactic frame of the lexical verb and the syntactic frame in which it is encountered (Gahl 2002), and that the likelihood of a garden-path "detour" during sentence processing is a function of the prior probability of a given constituent-structure assignment (e.g., reduced relative vs. main verb) combined with the transitivity bias of the lexical verb (Narayanan & Jurafsky 1998).

Such studies uphold the view, advanced by both Langacker (1987, 1991) and Bybee (2001), that linguistic knowledge is to a large extent the knowledge of routines. Significantly, such studies have also provided evidence that, as Bates and Goodman (1997: 59) put it, "grammatical and lexical forms are handled by the same large and heterogeneous processing system". In light of such findings, it is reasonable to ask what theory of grammar could best capture the properties of this non-modular representational system. Whatever the ultimate answer, it seems safe to say that it will almost certainly involve reference to grammatical constructions.

References

Bates, Elizabeth and Judith C. Goodman
1997 On the inseparability of grammar and the lexicon: Evidence from acquisition, aphasia and real-time processing. *Language and Cognitive Processes* 12: 507–584.

Bresnan, Joan
1994 Locative inversion and the architecture of universal grammar. *Language* 70: 72–131.
2001 *Lexical-Functional Syntax*. Oxford: Basil Blackwell.

Bybee, Joan
2001 *Phonology and Language Use*. Cambridge: Cambridge University Press.

Clark, Eve and Herbert Clark
1979 When nouns surface as verbs. *Language* 55: 767–811.

Croft, William
1990 *Typology and Universals*. Cambridge: Cambridge University Press.
Declerck, Renaat
1995 Is there a relative past tense in English? *Lingua* 97: 1–36.
Dowty, David
1979 *Word Meaning and Montague Grammar*. Dordrecht: Reidel.
1986 The effects of aspectual class on the temporal structure of discourse: Semantics or pragmatics? *Linguistics and Philosophy* 9: 37–61.
Fauconnier, Gilles and Mark Turner
1996 Blending as a central process of grammar. In: A. Goldberg (ed.), *Conceptual Structure, Discourse and Language*, 113–130. Stanford: CSLI Publications.
Fillmore, Charles J. and Paul Kay
1993 *Construction grammar coursebook*. Unpublished ms., Department of Linguistics, University of California, Berkeley.
Fillmore, Charles J., Paul Kay and Mary C. O'Connor
1988 Regularity and idiomaticity in grammatical constructions: The case of *let alone*. *Language* 64: 501–538.
Fillmore, Charles J., Paul Kay, Laura A. Michaelis and Ivan Sag
to appear *Construction Grammar*. Stanford: CSLI Publications.
Foley, William and Robert D. van Valin
1984 *Functional Syntax and Universal Grammar*. Cambridge: Cambridge University Press.
Gahl, Susanne
2002 The role of lexical biases in aphasic sentence comprehension. *Aphasiology* 16: 1173–1198.
Goldberg, Adele
1995 *Constructions: A Construction Grammar Approach to Argument Structure*. Chicago: The University of Chicago Press.
1997 The relationships between verbs and constructions. In Marjolijn Verspoor, Kee Dong Lee and Eve Sweetser (eds.), *Lexical and Syntactical Constructions and the Construction of Meaning*, 83–98. Amsterdam: John Benjamins.
Grimshaw, Jane
1979 Complement selection and the lexicon. *Linguistic Inquiry* 10: 279–326.
Harris, Roy and Talbot J. Taylor
1997 *Landmarks in Linguistic Thought 1: The Western Tradition from Socrates to Saussure*. London: Routledge.

Herweg, Michael
1991 a A critical account of two classical approaches to aspect. *Journal of Semantics* 8: 362–403.
1991 b Perfective and imperfective aspect and the theory of events and states. *Linguistics* 29: 969–1010.

Israel, Michael
1996 The *way* constructions grow. In: A. Goldberg (ed.), *Conceptual Structure, Discourse and Language*, 217–230. Stanford: CSLI Publications.

Jackendoff, Ray
1990 *Semantic Structures*. Cambridge, MA: The MIT Press.
1997 *The Architecture of the Language Faculty*. Cambridge, MA: The MIT Press.

Kay, Paul and Charles J. Fillmore
1999 Grammatical constructions and linguistic generalizations: The 'What's X doing Y' construction. *Language* 75: 1–33.

Lambrecht, Knud
1994 *Information Structure and Sentence Form*. Cambridge: Cambridge University Press.
1995 The pragmatics of case: On the relationship between semantic, grammatical, and pragmatic roles in English and French. In: Masayoshi Shibatani and Sandra A. Thompson (eds.), *Essays in Semantics and Pragmatics*, 145–190. Amsterdam: John Benjamins.

Lambrecht, Knud and Laura A. Michaelis
1998 Sentence accent in information questions: Default and projection. *Linguistics and Philosophy* 21: 477–544.

Langacker, Ronald W.
1987 *Foundations of Cognitive Grammar*, Volume 1: *Theoretical Prerequisites*. Stanford: Stanford University Press.
1991 *Foundations of Cognitive Grammar*, Volume 2: *Descriptive Application*. Stanford: Stanford University Press.

Levinson, Stephen
1983 *Pragmatics*. Cambridge: Cambridge University Press.

Marchman, Virginia A. and Elizabeth Bates
1994 Continuity in lexical and morphological development: A test of the critical mass hypothesis. *Journal of Child Language* 21: 339–366.

Michaelis, Laura A.
1994 A case of constructional polysemy in Latin. *Studies in Language* 18: 45–70.
1998 *Aspectual Grammar and Past-Time Reference*. London: Routledge.

2001 Exclamative constructions. In: Martin Haspelmath, Ekkehard König, Wulf Österreicher and Wolfgang Raible (eds.), *Language Typology and Linguistic Universals,* Volumes 1–3, 1038–1050. Berlin: Walter de Gruyter.

to appear Implicit and explicit type-shifting in Construction Grammar. *Cognitive Linguistics*.

Michaelis, Laura A. and Knud Lambrecht
1996 Toward a construction-based theory of language function: The case of nominal extraposition. *Language* 72: 215–247.

Michaelis, Laura A. and Josef Ruppenhofer
2001 *Beyond Alternations: A Constructional Model of the German Applicative Pattern*. Stanford: CSLI Publications.

Mourelatos, Alexander
1981 Events, processes and states. In: Philip Tedeschi and Annie Zaenen (eds.), *Syntax and Semantics,* Volume 14: *Tense and Aspect,* 415–434. New York: Academic Press.

Narayanan, Srinivas and Daniel S. Jurafsky
1998 Bayesian models of human sentence processing. In: Sharon J. Derry and Morton A. Gernsbacher (eds.), *Proceedings of the Twentieth Annual Meeting of the Cognitive Science Society*, 752–757. Mahwah, NJ: Lawrence Erlbaum.

Pullum, Geoffrey and Arnold Zwicky
1991 Condition duplication, paradigm homonymy and transconstructional constraints. In: Laurel A. Sutton, Christopher Johnson and Ruth Shields (eds.), *Proceedings of the Seventeenth Annual Meeting of the Berkeley Linguistics Society*, 252–266. Berkeley: Berkeley Linguistics Society.

Ritter, Elizabeth and Sara Rosen
1998 Delimiting events in syntax. In: Miriam Butt and Wilhelm Geuder (eds.), *The Projection of Arguments: Lexical and Compositional Factors*, 135–164. Stanford: CSLI Publications.

Slobin, Dan
1997 There's more than one way to talk about motion: Consequences of linguistic typology for narrative style. Paper presented at the Third Conference on Conceptual Structure, Discourse and Language, University of Colorado at Boulder, May 1997.

Smith, Carlota
1986 A speaker-based approach to aspect. *Linguistics and Philosophy* 9: 97–115.

1991 *The Parameter of Aspect.* Dordrecht: Kluwer Academic Publishers.

Talmy, Leonard
1985 Lexicalization patterns: Semantic structure in lexical meaning. In: Timothy Shopen (ed.), *Language Typology and Syntactic Description*, Volume 3, 57–149. Cambridge: Cambridge University Press.
1988 The relation of grammar to cognition. In: Brygida Rudzka-Ostyn (ed.), *Topics in Cognitive Linguistics*, 165–205. Amsterdam: John Benjamins.
Van Valin, Robert D. and Randy LaPolla
1997 *Syntax: Structure, Meaning and Function*. Cambridge: Cambridge University Press.
Vendler, Zeno
1967 *Linguistics and Philosophy*. Ithaca, NY: Cornell University Press.
Zwicky, Arnold
1994 Dealing out meaning: Fundamentals of grammatical constructions. In: Susanne Gahl, Andrew Dolbey and Christopher Johnson (eds.), *Proceedings of the Twentieth Annual Meeting of the Berkeley Linguistics Society*, 611–625. Berkeley: Berkeley Linguistics Society.

Metonymic sense shift: Its origins in hearers' abductive construal of usage in context

Kurt Queller

Abstract

Metonymy – the phenomenon whereby an expression that basically refers to one entity is used to indicate some other entity associated with it in a given domain – is frequently invoked as a factor in meaning change. Well-known examples include Middle English *bedes* ('prayers' > 'beads'), and Dutch *winkel* ('corner' > 'shop'). The present chapter argues that such sense shifts may involve no metonymic construal at all, on either speakers' or hearers' part. The model assumes speakers using words in their conventional senses, with hearers inferring innovative senses based on contextual meanings of usage events within which the words are commonly embedded. A dynamic usage-based analysis of semantic change is proposed, in which newer lexical meanings emerge through "semantic backformation" from contextualized utterance meaning.

Keywords: abduction, comprehension and production, emergence, idealized cognitive model, metonymy, semantic backformation, semantic change, usage-based model.

1. Introduction

One often finds discussions in the Cognitive Linguistics literature of metonymic usages like the following, in which a vehicle, trigger, or reference point entity, e.g., "your ham sandwich", provides mental access to an intended target entity, viz., "your customer (who ordered that item)".

(1) a. ***Your ham sandwich** left without paying.*
b. ***The vasectomy** in 312 is ready for his bath.*
c. *I picked up **Lakoff and Johnson** for five dollars.*

AUTHOR FOR WORK AUTHORED, exemplified in (1c), is included by Kövecses and Radden (1998) in their taxonomy of routine patterns of metonymic extension. Cases like (1a) and (1b), in contrast, are viewed as instances of metonymy grounded in idealized cognitive models (ICMs) involving "indeterminate relationships" (1998: 58–59). The connection between a menu item and a customer who orders it might fall under more general relations like POSSESSOR FOR POSSESSED, CONTROLLER FOR CONTROLLED, but the essential relationship emerges only within the nexus of an ICM specific to restaurants and restaurant workers.[1]

Although not primarily concerned with diachronic issues, Kövecses and Radden observe that "ICM-specific metonymies are a particularly frequent source of meaning changes", citing the origins of the word *tobacco* in the Carib (Arawakan) word *tobac*, meaning 'pipe'. Upon taking up the smoking habit, the Spaniards borrowed this word, seemingly shifting its meaning from the instrument used for smoking to the substance smoked. Though noting that they might have done this on the basis of an abstract conceptual metonymy such as CONTAINER FOR CONTAINED (as when *Will you drink a glass?* is used to offer wine), Kövecses and Radden consider this unlikely, suggesting rather that the Spaniards "probably had a specific 'pipe-smoking ICM' in mind" (1998: 59). The question arises, however, why they would have performed such a transfer in the first place. If, knowing that *tobac* meant 'pipe', they wanted to refer to the substance smoked in it, would not a composite expression, such as *hoja*

1. The distinction between the two kinds of metonymy may not be so clear-cut. One the one hand, usages like (1c), despite membership in the regular pattern AUTHOR FOR WORK AUTHORED, presuppose something like a "university/academic" ICM. On the other hand, the usages in (1a) and (1b) are thoroughly conventional within restaurant and hospital subcultures, requiring no special processing for comprehension. Cf. Sweetser & Fauconnier's (1996) treatment of both (1a) and (1c) types as involving similar sorts of "frame metonymy".

de tabaco 'pipe leaf', have been more likely?[2] I propose, instead, that the shift resulted as Spaniards unconsciously reanalyzed particular patterns of conventional usage that they heard in specific contexts, in a manner that left communication essentially unimpaired despite their inference of a new semantic schema for *tobac*. Though non-conventional, the newly inferred meaning was consistent not only with the relevant usage contexts, but also with ICMs familiar to the Spaniards which could easily have been construed as relevant for interpretation. The proposed process is sketched in Figure 1.

Kövecses and Radden suggest that the shift originates in speakers' strategic redeployment of the word *tobac* from one referent to another, given their association within a single highly specific ICM. I am suggesting instead that two distinct ICMs are involved – one invoked by speakers, who are using the word conventionally, and one invoked by hearers, who are re-construing the usage event in terms of cognitive models that seem to them to be relevant in the given context. For speakers, a request to "take the *tobac*" constitutes a conventional elaboration of the traditional (Carib) lexical schema [[PIPE]/[tobac]], employed in the context of a (likewise conventional) ICM associated with the *tobac* ceremony.[3] But the fortune-seeking Span-

2. Most instances of CONTAINER FOR CONTAINED metonymies (like *a glass* for *some wine*) are unlikely to result in diachronic sense shift. On the other hand, a composite expression like *hoja de tabaco* 'pipe leaf' might plausibly yield the symbolic pairing [[TOBACCO LEAF]/[tabaco]] by the process that Stern (1931: 275–276) called "shortening" through "omission of headword in binary combinations". Stern notes that shortenings of the type ((Noun + Prep) + Noun) are common in Romance (cf. French *bâteau à vapeur* > *vapeur*). Besides the abductive scenario outlined in this chapter, shortening constitutes a second plausible source for the *tobac* shift not involving figurative metonymy. The two scenarios are not incompatible; converging on the same endpoint by different routes, they may have reinforced each other. (On connections between referential metonymy and noun-noun compounds and on derivability of the one from the other by head-noun deletion, see Warren 1999.)
3. The notational conventions are those established in Langacker (1987). Square brackets [ ] enclose units (of whatever size) that are assumed to be entrenched in the mental lexicon, while parentheses ( ) enclose nonce elements. (Diagrams may use respectively squares and circles to designate these two categories.)

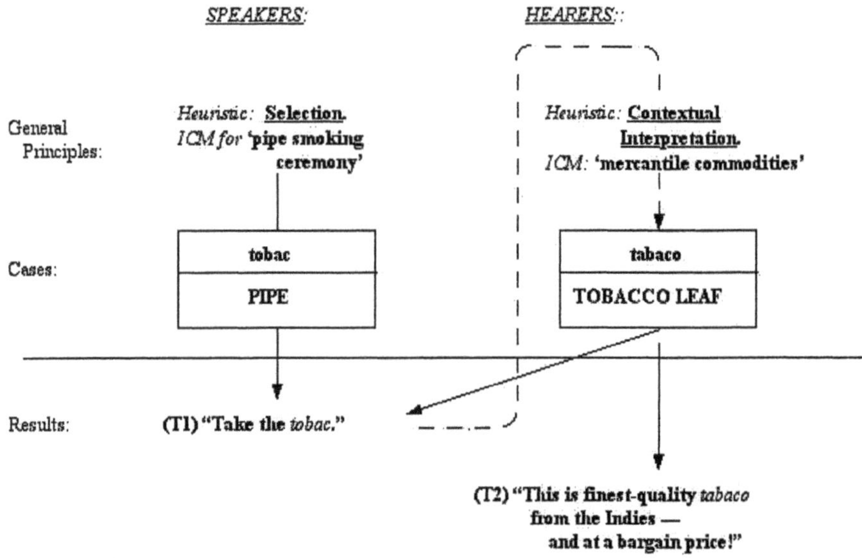

Figure 1. The *tobac* shift as context-based abductive reanalysis.

iards were more deeply acculturated to quite different cognitive models. Prominent among these was a "mercantile commodity" ICM, which comprised a constellation of cultural notions and practices pertaining to shipping and trade, commodities (precious metals, fine textiles, spices, cash crops, slaves...), commodity consumption and mass consumer markets, financing of mercantile enterprises, and wealth accumulation. The power of this ICM over the minds of the newcomers is evident; soon enough, many were seeking their for-

Symbolic units consist of a functional (semantic-pragmatic) specification, written in capital letters, paired with a formal (phonological-morphosyntactic) specification, noted in lower-case letters. When written horizontally in running text, the two are separated by a backslash (/). Within a given expression, curly brackets { } enclose a variable slot, for which a representative option is specified. In network diagrams like Figure 2 below, individual capital letters (A, B, C...) stand for schematic symbolic units (whether simple or compositional), while corresponding lower-case letters (a, b, c...) represent actual usage events that instantiate those schemas.

tunes through commodity trading not only in tobacco leaf, but also in Caribs – their erstwhile hosts.

The "mercantile commodity" ICM here proposed as the occasion for the *tobac* shift is quite distinct from the "pipe smoking" ICM invoked by the original speakers. On this account, there has been no strategic redeployment of the referring expression within an ICM. Although the outcome of the process might reasonably be called a metonymic shift, the process itself need not have involved any metonymic operation. It is worth considering whether figurative or conceptual metonymy (as cognitive process) and metonymic sense shift (as diachronic outcome) might not be entirely distinct phenomena (cf. Warren 1998).

The preceding sketch treats the *tobac* shift as an instance of what historical linguists call *abductive reanalysis*. The term goes back to Peirce (1935–66: 2: 263), who proposed abduction as a third basic form of reasoning alongside deduction and induction. While the classical deductive syllogism reasons from a general principle ("all men are mortal") through a particular case ("Socrates is a man") to a result ("Socrates is mortal"), induction works in the opposite direction, from a series of observed results ("Socrates, Plato, and Aristotle are dead") through corresponding cases ("Socrates, Plato, and Aristotle were men") to a general principle ("all men are mortal"). Abduction, in contrast, begins with an observed result ("Socrates was mortal"), invokes a general principle ("all men are mortal"), and infers what might well be the case ("Socrates was a man"). Abduction is in itself a very unreliable form of reasoning, since the principle invoked may be inappropriate (Socrates may have been a horse). Nonetheless, Peirce argued that abductive inferencing not only characterizes the psychological processes whereby humans construe their environment, but also underlies all new conceptualization. The construct of abductive reanalysis is by now standard in historical linguistics, having been used to elucidate phonological shifts (Andersen 1973) and morphosyntactic reanalyses (Lightfoot 1979; Hopper & Traugott

1993), as well as changes in lexical semantics (McMahon 1994: 177).[4]

In linguistic treatments of abduction, "results" involve concrete usage events, while "cases" correspond to particular linguistic rules or schemas. Within a cognitivist framework, one may think of "general principles" as a set of general heuristics for speech processing, together with all the ICMs relevant to the formulation and interpretation of usage events. Since speech production and comprehension are not mirror images of each other, the associated heuristics are presumably in part distinct. Speakers, who need to select schemas and assemble them into intelligible utterances, must have recourse to some set of *selection* heuristics. Hearers, meanwhile, must focus on linguistic and non-linguistic context to arrive at an interpretation of an utterance that is presumably consistent with the speaker's communicative intent, regardless of whether it directly reflects the speaker's selection process. I will have nothing further to say here about schema selection; Langacker (1988: 152–154) gives a useful sketch of some relevant principles, which need supplementing by a theory of onomasiology (cf. Grondelaers & Geeraerts, this volume) as well as by pragmatic heuristics (Traugott & Dasher 2002: 18–24). As for hearers, I propose the following heuristic:

(2) *Contextual interpretation*: Infer meanings for usage events that are to the greatest possible extent
  a. consistent with conventional usage,
  b. appropriate for the given context (linguistic and non-linguistic), and
  c. plausibly related to the ostensible intent of the speaker.

Ideally, the three desiderata will be equally satisfied, but one or another may sometimes be eclipsed without impairing successful communication. Contextually appropriate inference of speaker intent (2b,

4. McMahon even cites the semantic development of *bead* as a probable example of abductive sense shift. The account of abductive reanalysis given here relies heavily on Hopper and Traugott (1993).

c) does not always depend upon accessing precisely those conventional schemas selected by the speaker (2a). In the case sketched above, *Take the tobac* receives full sanction both from the conventional (speaker's) schema and from the innovative (hearer's abductively inferred) schema, and either will serve for immediate communicative purposes. Only later, when erstwhile hearers invoke the new schema as speakers in other usage contexts, does the change become evident (cf. the utterance at T2 in Figure 1). Yet there was never any link between the two *tobac* schemas, in anyone's mind. Neither speaker nor hearer has derived the one schema from the other. Hearers have, through successful contextual interpretation, inferred the new schema on the basis of speakers' contextually situated conventional usage, without having accessed the relevant component schema in its conventional sense.

Interest in metonymy and metaphor as creative responses of speakers to issues of linguistic coding has coincided with a second focal interest in Cognitive Linguistics: that of establishing motivated links among the multiple senses of a word or construction within a family resemblances network (Wittgenstein 1953; Rosch 1977), through a process of radial extension from a (logically and/or historically prior) prototype to peripheral (logically/historically derivative) schemas (Lakoff 1987; Taylor 1995). Consequently, semantic innovations embodied in metonymic sense shift tend to be regarded as if they resulted from speakers' creative solutions to issues of linguistic coding. One example is the well-known shift of the Middle English word *bede* 'prayer' to its modern meaning, 'bead', which Langacker (1987: 383–384) treats in terms of creative speaker responses to a perceived lexical gap. Another is the evolution of the Dutch word *winkel* from an earlier sense of '(street) corner' to its current sense of 'a shop', which Geeraerts (1997: 76–77) treats as involving a complex series of extensions including metonymy.

Sections 2 and 3 below argue that such metonymic shifts are best understood as resulting from hearers creatively reconstruing speakers' conventional usages, in the context of particular usage events. Sections 4 and 5 discuss the differences between such shifts and figurative or conceptual metonymy, and propose that accounting for them will require two adjustments within cognitive linguistic theory. First, lexical semantic changes must be understood as operating not on lexical items as abstract or isolated units, but on words and expressions as they are used in the context of particular collocations, constructions, and discourse environments. Second, while a dynamic usage-based model (Langacker 1988, 1999a) is well suited for this purpose, the model needs to refer to the distinctive role of hearers in construing plausible relations between linguistic expressions and situational contexts. Both goals can be achieved within a dynamic usage-based model that allows for abduction and "semantic backformation" of innovative lexical senses from contextually emergent meanings of larger syntagmatic units within which they occur.

2. The *beads* shift

A textbook case of metonymic sense shift is the splitting of Middle English *bede* into the meanings 'prayer' (the original sense) and 'bead' (a secondary sense which became the word's primary meaning when the 'prayer' sense was subsequently effaced, having been taken over by the French loanword *prayer*). The context in which this shift occurred is clear. In medieval Europe, prescribed cycles of formulaic prayers were associated with the rosary, a series of tiny balls threaded onto a circular thong; one kept track of progress through the prayer cycle by counting off the balls. Less clear is the mechanism behind the shift.

2.1. A speaker-based account: metonymic extension as a response to problems of linguistic coding

Langacker (1987: 383) sees the extension in terms of speakers resolving a problem of linguistic coding. In Langacker's model, speakers search the inventory of symbolic units for a match to the conceptualization in question. Sometimes, a fit is found such that the situation being conceptualized reflects (with greater elaboration) the semantic pole of some conventional symbolic unit. In such cases, the symbolic unit is said to be *fully schematic* for the target usage; conversely, the latter is said to be *fully sanctioned* by the former (cf. the solid-line arrows in Figure 2). In less straightforward cases, the speaker may find no unit in the language inventory [L] that is fully schematic for the intended conceptualization. A relationship of *partial sanction* (symbolized in Figure 2 by broken-lined arrows) is then established between the target usage (e) and the selected schema [C]. Similar relations of partial sanction may hold between the conventional schema [C] and a new, non-conventional schema (E), which is fully schematic for (e). Such partial sanction is always characterized by a greater or lesser amount of 'strain' (Langacker 1987: 69–70).

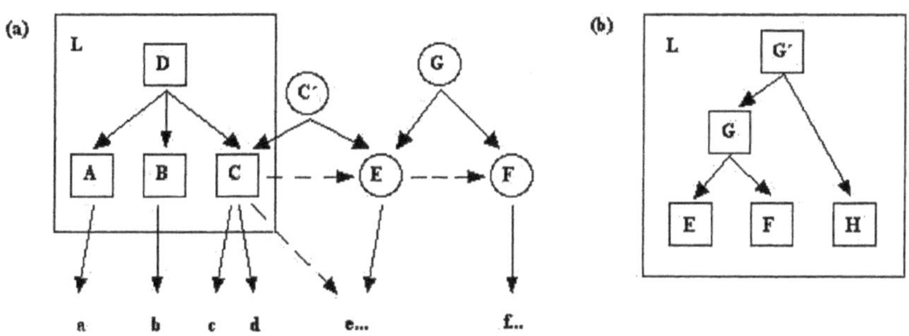

Figure 2. The *beads* shift: A speaker-based account.

In Langacker's model, metonymic shift (like all cases of radial extension from older to newer schemas) involves solutions to problems of linguistic coding in which speakers settle for partial sanction with some degree of strain, as in Figure 2. In the case of *bead*, we can imagine ourselves as speakers looking for a specific way of referring to the balls on a rosary. Lacking any schema that does just this, we search the schema inventory and come up with the schema [[PRAYERS]/[bedes]].[5] What we access is, however, not the general

5. I follow Langacker in using a Middle English spelling to designate the phonological pole of symbolic units involving this lexical item, regardless of

schema (corresponding to [D] in Figure 2), but rather the particular subschema that profiles individual prayers as items within a cycle that are related in a serial, one-to-one fashion with the little balls on the rosary (that is, [C]). Langacker observes that, abstracting away from the specific profiling of 'prayers' against this base representation, we can arrive at a representation that is fully schematic both for formulaic prayers in a fixed cycle and for rosary beads on a circular string. This more abstract schema (call it (C')) motivates an extension from the rosary subschema [[PRAYERS]/[bedes]] to the target schema ([BEADS]/[bedes]), which is schematically identical, except that it profiles the balls, rather than the prayers spoken in connection with them (that is, ([C] → (E)). As the latter schema becomes entrenched in the lexicon [E], it can serve as prototype for further extensions in usage contexts involving, not rosaries but, for example, necklaces or bracelets (F), and a new schema (G) accordingly emerges and ultimately itself becomes entrenched [G]. If, as happened with the word *bead*, the original schema complex ([D] and its instantiating subschemas) falls into disuse, we are ultimately left with the present situation, represented by Figure 2b (where [H] stands for still more recently conventionalized usages, such as *beads of sweat,* fully sanctioned by a higher-level schema [G'] that comprises small spherical objects apart from issues of solidity and perforation).

This account of the sense shift from 'prayers' to 'beads' raises a number of questions, both as a model of speaker choices and as an account of historical change. How likely is it that the apprehension of a lexical gap would have been sufficiently strong and widespread to have impelled a critical mass of speakers (whatever that might be) toward a common solution to the coding problem that involves such a degree of strain? If speakers did feel the need for a new schema, why would they have eschewed more conventional choices (e.g., *(little) balls*) in favor of such a strained solution? And how would their hearers have inferred the existence of the new schema? After all, the context (at least initially) is such that hearers might normally

---

the meaning attributed to it at the semantic pole. Otherwise, hypothetical Middle English utterance types will be represented in Modern English form.

assume the conventional schema. As an explanation of the historical shift, such a purely speaker-based account is problematic with respect not only to the actuation of the change, but also to its diffusion through the speech community.

2.2. A hearer-based account: abductive inferencing based on syntagmatic and situational context

These problems can be resolved by shifting focus from creative categorization judgments on the part of speakers to creative contextual inferencing by hearers. Following Jespersen (1922: 175), let us consider the Middle English verb-object collocation [tell/count {one's} *bedes*], originally meaning 'to count or recite one's prayers'. Imagine a speaker saying to a child,

(3) *Don't bother your grandma right now, she's telling her* **bedes**.

The expression is conventional, but the child, perhaps only vaguely aware of its status as an instantiation of [[PRAYER]/[bede]], sees grandma using the little balls as counter tokens, and infers that the expression means that she is 'counting her beads' (in the modern sense).

Or consider utterances like these:

(4) a. *This one here is your first "Hail Mary"* **bede**.
b. *I saw you skip that* **bede** *– go back and do it again*!

Again, *bede* may be assumed to have the conventional meaning 'prayer'. But in a context where indicating the physical token can count as a reference to the corresponding prayer, it is natural to infer that the referent is the object being pointed to. Having made such an inference, the erstwhile hearer may later say things like:

(5) a. *Which one did you say was my first "Hail Mary"* **bede**?
b. *Must you click your* **bedes** *so loud?*
c. *My rosary broke and the* **bedes** *rolled all over the floor.*

(5a) is ambiguous in just the way (4a) is, and a hearer lacking the new schema may notice nothing unusual.[6] In cases like (5b) and (5c), however, the acoustic and kinetic spatial imagery evoked by verbs like *click* and *roll* make it clear that a new schema has been extracted.

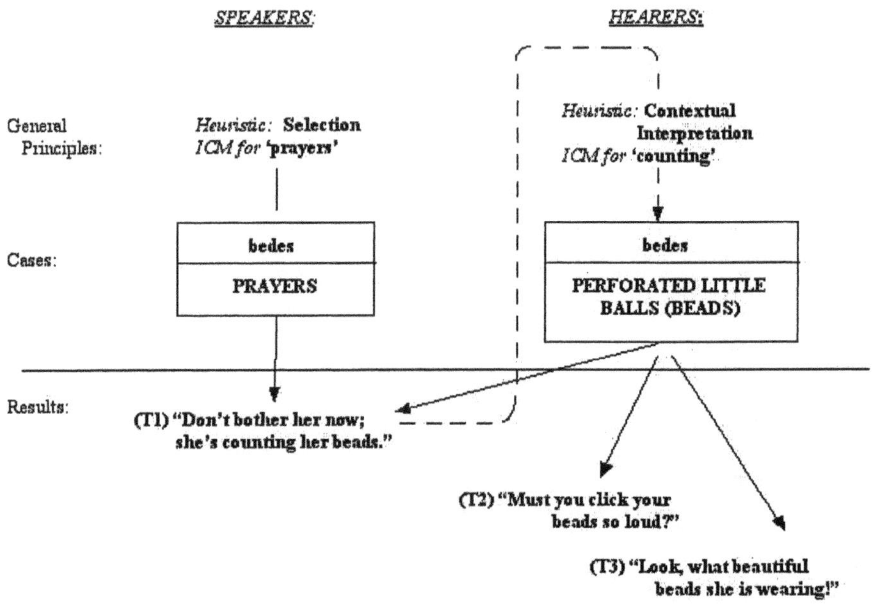

Figure 3. The *bedes* shift as context-based abductive reanalysis.

The process of schema extraction here proposed is essentially abductive, and can be diagrammed as in Figure 3. As in the *tobac* analysis, no direct mapping is posited between conventional and innovative schemas; the link is crucially mediated by contextualized usage

6. The OED entry for *bead* suggests a period during which the 'prayer' sense became restricted mainly to contexts associated with fixed cycles of formulaic prayers. (During this interim, presumably, the French loanword *prayer* gradually eclipsed most other 'prayer' uses of *bede.*) This may constitute evidence for the sort of granularity proposed both in Langacker's analysis and in the one offered here (as well as for the general thesis offered in Geeraerts 1996). In each, the point of departure for sense shift is located less in higher-level schemas than in elaborated subschemas. Such interim restriction would be accounted for on the assumption of a pre-existing subschema corresponding to the narrowed domain of usage.

events like that indicated at (T1). Having abandoned the mapping assumption, an abductive analysis also assumes (at the level of lexical semantics) no pair-wise establishment of contiguity links between parts of a single ICM (Kövecses & Radden 1998), domain matrix (Croft 1993), or frame (Koch 1999). For speakers, it is the "formulaic prayer" ICM that motivates selection of the conventional schema [[PRAYERS]/[bedes]]. The usage event also involves activation of a "counting" ICM, but that, in the speaker's conceptualization, is associated chiefly with the selection of the verb *tell* or *count*. The hearer's abductive inference of the new schema comes through reliance on this latter ICM in construing the event as a whole. Counting prototypically involves a *person* moving *tokens* from *one side to another* within a designated *counting space* (table or "counter" surface, abacus, rosary…) while *moving the lips* (with or without intelligible vocalization). All of these prototypical elements tend to be salient in the context of usage events of the present sort. Even for adult hearers whose lexicon contains the conventional schema [[PRAYERS]/[bedes]], it is thus conceivable that contextualized interpretation might yield the nonce schema ((BEADS)/[bedes]), through implicit invocation of the *tokens* component of the counting ICM.[7]

Contextual emergence of such a nonce schema need not vitiate the communication process. This is because within the formulaic prayer ICM, a circle of rosary beads stands in one-to-one correspondence with a cycle of formulaic prayers. But on the present account of the *bedes* shift, this token relationship is not the basis for a cognitive mapping process that derives the newer schema from the older one. Rather, it is simply an aspect of shared encyclopedic knowledge that allows communication to proceed without a hitch, despite hearers' abductive inference of a *bedes* schema unconnected with the conventional one invoked by speakers. Speaker and hearer can understand each other perfectly, even while having recourse to radically different schemas for the word in question, and without either party having

7. Or, in cases like (4a–b), by invoking a specific interpretation heuristic: "When someone utters a deictic expression like *this/that {X}* while pointing at an object, assume that *X* refers to the object indicated."

ever established any mapping between the two. Consider, for example, a conversational adjacency pair consisting of sentences (4a) and (5a) above (with or without intervening material):

(6)	A:	*This one here is your first Hail Mary* ***bede.***	[[PRAYER]/[bede]]
	B:	*Which one did you say was my first Hail Mary* ***bede?***	((BEAD)/[bede])

The dialogue can count as fully successful communication even if the two parties are accessing distinct schemas. The hearer has essentially grasped the speaker's intent, without having accessed the particular "case" (the symbolic schema) that had sanctioned the "result" (the target structure) in the latter's mind.

What makes such an abductive reanalysis account preferable to one based on speaker creativity? In the first place, it remains true to the traditional intuition that this sort of change does not hinge on any judgment of similarity, but that some kind of associative leap is involved. More importantly, it provides a plausible account of the activation and spread of the change. Since speakers are assumed to be behaving conventionally, the analysis depends neither on apprehension of a lexical gap, nor on the improbable scenario of many speakers converging upon the same rather strained schema-to-schema mapping in order to fill it. The *actuation* of change is instead located in contextual inferences that might plausibly be drawn separately by many hearers. The change's *spread* is also more straightforwardly accounted for. Even assuming that speakers had innovated a ((BEADS)/[bedes]) schema, hearers would still require evidence that they were invoking it, rather than the conventional one. At best, this would only become clear if a speaker subsequently re-invoked the innovative schema to sanction utterances that made no sense in terms of the conventional schema. But that would require that the innovative schema had meanwhile become so dissociated from the conventional one that the speaker could use the old word in the new sense with no sense of homonymic clash. On the abductive account, this problem need not arise, since the hearer has made no connection between older and newer schemas. The innovative schema thus has a far greater chance of moving from nonce to entrenched status, as it is reinforced by each successive usage event that can be successfully interpreted with reference to it. Hearers are also more likely to invoke the new schema to sanction utterances incompatible with the older schema. Utterances like those indicated at (T2) and (T3) in Figure 3 receive full sanction from the new schema, which from the start has no intrinsic connection with the conventional schema.

3. A further example: the Dutch *winkel* shift

Geeraerts (1997: 76–77) discusses several semantic changes in the history of Dutch as instances of what he (following Dik 1977) calls inductive change based on a salient subset of a word's overall extension. One involves the shift of *winkel* from its original sense 'angle' or 'corner' to the now current sense 'shop'. Geeraerts first outlines the shift in terms of a series of small, incremental steps forming a logical bridge from the one sense to the other, and then considers what sort of change might be involved in each step. The posited steps are shown in (7).

(7) a. 'a corner'
b. 'a street corner'
c. 'a building situated on a street corner'
d. 'a shop situated on a street corner'
e. 'a shop (wherever situated)'

In Geeraerts' analysis, the *winkel* case involves two stages at which a salient subset of a broader set of referents constitutes the point of departure for inductively based sense shift. First, within its general range of application (including all sorts of things construable as 'angles' or 'corners'), *winkel* gets prominently applied to 'street corners' (b). This forms the basis, via "inductive metonymy", for the sense 'building situated on a street corner' (c). Second, within the wider range of application of this new sense we have the salient subset 'shop situated on a street corner' (d). This finally forms the basis, via "inductive generalization", for the emergence of the general sense 'shop' (e).

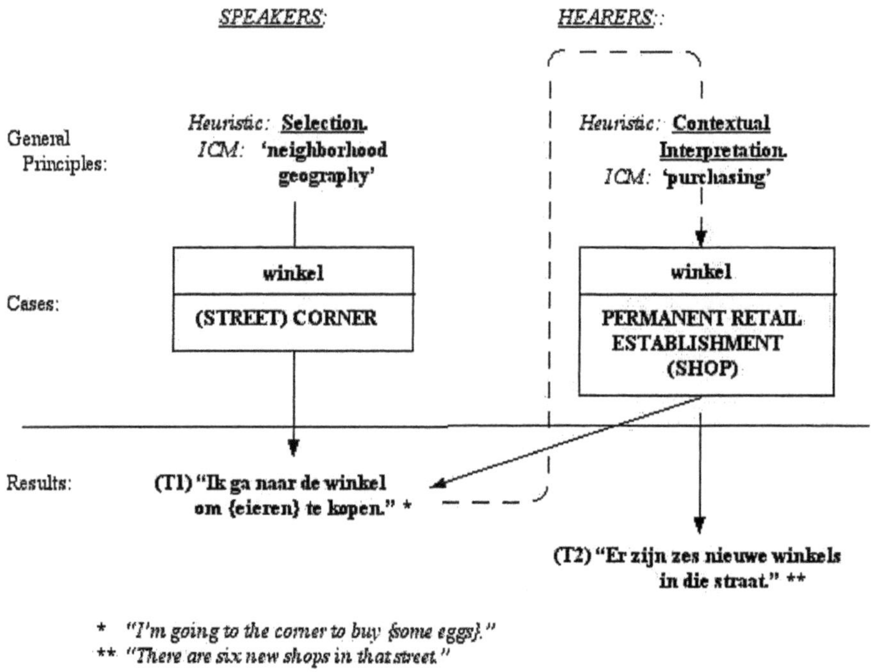

Figure 4. The *winkel* shift as context-based abductive reanalysis.

The analysis raises a number of questions. Are all these discrete steps needed? Who exactly is performing these inductive operations, and why? More fundamentally, is anyone really performing any sort of operation on symbolic units as such, so as to transform them into other symbolic units?[8] Finally, even granting that each of the posited

8. Geeraerts notes that "it is not excluded that the semantic development is psychologically taken in one step" (1997: 82, note 25). In a summary footnote to the whole section (note 27), he observes that the relationship between Dik's notion of inductive change and Peirce's concept of abduction needs further exploration.

operations might conceivably occur in the minds of individual speakers, how would this add up to a sense shift in the language?

Consider now the abductive reanalysis account outlined in Figure 4 above.[9] The crucial point of reference here involves situated utterances like:

(8) *Loop eens gauw naar de winkel om een doosje eieren.*
'Would you mind hopping down to the corner/the shop for some eggs?'

One might argue that such utterances are based on the metonymy LOCATION FOR BUILDING AT LOCATION, but any apparent metonymy is probably best understood in terms of referential vagueness.[10] The speaker assumes that, given a shared mental map of the neighborhood, the hearer will infer that *winkel* refers to the establishment located at the particular street corner where one can buy eggs (or whatever). Under the appropriate circumstances, hearers will have no trouble drawing the correct inference.[11]

---

9. I assume that 'street corner' is at the outset already an entrenched, fully conventional subsense of *winkel*. Nothing is lost if one assumes only the more general sense 'corner', supplemented by contextual inference.
10. Consider *I'm going downtown to meet some friends*. Normally, hearers will assume that the speaker's destination is some building situated downtown. Does this imply a metonymic extension LOCATION FOR BUILDING AT LOCATION? Not necessarily. The intended destination is simply "downtown" – a case of referential vagueness, which hearers construe in terms of world knowledge. The same applies to examples like *I'm going to the corner to buy eggs*, uttered in situations involving shared knowledge of neighborhood geography.
11. Cf. Langacker (1993) on metonymy as a reference point phenomenon, and Traugott and Dasher's (2002) model of semantic change based on invited inferences (Geis & Zwicky 1971). The present approach, however, does not depend on acts of oblique reference or implication by speakers. While such strategies may enter into the *winkel* scenario sketched here, nothing need be involved beyond referential vagueness (cf. the preceding footnote). In the *beads* case, hearers' inferences are even less likely to have been intentionally invited by speakers.

Hearer inferencing may even go further, yielding a novel construal of lexical meaning based on a rich understanding of the syntagmatic and situational context of the usage event as a whole. Imagine the following scenario. You are a Dutch speaker living at a time and place where the symbolic pairing [[STREET CORNER]/[winkel]] is established, but there is as yet no conventional schema [[PERMANENT RETAIL ESTABLISHMENT]/[winkel]]. Your neighborhood has two places where one can buy eggs: a traditional open-air market in the town square, where producers ply their wares on Wednesdays and Saturdays, and a permanent retail establishment that has recently opened for business on the ground floor of a building at the intersection of two local streets. On Monday, a family member or neighbor says to you, *Ik ga naar [xxxxx] om eieren te kopen*. (Assume that someone nearby coughed loudly at the precise moment when the destination is being specified.) You may not have accessed the speaker's particular solution to the encoding problem (viz., her/his choice of an expression meaning 'street corner'), but you have no trouble inferring her/his meaning. You note that the construction *ik ga naar {x} + {infinitival purpose complement}* implies going to a location for some purpose, and that the particular purpose complement (*om eieren te kopen*) implies buying something. Syntagmatic context alone thus enables you to construct provisionally ((PLACE FOR BUYING THINGS)/(xxxxx)). Encyclopedic knowledge (the fact that Monday is not market day) enables you to refine this further into the nonce specification ((PERMANENT RETAIL ESTABLISHMENT, i.e., SHOP)/(xxxxx)).

Now consider the same situation without the cough. Will your discernment of the word *winkel* necessarily change the process that you go through in inferring the speaker's meaning? You might of course fully reconstruct the speaker's solution to the coding problem; realizing that her/his reference is to a street corner, you proceed to infer that the corner in question must be the one with a shop on it. But your inferential process may remain just as in the "cough" scenario. The linguistic context (reference to intended purchase at a specified destination), together with situationally relevant world knowledge, impels you to jump straight to an appropriate contextual construal that by-passes the conventional symbolic pairing [[STREET CORNER]/[winkel]], yielding instead a nonce variant ((SHOP)/[winkel])). This is all the more likely if you are a child or a foreigner who has not yet fully acquired the conventional sense(s) of *winkel*. But if on-line contextual interpretation indeed involves parallel distributed processing (Rumelhart and McClelland 1986), even fully fluent adults may make such inferential "end runs" around lexical convention.

Other things being equal, such a nonce schema is likely to fade away. If, however, you keep hearing usage events that are interpretable with reference to it, it may undergo progressive entrenchment within your lexicon. You may well then access the new schema as a speaker in similar contexts. Since, however, this schema specifies only the notion "shop", you will likely use it indiscriminately for such establishments, regardless of location (cf. the utterance at (T2) in Figure 4). Far from relying on partial sanction to generalize a specific locational schema ((SHOP SITUATED ON A STREET CORNER)/[winkel]), you are simply applying your newly abduced schema with full sanction to new situations. Your hearers can now make one of two assumptions: either you're mad, or you are familiar with a conventional usage of *winkel* that had thus far escaped their notice. In the latter case, they will easily infer the relevant schema, and (depending upon sociolinguistic variables affecting the likelihood of their taking your usage as a model) they may even add it to their own repertoires.

Rather than a series of operations that progressively transform the sense '(street) corner' into 'shop' via intermediate senses like 'building/shop situated on a street corner', this abduction scenario essentially occurs in a single step. No mental operation of any kind has been performed on the conventional schema to derive the new one. The inference yielding the schema ((SHOP)/[winkel]) was based, not on a pre-existing schema involving *winkel*, but on richly contextualized interpretation within situated usage events. Elements intrinsic to a standard 'purchasing' frame (including notions of exchanging money for goods at particular locations established for that purpose) have been imported into the new schema for *winkel*, while core elements of the conventional schema (excepting only perhaps the very general feature of location) have simply disappeared, all at one blow.

Let us return to the questions originally posed with regard to a speaker-based analysis of the *winkel* shift. Even granting that the posited process might have occurred in the minds of a few speakers (the actuation problem), how do we account for such a shift spreading throughout an entire speech community? As far as actuation is concerned, we may suppose that many hearers, in the context of many separate usage events, would abductively extract the new schema. In a cultural setting where street corners are often occupied by retail establishments, an expression meaning ‘street corner’ is quite likely to crop up independently in many usage events involving purchase at a location. This provides considerable raw material for abduction, the more so if the particular expression used for ‘(street) corner’ is currently experiencing competition from an alternate expression (in this case, *hoek*).

As for spreading, there is a powerful dynamic favoring the propagation of the abductively derived schema. Anyone who (as hearer) has abduced the new schema is subsequently likely as speaker to begin applying it with full sanction in contexts where the old schema is inapplicable. Those who do not discount such usages as infelicitous will be inclined to induce the new schema and, under favorable sociolinguistic conditions (involving speaker-hearer relationships within local social networks), will begin applying it themselves. All in all, the usage-based abduction scenario offers a more compelling story about the actuation and spread of the change than do accounts that involve speakers progressively modifying a source schema toward a target schema.

4. Metonymic sense shift without metonymic construal?

The metonymic sense shifts just examined are different in nature from the figures of speech illustrated in (1). First, one may ask whether any of the latter represent a likely point of departure for the emergence of a new basic sense for the figuratively used expressions.

Concerning (1a), for example, what is the likelihood of the customer becoming renamed in the speech community as *Ham Sandwich*? Or what are the chances of our forgetting that *Lakoff and Johnson* (1c) is not really a book title? While the latter sort of designation is indeed conventional, and the former sort of situation does occasionally give rise to jocular nicknames that "stick", such usages remain obvious metonymies, and are hardly susceptible to reanalysis. Secondly (and more tellingly), one may ask whether a given ostensibly metonymic usage is in some contexts susceptible to a conventional, non-figurative interpretation. In (1a), can we assume that a sandwich has literally walked out of the restaurant? Surely not. We can however assume in cases like (3) and (8) that someone is literally counting her/his prayers or is literally headed for the corner. Our default assumption must be that such utterances were first said in a conventional, non-figurative sense.[12]

Shall we then say in such cases it is not speakers, but hearers who entertain a figurative construal of the expression?[13] This would be to assume that, given a conventional ("literal") and an innovative

12. Warren (1998) speaks of *implication* for cases where an expression is used literally, but where a secondary meaning typically associated with a particular context becomes conventionalized. (Example: someone who "hangs up" a telephone receiver is, by implication, ending the conversation.) Warren notes that in "implicational" shift (what Stern 1931 called "permutation", see below) the concomitance relation is not between entities, as in "referential" metonymy, but between contextualized propositions. For recent developments along similar lines, elaborating earlier work on strengthening and conventionalization of inferences that emerge in discourse (e.g., Traugott & König 1991), see Traugott and Dasher (2002). While sympathetic to this line of thought, I insist that the crucial hearer inferences have not necessarily (in cases like *winkel*) or even probably (in cases like *beads*) been "invited" by speakers. That presumption seems to be based on a model of change that requires direct mapping between earlier and later senses of an expression. It is precisely this requirement that I am questioning.
13. Koch (1999) might be interpreted in this sense. Koch recognizes the role of context-based hearer inferencing in such diachronic shifts, but (against Warren 1998, 1999) insists on the necessity of retaining discourse-based metonymic shifts (Warren's "implications"/Stern's "permutations") in the category of changes involving mapping between contiguous concepts within a larger frame.

("metonymic") sense of a word, someone must have derived the latter as a partially sanctioned extension from the former. Yet the cumulative force of the argument in sections 2 and 3 has been that no one, neither speaker nor hearer, has engaged in figurative construal. Each party accesses only one schema for the expression in question, and for each party, that single schema *fully* sanctions the expression's occurrence within the usage event. Speakers are speaking conventionally, and hearers, without misapprehending the communicative intent behind the usage event, are nonetheless contextually interpreting the word in question without reference to its conventional sense. What we have, in effect, is metonymic sense shift without any psychological process of metonymic construal.

5. Abduction in a usage-based model of semantic change

Langacker (1999a: 21–24) models the relationship between "compositional" and "contextual" values of a complex expression in a way that may contribute toward an understanding of how metonymic sense shift occurs in the absence of figurative or conceptual metonymy. In this final section, I first review Langacker's treatment of semantic extra-compositionality, and then show how the model, as it stands, nevertheless remains inadequate to the task of accounting for metonymic shift. Finally, I argue that the task can be accomplished through two adjustments to the dynamic usage based model: (i) extending its treatment of compositionality to comprise a phenomenon I call *semantic backformation*, and (ii) broadening its conception of usage events to comprise the distinctive role of hearers in construing relationships between contextualized speech and the linguistic system.

Langacker uses English instrumental nouns like *eraser* and *printer* to illustrate the distinction between compositional and contextual values of expressions (1999a: 19f, 23f). The relevant relationships may be visualized as in Figure 5. [C] represents an abstract compositional schema that is part of the grammar of the language [L], in the

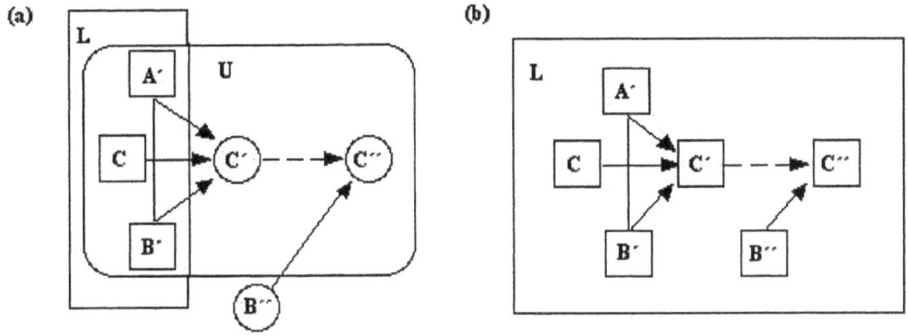

Figure 5. Semantic extra-compositionality and semantic backformation.

present case, a schema for suffixal derivation of deverbal nouns. It is composed of schematic elements [A] (the suffixal pattern) plus [B] (an abstract representation of the verbs that can elaborate it); for simplicity, these components are not shown in Figure 5 (see Langacker 1999a, Figures 8 and 9 for more detailed diagrams). (C') represents the purely compositional value of a new expression that is latently present in the language as an elaboration of the more abstract schema, and which speakers may choose to employ in the context of specific usage events (U). The instrumental noun *printer*, with the compositional meaning 'something that prints', would be a composite of the particular derivational schema [[SOMETHING THAT {v}s]/[{V}er]] and the particular verb *print* (cf. [A'] and [B'] respectively in Figure 5). (C") represents whatever additional, extra-compositional elements of meaning may accrue to the expression by virtue of routine use in particular sorts of context, for example, the special sense of 'device for producing hardcopy printouts of computer files'. The square boxes in Figure 5b represent the outcome of the process whereby both compositional and contextual values become entrenched in linguistic convention [L] through constant usage in similar contexts.

One last point, thus far not explicit in Langacker's model of semantic extra-compositionality, is crucial for an adequate understanding of metonymic sense shift. Emergence of the contextual sense (C") implies a potential for "semantic backformation" of a new, more elaborated schema for the autonomous component [B'], which, if realized, may be designated as (B"). In the present case, this would yield a new schema for *print* with the sense 'to produce a hardcopy printout of a computer file'.[14] These facts are summarized in (9):[15]

(9) A': [[SOMETHING THAT {V}S]/[{V}er]]
B': [[TO PRINT]]/[print]]
C': [[SOMETHING THAT PRINTS]/[printer]]
C": [[DEVICE FOR PRODUCING HARDCOPY OF COMPUTER FILES] /[printer]]
B": [[TO PRODUCE HARDCOPY OF A COMPUTER FILE]/[print]]

Langacker points out that [C"], in all its extra-compositional specificity, is crucial to any description of the instrumental noun *printer* in present-day English. (Pairings like *((PRINTING PRESS)/[printer]), which [C'] might otherwise sanction, are not sanctioned.) Nonetheless, the purely compositional schema [C'] is hardly eclipsed, since *printer* has not lost its motivated status as an instantiation of the general schema [A']. Thus, Langacker argues, the relevant sense of *printer* may best be represented by the complex schema [[C'] → [C"]].

How might this aspect of the dynamic usage based model help elucidate the sense shifts presently under discussion? (10) and (11) show a plausible representation of the facts:

14. Cf. the well-known process whereby a verb like *babysit* is derived by backformation from a composite agentive noun like *babysitter* (originally *baby* + *sitter*). Semantic backformation differs from such examples only in that the formal result is isomorphous with one of the original input forms (i.e., [print]" = [print]'). In the present case, a specific computer sense for *print* conceivably preceded the entrenchment of *printer* in its computer-related sense. The semantic backformation treatment here has a heuristic purpose, as will become apparent.

15. C', C", and B" begin as nonce schemas ( ); for simplicity, only their subsequent entrenchment [ ] is represented here.

(10) A': [[TO COUNT {SOMETHING}]/[tell {NP}]]
B': [[PRAYERS]/[bedes]]
C': [[TO COUNT ONE'S PRAYERS]/[tell one's bedes]]
C'': [[TO COUNT ONE'S BEADS]/[tell one's bedes]]
B'': [[BEADS]/[bedes]]

(11) A': [[GO TO {LOCATION} (TO {DO STH})]/[naar {LOCATION} gaan ({iets doen})]]
B': [[THE (STREET) CORNER]/[de winkel]
C': [[GO TO THE CORNER (TO BUY {STH})]/[naar de winkel gaan (om {iets} te kopen)]]
C'': [[GO TO THE SHOP (TO BUY {STH})]/[naar de winkel gaan (om {iets} te kopen)]]
B'': [[THE SHOP]/[de winkel]]

In many respects, the situation is parallel to that shown in (9), despite the fact that the composite structure [C'] involves a derivational morphological schema in the one case and a syntactic schema in the others. But is the meaning best characterized as [[C'] → [C'']], as in the case of *printer*? After all, C'' in (10) and (11) does not merely represent a more highly specified elaboration of C'. (The same is all the more true for B' and B''.) Despite formal identity, we have here a marked discontinuity between contextual and compositional meanings. Is anyone likely to have had the two schemas in mind at once?

At least one authority on semantic change seems to have answered these questions in the affirmative. Gustaf Stern (1931) distinguished figurative metonymies (which he called "metaphors based on other relations" [viz., other than similarity]) from "permutations" like that involved in the *beads* shift (1931: 326ff, 351ff). He moreover recognized the latter as crucially involving an unconscious reapprehension of the given word's meaning within the context of a larger phrasal usage, in situations where either the conventional or the innovative sense of the word may be assumed without affecting the sense of the phrase as a whole. His analysis of the *beads* shift is thus like that presented here, except that he stipulates that it must have occurred primarily in the minds of speakers, not hearers.[16]

While denying that speakers who utter phrases like *tell {one's} beads* intentionally set about using an old word to express a new meaning, Stern's analysis does require that the shift be based upon the emergence in speakers' minds of something like the complex schema [[C'] → [C'']] in (10) above, with ultimate suppression of the compositional sense [C'] in favor of the contextually based extra-compositional sense [C'']. The trick, for Stern, is that the two senses must not be activated at once, lest the speaker become conscious of the radical discrepancy between the emergent component word-level schema (B'') and the conventional one [B']. For Stern, the shift thus requires a lengthy "period of preparation" during which, within the context of the relevant phrasal usages, the speaker's lexical representation imperceptibly slips from the one meaning to the other. Besides this problem, there is the issue of how to account for the ultimate spread of the new sense beyond the sorts of contexts that had originally licensed its emergence. In order for the same speakers to begin using *beads* with reference to necklaces (or *winkel* for shops in general), yet a further process of change must intervene, which Stern (1931: chap. 14) terms "adequation".

These problems vanish when one drops the assumption that it is necessarily speaker choice (conscious or not) that drives semantic change. Psychologically speaking, there is no strain (and no need for Stern's period of preparation) on a hearer-based account, because no

16. Stern's reasoning on this point is unclear. He asserts without argument that hearer misapprehension of a word's conventional semantic value would not constitute a "normal psychic process", suggesting that "permutations are too common to be due to misunderstandings", and that "[t]he hearer, like the speaker, must be assumed to know his native language" (1931: 36). Ultimately, his rejection of any crucial role for hearers appears to be based on a doctrinaire preconception that any scientific theory of semantic change must be grounded solely in the communicative and expressive purposes to which speakers put language (1931: 182 *et passim*). Nonetheless, in discussing causes of semantic change (1931: 173–174), he does suggest that permutations differ from most other semantic shifts precisely in involving a crucial element of hearer interpretation.

direct link between C' and C'' (let alone between B' and B'') need ever be established in anyone's mind. By the same token, there is no need for any separate adjustment process (Stern's adequation) in order to free the innovative sense from the particular contextual nexus that gave rise to it. Once hearers have abduced the new schema [[BEADS]/[bedes]] – or [[SHOP]/[winkel]] – it is immediately applicable, without strain (i.e., with full sanction), in the full range of relevant environments.

What then of Stern's objection that "[t]he hearer, like the speaker, must be assumed to know his native language" (1931: 360)? In the context of a usage event, speakers presumably have the relevant lexical conventions more firmly in mind than hearers. Since it is speakers who have selected the component schemas for assembly, they will normally be more immediately cognizant of their conventional senses. Hearers, on the other hand, often arrive at an adequate construal of contextual meaning (and of speaker intent) without analyzing each individual component of the utterance in terms of semantic convention.

By virtue of its attention to contextually emergent extra-compositional meaning, Langacker's dynamic usage based model thus proves very useful in analyzing the process of metonymic sense shift. Several otherwise vexatious problems disappear when one assumes that innovative lexical senses emerge through semantic back-formation from extra-compositional meanings of phrasal assemblies within which they routinely occur. The success of this approach, however, suggests a need for reassessing the model's conception of usage events.

Langacker defines a usage event as "the pairing of a vocalization, in all its specificity, with a conceptualization expressing its full contextual understanding", adding that "for present purposes, it makes no difference whether we consider the speaker or the addressee, since each has to establish some connection between the linguistic system and a usage event that supposedly manifests it" (1999a: 7–8). Yet for purposes of understanding semantic change, this distinction does evidently make a difference, as does the precise nature of the established connection. We have seen that it is in the minds of hearers that contextually emergent meanings are most likely to gain ascendancy over purely compositional ones, since speakers are relatively constrained by the conventional senses of the individual items that they have selected in formulating the utterance. Though extra-compositional meanings are by no means excluded for speakers, they are less likely to become unmoored from more conventional and fully compositional senses. Given that some sorts of semantic change appear to involve just such an unmooring of contextual from compositional meaning, it would seem advisable to elaborate the dynamic usage-based model in a manner that recognizes the distinctive concerns and strategies that hearers bring to the contextual interpretation of usage events.

Indeed, usage events are best understood not only as a manifestation of the speaker's conceptualization and selection process, as if the hearer's role were simply to recapitulate that process in reverse. Rather, usage events should be treated as the focal point for a reciprocal negotiation of meaning, with hearers crucially and creatively involved in ways that do not simply mirror the cognitive activity of speakers. Such an adjustment is profoundly consistent with the spirit of the usage-based model, particularly with its character as a bottom-up approach grounded in concrete human problem-solving behavior. It also enables us (*pace* Stern) to understand contextually based abductive reanalysis by hearers as a "normal psychic process" that plays an important role both at the micro-level of everyday conversational interactions and at the macro-level of long-term systemic change.[17]

---

17. Abductive reanalysis may figure in semantic shifts other than those conventionally termed metonymic. Queller (2001: 70–73) argues that apparent garden-variety metaphorical extensions like *The children are fighting* ***over*** *who gets to go first* are better understood as products of abductively derived schemas that are no longer even metaphorically spatial in nature. Queller (in prep.) argues that abductive accounts of radial extension within the *over* network are generally preferable to ones invoking image-schema transformations and metaphorical construal.

References

Andersen, Henning
1973 Abductive and deductive change. *Language* 49: 765–793.

Croft, William
1993 The role of domains in the interpretation of metaphors and metonymies. *Cognitive Linguistics* 4: 335–370.

Dik, Simon
1977 Inductive generalisation in semantic change. In: Paul J. Hopper (ed.), *Studies in Descriptive and Theoretical Linguistics: Festschrift for Winfred P. Lehmann,* 283–300. Amsterdam: John Benjamins.

Geeraerts, Dirk
1997 *Diachronic Prototype Semantics: A Contribution to Historical Lexicology*. Oxford: Clarendon Press.

Geis, Michael L. and Arnold M. Zwicky
1971 On invited inferences. *Linguistic Inquiry* 2: 561–566.

Grondelaers, Stefan and Dirk Geeraerts
this volume Towards a pragmatic model of cognitive onomasiology.

Hopper, Paul J. and Elizabeth C. Traugott
1993 *Grammaticalization.* Cambridge: Cambridge University Press.

Jespersen, Otto
1922 *Language: Its Nature, Development and Origin*. London: Allen & Unwin.

Koch, Peter
1999 Frame and contiguity: On the cognitive bases of metonymy and certain types of word formation. In: Klaus-Uwe Panther and Günter Radden (eds.), *Metonymy in Language and Thought*, 139–167. Amsterdam: John Benjamins.

Kövecses, Zoltán and Günter Radden
1998 Metonymy: Developing a cognitive linguistic view. *Cognitive Linguistics* 9: 37–77.

Lakoff, George
1987 *Women, Fire, and Dangerous Things*: *What Categories Reveal about the Mind.* Chicago: The University of Chicago Press.

Langacker, Ronald W.
1987 *Foundations of Cognitive Linguistics*, Volume 1: *Theoretical Prerequisites*. Stanford: Stanford University Press.
1988 A usage-based model. In: Brygida Rudzka-Ostyn (ed.), *Topics in Cognitive Linguistics*, 127–161. Amsterdam: John Benjamins.
1993 Reference point constructions. *Cognitive Linguistics* 4: 1–38. (Reprinted in Langacker, 1999b, 171–202.)

1999 a A dynamic usage-based model. In: Michael Barlow and Suzanne Kemmer (eds.), *Usage Based Models of Language,* 1–63. Stanford: CSLI Publications. (Reprinted in Langacker, 1999b, 91–145.)

1999 b *Grammar and Conceptualization*. Berlin: Mouton de Gruyter.

Lightfoot, David
1979 *Principles of Diachronic Syntax.* Cambridge: Cambridge University Press.

McMahon, April M.S.
1994 *Understanding Language Change.* Cambridge, MA: Harvard University Press.

Peirce, Charles S.
1935–66 *Collected Papers of Charles Sanders Peirce* (C. Harshorne, P. Weiss and A. W. Burks [eds.]). Cambridge, MA: Harvard University Press.

Queller, Kurt
2001 A usage-based approach to modeling and teaching the phrasal lexicon. In: Martin Pütz, Susanne Niemeier and René Dirven (eds.), *Applied Cognitive Linguistics,* Volume 2: *Language Pedagogy,* 55–83. Berlin: Mouton de Gruyter.

in prep. Usage, abduction and the nature of polysemy.

Rosch, Eleanor
1977 Human categorization. In: N. Warren (ed.), *Studies in Cross-Cultural Psychology*, 3–49. London: Academic Press.

Rumelhart, David E. and James L. McClelland
1986 *Parallel Distributed Processing: Explorations in the Microstructure of Cognition*, Volume 1: *Foundations*. Cambridge, MA: MIT Press.

Stern, Gustaf
1931 *Meaning and Change of Meaning.* Bloomington: Indiana University Press.

Sweetser, Eve E. and Gilles Fauconnier
1996 Cognitive links and domains: Basic aspects of mental space theory. In: Gilles Fauconnier and Eve E. Sweetser (eds.), *Spaces, World and Grammars,* 1–28. Chicago: The University of Chicago Press.

Taylor, John
1995 *Linguistic Categorization: Prototypes in Linguistic Theory*, 2nd edition. Oxford: Clarendon Press.

Traugott, Elizabeth C. and Richard B. Dasher
2002 *Regularity in Semantic Change.* Cambridge: Cambridge University Press.

Traugott, Elizabeth C. and Ekkehard König
1991 The semantics-pragmatics of grammaticalization revisited. In: Elizabeth C. Traugott and Bernd Heine (eds.), *Approaches to Grammaticalization,* Volume 1, 189–218. Amsterdam: John Benjamins.

Warren, Beatrice
1998 What *is* metonymy? In: Michael Hogg and Linda van Bergen (eds.), *Historical Linguistics 1995*, 301–310. Amsterdam: John Benjamins.
1999 Aspects of referential metonomy. In: Klaus-Uwe Panther and Günter Radden (eds.), *Metonymy in Language and Thought*, 121–135. Amsterdam: John Benjamins.

Wittgenstein, Ludwig
1953 *Philosophical Investigations*. New York: Macmillan.

Growth of a lexical network: Nine English prepositions in acquisition

Sally Rice

Abstract

The early development of multiple sense types for the English prepositions *in*, *on*, *at*, *to*, *for*, *from*, *with*, *by*, and *of* has been charted on the basis of longitudinal data obtained from the CHILDES corpus for two English-speaking children. In Cognitive Linguistics, prepositions are assumed to be complex lexical categories each associated with a range of polysemous senses. This set of prepositions was selected on the basis of differences in the concreteness of their locative meaning, their varying semantic transparency across a range of sense types, their differing grammatical function, pragmatic relevance, frequency of occurrence, and overall shared monosyllabic shape. While inter-prepositional correspondences and discrepancies are of some interest, the discussion focuses on intra-prepositional commonalities and differences between these two children and addresses implications findings like these have for researchers in cognitive lexical semantics. Even a broad picture such as this of the progress of lexical acquisition by two children calls into question the applicability of certain cognitive mechanisms such as metaphor, metonymy, and schematization deemed to be responsible for the (uni-)directionality of semantic extension observed historically. These mechanisms, while not claimed to be teleological, can take a linguistic form with a concrete lexical meaning and eventually render it reduced, abstract, and highly grammaticalized in function. Such mechanisms are also assumed to have motivated lexical organization synchronically, i.e., in the adult speaker's mental lexicon (as given in lexical network models in Cognitive Linguistics). However, the data presented here suggest that each child seems to have his or her own starting point within a lexical category – one which may not be conceptually basic – with additional senses appearing in a piecemeal fashion, usually as part of a favorite fixed expression, rather than through stepwise semantic extension driven by processes such as metaphor and schematization.

Keywords: cognitive mechanisms, fixed expression, frequency, grammatical function, lexical acquisition, lexical category, linguistically motivated extension, locative meaning, metaphor, metonymy, monosyllabic, network model, non-basic sense, pragmatic relevance, prepositions, schematization, semantic extension, semantic transparency, sense types, uni-/directionality.

1. Introduction[1]

This paper is the initial report of a longitudinal study investigating how, when, and why two non-impaired, middle-class, American children have acquired different usages of locative particles, in this case, nine of the English prepositions.[2] Prepositions are widely asserted by cognitive linguists to be highly polysemous, and their multiple senses are assumed to be related semantically via a variety of construal mechanisms, including metaphor, metonymy, instantiation, schematization, image-schematic transformations, and so forth. Since this is the accepted wisdom in Cognitive Linguistics (henceforth, CL) and since I have long been interested in the meaning potential of locative terms, I have felt an imperative to investigate the nature of the early lexical acquisition of prepositions. By studying trends or sequences in a child's development of a lexical item, it is hoped that we can gain empirical grounds for evaluating many CL assumptions about polysemous lexical items, but at the very least have some inde-

---

1. This research was partially supported by grant #410-930205 from the Social Science Humanities Research Council of Canada. I would also like to thank the University of Antwerp (UFSIA) for their generous logistical support during my sabbatical stay there during the fall of 1996. Thanks, too, to two anonymous reviewers, whose careful and cogent comments helped me focus the ideas presented in this paper. Any remaining inadequacies are entirely my own.
2. An earlier version of this paper was presented at the "Workshop on Cognitive Approaches to Lexical Semantics" during the 16th Scandinavian Linguistics Conference held at the University of Turku, Finland, 15 November 1996.

pendent basis for formulating, testing, and evaluating our lexical models, especially network models.

The organization of this paper is as follows. In section 2, I make a case for bridging two separate gaps which weaken CL theory and which the discipline should begin to address as a maturing school of linguistic thought: (i) the gap between observations about what is essentially adult lexico-grammatical description (albeit semantically based) and child language data and (ii) the gap between theoretical claims and empirical evidence. While I do not presume that the fairly anecdotal and highly qualitative child language data presented here should actually influence the construction of theoretical models, I do believe that they can and should call into question many assumptions about semantic extension that are too often accepted unconditionally by adherents (e.g., that it is largely conceptually rather than linguistically motivated). In section 3, I recount how the language data for the two children in this study were collected, coded, and tabulated. I also summarize the findings in a general fashion. In section 4, I turn to specific points of similarity and contrast between the two children with respect to their learning to use a particular preposition. In section 5, I itemize factors which seem to affect the acquisition of multiple sense types for the nine prepositions under study here and, in section 6, I emphasize the need to incorporate these factors within a less unidimensional approach to the structure and evolution of lexical networks, that is, one based on multiple constraint satisfaction.

2. Theoretical context: Can acquisition data say anything about lexical networks?

The central assumption motivating the present study is that lexical acquisition data can contribute meaningfully to the discussion on the nature of lexical networks proposed by cognitive linguists. Whether explicitly stated as such or not, most lexical network models in CL are treated as representational models of the mental lexicon and are thus assumed to have some degree of psychological correspondence and relevance.[3] Although CL per se is less a well-integrated and fully realized linguistic framework than a theoretical stance taken partly in opposition to more form-based or generative paradigms in the field, it is highly compatible with well-accepted findings in cognitive psychology having to do with categorization by prototype (cf. Rosch 1975, 1978; Lakoff 1987; Taylor 1989; MacLaury 1991). This is especially evident in CL research on individual lexical items and constructions. I think it would be fair to summarize the major CL assumptions about the lexicon as follows (cf. Lakoff 1987; Langacker 1987, 1991a, 1991b; Goldberg 1996):

(a) most lexemes constitute complex categories having internal structure (i.e., all things considered, most words are polysemous, having multiple related senses);
(b) the multiple senses of a lexical item are distributed nonrandomly in some type of sense space, usually construed as a semantic network (i.e., the senses are organized horizontally around a prototypical sense or set of senses and vertically in relation to more schematic types or more specific tokens);
(c) the most prototypical senses tend to be those which are experientially grounded (i.e., somehow conceptually basic);
(d) additional senses (both abstract and novel ones) arise through either schematization or instantiation processes;
(e) lexical boundaries are porous and often indeterminate (i.e., since natural category boundaries are fuzzy, a word's meaning should be ambiguous or indefinite at the periphery of the category);
(f) and, more broadly, grammatical and lexical systems more or less directly reflect both conceptualization and conventional usage pressures rather than some innately given structural requirements.

3. See Sandra and Rice (1995), Rice (1996), and Sandra (1998) for a full description and critique of lexical network models in CL.

In truth, however, it is rather disingenuous to refer to a separate lexicon in CL. Grammar and lexicon are construed more or less equivalently, if indeed they are construed at all as atomic subcomponents of linguistic knowledge. In short, grammar and lexicon are one and the same. Linguistic knowledge has been best and most pithily characterized as "a structured inventory of symbolic units" (Langacker 1987: 57) rather than as a constructive device. Essentially a list of symbolic resources that a speaker uses to produce and comprehend both conventionalized and novel utterances, this inventory contains both specific expressions and schematic ones based on abstracted usage patterns (the latter are similar, perhaps, to generative rules or constructional templates) noted by the language user. Some version of this general view is adopted by most researchers in CL.

Thus far, the output of CL research has been generally descriptive and overwhelmingly synchronic. Although multiple points of correspondence are emerging between CL and research in what has come to be called grammaticalization theory in terms of the import placed on conceptualization strategies for shaping linguistic form (cf. Croft 1995 or Jurafsky 1996 for an overview), there is still a wide gap between CL theory and psychological claims about the nature of linguistic representation and processing (cf. Sandra & Rice 1995; Cuyckens, Sandra & Rice 1997; Sandra 1998; and Rice, Sandra & Vanrespaille 1999). Nevertheless, there are a number of empirical proving grounds available to CL, each with its virtues and limitations. Diachronic studies have allowed scholars to propose non-teleological mechanisms of linguistic change, lexical shift and expansion, and grammaticalization, although these mechanisms do not necessarily enjoy any appreciable degree of psychological reality in the minds of contemporary speakers and therefore should not be deployed automatically as either synchronic or developmental explanations of data patterns. Cross-linguistic verification of cognitive linguistic hypotheses is also required. Although few proposals in the theory are intended to have predictive power or universal scope (by virtue of being wedded to usage-based description), this limited applicability is at odds with the theory's general claims about cognitive motivation. Surely, the same mechanisms must be in evidence in a broad range of linguistically diverse languages or the very cognitive basis of CL would be in doubt. *Controlled psycholinguistic experimentation* is obviously an efficient and reliable means for collecting data for testing hypotheses. However, the results from any single experiment are necessarily inconclusive due to the likely potential for methodological flaws or task-related artifacts. Neither cognitive psychology nor psycholinguistics as generally practiced seem especially equipped or predisposed to study the particulars of word meaning beyond obvious cases of homonymy (i.e., ambiguity resolution). Therefore, it is incumbent upon cognitive linguists to lead the way in asking psychologically testable questions of its theory and identifying relevant experimental stimuli. Finally (and this is the empirical arena under discussion in this paper), *child language acquisition studies* can possibly shed light on questions about the nature of word meaning in the mental lexicon and the soundness of CL models about lexical representation.

Only through converging lines of evidence will we be able to have any confidence in our claims about the conceptual forces which shape linguistic (and lexical) systems. Conversely, it could very well be the case that empirical results from these four domains of inquiry give us diverging accounts of polysemy, conceptual similarity and distance, and semantic extension. For example, it could be found that cognitive mechanisms which operate(d) diachronically and typologically are not the same as those which operate in the mind of the adult speaker or developing child. Carpenter (1992) discusses cases in which the historical evolution of classifier systems does not mirror children's acquisition of those systems, thus calling into question much of CL's tacit assumption that phylogeny recapitulates ontogeny when it comes to semantic extension (cf. Slobin 1985 [a position which he later repudiates in Slobin 1997]; Sweetser 1990; Ziegeler 1997). Whereas facts like these are not fatal to CL theorizing, they do require much needed refinement to claims about the interaction between cognition and language, especially when language is undergoing change as it does over broad expanses of time within a given speech community or over more compressed episodes in the mind of the developing language user.

As it stands now, much of the CL literature describing the prevalence of polysemy in synchronic analyses of lexical and constructional categories claims that semantic extension is motivated by cognitive processes such as metaphor, metonymy, schematization, pragmatic inference, and the like. This research is highly consonant with findings in grammaticalization theory and most cognitive linguists are comfortable with an implicit notion that the synchronic array of polysemy patterns reflects historical development (which of course encompasses not just conceptually based abduction processes [see Queller, this volume], but borrowing, frequency, and cultural pressures as well). Historical linguists as far back as Meillet (1912 [1958]) have proposed clines of grammaticality or diachronic hierarchies which predict that a strong degree of unidirectionality obtains cross-linguistically with respect to semantic and/or functional change. Examples abound in the grammaticalization literature showing how various grammatical affixes have evolved from some unbound lexical item in the following general fashion: content item > grammatical word > clitic > inflectional affix (Hopper & Traugott 1993: 7). However, each grammaticalization theorist seems to have posited his or her own cline or hierarchy of change.[4] The unidirectionality claim is by no means without exception, but it is a powerful predictor of which of two general senses of an item (e.g., a locative versus a conjunctive usage of an adposition) was likely to have emerged first historically. Moreover, unidirectionality as a claim does not mean that sense A will inevitably turn into sense B as it changes semantically or recategorizes into a different form class. Both the A and B senses of an item can co-exist and even evolve into separate, newer senses. Nevertheless, it is to grammaticalization the-

4. Heine, Claudi and Hünnemeyer (1991) propose one whereby senses of an item or construction having to do with PERSONS outrank or are prior to those for OBJECTS > ACTIVITIES > SPACE > TIME > QUALITY. For Traugott (1982) and Traugott and König (1991), the hierarchy is not based on properties of the referent, but properties of the situation: EXTERNAL > INTERNAL, EXTERNAL/INTERNAL together > TEXTUAL/METALINGUISTIC, and all of the above > SPEAKER'S SUBJECTIVE BELIEF STATE. In short, usages having propositional content precede those with textual or expressive power.

ory (rather than CL) that we must turn for any explicit predictions about the order of emergence of different sense types of a linguistic form such as the nine English prepositions under investigation in the present lexical acquisition study.

Historically and typologically, there is a plethora of evidence accumulating that adpositions are notoriously polysemous and especially vulnerable to grammaticalization.[5] Multiple articles in the (1991) two-volume collection, *Approaches to Grammaticalization* edited by Traugott and Heine, attest to the fact that, all things being equal, adpositions evolve additional meanings and functions beyond their basic locative, lexical ones in the orders summarized in Table 1 (cf. in particular those studies by Hopper, Lichtenberk, Carlson, Genetti, and Craig).

Table 1. Some historically attested order-of-emergence patterns for divergent senses (S) and/or functions (F) of adpositions [> = precedes].

S1/F1	>	S2/F2
concrete	>	abstract
transparent *(i.e., referring to present situation)*	>	opaque *(i.e., non-referring; wholly conventionalized)*
spatial *(e.g., locative, directional)*	>	non-spatial *(e.g., dative, instrumental, purpose)*
spatial	>	temporal
adposition	>	particle *(e.g., conjunction, complementizer)*
lexical usage	>	grammatical usage
use in specific collocation	>	generalized application

The gap between CL theory and psychological claims about lexical polysemy is especially notable with respect to the nature of language acquisition, either by children or second language learners. There is a

5. These two findings are, of course, not at all independent.

general lack of research by cognitive linguists on the subject of acquisition (Carpenter 1992 and Ziegeler 1997 are rare exceptions), despite assertions elsewhere that the general cognitive approach is usage-based and speaker/conceptualizer-centered (cf. Tomasello 1992: 2–8). Indeed, the theoretical CL literature contains only a handful of explicit claims about the acquisition process, so few in fact that I will indulge in quoting one at length here:

> ...[the] model is said to take a "bottom up" approach. What this amounts to is a redistribution of emphasis: instead of being almost solely concerned with general rules and principles, we must also give substantial weight to their arrays of conventional instantiations, investigating the actual extension of the patterns in question and the factors that influence it. Furthermore, since patterns are abstracted from specific instances, we need to investigate the schematization process. We know, for example, that *speakers learn and manipulate specific expressions; but we do not know, in any direct way, precisely what degree of schematization they achieve, i.e. how abstract and general the rules are that they manage to extract from more specific structures. I suspect that speakers differ somewhat in this regard, and do not invariably arrive at the highest-level schemas that the data would support.* In any event, the omnipotence of high-level generalizations is not a matter of apriori necessity. Though regularities are obviously noted and employed in the computation of novel expressions, it is quite conceivable that low-level schemas are more important for this purpose than highly abstract schemas representing the broadest generalizations possible. If high-level schemas are extracted, they may be of only secondary significance, serving more of an organizing function than an active computational one. (Langacker 1991b: 265; emphasis mine)

CL lacks an explicit theory about the time-course, nature, and mechanics of language acquisition except for the rather minimalist comment by Langacker and statements by Tomasello which speak of CL's compatibility with cognitive and socio-cognitive models of acquisition. In short, the claim that grammar is meaning- and usage-based as well as experientially grounded, while sensible and plausible and accepted as an article of faith by adherents of CL, must be supported with empirical evidence. Grammar is deemed to be conceptually based, but such a claim may prove as vulnerable as the long vilified Derivational Theory of Complexity, the difference being that the primary domain under consideration is not one of structural, but conceptual complexity. More flesh needs to be put on a statement like the one given above if it is to carry any degree of descriptive let alone explanatory weight. In the absence of any other explicit claims about the acquisition of prepositional sense types in the CL literature, we could take the individual, pairwise, and *historical* orderings in Table 1 as a set of hypotheses about the order of emergence of sense types by *children*. Unfortunately, few of these specific ordering relations are borne out by the developmental data reported on in section 4 below. The theoretical ramifications of this incompatibility between historically prevalent patterns and the actual patterns of emergence shown by the two children in the present study are addressed in section 5.

3. Data collection and analysis

Previous developmental studies on lexical and grammatical acquisition have typically included data from select prepositions, notably *in* and *on*, concentrating especially on their basic spatial senses. Although Brown (1973) and Clark (1973) drew attention to the acquisition of prepositions early on, comparatively little work has been conducted on this word class. Most extant research has looked at the category *interlexemically*, comparing the overall onset patterns of different prepositions (cf. Johnston & Slobin 1979; Dromi 1979; and Furrow, Murray & Furrow 1985/6) rather than *intralexemically*, comparing onset patterns of different senses of a single preposition. There are a few notable exceptions of studies which have looked beyond the purely spatial in examining prepositional usage by young children (cf. Bloom, Tackeff & Lahey 1984; Tomasello 1987; and Clark & Carpenter 1989). I have long been interested in lexicosyntactic properties of prepositions as a class, including their extended uses. In this study, the acquisition of the prepositions *in, on, at, to, for, from, with, by*, and *of* was targeted and was done so for a variety of reasons. These nine prepositions are of relatively different frequency in the adult language; they differ also in their retainment of a basic spatial sense (although synchronically they can all still be used spatially, even *of* in limited cases), in the degree of abstraction they have attained when considering their entire usage potential, and in the degree of grammaticalization they have undergone (e.g., *on* is a verb particle as well as a preposition, *to* and *for* have become complementizers, *by* is used to mark agents in passive clauses, *of* marks partitive relations among others). Yet they are all monosyllabic, typically unstressed, and they tend to appear within the first two and a half years of an English-speaking child's life.

The data were taken from transcript files found in the CHILDES Archive (MacWhinney & Snow 1990).[6] The two children whose prepositional usages were examined for this study are Naomi (Sachs 1983) and Abe (Kuczaj 1976). These children were selected because their spontaneous utterances were regularly sampled in a home setting over the course of several years. Thus, we have both naturalistic and extensive production data on them.[7] (Most of the other longitudinal studies of non-impaired English-speaking children in the corpus do not cover such a wide period, or the sampling period begins well after the prepositions were first being used.) As shown in the first row of Table 2, the sampling window covers a period of well over two and a half years for both children. A cursory examination of Table 2 reveals that the age of onset for each preposition as well as the actual order of onset differs considerably for the two children. The operational criteria used for establishing age of onset (or first emergence) was either (i) the age at which two spontaneous usages occurred in a single sampling episode or (ii) the age at which at least one spontaneous usage was produced in an episode subsequent to a usage in a previous episode.

6. Roughly, the sampling intervals were monthly for most of the sampling period. In the case of Naomi, however, the available CHILDES files during her third year of life reflect approximately a bimonthly sampling interval and there is a gap of over a year between the penultimate and last transcript files for Naomi.
7. Only data from files sampled at (roughly) biweekly intervals were used in this study.

Table 2. The approximate age of onset for the nine prepositions by Naomi and Abe.

Age (yr; mo)	Naomi (1;3–4;8)	Abe (2;5–5;0)
1;7		
1;9		
1;11	on, in, at	
2;1	to	
2;3		
2;5	of, for	to, in, for
2;7	by	with, on, at, of
2;9	from	by
2;11		
3;1		from
3;3		
3;5	with	

Only prepositions used in combination with other words were coded and tabulated. Single-word or holophrastic utterances containing prepositions were extremely rare, but if present were coded as indeterminate and not further analyzed. Each contextualized usage of one of the targeted prepositions was coded for a wide variety of factors (similar to those used by Tomasello 1987 and Clark & Carpenter 1989). These factors encompassed both morphosyntactic and conceptual categories such as imitative usages, repetitions, errors, innovations, spatial usages (to mark static LOCATION as well as the SOURCE or GOAL of motion), temporal usages (to mark location in TIME, DURATION, FREQUENCY), abstract usages (to mark the SOURCE or GOAL of a transfer or communicative act, for example, or to mark relations as diverse as COMITATIVE, INSTRUMENTAL, DATIVE, BENEFACTIVE, PURPOSE, REASON, etc.), usages in fixed expressions, usages to mark ASPECT, grammatical usages (as a COMPLEMENTIZER or PARTITIVE marker), and so forth. Some of these factors are listed in Table 3 along with actual examples to illustrate.

Table 3. Factors for which prepositional usages were coded.

Coded factors	Sample utterances
SPATIAL LOCATIVE (S-LOC)	*Where's my other bag **at**? I want-ta do this* on *the table right now; No, I didn't tee-tee **in** my pants*
SPATIAL GOAL (S-GOAL)	*I need some **in** here, Mom, Throw it **on** the floor*
SPATIAL SOURCE (S-SOURCE)	*Take the toys **from** the bin; Here's a letter **from** Abe to Stan*
ABSTRACT LOCATIVE (A-LOC)	***on** TV, the girl **on** the tape-recorder*
ABSTRACT GOAL (A-GOAL)	*What is Mommy listening **to**? Pay attention **to** me*
ABSTRACT SOURCE (A-SRCE)	*Daddy, can we make something **with** this wood? I'm gonna get it **from** (by means of) this chair*
TEMPORAL (TEMP)	*She won't feel bad **in** the nighttime*
DURATION (DUR)	*He cried and cried **for** hundreds of weeks; We're going to the cabin **for** some days*
DATIVE (DAT)	*Give it **to** me*
BENEFACTIVE (BEN)	*And I got something **for** me*
COMITATIVE (COMIT)	*Sing **with** me*
ATTRIBUTIVE (ATTRIB)	*I like them **with** colors; the one **with** all the sand in it*
INSTRUMENTAL (INST)	*I'm gonna scrape the fish **with** this; We built a road **with** this truck*
PURPOSE	*What are these ones **for**? It's a cover **for** the teapot*
PHRASAL VERB	*look **at**, wait **for**, play **with***
FIXED EXPRESSION (FIX)	*Happy Birthday **to** you; Just **in** case; something is **on** fire; I don't think it's silly **at** all; Cutted a hole out **of** that thing*
INFINITIVE (INF)	*How about a fork **to** make designs*
COMPLEMENTIZER	*too frightening **for** me to tell it; She left **for** me to pick up the living room*
ERRORS (ERR)	*You can take it *__at__ (__to__) school and show your friends, You found it for me *__from__ (__in__) the tent*

Clearly, some usages of a preposition could be assigned multiple codes. Each code assignment is as subjective as its assessor, and no coding decision or coding scheme is uncontroversial or without limitations. The problem of sense determination plagues lexicographers and lexical semanticists as well and is an issue I have addressed elsewhere in print (cf. Rice 1996). For the purpose of this rather modest study, codes were chosen which were generally recognizable, had been used in other child language studies, or were applicable across multiple prepositions. Also for present purposes, usages which seemed to pertain to specific lexical collocations were treated and tabulated separately; for example, *at* in the expression *look at*. Each coded usage type was tallied as a percentage of overall uses of a particular preposition by a child. This allowed a number of specific comparisons to be made, for example, the usage context or sense type of the first appearance of a preposition, the overall range of sense types achieved by the end of the sampling period for a given preposition, the relative frequency of individual sense types, the percentage of spontaneous to non-spontaneous usages of a preposition or prepositional sense type, etc. It was hoped that these cross-child and cross-lexical comparisons would reveal something about conceptual versus linguistic transparency and complexity or, at the very least, some sort of developmental pattern.

Patterns observed for these two children and for these prepositions suggest that onset and, presumably, mastery of a particular sense type of a given item of this alleged lexical class is partly regular and partly idiosyncratic; is motivated by conceptual, linguistic, and pragmatic factors (such as communicative or interactional usefulness to the child or frequency in the adult input); can be rapid or slow; and that the successful acquisition of other parts of a child's lexicon plays a big role in the acquisition of individual prepositions. In short, not a lot of pattern was noted. Both children displayed rather distinctive styles and sequences of prepositional acquisition. For example, Abe is appreciably more verbose and linguistically innovative compared to Naomi. However, we have an incomplete picture of Abe's prepositional development since he already had started to use *to*, *in*, and *for* by the time spontaneous speech data were first collected on him.

By contrast, we do have a record of Naomi's language prior to and during her first uses of all nine prepositions under study. The actual preposition and sense type acquisition sequences for the two children are detailed in the next section.

4. Points of correspondence and contrast between Naomi and Abe

In this section, I will focus on several findings in particular: (i) the order of emergence of sense types for the nine prepositions by each child, (ii) the comparative frequency of the nine prepositions for each child, (iii) any trends observed in the data, and (iv) idiosyncratic features of each child's use of a specific preposition.

Figure 1 below compares the overall prepositional tokens produced by the two children.

Because Abe had over twice as many prepositions in his sampled utterances as did Naomi and because his ratio of spontaneous to non-spontaneous usages was consistently high, the prepositions are ordered horizontally in descending order based on Abe's usage. I have differentiated between spontaneous and non-spontaneous usages, the latter being comprised of self-repetitions or immediate imitations of the adult input (determined on the basis of having occurred within the last two conversational turns or the child's last three utterances). Neither errors nor non-spontaneous usages entered into the order-of-emergence compilation of sense type described below because the former were rare and because one cannot have much confidence that the latter are representative of the child's native linguistic ability at a given point in time.

Below, I describe for each preposition the first and subsequent sense types or usage contexts as they emerged for the two children during the sampling time-frame. The prepositions are presented in a somewhat random order based loosely on the fact that in their purported "basic" spatial senses, *on*, *in*, and *at* typically predicate static relationships such as contact between an entity and some landmark location (not to mention that *in* and *on* are widely believed to be the first prepositions to emerge in young children's speech); *to*, *for*, and *from* typically predicate dynamic relationships such as an entity's destination or origin of motion (Choi and Bowerman (1991) suggest that motion is conceptually more salient to a child than is static location so one might expect relationships involving motion to be coded before those involving stasis); while *with*, *by*, and *of* largely predicate abstract or grammaticalized relationships in Modern English such as instrumental, manner, agency, possession, association, comitative and only retain vestiges of their original spatial senses.

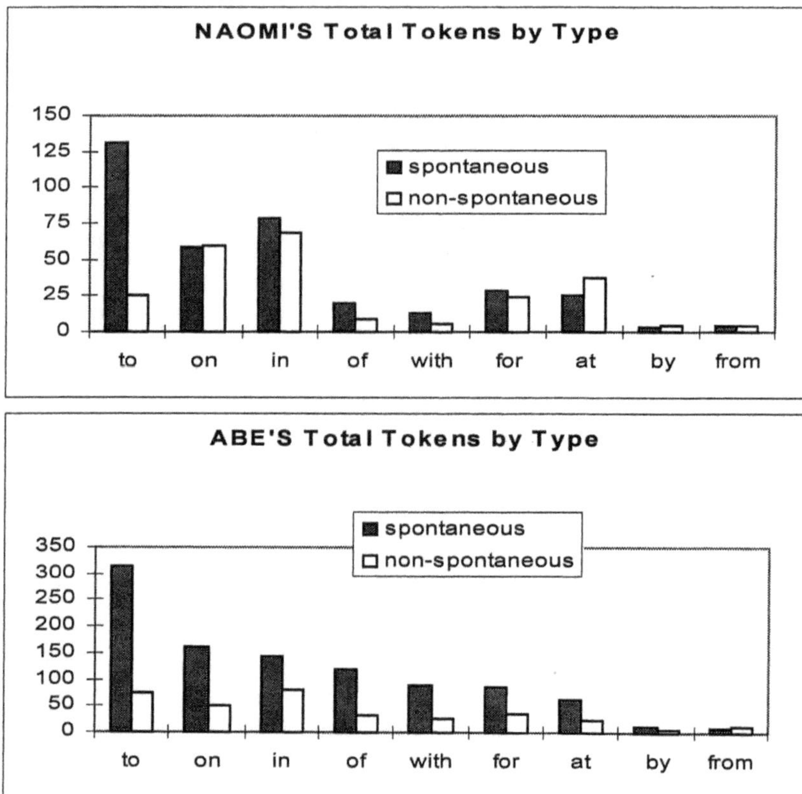

Figure 1. The overall prepositional tokens produced by Naomi and Abe.

For each preposition, I give two tables. The first table indicates the order of emergence and approximate age of the *first* recorded usage of each major sense type for the two children as reflected in their spontaneous speech. Note that this criterion is much less stringent than the one used for tabulating order of emergence by preposition in Table 2. The second table summarizes each child's overall usage frequency for a given preposition, including a breakdown of the non-spontaneous utterances and all the spontaneous ones subcategorized by sense type. In some cases, a preposition is only used in a specific, fixed expression such as *by* in *by myself*. In those cases or when the usage is limited to a particular domain such as *on* in *put CLOTHES on*, the actual usage context is spelled out rather than assigning it an abstract sense type such as SPATIAL LOCATION, whose code nomenclature is meant to reflect that the child has partially generalized the preposition in this subcategory.

ON. As shown in Figure 1, Abe had nearly twice as many usages of *on* in the sampled CHILDES files as did Naomi. Moreover, more than half of Naomi's uses of this item consisted of repetitions or imitations. Their respective emerging sense sequences are given in Table 4.

Table 4. Order of first emergence of major sense types of *on* by Naomi (N) and Abe (A).

N	*has CLOTHES on* (1;10)	*put CLOTHES on* (2;0)	S-GOAL (2;0)	S-LOC (2;3)	*turn MACHINE on* (2;6)	ASPECT (4;8)
	>	>	>	>	>	
A	S-GOAL (2;6)	S-LOC & *put CLOTHES on* (2;7)	*turn MACHINE on* (2;10)	*on TV* (2;11)	*has CLOTHES on* (3;2)	TEMP (4;11)

Table 5 shows the frequency of individual senses or usage types of *on* by each child.

Table 5. Child usage frequency of *on* [shaded lines indicate non-spontaneous or uncodable uses].

Sense type	Naomi		Abe	
imitations	20%		2%	
repetitions	14%		19%	
indeterminate usages	15%		3%	
errors	2%		0%	
S-LOC	14%		29%	
S-GOAL	11%		19%	
put CLOTHES *on*	7%		6%	
have CLOTHES *on*	3%		0%	
on TV	3%		7%	
fixed expressions	9%		11%	
Other	2%		4%	
Total of all uses	100%	(N = 119)	100%	(N= 211)

Both Naomi and Abe have developed a healthy repertoire of *on* uses by the end of the sampling period, although they are not quite the same uses. Clearly, the experientially basic (and highly frequent!) act of putting clothes on or the simple state of wearing clothes (e.g., *having a hat on*) provides a powerful bootstrap into this lexical category. Moreover, the preposition is phonologically salient in these contexts by virtue of it functioning primarily as a verb particle in *have X on* or *put X on* constructions. In these contexts, it is uttered in phrase-final position and receives primary stress. However, whether this bootstrap is conceptual, phonological, linguistic, or merely pragmatic remains to be seen. Not surprisingly, SPATIAL GOAL and SPATIAL LOCATIVE usages are prevalent and regularly generalizable. Moreover, SPATIAL usages precede TEMPORAL ones and other ABSTRACT usages. All in all, Naomi and Abe's developmental patterns for *on* seem quite consonant with the historical pattern evidenced by *on* and predictions emanating from the grammaticalization literature.

IN. Table 6 presents the developmental sequence for the emergence of different sense types of the preposition *in* by Naomi and Abe.

Table 6. Order of first emergence of major sense types of *in* by Naomi (N) and Abe (A).

N	S-GOAL (1;9)	S-LOC (2;0)	TEMP (3;2)	
	>	>	>	
A	S-LOC (2;5)	S-GOAL (2;7)	A-LOC & TEMP (3;0)	DURATION (3;2)

Table 7. Child usage frequency of *in* [shaded lines indicate non-spontaneous or uncodable uses].

Sense type	Naomi		Abe	
imitations	4%		3%	
repetitions	33%		32%	
indeterminate usages	9%		2%	
errors	0%		0%	
S-LOC	27%		23%	
S-GOAL	24%		24%	
A-LOC	0%		6%	
TEMP	1%		3%	
DURATION	0%		2%	
fixed expressions	2%		5%	
Other	0%		0%	
Total of all uses	100%	(N = 146)	100%	(N= 226)

As shown in Figure 1 and Table 7, nearly half of Naomi's uses of *in* were in non-spontaneous utterances. GOAL-directed usages preceded static LOCATIVE ones and there were very few TEMPORAL usages at all. By contrast, Abe used *in* for marking location before destination (GOAL). He also produced more ABSTRACT usages such as the following: *I'm in another quiet mood* (3;10.18) (ABSTRACT LOCATION); *because I didn't know anything to dream in the daytime, to sing in the nighttime* (3;7.21), *Daddy do you remember where I putted that surprise you gotted me in the morning* (4;1.15) (TEMPORAL); *We haven't color that in a long, long time* (3;1.22) (DURATION). Both children seemed to generalize SPATIAL GOAL usages with *in*, that is, they did not persist in using them exclusively with verbs such as *put*. A more complete picture of Naomi and Abe's respective proportion of different *in* usages is given in Table 7 above.

AT. For both children, *at* is a relatively low frequency item despite its early emergence, as shown in Table 2 and Figure 1 respectively. The majority of Naomi's usages of *at* were non-spontaneous (in fact, they were self-repetitions of utterances containing the expression *look at*, which turned out to be her dominant spontaneous usage of *at* as well). Table 8 summarizes Naomi and Abe's development sequence for this preposition and Table 9 gives the relative proportion of usages of *at* by Naomi and Abe.

Although the first usages of *in* and *on* for both children were SPATIAL, the first usages to emerge for *at* did not seem to be spatial at all and were only marginally prepositional (synchronically speaking). The developmental pattern for *at* is remarkable in the fact that both children began by using this preposition in the collocation *look at* and this usage either dominated or persisted as the major usage throughout the sampling period. Indeed, all of Naomi's repetitions involved *look at*. The phrasal verb *look at* has a great deal of pragmatic utility for any young child trying to draw the attention of caregivers. It is therefore not surprising that *at* should emerge first in this context. The near exclusivity of *at* in a *look at* collocation is consistent with Tomasello's Verb Island hypothesis whereby a morphosyntactic marker or associated lexical item first occurs exclusively with or in the context of a particular verb (Tomasello 1992). This hypothesis suggests that underextensions are the norm in child language acquisition, at least with respect to inflectional and relational items (cf. Bloom, Lifter & Hafitz 1980; Bybee 1985: 50–51, *passim*). CL theory would probably add that the first-to-emerge underextended form should be experientially grounded (which *look at* certainly is). Of course, one could argue that the child has not acquired *at* at all, merely the expression *look at*, in which the second morpheme is phonologically reduced compared to its pronunciation as head of an independent prepositional phrase such as *I found it at*

Table 8. Order of first emergence of major sense types of *at* by Naomi (N) and Abe (A).

N	*look at* (1;11)	S-LOC (2;5)	*at mealtime* (3;0)			
	>	>	>	>	>	
A	*look at* (2;6)	S-LOC (2;7)	TEMP (3;1)	*at the same time* (3;2)	*throw at* (3;5)	*at all* (3;11)

Table 9. Child usage frequency of *at* [shaded lines indicate non-spontaneous or uncodable uses].

Sense type	Naomi		Abe	
imitations	0%		2%	
repetitions	60%		10%	
indeterminate usages	0%		1%	
errors	0%		14%	
S-LOC	5%		40%	
TEMP	6%		6%	
look at	29%		20%	
fixed expressions	0%		7%	
Other	0%		0%	
Total of all uses	100%	(N = 63)	100%	(N= 87)

school. Spatial usages quickly emerged for both children as did TEMPORAL ones, thereby suggesting that conceptual basicness correlates with developmental priority. On the other hand, extremely ABSTRACT, semantically opaque usages such as *at the same time* or *at all* were soon produced by Abe as well, suggesting either that a lot of language production is the consequence of rote learning or that parental input and background frequency are important factors in shaping a lexical category along with conceptual basicness.[8]

8. A finding thoroughly supported by additional research of mine comparing the acquisition and usage frequency of different senses of *to* and *for* by thirty Brit-

TO. Figure 1 reveals *to* as the most frequently used of the nine prepositions by both Naomi and Abe. It was nearly twice as common as the next most frequent item. However, it is arguable as to whether or not two separate lexical items, a preposition and an infinitive marker, were being coded and counted as different instantiations of the same morpheme. Nevertheless, *to* is the only case in which Naomi and Abe's patterns were identical in terms of sense types achieved, order of emergence, and relative proportion of sense type use vis-à-vis all the senses in the lexical category. This parallelism can be seen in both Tables 10 and 11.

Table 11 indicates just how prevalent the heavily grammaticalized and purportedly semantically opaque INFINITIVAL sense of *to* is for both children. Taken at face value, this finding flies in the face of what grammaticalization theory would predict since lexical senses of an item predate grammatical ones historically. On the other hand, SPATIAL GOAL-of-motion usages do precede more ABSTRACT usages in transfer predications such as DATIVE uses as in *give to.* Nevertheless, we might want to question seriously whether or not INFINITIVAL *to* should even be considered an extended sense of the preposition *to.* This seems to be carrying polysemy too far for some. Cross-linguistically, however, complementizers routinely grammaticalize from locatives, especially from GOAL-markers (cf. Carlson 1991; Craig 1991; and Genetti 1991), so a connection is not unexpected. Moreover, there is precedence in the child language literature for assuming that English-speaking children might treat INFINITIVAL *to* as a special case of the preposition. Bloom, Tackeff and Lahey (1984) found that in four children's spontaneous speech, INFINITIVAL *to* emerged only in the context of a small number of verbs (reminiscent of Tomasello's Verb Island hypothesis discussed earlier) and did not behave as a meaningless syntactic marker. They reasoned, "Inasmuch as the preposition *to* in noun contexts in the children's speech always meant 'direction towards', the fact that they learned *to* in verb contexts at essentially the same time that they learned *to* in noun con

---

ish children with the usage frequency in their respective households (cf. Rice 1999).

Table 10. Order of first emergence of major sense types of *to* by Naomi (N) and Abe (A).

N	INFINITIVE (2;1)	S-GOAL (2;2)	misc. PHRASAL VERBS (2;5)	DATIVE (4;8)
	>	>	>	
A	INFINITIVE (2;5)	S-GOAL (2;6)	misc. PHRASAL VERBS (2;7)	DATIVE (3;0)

Table 11. Child usage frequency of *to* [shaded lines indicate non-spontaneous or uncodable uses].

Sense type	Naomi		Abe	
imitations	4%		4%	
repetitions	14%		14%	
indeterminate usages	3%		1%	
errors	0%		1%	
S-GOAL	9%		14%	
phrasal verbs	2%		5%	
DATIVE	2%		2%	
fixed expressions	7%		3%	
infinitive marker	59%		56%	
Total of all uses	100%	(N = 149)	100%	(N= 385)

texts added support to the conclusion that they learned *to* in verb contexts with that meaning" (1984: 403). There are certainly instances of INFINITIVAL *to* produced by Naomi and Abe that suggest it is an isolable, salient lexical item with GOAL- or PURPOSE-marking properties: *I wanna have something to eat* (3;2.21); Mother: *Why did you have your jacket on?* Abe: *Because why. To go outside* (3;5.17); or *I want something to get, to bring, to put in the truck* (4;8.14). I report similar acquisition results for *to* by thirty British-speaking children in Rice (1999).

FOR. *For* was one of Abe's first acquired prepositions, but except for an isolated use at 2;1, Naomi did not really start using it until she was almost two and a half. Neither child used it with much frequency except in collocations with *look for*. Nevertheless, as shown in Tables 12 and 13, each child achieved quite a range of different usages, most of which are highly abstract.

Table 12. Order of first emergence of major sense types of *for* by Naomi (N) and Abe (A).

N	BEN (2;1)	misc. FIXED & PURPOSE (2;5)	*look for* (2;8)	*for meal* & COMIT (3;2)	DURATION (4;8)		
	>	>	>	>	>	>	
A	BEN (2;6)	COMIT (2;7)	*for meal/ day* (2;11)	REASON (3;1)	DURATION (3;2)	*look/wait for* (3;3)	COMP (3;8)

Table 13. Child usage frequency of *for* [shaded lines indicate non-spontaneous or uncodable uses].

Sense type	Naomi		Abe	
imitations	4%		6%	
repetitions	38%		20%	
indeterminate usages	2%		4%	
errors	0%		0%	
BENEFACTIVE	22%		26%	
PURPOSE	4%		13%	
COMITATIVE	7%		5%	
DURATION	5%		7%	
REASON	0%		2%	
look/wait for (phrasal verb)	5%		5%	
for MEAL/HOLIDAY	2%		4%	
fixed expressions	9%		5%	
complementizer	2%		3%	
Total of all uses	100%	(N = 54)	100%	(N= 119)

While a considerable range of usages emerged for *for*, only BENEFACTIVE senses were used with much frequency. Curiously,

BENEFACTIVE usages of *for* emerged much earlier for both children than did somewhat comparable DATIVE usages of *to*, suggesting that linguistic factors, rather than purely conceptual ones, are partly responsible for extension within a lexical category. Furthermore, unlike the child reported on in Tomasello (1987), neither Naomi nor Abe used *for* erroneously (e.g., substituting *for* for *to* in a *give* construction).

FROM. From the information given in Table 2, Figure 1, and Tables 14 and 15, one sees that *from* was both a late acquired preposition for

Table 14. Order of first emergence of major sense types of *from* by Naomi (N) and Abe (A).

N	S-SOURCE (2;8)			
	>	>	>	
A	S-SOURCE (3;0)	*from Abe* (3;0)	A-SOURCE (by means of) (3;5)	*a day off from school* (4;5)

Table 15. Child usage frequency of *from* [shaded lines indicate non-spontaneous or uncodable uses].

Sense type	Naomi		Abe	
imitations	13%		14%	
repetitions	25%		18%	
indeterminate usages	13%		10%	
errors	0%		10%	
S-SOURCE	49%		28%	
A-SOURCE	0%		15%	
fixed expressions	0%		5%	
Total of all uses	100%	(N = 8)	100%	(N= 21)

both children and it manifested just about the overall lowest frequency despite the fact that it retains a strong SPATIAL sense in English. Moreover, the total number of spontaneous usages was just about equivalent to the non-spontaneous ones. Table 14 reveals that Naomi never produced any usages beyond a handful of SPATIAL ones, while Abe seems to have acquired a few more ABSTRACT usages. Table 15 gives the proportion of use by usage type of *from*.

BY. The preposition *by* was the least used of all nine items in this study. The order of emergence patterns are given in Table 16 and the proportion of usage types is presented in Table 17.

Table 16. Order of first emergence of major sense types of *by* by Naomi (N) and Abe (A).

N	*by myself* (2;3)			
	>	>	>	
A	S-LOC (2;5)	*by -self* (3;5)	PASSIVE AGENT (3;8)	TEMP (4;10)

Table 17. Child usage frequency of *by* [shaded lines indicate non-spontaneous or uncodable uses].

Sense type	Naomi		Abe	
imitations	14%		6%	
repetitions	29%		16%	
indeterminate usages	14%		6%	
errors	0%		0%	
S-LOC	0%		17%	
by –self	43%		16%	
by mistake	0%		17%	
passive agent	0%		16%	
TEMP	0%		6%	
Total of all uses	100%	(N = 7)	100%	(N= 18)

For the preposition *by*, its use by Naomi was confined throughout the sampled files to the expression, *by myself*, whereas Abe first used it as a SPATIAL LOCATIVE, then in productive *by -self* constructions, and then rather unexpectedly but completely spontaneously as a marker of a passive agent, *A baby butterfly was killed by a bird* (3;7.21). Finally, Abe had one instance of a TEMPORAL usage: *You were there by then when I was carving the top [of the pumpkin] off* (4;10.15). Because Abe is so expressive and precocious linguistically, it is difficult not to conclude that many of these abstract sense types are probably being used idiomatically.

WITH. With *with*, we have more evidence to support Tomasello's Verb Island Hypothesis. Dynamic uses of *with* with verbs of coming and going were the initial sense types for both children. Moreover, the experientially basicness and pragmatic utility of *playing with someone* or doing things with things (INSTRUMENTAL) or with other people (COMITATIVE) clearly motivated the majority of the instances of *with*. These uses emerged in the order given in Table 18. Their overall frequency is indicated in Table 19.

Table 18. Order of first emergence of major sense types of *with* by Naomi (N) and Abe (A).

N	*go with* (2;5)	*play with* (3;4)	INST (3;4)	ATTRIB (3;4)	*come with* (3;6)	
	>	>	>	>	>	
A	*come/go with* (2;7)	*play with* (2;8)	COMIT (2;8)	INST (2;11)	ATTRIB (3;1)	*make/build with* (3;7)

In addition, both Naomi and Abe used *with* to mark ATTRIBUTIVE relations such as *because you can shoot with your eyes closed* (3;9.19) or *[I want] toast with honey* (3;9.19). However, these uses are considerably more abstract and did emerge later, in keeping with what the grammaticalization evidence might predict.

Table 19. Child usage frequency of *with* [shaded lines indicate non-spontaneous or uncodable uses].

Sense type	Naomi		Abe	
imitations	0%		9%	
repetitions	17%		14%	
indeterminate usages	11%		0%	
errors	6%		0%	
INSTRUMENT	17%		20%	
ATTRIBUTIVE	6%		14%	
go/come with	11%		8%	
play with	21%		25%	
other COMITATIVE	11%		6%	
SOURCE	0%		4%	
Total of all uses	100%	(N = 18)	100%	(N= 115)

OF. Finally, *of*, arguably the most abstract and grammaticalized of all the prepositions under consideration here, was neither very late to emerge nor of particularly low frequency. The emergence pattern for *of* is shown in Table 20 and the overall proportion of usage types is shown in Table 21. Of course, *of* never really heads its own preposition phrase so much as it exists in an array of highly frequent collocations, to mark quantities (both quantals as in *half of the cookie* and sortals as *in a glass of milk*) and partitive relations (*the top of the refrigerator*). Both of these usages generalized early for both children.

Table 20. Order of first emergence of major sense types of *with* by Naomi (N) and Abe (A).

N	misc. FIXED (2;5)	QUANTIFIER (3;2)	
	>	>	
A	QUANTIFIER (2;6)	SORTAL (2;8)	misc. FIXED (3;0)

Table 21. Child usage frequency of *of* [shaded lines indicate nonspontaneous or uncodable uses].

Sense type	Naomi		Abe	
imitations	3%		6%	
repetitions	28%		14%	
indeterminate usages	0%		2%	
errors	0%		0%	
quantifier	41%		44%	
sortal/partonymic	0%		13%	
fixed expression	28%		21%	
Total of all uses	100%	(N = 29)	100%	(N= 152)

This is by no means a definitive study. It lacks the thoroughness, for example, of a case study like that reported in Tomasello (1987, 1992), or Moerk (1992). Not only were the sampling intervals fairly wide, but data from only two children were examined and not at a very finely-grained lexical or contextual level of detail, only at a broad semantic one. The pattern of prepositional errors and innovations, which have not yet been analyzed, should eventually yield some interesting data that may help indicate the role of conceptualization in the acquisition process. Although these findings remain largely anecdotal, they accord with conclusions drawn by other researchers tracking lexical development, viz., that inter-child and inter-item variability is great and so it is unlikely that conceptual predispositions drive the acquisition process as much as other factors (Van Geert 1985/6). The patterns of lexical growth for these nine items evidenced by Naomi and Abe differ from each other as well as from Tomasello's daughter (1987). Thus, they certainly underscore one aspect of the Langacker quote given in section 2: There may be considerable individual variation with respect to the specific structures (schemas or extensions) that speakers ultimately arrive at.

5. Summary of factors affecting the acquisition of prepositions

Despite the narrowness of the present case study, some preliminary conclusions can be drawn. There are significant speaker differences in the emergence and usage patterns for the majority of the nine prepositions studied. More often than not, each child manifests a different point of entry into one of the nine lexical categories. In addition, underextensions involving specific verbs or objects seem to be the norm. There are also significant differences among the nine prepositions in terms of whether a basic spatial sense or some more abstract or grammaticalized sense emerges first. The relative role that adult frequency and other input factors play is as yet unknown, so we should not put too much stock into wholly conceptually-driven acquisition mechanisms unless we are prepared to expand our characterization of and/or operationalize such mechanisms. Perceptual salience, experiential basicness, and conceptual complexity are hard concepts to qualify, let alone quantify. While a cursory examination of the error pattern reveals some early conceptual influence on the use of a particular preposition in a particular context, there also seems to be a large linguistic component to the acquisition process (i.e., items may emerge in idiomatic or fixed expressions without regard to their meaning or function, or because the child has developed an affinity for a particular verb or expression, or because of contrastive pressures exerted by another lexical item in the same category), as well as an even larger experiential component (i.e., a child may use a form purely on the basis of frequency of exposure to the adult target or because it is associated with an activity or social interaction that is highly routine or of great importance psychologically to him or her).

These findings, although not very robust, do suggest that semantic extension within a lexical category by a young child proceeds outwardly only partially (if at all) from some basic, concrete sense by the application of a series of metaphorical image-schematic transformations or other construal processes. This is the dynamic claimed to underlie historical patterns of development. As shown in Table 22, the child language evidence presented here are, at the very least, inconclusive about any parallelisms which might obtain between developmental and diachronic extension. They tend, however, to point in the direction that ontogeny does not recapitulate phylogeny when it comes to the development of polysemous senses of a preposition.

Table 22. Presence (□), absence (*), or indeterminacy (?) of correspondence between historically attested order-of-emergence patterns (from Table 1) and Abe and Naomi's developmental orders.

	S_1/F_1	>	S_2/F_2
?	concrete	>	abstract
*	transparent	>	opaque
*	spatial	>	non-spatial
□	spatial	>	temporal
?	adposition	>	particle
*	lexical usage	>	grammatical usage
□	specific meaning	>	generalized meaning

Returning to the Langacker quote given in section 2 above, the data presented here certainly reinforce his central message that "speakers learn and manipulate specific expressions". In this regard, Cognitive Grammar, with its basic tenet of being usage-based, may be far from having an underspecified theory of language acquisition. Rather, it may have already axiomized what looks to be true: Usage patterns may differ appreciably from speaker to speaker so the model must remain bottom-up in its approach rather than seek the highest level of generalization possible (e.g., generalizations such as "SPATIAL usages emerge before NON-SPATIAL ones", "PREPOSITIONAL usages emerge before PARTICLES", or "the central/basic meaning of the preposition *to* is to mark SPATIAL GOALS"). The kind of methodology relied upon in this study is not without precedent (cf. Bloom et al. (1994), who argued for evidence of young children's knowledge of and adherence to certain pronominal binding principles on the basis of spontaneous speech data from the CHILDES corpus for 3 children, or Tomasello's (1987) study of prepositional use by a single child). However, any conclusions about the mechanisms underlying lexical acquistion drawable from spontaneous speech data can and should be strengthened by:

- analyzing longitudinal data from additional children;
- looking in more detail at specific contexts surrounding a particular usage type;
- normalizing the results for each child on the basis of MLU or tokens per 100 words (percent scores);
- looking for correlations in onset and sequence of individual prepositions and usages;
- examining the adult input;
- examining acquisition of similar locative items cross-linguistically.

These additional investigations form the basis of ongoing and future work as part of my long-term research into prepositional semantics and the representation of meaning in the mental lexicon.

6. Ramifications for lexical network analyses of prepositions

This paper took as its point of departure the idea that the center of a multi-faceted, polysemous lexical category such as an English preposition is often assumed to be a semantically basic (and generally historically prior) sense and that additional senses probably arise on the basis of conceptual pressures of some sort. This is what is assumed throughout the CL literature and detailed in a host of well documented grammaticalization studies. If true, I questioned whether or not acquisition patterns might reflect the diachronic pattern. If not true, then one is left wondering what influences the growth of a lexical category developmentally.

On the whole, these findings suggest that semantic extension within a developing lexical category appears to be only partially conceptually driven for the young child. The emergence of a lexical item's initial and subsequent sense types seems to be motivated as much if not more by frequency of exposure, favorite expressions, or contrastive pressures exerted by other lexical items than by purely semantic factors. As Carpenter states in her diachronic vs. developmental comparison of evolving classifier systems, "Learning a language is not simply a process of mapping linguistic forms onto salient cognitive categories. Many conceptually salient categories are not grammaticalized in all languages, or even in all systems of a single language, and the child must learn which ones are linguistically significant and which ones are not" (1992: 146). The child's task is to learn a "conventional, pre-existing system, with a targeted end-state" (1992: 145), so it is of no great surprise that the forces shaping a lexical system diachronically should not be the same as those that a child uses to fill in or acquire some approximation of that system developmentally. Bowerman (1989) has reached a similar conclusion on the basis of cross-linguistic developmental research: The conceptual categories that are considered basic for a child, that seem to motivate acquisition in the first place, including error patterns and innovations, are those that the *target language* distinguishes; i.e., they are language-specific, not universal.

Cognitive Linguistics needs to pay more attention to acquisition, which for psychologists and both generative and functionalist linguists alike has long been a testing ground for hypotheses about the role that cognition (as opposed to purely linguistic factors such as morphosyntactic regularity, high frequency, etc.) plays in language development. After all, the CL movement places a great deal of theoretical weight on the idea that conceptualization shapes grammar and that most linguistic categories are complex, internally structured, and generally display prototype effects. The data presented here are suggestive of the notion that a lexical category for a young child does not start out as either monosemous or polysemous, but as potentially very homonymous. Additional senses do not emerge through extension. Rather, they *may* be integrated through some sort of schematization process at a much later date. Any CL-sanctioned model of a lexical network that assumes the single dimensionality of semantic extension via conceptually-motivated extensions in semantic/associative memory will probably not receive wide support by evidence from developmental studies. CL needs to integrate into the model the idea that multiple factors constrain and license semantic extension. Some of these candidate factors are frequency, semantic contrast, pragmatic utility, ease of articulation, lexical preference, conventionalization, and so forth. We need more integration of independent empirical findings into our models of lexical semantic knowledge. There should be efforts to refine terms like "cognitive salience" and "conceptual basicness/complexity" and even "metaphorical extension". Certainly, there should be more care in using labels like these as all-purpose explanatory mechanisms driving language growth and change.

References

Bloom, Lois, Karin Lifter and Jeremy Hafitz
1980 Semantics of verbs and the development of verb inflection in child language. *Language* 56: 386–412.

Bloom, Lois, Jo Tackeff and Margaret Lahey
1984 Learning *to* in complement constructions. *Journal of Child Language* 11: 391–406.

Bloom, Paul, Andrew Barss, Janet Nicol and Laura Conway
1994 Children's knowledge of binding and coreference: Evidence from spontaneous speech. *Language* 70: 53–71.

Bowerman, Melissa
1989 Learning a semantic system: What role do cognitive predispositions play? In: Richard L. Schiefelbusch and Mabel L. Rice (eds.), *The Teachability of Language*, 133–169. Baltimore: Paul H. Brooks.

Brown, Roger
1973 *A First Language: The Early Stages*. Cambridge, MA: Harvard University Press.

Bybee, Joan
1985 *Morphology*. Amsterdam: John Benjamins.

Carlson, Robert
1991 Grammaticalization of postpositions and word order in Senufo languages. In: Elizabeth C. Traugott and Bernd Heine (eds.), *Approaches to Grammaticalization*, Volume II, 201–223. Amsterdam: John Benjamins.

Carpenter, Kathie
1992 Two dynamic views of classifier systems: Diachronic change and individual development. *Cognitive Linguistics* 3: 129–150.

Choi, Soonja and Melissa Bowerman.
1991 Learning to express motion events in English and Korean: The influence of language specific lexicalization patterns. In: Beth Levin and Steve Pinker (eds.), *Lexical and Conceptual Semantics*, 83–121. Oxford: Basil Blackwell.

Clark, Eve and Kathie Carpenter
1989 The notion of source in language acquisition. *Language* 65: 1–30.

Clark, Herbert
1973 Space, time, semantics, and the child. In: Timothy E. Moore (ed.), *Cognitive Development and the Acquisition of Language*, 65–110. New York: Academic Press.

Craig, Colette
1991 Ways to go in Rama: A case study in polygrammaticalization. In: Elizabeth C. Traugott and Bernd Heine (eds.), *Approaches to Grammaticalization*, Volume II, 455–492. Amsterdam: John Benjamins.

Croft, William
1995 Autonomy and functionalist linguistics. *Language* 71: 490–532.

Cuyckens, Hubert, Dominiek Sandra and Sally Rice
1997 Towards an empirical lexical semantics. In: Birgit Smieja and Meike Tasch (eds.), *Human Contact through Language and Linguistics*, 35–54. Frankfurt am Main: Peter Lang.

Dromi, Esther
1979 More on the acquisition of locative prepositions: An analysis of Hebrew data. *Journal of Child Language*, 6: 547–562.

Furrow, David, Patricia Murray and Melissa Furrow
1985/6 Spatial term use and its relation to language function at two developmental stages. *First Language* 6: 41–51.

Genetti, Carol
1991 From postposition to subordinator in Newari. In: Elizabeth C. Traugott and Bernd Heine (eds.), *Approaches to Grammaticalization*, Volume II, 227–256. Amsterdam: John Benjamins.

Goldberg, Adele
1996 Jackendoff and construction-based grammar. *Cognitive Linguistics* 7: 3–19.

Heine, Bernd, Ulrike Claudi and Friederike Hünnemeyer
1991 *Grammaticalization: A Conceptual Framework*. Chicago: University of Chicago Press.

Hopper, Paul
1991 On some principles of grammaticalization. In: Elizabeth C. Traugott and Bernd Heine (eds.), *Approaches to Grammaticalization*, Volume I, 17–36. Amsterdam: John Benjamins.

Hopper, Paul, and Elizabeth C. Traugott
1993 *Grammaticalization.* Cambridge: Cambridge University Press.

Johnston, Judith R. and Dan Slobin
1979 The development of locative expressions in English, Italian, Serbo-Croatian, and Turkish. *Journal of Child Language* 6: 529–545.

Jurafsky, Daniel
1996 Universal tendencies in the semantics of the diminutive. *Language* 72: 533–578.

Kuczaj, Stan
1976 -ing, -s, *and* -ed: *A study of the acquisition of certain verb inflections.* Unpublished doctoral dissertation, University of Minnesota.

Lakoff, George
1987 *Women, Fire, and Dangerous Things: What Categories Reveal about the Mind.* Chicago: The University of Chicago Press.

Langacker, Ronald W.
1987 *Foundations of Cognitive Grammar*, Volume 1: *Theoretical Prerequisites.* Stanford: Stanford University Press.
1991 a *Foundations of Cognitive Grammar*, Volume 2: *Descriptive Application.* Stanford. Stanford University Press.
1991 b *Concept, Image, and Symbol: The Cognitive Basis of Grammar.* Berlin: Mouton de Gruyter.

Lichtenberk, Frantisek
1991 On the gradualness of grammaticalization. In: Elizabeth C. Traugott and Bernd Heine (eds.), *Approaches to Grammaticalization*, Volume I, 37–80. Amsterdam: John Benjamins.

MacLaury, Robert
1991 Prototypes revisited. *Annual Review of Anthropology* 20: 55–74.

MacWhinney, Brian and Katherine Snow
1990 The Child Language Data Exchange System: An update. *Journal of Child Language* 17: 457–472.

Meillet, Antoine
1912 [1958] L'évolution des formes grammaticales. *Scientia* (Rivista di Scienza) 12, No. 26, 6. (Reprinted in Antoine Meillet, *Linguistique Historique et Linguistique Générale*, 130–148. Paris: Champion.)

Moerk, E
1992 *A First Language Taught and Learned.* Baltimore: Paul H. Brookes.

Queller, Kurt
this volume Metonymic sense shifts: Its origin in hearers' abductive construal of usage in context.

Rice, Sally
1996 Prepositional prototypes. In: Martin Pütz and René Dirven (eds.), *The Construal of Space in Language and Thought,* 135–165. Berlin: Mouton de Gruyter.
1999 Patterns of acquisition in the emerging mental lexicon: The case of *to* and *for* in English. *Brain and Language* 68: 268–276.

Rice, Sally, Dominiek Sandra and Mia Vanrespaille
1999 Prepositional semantics and the TIME IS SPACE metaphor. In: Masako Hiraga, Chris Sinha and Sherman Wilcox (eds.), *Cultural, Typological, and Psycholinguistic Issues: Proceedings of the Fourth International Cognitive Linguistics Conference*, 107–127. Amsterdam: John Benjamins.

Rosch, Eleanor
1975 Cognitive representations of semantic categories. *Experimental Psychology: General* 104: 192–233.
1978 Principles of categorization. In: Eleanor Rosch and Barbara Lloyd (eds.), *Cognition and Categorization*, 27–48. Hillsdale, NJ: Lawrence Erlbaum.

Sachs, Jacqueline S
1983 Talking about the there and then: The emergence of displaced reference in parent-child discourse. In: Keith E. Nelson (ed.), *Children's Language*, Volume 4, 1–28. Hillsdale, NJ: Lawrence Erlbaum.

Sandra, Dominiek
1998 What linguists can and can't tell you about the human mind: A reply to Croft. *Cognitive Linguistics* 9: 361–378.

Sandra, Dominiek and Sally Rice
1995 Network analyses of prepositional meaning: Mirroring whose mind – the linguist's or the language user's? *Cognitive Linguistics* 6: 89–130.

Slobin, Dan
1985 Crosslinguistic evidence for the language-making capacity. In: Dan Slobin (ed.), *The Crosslinguistic Study of Language Acquisition*, Volume 2: *Theoretical Issues*, 1157–1256. Hillsdale, NJ: Lawrence Erlbaum.

1997 The origins of grammaticalizable notions: Beyond the individual mind. In: Dan Slobin (ed.), *The Crosslinguistic Study of Language Acquisition,* Volume 5*: Expanding the Contexts*, 265–323. Mahwah, NJ: Lawrence Erlbaum.

Sweetser, Eve
1990 *From Etymology to Pragmatics: Metaphorical and Cultural Aspects of Semantic Structure.* Cambridge: Cambridge University Press.

Taylor, John
1989 *Linguistic Categorization: Prototypes in Linguistic Theory.* Oxford: Clarendon Press.

Tomasello, Michael
1987 Learning to use prepositions: A case study. *Journal of Child Language* 14: 79–98.
1992 *First Verbs: A Case Study of Early Grammatical Development.* Cambridge: Cambridge University Press.

Traugott, Elizabeth C.
1982 From propositional to textual and expressive meanings: Some semantic-pragmatic aspects of grammaticalization. In: Winfred P. Lehmann and Yakov Malkiel (eds.), *Perspectives on Historical Linguistics*, 245–271. Amsterdam: John Benjamins.

Traugott, Elizabeth C. and Bernd Heine (eds.)
1991 *Approaches to Grammaticalization*, Volumes I–II. Amsterdam: John Benjamins.

Traugott, Elizabeth and Ekkehard König
1991 The semantics-pragmatics of grammaticalization revisited. In: Elizabeth C. Traugott and Bernd Heine (eds.), *Approaches to Grammaticalization*, Volume I, 189–218. Amsterdam: John Benjamins.

Van Geert, Paul
1985/6 *In, on, under*: An essay on the modularity of infant spatial competence. *First Language* 6: 7–28.

Ziegeler, Debra
1997 Retention in ontogenetic and diachronic grammaticalization. *Cognitive Linguistics* 8: 207–241.

Image schemas and category coherence: The case of the Portuguese verb *deixar*

Augusto Soares da Silva[1]

Abstract

This paper offers a conceptual analysis of the many different senses of the Portuguese verb *deixar* 'to leave, to let'. Two clusters of meanings are identified, corresponding, roughly, to English 'to leave' and 'to let'. The analysis applies force-dynamic notions and is framed in terms of image schemas and their transformations. In the second half of the chapter, the diachronic development of the present-day complex is traced from the Latin etymon *laxare* 'to let go'. Finally, methodological conclusions are drawn on the proper treatment of polysemous and multifunctional lexical items.

Keywords: dehomonymization, deprototypicalization, force dynamics, homonymy, image schema, image-schema transformation, prototypicality.

1. I am greatly indebted to Dirk Geeraerts and John Taylor for their valuable comments on earlier versions of this paper. This article is partly based on sections of my Ph.D. dissertation (Soares da Silva 1999) supervised by Dirk Geeraerts and Mário Vilela, to whom I express my gratitude. A short version of this paper was presented at the Fifth International Cognitive Linguistics Conference in Amsterdam, in July 1997. I would also like to thank two anonymous reviewers for their thorough and illuminating comments, as well as Brygida Rudzka-Ostyn, Nicole Delbecque, Béatrice Lamiroy, Ludo Melis, and Willy Van Hoecke, from the University of Leuven, all of whom provided useful observations. Any remaining errors are of course my own. Finally, I would like to thank the Calouste Gulbenkian Foundation and the Camões Institute for their financial support.

1. Introduction

In Cognitive Semantics, considerable theoretical weight is given to the role of image schemas and their transformations in both everyday thought and in word meaning. These concepts are important to lexical-semantic analysis, as numerous descriptive studies have shown. Among these are the pioneering study on *over* by Brugman (1981), elaborated by Lakoff (1987: 416–461) and Dewell (1994), the analysis of *take* by Norvig and Lakoff (1987), and of *stand* by Gibbs et al. (1994). Recently, Gibbs and Colston (1995) and Beitel, Gibbs and Sanders (2001) presented experimental data as evidence for the cognitive-psychological reality of image schemas and their transformations.[2]

Image schemas are imaginative, non-propositional, and dynamic patterns of our bodily movements through space, manipulations of objects, and perceptual interactions (Johnson 1987, 1993; Lakoff 1987, 1990). They have an internal structure and can be metaphorically elaborated to provide for our understanding of abstract concepts. This paper applies to the notion of image schemas, and their transformations, to a study of the Portuguese verb *deixar*.

2. The meanings of *deixar*

The Portuguese verb *deixar* is cognate with Spanish *dejar*, French *laisser*, and Italian *lasciare*, and has two equivalents in English, *to leave* and *to let*. The verb exhibits a wide and diversified range of

2. On the importance of image schemas in cognitive semantics, see also Cienki (1997, 1998) and Clausner and Croft (1999). Other studies highlight the role of image schemas in the transition from perception to concepts in child development (Mandler 1992) and in gesture (McNeill 1992). Edelman (1992: 247–250) recognizes the neurobiological plausibility of image schemas. Langacker's (1987, 1991, 1999) notion *imagery* (the ability to construe a conceived situation in alternate ways) and Talmy's (1988) patterns of *force dynamics* are also consonant with schematic mental images, despite being theoretically distinct concepts.

senses, which cluster in two main groups, referred to henceforth as *deixar*I and *deixar*II. The principal senses are exemplified below:[3]

***Deixar*I** (equivalent to English *to leave*)

(1) 'to go away' (to move away from a place)
O João deixou a sala, quando ela entrou.
'John left the room when she came in.'

(2) 'not to take (something or someone) with one (when one moves away from a place)'
a. *Deixei a (minha) pasta no carro.*
'I left my briefcase in the car.'
b. *Tenho de voltar à estação, porque deixei a minha pasta no combóio.*
'I have to go back to the railway station because I left my briefcase on the train.'

(3) 'to (unintentionally) cause signs of one's presence to remain after one has left (a place)'
O assaltante deixou marcas de sangue no chão.
'The burglar left blood stains on the floor.'

(4) 'to cause (something or someone) to remain'
a. *Pode deixar os livros em cima da mesa.*
'You may leave the books on the table.'
b. *Deixei a Maria no colégio, e depois fui ao Porto.*
'I left Mary at the school and then went to Oporto.'

(5) 'to abandon, to sever a relation'
a. *O João deixou a sua mulher.*
'John left his wife.'
b. *O João deixou o emprego/o partido comunista/os estudos.*
'John left his job/the communist party/gave up his studies.'

3. The analysis is based on a corpus of 5,000 contextualized occurrences. The characterization of each of the seventeen senses is given in a simple paraphrase; more specific senses are discussed in section 4.

(6) 'not to alter (the state of a person or object)'

a. *Deixei-o a ver televisão/naquele estado, quando saí de casa.* 'I left him watching television/in that state, when I left home.'

b. *Ele saiu e deixou a porta aberta/a luz ligada.* 'He went out and left the door open/the lights on.'

(7) 'to (unintentionally) cause a part of oneself to remain after leaving'

a. *Em várias partes do mundo, continua viva a cultura portuguesa deixada pelos descobridores.* 'The culture left by the Portuguese discoverers is alive today, in many parts of the world.'

b. *Morreu sem deixar descendentes directos.* 'He died without leaving any direct descendants.'

c. *Ele deixou(-nos) uma boa recordação/muitas saudades.* 'He left us with good memories of himself/We miss him a great deal.'

d. *A ferida deixou uma cicatriz na cara.* 'The injury left a scar on his/her face.'

(8) 'to cause (something or someone) to remain in an altered state'

a. *Deixou-me sem palavras/nervoso/escandalizado com o que me disse.* 'He left me speechless/He made me nervous/I was scandalized by what he told me.'

b. *O mecânico deixou o carro como novo.* 'The mechanic left the car like new.'

c. *O jogo deixou-o rico/na miséria.* 'Gambling made him rich/poor.'

(9) 'not to approach, or go to (a place)'

Deixei Paris à esquerda e segui para Amsterdão. 'I left Paris on my left and proceeded to Amsterdam.'

(10) 'not to take away'

a. *Deixou a sua pasta em casa/no hotel para não ser assaltado.*

'He left his briefcase at home/at the hotel so that no one could rob him.'

b. *Deixa o carro em casa e vai de metro!*
'Leave your car at home and take the underground!'

(11) 'not to take'
Ele comeu o bife e deixou as batatas.
'He ate the steak and left the potatoes.'

(12) 'not to alter (the state of something or someone)'

a. *Não mexas em nada; deixa tudo como estava!*
'Don't touch anything! Leave everything as it was!'

b. *Não me chateies; deixa-me em paz!*
'Don't bother me! Leave me alone!'

(13) 'to transfer possession (especially when one moves away)'

a. *O pai deixou-lhe uma casa no Algarve.*
'His father left him a house in the Algarve.'

b. *Quando saíres, deixa-me as chaves!*
'When you go out, leave the keys with me!'

c. *Levantei-me para deixar o lugar ao velhinho.*
'I got up to leave my seat free for the old man.'

d. *Não posso ir ao cinema, porque não tenho ninguém a quem deixar as crianças.*
'I cannot go to the cinema because I do not have anyone to leave the children with.'

(14) 'not to take possession of'

a. *Deixa-lhe o que não te pertence!*
'Leave him what does not belong to you!'

b. *Deixa esse problema para os entendidos!*
'Leave that problem to the experts!'

***Deixar*II** (equivalent to English *to let*)

(15) 'not to prevent, not to impede'
O João pôs-se a fazer disparates, e eu deixei-o fazer.
'John started fooling around, and I let him do it.'

(16) 'to allow' (to permit, to consent, to authorize)
A Maria pediu-me para ir ao cinema, e eu deixei-a ir.

'Mary asked me if she could go to the cinema, and I let her go.'

(17) 'to let go' (to release, to free, to stop impeding, to drop)

a. *Ele deixou o pássaro voar (abrindo a gaiola).*
'He let the bird fly out (by opening the birdcage).'

b. *Segura-o bem, para não o deixares cair!*
'Hold it carefully so that you won't let it fall!'

c. *Não deixes a corda/as rédeas do cavalo!*
'Don't let go of the rope/of the horse's reins!'

Essentially, the two groups differ with respect to the construal of the landmark entity. Schematically, *deixar*I means 'to suspend interaction with what is characterized as static', whereas the schematic meaning of *deixar*II is 'not to oppose what is presented as dynamic'. Accordingly, both groups implement a similar force dynamic schema (Talmy 1988): a stronger force entity, the Antagonist, encoded by the subject of the verb, fails to exert a force that might interfere with the natural disposition of a second entity, the Agonist; they differ in that the Agonist in *deixar*I is disposed to rest, while in *deixar*II it is disposed to motion (or, more generally, change). The landmark of *deixar*I is expressed by a nominal complement, either in a bivalent structure with a locative or a non-locative object (cf. examples 1, 9, and 3, 5, 7, 11), or in a trivalent structure involving a locative (2, 4, 10), a predicative (6, 8, 12), or a dative (13, 14a).[4] The landmark of *deixar*II, on the other hand, is expressed by a verbal complement, either an infinitive clause or, less frequently, a *that*-clause.[5]

Another dimension, which cross-classifies the *deixar*I and *deixar*II groups, concerns the (degree of) activity of the subject entity. The subject can take on an "active" attitude. In *deixar*I, this is the case in examples (1)–(8) and in (13), where the subject moves away from a

4. Examples (3), (7), and (14b) are only apparently trivalent, since the locative and the dative phrases are not verb complements.

5. The different infinitival constructions with *deixar*II – VOV, with inflected or uninflected infinitive, and VVO, with the causee in the accusative or the dative, and with an uninflected infinitive – though interesting in themselves, are not relevant to differentiating the principal senses of the verb.

place, abandons or severs a relation, transfers possession to someone else, and so on; these uses can be represented schematically as 'to actively suspend interaction'. With *deixar*II, the active attitude of the subject is present in (16) and (17): in (16), the subject gives permission to someone; in (17), the subject releases (frees, drops, ceases to impede) the object. Schematically, the subject 'does not actively oppose' a process to be fulfilled by another entity. The subject can also adopt a "passive" attitude. Such is the case in examples (9)–(12) and (14) of *deixar*I, in which the subject does not go near a place, abstains from taking away, altering, taking, or picking up an object, does not take possession of the object, etc. Schematically, these uses can be represented as 'to passively suspend interaction', that is, 'to suspend the intention of interacting', or 'not to interact'. In *deixar*II, the subject's passive attitude is exemplified by (15): the subject does not prevent an object from continuing with the fulfillment of a process; in other words, it "does not oppose" an already existing or ongoing process. In terms of Talmy's (1988) force dynamics, the opposition is between the cessation of impingement (removal of barrier), in the active cases, and the non-occurrence of impingement (absence of barrier) in the passive cases.

Those uses which express the subject's active attitude can be subdivided further. In *deixar*I examples (4), (3), (8), (7), and (13) and in *deixar*II example (17), the activity of the subject occurs after a previous action upon the object: in particular, in the *deixar*I examples, the subject moves away (or abandons the object) after having moved, altered (the state of), or transferred (possession, use, control of) the object; in *deixar*II example (17), the subject ceases to impede (lets go, releases, drops) the object. In the remaining uses (cf. examples 1, 2, 5, 6, and 16), the subject's active attitude is not preceded by a previous intervention with the object. It is worth noting that sentences such as *O João deixou os livros em cima da mesa* 'John left the books on the table', *O João deixou a Maria triste* 'John made Mary unhappy', and *Deixei-o sair* 'I let him go out' are ambiguous with respect to the three values that can be assigned to the subject's activity (i.e., "active with previous intervention", "active without previous intervention", and "passive").

Combining the dimensions we have just identified – the two values of "construal of the object" and the three values of "(degree of the) subject's activity" – a preliminary systematization of the semantic range of *deixar* can be proposed. It is presented in Table 1, and is based on examples (1)–(17).

Table 1. Systematization of the basic semantic range of *deixar*.

	Actively		**Passively**
	Without previous intervention	With previous intervention	
***Deixar*I:** 'suspend interaction with what is static'	1. go away 2. not take with one 5. abandon relation 6. not alter	4. cause to remain after having moved 8. cause to remain after having altered 13. transfer possession 3. cause a part of oneself to remain 7. cause a part of oneself to remain	9. not approach 10. not take away 11. not take 12. not alter 14. not take possession of
***Deixar*II:** 'not oppose what is dynamic'	16. allow (permit, authorize)	17. let go (stop impeding)	15. not prevent, not impede

Two essential features of the semantics of *deixar* should now have become clear: causation and negation, both construed in force dynamic terms. In other words, what unifies the senses of the verb is the notion of negative causation, in the sense that the Antagonist does not exert a force that may impinge (in the passive cases), or exerts a force in order to stop impingement (in the active cases), on the natural disposition of the Agonist. It is precisely because of this non-interference that the Agonist is "left free" to follow its own natural course. Note that the active and passive options for negative causation are grammaticalized by the Iberian periphrasis *deixar de/dejar de* + infinitive: *deixar de fumar* 'quit smoking' vs. *deixar de ir ao cinema para me ajudar* 'refrain from going to the cinema in order to help me'.[6]

There are still other dimensions involved in the semantic structure of *deixar*. One concerns the contrast between the spatial and non-spatial domains; another is the "absolute vs. partial autonomy" dimension. These dimensions are more relevant to *deixar*I, but they can also be found in *deixar*II. In section 4, I will address them in more detail.

Finally, two more points are worth mentioning in the discussion of the semantics of *deixar*. First, the two categories of senses are functionally different: *deixar*II results from a process of (semi-)grammaticalization in order to express a special type of causation, whereas *deixar*I is a lexical category (though presenting some grammaticalized uses). Second, as I will explain in section 4, the active and non-spatial senses are the prototypical senses of *deixar*I, whereas the prototypical sense of *deixar*II is passive.

3. Image schemas of *deixar* and their transformations

Let us now try to find a diagrammatic representation which not only allows us to better distinguish the six poles of the semantic structure of *deixar,* but also to understand the coherence of this complex. Table 2 presents six image schemas (IS) which correspond to the six poles in Table 1. P_1 and P_2 designate the Antagonist and Agonist, while the arrows indicate movement.

In IS1, IS2, and IS3 (representing the uses of *deixar*I), it is the subject participant (P_1) that moves; in IS4, IS5, and IS6 (representing the uses of *deixar*II), it is the object participant (P_2) that is construed as moving. The image schemas in the two left columns (involving an active subject) depict a starting situation in which P_1 and P_2 are in contact, while in the image schemas on the right (involving a passive subject), P_1 and P_2 are represented as separate from the outset and

6. Soares da Silva (1999, 2000, in press a) develops the analysis of "letting" causation from a force dynamic perspective.

remaining so. The passivity of P_1 consists in the fact that P_1 does nothing to do away with this separation. P_1's activity either consists in moving away from some place, thus ceasing to be in contact with the object (*deixar*I), or in creating the necessary conditions for the object to move away (*deixar*II). Some of the image schemas involving an active subject also introduce a previous time segment, during which P_1 moves/transports P_2 (*deixar*I), or P_2 gets closer to P_1 and is blocked by the latter (*deixar*II).

Table 2. Image schemas of *deixar*.

	Actively		**Passively**
	Without previous intervention	With previous intervention	
***Deixar*I:** 'suspend interaction with what is static'	IS 1 ('go away') 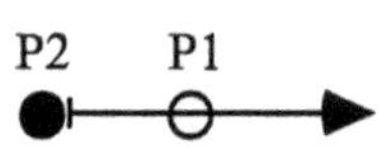	IS 2 ('cause to remain after having moved') 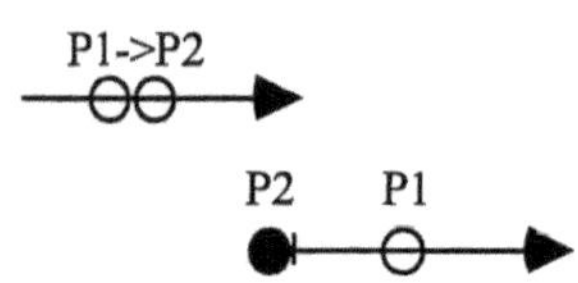	IS 3 ('not approach') 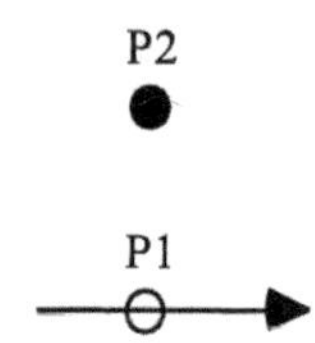
***Deixar*II:** 'not oppose what is dynamic'	IS 4 ('allow') 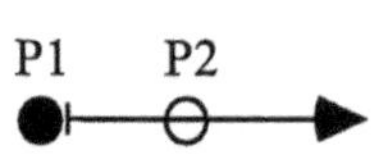	IS 5 ('let go') 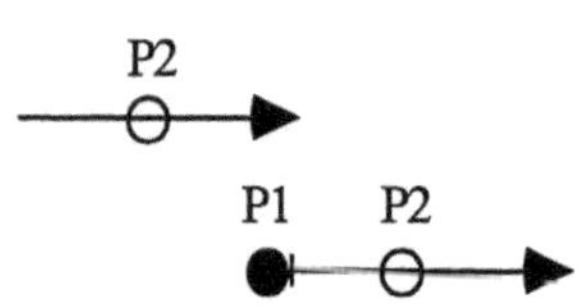	IS 6 ('not impede') 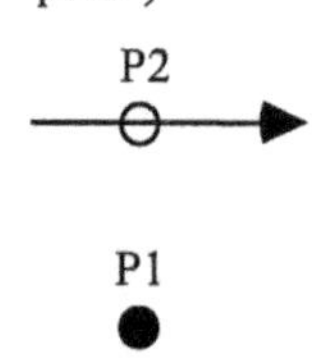

What essentially distinguishes the two clusters of senses, then, is the movement of P_2. In *deixar*I, P_2 is presented as being essentially static, whereas in *deixar*II, P_2 is construed as being dynamic, and subject to an inevitable dynamic tendency. We may observe this contrast, for example, between *deixar a Maria no cinema* 'to leave Mary at the cinema' and *deixar a Maria ir ao cinema* 'to let Mary go to the cinema'. In both cases, the Antagonist (P_1) fails to engage the Agonist (P_2). The difference is that in the first case, the Agonist (Mary) is construed statically, as an entity that is not engaged, while in the second case, it is construed dynamically.

The fundamental opposition between *deixar*I and *deixar*II is iconically expressed in the syntactic nature of the complements. With *deixar*II, the complement is verbal – *deixar* P_2 *V* (or *deixar V* P_2) – which encodes the participation of P_2 in a process. With *deixar*I, the complement is nominal – *deixar* P_2, or *deixar* P_2 *in a place/in a state/to* P_3 – thus expressing the static condition of P_2 (P_2 is a place, as in IS1 and IS3, or is/comes to be in a place which P_1 moves away or keeps away from).

In *deixar*I as well as in *deixar*II, P_2 has to be construed as having a certain disposition to behave in a particular way. With *deixar*II, P_2's disposition may manifest itself as its independent will to do something, with subconscious emotions, as an already existing process, or even as a physical process that P_2 cannot resist (for example, the force of gravity in *deixar cair* P_2 'drop'). In any case, what characterizes *deixar*II is P_2's inevitable dynamic tendency or, alternatively, P_2's aspiration to do something. With *deixar*I, on the other hand, P_2 is disposed to rest. In both cases, P_2's disposition is considered to be natural in some way. That is why it is not possible to say, in normal contexts, *deixar subir o livro* 'to let the book go up'. It is also why *deixar a Maria em paz* 'to leave Mary alone' and *deixar o assento livre* 'to leave the seat free' presuppose that the natural state of a person is to be at ease, and that the natural state of a seat is to be unoccupied.

Cases such as *deixar alguém na dúvida* 'to leave someone in doubt', implying the passivity of the subject, also fall within *deixar*I and not *deixar*II. *Na dúvida* 'in doubt' does not express the dynamic tendency typical of the object of *deixar*II; the doubt is presented as a state (a place, not a movement), and the natural disposition of P_2 is to be (or remain) in a state of doubt.

At the same time, one has to acknowledge that this example is not a prototypical instance of *deixar*I; i.e., it positions itself at the boundary between the two categories. Prototypically, P_2 in *deixar*II is not only dynamic, but acts voluntarily and consciously; in this respect, *deixar cair P_2* '[to let fall P_2] to drop P_2' is less typical than *deixar P_2 ir-se embora* 'to let P_2 go'. In addition, the use of *deixar*II presupposes that P_2's activity is considered by P_2 himself as being beneficial for P_2. On the other hand, P_2 in *deixar*I is prototypically static by nature and cannot exert movement; a prototypical example would be *deixar o carro em casa* 'to leave the car at home'. The reason why *deixar alguém na dúvida* 'to leave someone in doubt' is a boundary case is that it is quite possible to imagine that there is activity on the part of the object: P_2 questions him-/herself, tries to find a solution, his/her thoughts do not rest. However, this dynamic aspect of P_2 is not construed as leading him/her anywhere: the activity is therefore construed as a state, albeit one involving activity. In contrast, *deixar alguém enganar-se* 'to let someone make a mistake', while no doubt similar in truth conditional terms to *deixar alguém na dúvida*, falls within *deixar*II, since the object is construed dynamically. But this case is not typical of *deixar*II, since it does not involve a conscious, voluntary activity, nor does it benefit P_2.[7]

Further cases of conceptual overlap between *deixar*I and *deixar*II occur when the verbal complement (V_2) of *deixar*II designates a state; in this case, the difference between *deixar*I and *deixar*II becomes subtle, or even disappears (in contrast, a V_2 designating a dynamic process maximizes the contrast). For instance, *deixar estar/ficar a porta aberta* 'to let the door be/remain open' and *deixar a porta aberta* 'to leave the door open' are no doubt truth conditionally equivalent, and the first example may even be genuinely indeterminate as far as its membership in either one of the two *deixar* categories is concerned. However, it is possible that the circumstances in which the two constructions are used are not exactly the same. Given the door's disposition to close, *deixar estar/ficar a porta aberta* may

7. The prototypicality judgments expressed here should not be understood in terms of the frequency of use of the respective senses, but rather in the context of an extreme differentiation between the cases represented in Table 2.

be preferred in a context in which something has to be done to prevent the door from closing.

A distinction must also be made between the superficial syntax and the semantics of the construction. Even though in the sense 'to release, to let go', *deixar*II takes a nominal complement, e.g., *deixar a presa/a mão/a corda/as rédeas do cavalo/o volante* 'to let go of the prey/the hand/the rope/the reins/the steering wheel', P_2 in this nominal construction continues to be conceived as a participant in an independent dynamic activity. What matters therefore is the particular construal of the event, and of P_2, that is rendered by the syntactic construction.

Let us now examine the relationships among the six image schemas (ISs) which have been proposed, and in particular whether they are interrelated through image-schema transformations. As can be easily verified in Table 2, the ISs of *deixar*I and *deixar*II are inverses of each other. This suggests that an inversion transformation operates between the ISs of the two categories, involving the inversion of the dynamic participant (the one who carries out the movement), i.e., P_1 (the subject) in *deixar*I and P_2 (the object) in *deixar*II. Inversion occurs between each of the following pairs: IS1 – IS4, IS2 – IS5, IS3 – IS6 (and IS1 – IS5, and IS2 – IS4). But the central inversion transformation (the simplest and the most easily explainable) is between IS1 ('to go away') and IS5 ('to let go'). In fact, 'to move away from' develops through the inversion of the dynamic participant into 'to allow *x* to go away', and the latter, in turn, develops by implication into 'to let go'. Conversely, 'to let go' implies 'to allow *x* to go away' which develops, owing to an inversion of the dynamic participant, into 'to go away'. It is on the level of the semasiological realization of these image schemas, and due to the grammaticalization of *deixar*II, that this inversion shifts from IS1 to IS5, and, by extension, from *deixar*I to *deixar*II. It is at this level that restrictions are found on the symmetry which is characteristic of an inversion relationship.

It is, therefore, the inversion transformation involving P_1 – P_2 which is at the basis of the very existence of the two categories *deixar*I and *deixar*II. At the same time, this transformation also unites them. In fact, an inversion (or any other antonymic relation) not only dissociates but also associates, in that any opposition presupposes some similarity between the contrasting elements. At times, the two opposing perspectives can fuse together: *deixa-me!* ('leave me alone' vs. 'let me go').

There is yet another inversion transformation to be considered, the one which occurs, intracategorially, between IS1 ('go away') and IS3 ('not approach'), and between IS4 ('allow') and IS6 ('not impede'). This transformation involves inversion of P_1's role, which is active in IS1 and IS4 (i.e., P_1 ceases to be in contact with the object), and passive in IS3 and IS6 (i.e., P_1 maintains the initial situation of non-contact). If we take into account the prototypical value of the respective semantic instantiations of these image schemas, the direction of this transformation in *deixar*I is from IS1 to IS3, that is, P_1's active attitude is transformed into a passive attitude. Conversely, in *deixar*II, the direction of operation is from IS6 to IS4 and, correspondingly, P_1's passive attitude is transformed into an active one. A further transformation consists of the addition/suppression of a previous time segment, T, at which a previous intervention takes place. With *deixar*I, the addition of T broadens IS1, resulting in IS2 (this direction is more salient than the opposite one, owing to the centrality of IS1, which is incorporated into IS2). On the other hand, with *deixar*II, the suppression of T restricts IS5, resulting in IS4 (this direction is more salient than the opposite one, given the centrality of IS5 in this chart of diagrammatic representations). This addition/suppression transformation accompanies the central transformation mentioned above, i.e., the one which operates between IS1 and IS5.[8]

A final transformation, less important for the internal coherence of *deixar*, is the multiple subject transformation, which lies at the basis of the opposition between the bivalent and the trivalent constructions

8. In this third case, more perhaps than in the previous ones, another interpretation of the variations in image schemas is possible. We may speak here of the process of foregrounding certain portions of an event-frame, referred to by Talmy (1996) as the *windowing of attention*, whereby different facets of the non-interference event-frame, such as the previous moment, the initial or final object state, and the final result are *windowed* for attention or, conversely, are backgrounded or *gapped*.

of *deixar*I. In the bivalent constructions, there is only one trajector; in the trivalent constructions, however, there are two trajectors: one primary, the subject, and the other secondary, the object. Some trivalent constructions which express a movement of the object at the previous moment (T) fall within IS2, e.g., (4) 'to cause (something or someone) to remain after having moved them'; other trivalent constructions fall within IS1 and IS3, where the object does not undergo change, e.g., (2) 'to go away without taking' and (10) 'to abstain from taking away'.

4. Metaphorical elaborations of image schemas, prototypicality, and meaning relations

Let us now examine how the six image schemas represented in Table 2 manifest themselves in the semasiological complex of *deixar*, which is systematized in Table 1 and exemplified in (1)–(17). Figure 1 presents the instantiations and the metaphorical elaborations of the proposed image schemas (the boxes in bold indicate prototypical senses).

All of *deixar*I's schemas are instantiated by one (or more) spatial senses. Thus, IS1, IS2, and IS3 are instantiated in the senses exemplified in (1), (4), and (9) and, through the above mentioned multiple subject transformation, in the equally spatial examples (2), (3), and (10). It should be added that (2) 'not to take (something or someone) with one' – whether intentionally (as in 2a) or out of forgetfulness or carelessness (as in 2b) – in which *deixar* acquires the nuances 'to forget', 'to lose', as well as (10) 'to abstain from taking away (something or someone)', represent a metonymic extension of (1) 'to go away' and (9) 'not to approach', respectively, through *perspectivization of an implication* (Taylor 1995a: 126). When someone moves away from a place, or does not come near a place, they also distance themselves from, or keep themselves at a distance from, the entities that may be in that place. As far as *deixar*II's schemas are concerned, IS5 is instantiated in spatial sense 'to let go' exemplified in (17), but IS4 and IS6 are basically not spatial.

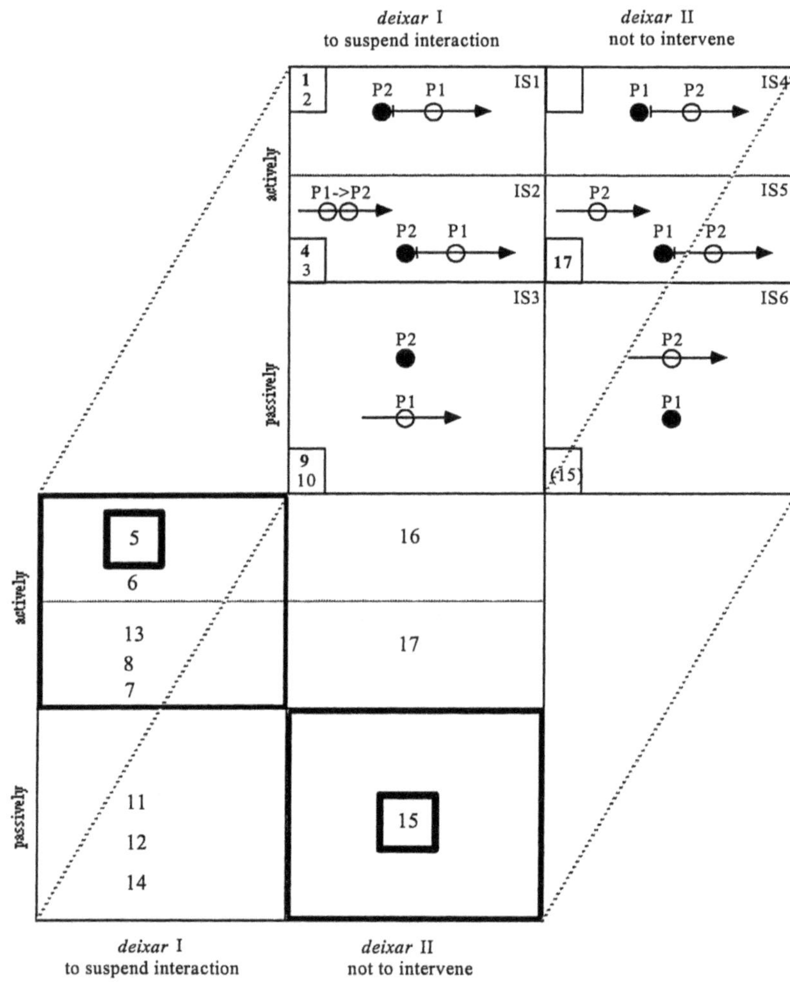

1. go away
2. not to take (go without taking)
3. cause signs of one's presence to remain after leaving
4. cause to remain after having moved
5. abandon relation
6. not to alter
7. cause a part of oneself to remain after leaving (leave a legacy, be survived by, produce an effect)
8. cause to remain after having altered
9. not to approach
10. not to take away (abstain from taking away)
11. not to take (abstain from taking)
12. not to alter (abstain from altering)
13. transfer possession (bequeath, cede, entrust)
14. not to take possession of
15. not to impede, not to prevent
16. allow (permit, consent, authorize)
17. let go (release, stop impeding, drop)

Figure 1. Image schemas of *deixar* and their metaphorical elaborations.

Secondly, all of the ISs are metaphorically projected onto various abstract domains, giving rise to additional senses of *deixar*. The more basic ones are shown in the foreground of Figure 1. Thus, IS1 is metaphorically projected onto (5) and (6); IS2 onto (13), (8), and (7), and so on. They are conventionalized metaphorical extensions of both motion (movement away from a place and keeping away from a place) and force dynamic interactions, and they occur, among others, in the following domains:

(a) *Interpersonal and functional relationships*. Included here are: the abandonment of a marital, sentimental, or other interpersonal relationship (5a), the abandonment of a functional relationship (5b), or the mere interruption of a relationship or function (e.g., *Eram 17 h quando deixei a minha casa/o meu amigo/o emprego* 'I left home/my friend/work at 5 p.m.', *Deixei o que estava a fazer para o ajudar* 'I left what I was doing to help him'). Note that (5) 'to abandon, to sever a relation' not only constitutes a metaphorical but also a metonymical extension of (1) 'to go away': to leave someone or to leave a function puts the focus on the outcome or effect of the event, rather than on its cause. The same applies to the other non-spatial active senses and to the passive correlates of (9) 'not to approach'. As such, (1) and (9) are always present in the corresponding non-spatial senses of *deixar*I, and, conversely, the non-spatial senses of *deixar*I represent a metonymic-metaphorical projection of the spatial senses.

(b) *Death,* conceptualized as a departure: *deixar a vida/este mundo* 'to leave this life/this world'. This use of *deixar* is directly associated with (5). The same metaphorical conceptualization of death is presupposed in specific uses of (13) and (7), i.e., 'to leave a legacy, to bequeath, to donate' (cf. 13a) and 'to transmit a legacy (or to leave as a legacy), to leave something for posterity, to be survived by' (examples (7a–b), *deixar uma fortuna* 'to leave a fortune', *deixar uma obra de grande valor* 'to leave a work of great value', and *deixar uma mulher e dois filhos* 'to leave a wife and two children').

(c) *Possession and transfer of possession*, involving property, access, and responsibility. This characterization unites the various specific uses of (13): 'to leave a legacy, to bequeath, to donate' (13a), 'to cede, to give up' (13c), 'to put at someone's disposal, to lend' (*deixar-lhe a bicicleta quando for de férias* 'to leave him the bicycle while on holiday'), 'to sell for a low price' (*deixar-lhe isso por um bom preço* 'to let him have it for a good price'), 'to send, to give' (13b), 'to trust' (13d), 'to put in charge of' (*deixar-lhe a tarefa de* 'to leave the task to him'), 'to convey a message' (*deixar recado/uma ideia* 'to leave a message/an idea'). A further form/manifestation of possession is that of 'non-appropriation'; this sense is captured by (14), with its specific uses 'not to deprive of' (*deixar-lhe a esperança/a vida* 'to leave him with hope/spare his life', *deixar-lhe caminho livre/a possibilidade de* 'to leave the way open to someone/to leave someone the chance to') and 'to reserve for, not to take upon yourself what is the responsibility of another' (14b), and it is also captured by (the more marginal use of) (11). Specific uses of (7) and (5) express termination of possession, not only alienable possession (*deixar uma fortuna no casino* 'to lose a fortune at the casino'), but also inalienable possession (*deixar a vida em combate* 'to die in combat', *deixar aí a sua juventude* 'to leave behind one's youth', *a árvore deixa as folhas no Outono* 'the tree lets its leaves fall in Autumn').[9] It is worth noting that *deixar*I's senses 'to transfer possession' (13) and 'not to take possession' (14), expressed syntactically by a dative construction, form a group that is relatively distinct from the other

9. In terms of Seiler's (1983) reinterpretation of the traditional distinction between alienable and inalienable possession, *deixar* expresses both *established* (active, acquired) possession, particularly through senses (13) 'to transfer possession' and (14) 'not to take possession', and *inherent* (stative, self-oriented, given) possession, particularly in sense (7) 'to cause a part of oneself to remain after leaving'. It is interesting that the established possession of (13) tends to be conceived as an integral part of the subject (inherent possession), while the inherent possession of (7) sometimes assumes the character of established possession.

senses. In (13) and (14), the object is "partially autonomous", as it may be transferred into someone else's control (13), or remain under someone else's control (14); this is in contrast to the other senses, which express "absolute autonomy" of the object.[10]

(d) *Modality – permission*, involving permission granting, consent, authorization, agreement (16), and even tolerance and resignation (15) (*deixá-los viver na sua crença* 'to let them live according to their beliefs', *deixar-se prender/matar* 'to let oneself get arrested/killed'). In sense (16), *deixar* therefore behaves like a verb of permission in the strict sense, i.e., like a normative and directive verb that establishes the (deontic) permissibility of an action. Unlike the force dynamic patterns of barrier removal ('to let go', 17) or of the non-occurrence of a barrier ('not to prevent', 15), sense (16) constitutes a force dynamic pattern, and type of negative causation, whereby the opposing force is a socially acknowledged authority with the moral power to forbid/permit, and the focal force is an individual's desire or request to perform a future and controllable action. This is a more indirect and complex causation than the non-preventive causation of (15) and the unblocking causation of (17). In fact, what the subject (Antagonist) of (16) 'allow, permit' does, by exerting its authority, constitutes not so much the (only or real) cause of the action, but rather its social and moral legitimation. In contrast, what the Antagonist does or does not do in (15) and (17) is viewed as *the* cause of the action taking

10. This dimension of the object's "autonomy" is indirectly reflected in *deixar*II: in (16) 'to allow, to permit, to authorize', the object's autonomy is partial, to the extent that it is granted some freedom within a field of deontic possibilities; on the contrary, in (15) 'not to prevent' and in (17) 'to let go', the object's freedom is (continues to be/becomes) total. Considering the structure of *deixar* as a whole, three situations where there is autonomy of the object (directly related to the activity of the subject) can be distinguished: (i) increased autonomy (resulting autonomy) in *deixar*I, as a result of the subject's movement away or non-interaction; (ii) permanent autonomy (primary autonomy) in *deixar*II, resulting from the non-opposition of the subject; (iii) and permanent partial autonomy in (13) and (14), as a result of transfer/non-appropriation.

place.[11] This means that the *deixar*II cluster comprises both *deixar* as a codification of "cause" (causal *deixar*, senses 15 and 17) and *deixar* as a codification of "norm" (deontic *deixar*, sense 16). As we will see in the next section, the deontic meaning is the result of a metaphorization of the causal meaning, whereby the intentional/social world is modeled after the causal/natural world.

(e) *Negative conduct*, such as passivity, negligence, irresponsibility, slackness, laxness, and other similar, morally negative attitudes, i.e. "not doing what should be done". These kinds of behavior, closely related to the modal senses above, are implied in the uses of *deixar*II (in cases like *deixar andar* 'to let things go on as they are', *deixar correr* 'to let things run as they are', *deixar-se levar/tentar/vencer* 'to let oneself be taken in/be tempted/be beaten' [by something that is easy, agreeable or seductive], *deixar fazer tudo o que ele quer* 'to let someone do whatever they want to', *deixar crescer o cabelo e a barba* 'to let one's hair and beard grow' [out of carelessness or intentionally]), as well as in those of *deixar*I (*deixar a porta aberta/a torneira aberta* 'to leave the door open/the tap on' [instead of closing the door and turning the tap off], *deixar isso para mim* 'to leave that to me' [instead of doing it oneself], *deixar isso a meio/por acabar* 'to leave something midway/unfinished', *deixar ao abandono/ao deus-dará* 'to abandon/to leave something to fate').[12]

---

11. It should be pointed out that the strictly permissive sense (16) of *deixar* expresses a notion that is closely related to causation, namely enablement. Following Sweetser's (1990: 53) distinction between the two types of enablement present in the modal verbs *can* and *may*, sense (16) encodes a *positive enablement* – an interpretation also permitted by the active sense (17) 'let go', while the non-preventive passive sense (15) encodes a *negated restriction*.
12. But the passivity of the subject of *deixar* is morally positive when the situation of the object is evaluated as positive, that is, when the subject 'does not disturb' or 'does not resist/no longer resists' something that affects him/her positively (*deixá-lo em paz* 'to leave him in peace/alone', *deixar-se medicar* 'to accept medical treatment', *deixar-se tocar por Deus* 'to allow oneself to be touched by God').

(f) *Mental activity*, as in the omission of a component of a mental or psychological act, for instance when details, improprieties, or problems are left "out" or left "aside". These cases also involve metaphorization of laterality ("the lateral is secondary") and the *conduit* metaphor (the ideas, the arguments, the words, the psychological states are conceptualized as containers).
(g) *Time*. Included here are metaphorical conceptualizations such as 'postponement' (*deixar para depois* 'to leave for later') and 'leaving something for posterity' (see especially the examples in (7), where the process is accomplished not in space but in time).

At this stage, the question arises whether the group of spatial instantiations of the image schemas and the group of their metaphorical extensions have the same semasiological salience or prototypicality, i.e., whether these two groups of senses are equally representative within *deixar*'s range of application. It will be seen that they are not. In fact, if representativity, and hence prototypicality, is measured in terms of frequency, it can be observed that the frequency of the non-spatial uses is vastly superior to that of the spatial uses: in our corpus of Modern Portuguese (with nearly 3,000 occurrences), out of a total of 1,312 transitive occurrences of *deixar*I, 72.9% are clearly non-spatial, whereas the essentially spatial uses only amount to 12.1%.[13] In addition, *deixar* is intuitively felt by Portuguese speakers to be a verb of the psycho-social domain, to the extent that its more spatial uses acquire psycho-social nuances[14] (this is in contrast to *leave*, which is basically a spatial verb).

As such, then, the spatial senses of *deixar*, although conceptually basic in that other senses derive from them, are not prototypical. This is exactly what is suggested in Figure 1: the six image schemas, instantiated in their respective spatial senses, are the structural support,

13. The remaining cases are indeterminate, involving neutralization or merger of the opposition in question. The same applies to the frequencies cited subsequently in this section.
14. Questionnaires presented to Portuguese speakers confirmed that spatial uses were interpreted as extensions of non-spatial uses.

the underlying images for the conceptualization of *deixar*; but it is the metaphorical elaborations of these image schemas that represent the most salient uses of *deixar*.

Let us now look in more detail at the semasiologically most salient, that is, most prototypical or representative, uses of *deixar*. It can be observed that within this set of non-spatial uses of the verb, some are more representative than others. In our corpus, the uses of *deixar*I which express an active attitude on the part of the subject have a frequency rate of 70.9% and are, therefore, more representative than those uses which express a passive attitude on the part of the subject, whose frequency rate only stands at 14.1%. Incidentally, among the strictly spatial uses, the active sense 'to go away' is also more representative than the passive counterpart 'not to approach', with frequencies of 4.4% against 0.5%, respectively. There is thus a general prototype which can be characterized as 'to actively suspend non-spatial interaction'. This prototype is instantiated in three focal points: (5) 'to abandon, to sever a relation', (13) 'to transfer possession', and (8) 'to cause something or someone to remain after having altered (the state of the object)'. At the same time, 'to abandon, to sever a relation' is the specific prototype of *deixar*I: not only does it occur in bivalent constructions, as in the examples in (5), but it is also present in trivalent constructions (for this reason, its frequency in the corpus is far greater than the rate of 9.2% in bivalent constructions). It can be seen, then, that degree of representativity may be detected at hierarchically different levels of a word's semantic structure; in *deixar*, it is located at the level of the uses that can be regarded as psychologically more "real" (that is, at the level I have previously classified as being that of the principal senses), but it also occurs at the higher, schematic level of semantic content; in Figure 1, (groups of) semasiologically salient uses have been indicated by bold-faced lines.

In turn, the prototypical sense of *deixar*II is (15) 'not to prevent, not to impede': out of a total of 796 occurrences with an animate subject and a verbal complement, 44.5% instantiate the passive sense, whereas the active senses (16) 'to allow, to permit, to authorize' and (17) 'to let go' have frequencies of 27.3% and 13.9%, respectively.

From an onomasiological perspective, it should be added that, in relation to *abandonar* 'to abandon', *deixar* expresses 'abandonment' with a lesser intensity and emotional density, hence *deixar* can be used as a euphemism for the processes conveyed by *abandonar*. Furthermore, there is no other verb in Portuguese which so perfectly expresses in positive terms the notion of 'non-preventing', nor the whole extension (and intension) of (passive) 'non-intervention' – from the most passive attitude to the decision not to intervene. In contrast, with the normative meaning (16), *deixar* occupies the semantic space of the permissive verbs *permitir* 'to permit', *consentir* 'to consent to', and even *autorizar* 'to authorize'. Still, it presents some advantages over its synonyms: *deixar* belongs to a non-formal register, and presupposes a more familiar or personal authority. Moreover, it possesses the advantages which result from its relative grammaticalization.

In sum, the semasiological structure of *deixar* shows a contrast between an active prototypical center (of *deixar*I) and a passive one (of *deixar*II) (shown in Figure 1 through the lines in bold type). It is this opposition (or inversion) of prototypical structures which reinforces the dissociation of the two categories *deixar*I and *deixar*II, thus highlighting the homonymic tension that characterizes the current semasiological complex of *deixar*.

There are, however, intra- and intercategorial prototypicality effects which lead to a certain approximation between *deixar*I and *deixar*II. Differences of salience among the senses of each category and also, as seen in the previous section, in relation to what essentially distinguishes the two categories (the static/dynamic construal of its object) result in categorization difficulties and overlapping areas. Recall the cases of *deixar alguém na dúvida* 'to leave someone in doubt' and *deixar alguém enganar-se* 'to let someone make a mistake', which are situated on the periphery of the respective categories (we shall subsequently refer to other cases).

In addition to the inversion relation referred to above, other meaning relations can be found between the two categories, which allow the two (discrete) categories to be viewed as continuous.

(a) *Metonymy*. 'To transfer the right to intervene' leads, by implication (strictly, an implicature), to 'not to intervene': the person who transfers the right of possession, use, or responsibility (or any other right of intervention) to another person can no longer intervene (at least not directly) and, thus, allows or does not prevent someone else from intervening. Conversely, 'not to intervene' leads, by implicature, to 'to transfer the right of intervention', for the person who does not intervene gives someone else the possibility of intervening. It is in this way that specific readings of 'to transfer/not to appropriate the right to intervene' carry, some more clearly than others, the nuances of permission, consent, or non-preventing, characteristic of *deixar*II. As such, apparently disparate concepts such as "possession" and "permission" are connected after all. In our moral and cultural models, possession involves a set of conventional rights and duties which govern the behavior of individuals in relation to the objects they possess.

(b) *Non-metaphorical similarity* between the two poles of the subject's passivity ('to passively suspend interaction' and 'to passively not intervene'). 'To passively suspend interaction (not to interact)' can be read as 'not to intervene passively' in relation to what is presented as static. In turn, 'to passively not intervene' can be read as 'to passively suspend interaction (not to interact)' with what is characterized by a dynamic tendency. 'To passively not intervene' has, as its object, an already existing process, and that pre-existing process, in which the subject of *deixar*II does not intervene, is similar to the naturally pre-existing situation or state with which the subject of *deixar*I does not interact. It is worth noting that this similarity between the passivity poles (which is non-metaphorical because it does not, in itself, involve a change in domain) gives rise to several categorization difficulties exemplified in cases such as *deixar* *na dúvida* 'to leave someone in doubt', *deixar em paz* 'to leave someone alone', *deixar o miúdo a brincar* 'to leave the child playing' (which is different from *deixar brincar o miúdo* 'to let the child play'), *deixar-se ficar* 'to allow oneself to stay', and so on.

(c) *Metonymic-metaphorical extension* from (1) 'to go away' – and, by extension, from the very category *deixar*I – to 'not to intervene' and, therefore, to *deixar*II. This extension is metonymic in that an entity that moves away is no longer able to intervene; at the same time, this extension is metaphorical since there is a change in the domain of the movement towards that of non-opposition. This extension can be interpreted as a follow-up of the metonymic-metaphorical extension from the spatial senses to the non-spatial senses of *deixar*I.

(d) *Weakening/strengthening* of the subject's degree of activity. Intracategorially, there is a weakening in *deixar*I, as the trajectory goes from the activity pole (the most prototypical one, as we have seen) to the passivity pole, passing through 'to transfer possession' (which denotes a certain weakening or relaxation of the subject's activity); there is a strengthening in *deixar*II, as the trajectory goes from the passivity pole (which is more prototypical) to the activity pole (from "without previous intervention" to "with previous intervention"). Intercategorially, there is a weakening of the subject's activity, from *deixar*I to *deixar*II; there is strengthening of the subject's activity, from *deixar*II to *deixar*I (note that this strengthening is less salient by virtue of the grammaticalization of *deixar*II).

In order to represent the semasiological structure of *deixar*, while accounting for the various facts I have just described (i.e., salience effects among readings or prototypicality, overlaps, hierarchical semantic links of schematization and specialization, and non-hierarchical semantic links, whether metaphorical or metonymic), I have made use of Langacker's (1987, 1991) network model of category structure (cf. also Taylor 1995b). Figure 2 represents the greater part of the semantic network of *deixar*. The heavy-line boxes indicate prototypical senses and the broken-line boxes non-salient senses. The solid arrows mark specifications, and the dashed arrows represent metonymic, metaphorical, or other non-hierarchical extensions.

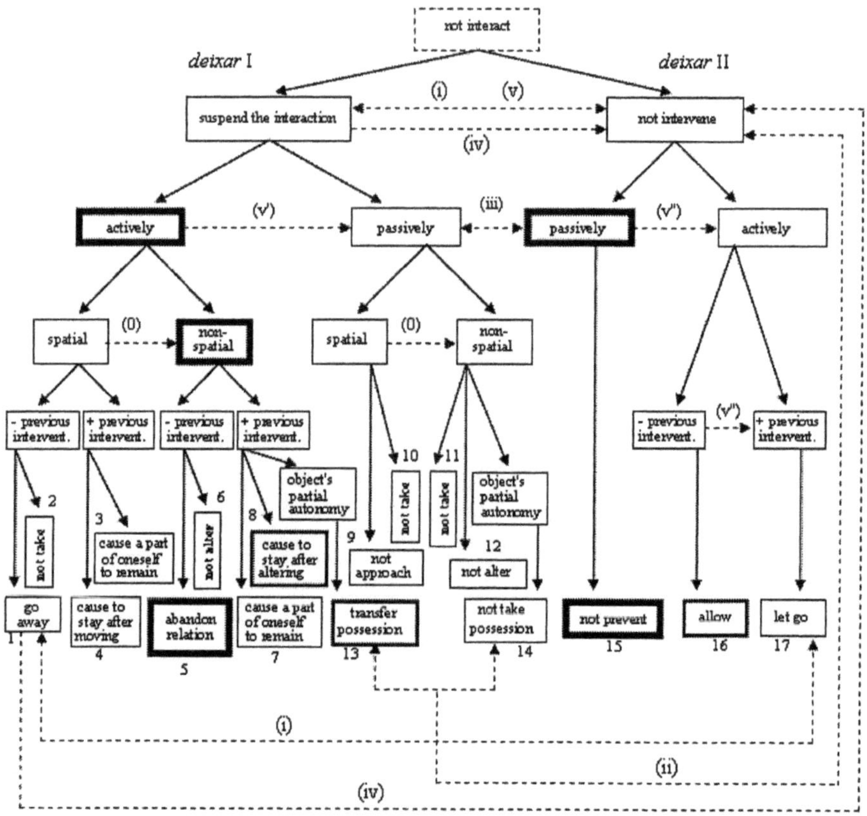

(0) metonymic-metaphorical extension
(i) inversion
(ii) metonymy
(iii) non-metaphorical similarity
(iv) metonymic-metaphorical extension
(v) weakening/strengthening
(v') weakening
(v'') strengthening

Figure 2. The semantic network of *deixar*.

This semantic network is, more properly speaking, a diagrammatic representation of the internal structure of *deixar*, not a very elegant one, but one which is as systematic as possible.[15] It need not be understood as a network that is mentally represented in the speaker's mind (cf. Rice, this volume).

5. The semantic development of *deixar*

In this section, I will consider the historical processes which have led to the semasiological structure of *deixar* in present-day Portuguese. *Deixar* comes from the Latin etymon *laxare* 'to loosen, to slacken' (bonds, fastenings, bolts, ropes, cables, attachments; body, mind) and originally also 'to widen, to enlarge', and entered Old Portuguese mainly in the form of *leixar*. A corpus of more than 2,000 occurrences (from Post-Classical and Late Latin and from Old and Classical Portuguese) suggests that it was probably on the basis of 'to let go' ('to release'), a metonymic development from *laxare* which became prototypical around the second century AD, that two groups of senses ('leave' and 'let'), which still occur in Modern Portuguese, were formed. This formation started in Post-Classical and Late Latin, and comprised at first the following two groups of senses: (i) 'to grant (peace, truce, leave, and rights)' and 'to forgive (sins, debts)' – senses formed mainly within the language of the Church but which were to disappear in the Romance verb – and also 'to allow, to consent, to authorize', formed with the infinitive from the sixth century onwards as *laxare* + infinitive then replaced *sinere* ('to let, to allow'); (ii) in competition with *relinquere* 'to leave' and finally substituting for it, the senses 'to go away, to abandon' (from the third or fourth century, or maybe earlier, as a nuance of 'to let go': when somebody drops, lets go, or releases an object, they also become separated from it), 'to leave somewhere or in a state (to move away afterwards/without having moved or altered the object)', 'to abandon

15. On this and other representational formats which have been used in cognitive semantics for the representation of the semasiological structure of lexical items (the network model, the radial set model, and the overlapping sets model), see Geeraerts (1995).

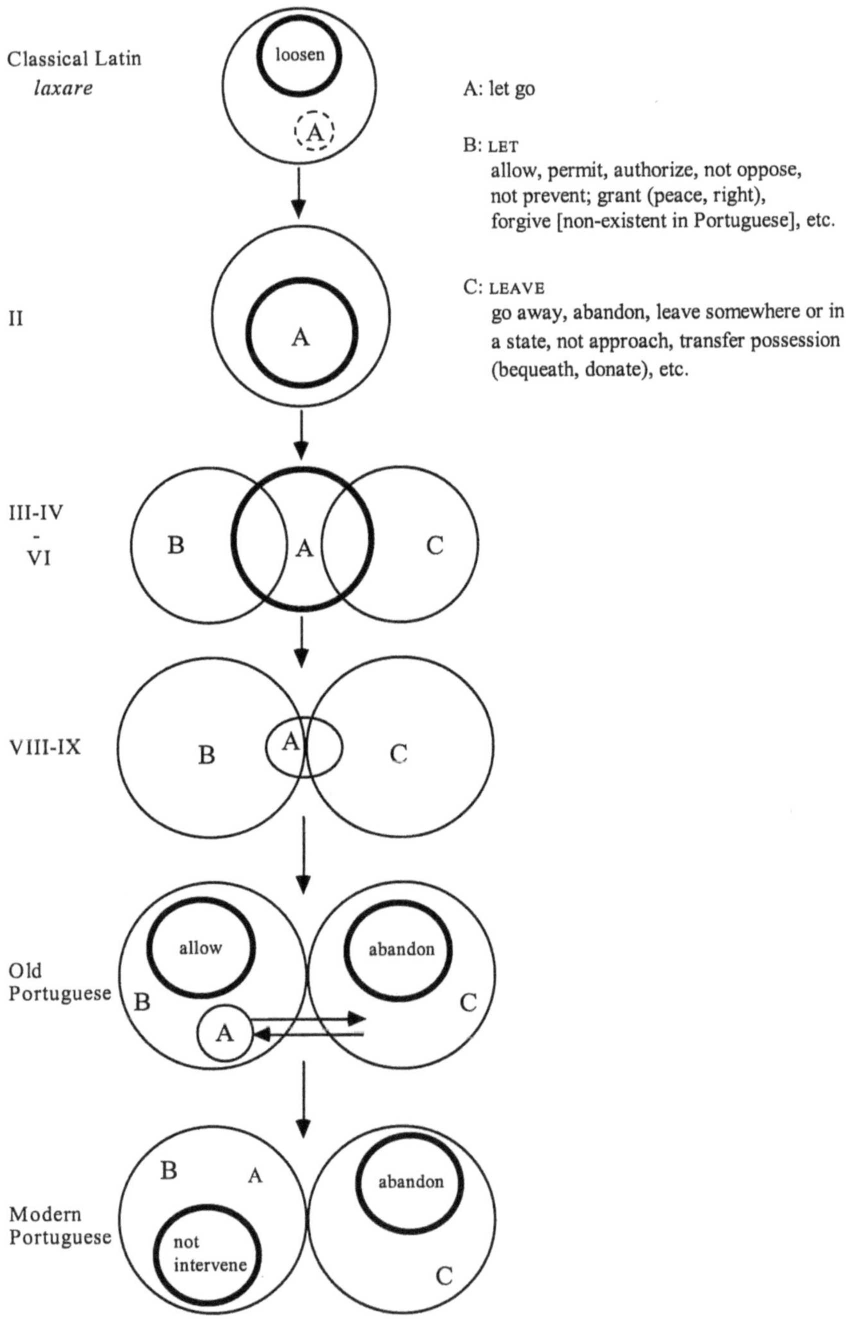

Figure 3. Schematic representation of the semantic development of *deixar*.

(to renounce, to cede) possession of', and, with clear evidence only from the eighth or ninth century, 'to transfer due to death, to bequeath, to donate'. It appears, then, that it was already in Latin that almost all the present-day senses of *deixar* had developed.

From Late Latin to Portuguese, there followed a process of *deprototypicalization* of 'to let go', which led to the consolidation of the two groups into two prototypical semasiological restructurings, and to a homonymic tension between them. Figure 3 systematizes the semantic development (the circles in bold type indicate prototypical centers).

Let us now consider the first part of *deixar*'s development in detail, that is, the formation, still in Latin, of the new meanings. Figure 4 represents the image-schema transformations shown as (a) to (g), which underlie the main stages in the semantic development of Latin *laxare*, from the prototypicalization of 'to let go' (second century), represented in IS1, to the appearance of the two groups of senses (in the third and fourth centuries, and in the sixth and seventh centuries), represented in IS2 – IS3 and IS4 – IS6. Please note that the image schemas in the semantic development of *deixar* are labeled differently from the synchronic image schemas in Table 2.

Three types of transformation can be pointed out:

(a) suppression (cf. [a], [c], and [f]) of the previous moment (T) of blocking (in IS1) or transportation (in IS5), and, concomitantly, restriction to IS1's and IS5's second part; addition (cf. [e]) of the previous moment of transportation;

(b) inversion of the movement of $P_1 - P_2$ (cf. [c] and [d]), that is, from the movement of P_2 and non-movement of P_1 to the movement of P_1 and non-movement of P_2;

(c) inversion of the attitude (and of the initial situation) of P_1 (cf. [b] and [g]), that is, from an active attitude (of P_1) and an initial situation of contact (with P_2) to a passive attitude (of P_1) and an initial situation of non-contact (with P_2).

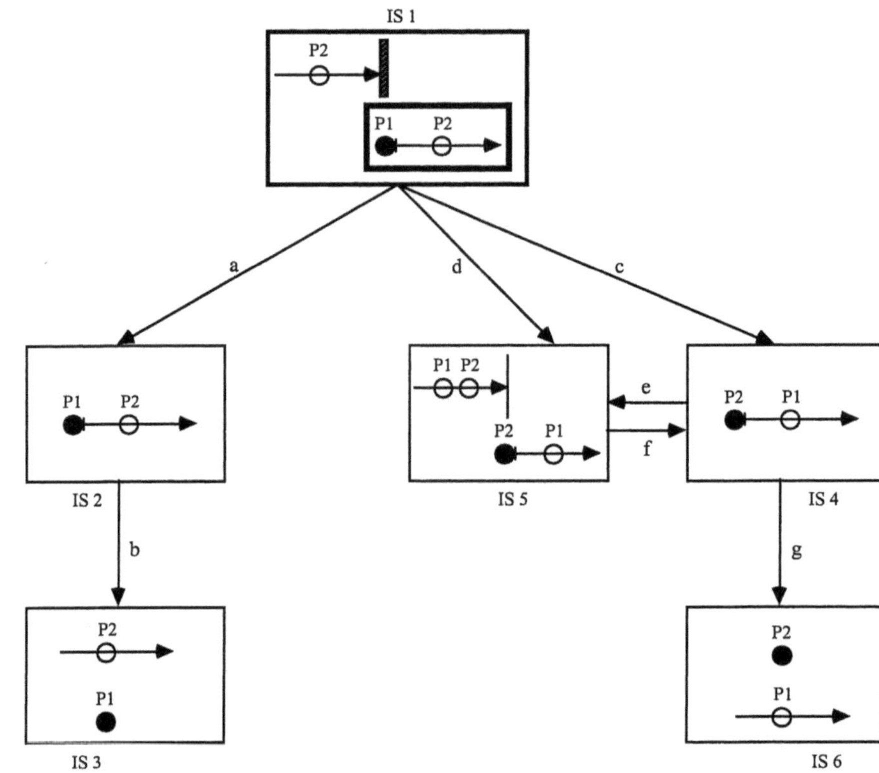

IS 1: let go
IS 2: grant (peace, right), forgive
allow, permit, authorize (*laxare* + infinitive)
IS 3: not to oppose, passively (*laxare* + infinitive)
IS 4: go away, abandon
go away without taking (/without altering)
IS 5: go away after having moved
(go away after having altered)
(go away after having transferred possession: bequeath, convey, grant)
IS 6: not to approach
abstain from taking (/from altering)

P1: subject
P2: direct object

a: suppression of T
b: P1 inversion
(passivization of P_1's role)
c: suppression of T + $P_1 - P_2$ inversion
d: $P_1 - P_2$ inversion
e: addition of T
f: suppression of T
g: P_1 inversion
(passivization of P_1's role)

Figure 4. Image-schema transformations in the semantic development of *laxare*.

The inversion of the participant carrying out the movement ($P_1 - P_2$ inversion) was the essential transformation that gave rise to the group of senses in which the object is disposed to rest, i.e. the group of 'leave'. And it is this inversion which caused *deixar*'s semantics to diverge, with on the one hand IS2, IS3, and also IS1, where the object (P_2) is dynamically construed ('let'), and on the other hand IS4, IS5 and IS6, where the object (P_2) is statically construed ('leave'). The inversion of the subject participant's attitude (P_1 inversion) was probably the last to occur.

It is important to note that the initial prototype of *laxare* ('to let go') unites (rather than separates) the two image schemas of *deixar* through the relation of inversion that exists between the object's dynamism (the movement of P_2) and that of the subject (the movement of P_1). In fact, *laxare* is originally neutral in relation to the two images: 'to let someone free' can occur by leaving a person (IS4), or by allowing them to go away (IS2). Although the latter image (IS2) predominates, the two image schemas are compatible with the 'let go' sense of *laxare*, without any ambiguity being present. The polysemy of *laxare* arises later, when the two instantiations of 'let go' developed different uses. This means that, from a diachronic perspective, this relation of inversion – this auto-antonymy – is not an autonomous mechanism of semantic extension (to the same extent as the metaphorical and metonymic extension mechanisms), but rather an epiphenomenon.[16]

Let us now consider the second part of the history of *deixar* and return to Figure 3. In the period from Late Latin to Old Portuguese, the disappearance of the original meaning 'to loosen, to slacken' and, above all, the deprototypicalization of 'to let go' caused *deixar*'s prototype(s) to shift from the spatial domain to the psycho-social and moral domains, giving rise to, on the one hand, the prototypicalization of 'to allow, to permit, to authorize' and, on the other hand, the prototypicalization of 'to abandon'. Simultaneously, a new redis-

16. Theoretically speaking, it is difficult to determine whether auto-antonymy is an autonomous mechanism of semantic extension (as some historical linguists suggest), or an effect of traditional semantic extensions.

tancing could be observed of the two semantic groups which had developed in Latin and which were now organized around these two new prototypes. Let us look in detail at this restructuring. In the corpus of Old Portuguese, the relational and functional sense of 'to abandon' registers a frequency rate of 17%, but given that this semantic value is present in other senses of *leixar*, its frequency is far higher. In turn, the strictly spatial senses only account for 11.4% (only 4.3% for 'to go away'). In *leixar*'s other semantic group, the active sense 'to allow, to permit, to authorize' has a frequency rate of 17.5%, whereas the passive sense 'not to prevent, not to impede' adds up to only 6.4%. The semasiological salience of 'to abandon' and 'to permit, to authorize' is further highlighted by the onomasiological salience of *leixar* in lexicalizing these two groups of semantic content; indeed, it is only at a later stage that they find genuine alternatives in the lexical items *abandonar* 'to abandon' (a Gallicism) and *permitir* 'to allow, to permit' (a juridical Latinism and even today a formal term).

As can be seen in Figure 3, the deprototypicalization of 'to let go' (evident from its low frequency of 5.2%) was accompanied by a movement towards the group of 'to let', formed with the infinitive, with which it had more in common both semantically and syntactically; however, this did not prevent it from associating itself with the group of 'to leave', given that its complement can be expressed nominally.[17] Old Portuguese also saw the schematic senses referred to in section 2 first emerging. These senses, which arose in both semantic groups, and only after *leixar*'s specific uses had become well-established, brought the two groups closer (I will designate the group characterized as 'to abandon' by *leixar-deixar*I and the group characterized 'to allow' by *leixar-deixar*II). Furthermore, it is only during this period that (i) the aspectual periphrasis *leixar de* + infinitive 'not to go on, to cease' and 'not to do, refrain from doing' emerged,

17. Different from this solution was what happened in French: instead of a semasiological demotion, there was an onomasiological change; that is, 'to let go', together with the primitive sense 'to loosen, to slacken', became onomasiologically distinct and autonomous, being expressed later by *lâcher*, cognate with *laisser*.

thereby grammaticalizing the dimensions of activity and passivity of the subject of *leixar*I, and that (ii) the causative construction *leixar* + infinitive (the most typical syntactic construction of *leixar*II), of Latin origin, was grammaticalized to a greater extent.[18]

From Old Portuguese to Modern Portuguese, a new reorganization of prototypes can be observed, prompted, above all, by the strengthening of the passive attitude of the subject. The frequency of all such passive occurrences (in either category) increased from 16.4% in Old Portuguese (10% in *leixar*I and 6.4% in *leixar*II) to 27.3% in sixteenth and seventeenth century Portuguese (16.3% in *deixar*I and 11% in *deixar*II), and amounts to 25.6% (8.8% in *deixar*I and 16.8% in *deixar*II) in Modern Portuguese. But on the whole, it is the passive reading of *leixar-deixar*II, i.e., 'not to prevent, not to intervene', which was comparatively more reinforced. In effect, in sixteenth and seventeenth century Portuguese, this passive reading was slightly more frequent than the active reading 'to allow, to permit, to authorize' (11% as against 10.3%), whereas in Old Portuguese the distribution of these two uses was, as we have seen, clearly the contrary. And in Modern Portuguese (cf. section 4), 'not to prevent, not to intervene' occurs far more frequently than 'to allow, to permit, to authorize'.

It should have become clear, then, that the passive uses, which chronologically postdate the active ones, have occupied an increasingly important position in *deixar*'s general semantic structure. Although one might argue that the original passivity of *laxare* 'to loosen, to slacken' has been re-established, it would be more accurate to see *deixar* developing towards the passivity of its agent.

Meanwhile, the promotion of passivity in *deixar*II, helped most probably by the entry into Portuguese of *permitir* 'to allow, to permit' in the fifteenth century, has given rise to a structural asymmetry of prototypical values (cf. Figure 3). Whereas in Old Portuguese the two prototypical senses (i.e., 'to abandon' and 'to allow') were both

18. It is from Old Portuguese, and along with the construction *leixar* + causee + infinitive (VOV) that the monoclausal structure *deixar* + infinitive + causee (VV) appears and the subject of the transitive infinitive begins to be formed like an indirect object or dative.

active, from Classical Portuguese onwards, the prototypical reading of *deixar*II ('not to prevent, not to intervene') has become passive, while the active prototype ('to abandon') in *deixar*I has been retained. This has given rise to a greater homonymic tension between the two categories. At the same time, the late entry into Portuguese of *permitir* 'to allow, to permit' and *abandonar* 'to abandon' has positioned the prototypical senses of *deixar* on hierarchically more schematic levels (cf. section 4), leading to the consolidation of *deixar*'s schematic contents and to intercategorial associations between *deixar*I and *deixar*II (referred to in section 4); and although these associations already existed prior to *permitir*'s and *abandonar*'s entry into the language, it is only afterwards that they have become increasingly necessary semasiologically (to prevent homonymic split) – in spite of the fact that they are not so close to each other.[19]

6. Conclusion: *deixar* and polysemy research

Deixar raises some important questions for lexical semantics in general and for polysemy research in particular. One important issue that is intrinsically bound up with the question of polysemy concerns the coherence of a lexical category. *Deixar* shows that, in spite of the homonymic tension that characterizes its present-day semasiological structure, the category retains a certain internal coherence. In part, the coherence of *deixar* can be grounded in its prototype organization, in the various dimensions that structure its two semantic groups, and in the meaning relations between these groups. But the principal factor lending internal cohesion to *deixar* is the image-schema transformations that bind the two groups of senses together.

The homonymic tension in *deixar* manifests itself in the existence of two categories (*deixar*I 'to suspend interaction with what is characterized as static', and *deixar*II 'not to oppose what is presented as dynamic'), which exhibit different prototypical structures (an active

19. For a detailed comparison of the semantic history and structure of the Romance cognate verbs, see Soares da Silva (in press b).

prototypical center in *deixar*I and a passive prototypical center in *deixar*II). As we saw in the previous section, this homonymic tension results from a historical process of deprototypicalization of 'to let go', which may thus constitute the first step towards a homonymic split. But the homonymization of *deixar* is not yet complete, as evidenced by the fact that the verb still presents some internal coherence.

It is of theoretical import to note that the process of deprototypicalization (as a process of split) mirrors the process of prototypicalizing merger described in Geeraerts (1997: 130–150). In truth, *split* and *merger* are complementary processes: the former leads (or can lead) to homonymy, the latter leads to a dehomonymization and to polysemy. What links them more than anything else, though, is the fact that prototypicality plays a major role in both types of semantic development. In the merger described by Geeraerts (Dutch *verduwen*, whose range of senses results from the conceptual merger of two etymologically distinct words), a new prototype constitutes the center of the emerging category. In the case of *deixar,* the deprototypicalization constitutes the first step in the direction of possible eventual homonymy.

The semasiological structure of *deixar* in Modern Portuguese results from two restructurings of the semasiological complex of Latin *laxare* around two new prototypical centers. As we have seen, intra- and intercategorial prototypicality effects may link up the two categories (*deixar*I and *deixar*II). But what constitutes the basis for the coherence of *deixar* is not so much its prototypical structuration, but the phenomenon of image-schema transformations. In this respect, I have shown that the two categories (*deixar*I and *deixar*II) are systematically linked by an inversion of the respective image schema's dynamic participant. Additional links between *deixar*'s two semantic poles come from the inversion of the subject participant's attitude, as well as the addition and the suppression of parts of image schemas. Theoretically, these findings are important in that they make us aware that prototypicality is not the only phenomenon that can provide the basis for the coherence of a category.

The image schemas and the proposed image-schema transformations demonstrate the coherence of not just any polysemic complex, but of a polysemic complex that tends towards homonymy (or, if one prefers, of a semasiological complex that situates itself between polysemy and homonymy). They therefore allow us to put into evidence the flexibility and cognitive efficiency of the polysemic categories, as well as their complexity and heterogeneity.

They also allow an explanation of the syntactic behavior of *deixar*, which can take either a nominal or a verbal complement. A transitive construction with nominal complementation codes the subject participant's movement and the object participant's static construal, whereby a bivalent (transitive) construction lexicalizes the subject's movement and a trivalent (transitive) construction adds the circumstance in which the object continues to be or comes to stay. In neither of these cases is the transitivity of *deixar* prototypical, due precisely to the image of the subject's moving away or keeping away. Secondly, a construction with verbal complementation lexicalizes the image of the object participant's dynamic tendency (or movement), and the force dynamics of non-impediment (or the cessation of impediment) of this movement implies the causative construction. Finally, the image inversion of the dynamic participant allows us to perceive the conceptual affinity between non-prototypical transitivity, characterized by the subject's moving away or keeping away, and negative causation (itself also non-prototypical). This connection between the image schemas and the syntactic constructions constitutes one more manifestation of the internal coherence of the verb.

The image schemas represent a paradigmatic example of force dynamics, that of not exerting a force that might impinge upon the natural disposition of an entity, and also of variations in this dynamic schema (some of which are identified by Talmy 1988). In addition, they help us understand other aspects of the semantics of *deixar*, which were summarily analyzed: the cognitive model of negative causation and specific forms of letting causation; the metaphorical elaborations of motion and non-impingement in various abstract domains, especially the metaphorical construal of (rupture in) interpersonal relations, of death, of passivity, of laxity, as well as of permission and possession. All these aspects are manifestations of the internal coherence of *deixar*'s semasiological complex.

As I pointed out earlier, the spatial senses of *deixar* are structurally basic but not prototypical, this being the result of a historical process in which prototypes undergo change. This idea of a conceptually basic, but not prototypical meaning is theoretically very important, and has a number of important implications. Firstly, it allows us to put into evidence the problems involved in the *derivational* model of polysemy, widely practiced and defended by many authors (for an extensive critique, see Geeraerts 1993: 255–258). According to this model, polysemy involves permanently stored meanings rather than surface-structure interpretations, and what can be derived procedurally from stored information need not itself be stored. Put differently, a particular interpretation constitutes a distinct meaning if it cannot be derived by rules. Now, the non-spatial senses of *deixar* are not only derivable (metonymically and metaphorically from spatial senses), but they also constitute stored meanings which are more prototypical than those from which they may have derived. *Deixar*'s non-spatial senses would have to be considered, then, as meanings as well as non-meanings. *Deixar* is thus a good example of what Langacker (1987: 29) has called the "rule/list fallacy". Secondly, the fact that the spatial senses of *deixar* are structurally basic but not prototypical runs counter to the intuitive, and even theoretical distinction between literal and figurative meanings, whereby the first are more autonomous and salient than the second. At the very least, it demonstrates the problematic character of this distinction. Thirdly, *deixar* shows that the prototypical members of a category can be situated within the area of category (meaning) extension; in other words, the prototypical center of a category need not coincide with its basic conceptual and diachronically primary center.

The image schemas of *deixar* are imaginary, non-propositional, and experiential gestalts, and have been studied extensively in cognitive linguistics: LINKAGE, CONTACT, DETACHMENT, SEPARATION, DISTANCE, CONTAINER, and PART-WHOLE; image schemas of spatial orientation such as AWAY, BACK, BEHIND, ASIDE, and OUT; image schemas of force such as ABSENCE OF RESTRAINT, REMOVAL OF

RESTRAINT or OF BLOCKAGE, RUPTURE, and SLACKENING/LOOSENING. Although they are not discussed in the literature on the subject, the image-schema transformations of inversion and of addition/ suppression that were introduced in this paper are simple and natural.

The semantic analysis of *deixar* allows for the elucidation of other quantitative and qualitative aspects and problems of a polysemous cluster. Quantitatively, it documents the existence of categories with more than one prototypical center, the localization of prototypicality at different hierarchical levels, and the problems concerning the hypothesis of a unitary meaning. In regard to this last aspect, postulating that *deixar* means essentially 'not to interact' (or 'not to interfere') is to say little about its meaning. This, or any other, single common denominator ends up being neither semasiological unitary (only with difficulty can it be the basis for predicting or deriving the diverse readings of the verb), nor onomasiologically distinctive (because it is unable to distinguish *deixar* from other verbs), nor psychologically relevant (because speakers do not need it to use and interpret the verb).

Qualitatively, *deixar* is a good example of the structural multidimensionality of a polysemic category. It is also a good example of the variety and complexity of the relations that can link the uses of a lexical item: metaphorical and metonymical relations, non-metaphorical similarity relations, hierarchical relations (schematization/ specialization), and also image-schema transformations and non-canonical relations such as inversion and weakening/strengthening. Another important point is that the very possibility of relating the different uses of *deixar* rests on the availability of encyclopedic knowledge and of cognitive processes. This demonstrates the inseparability of conceptual and linguistic knowledge.

Our analysis of *deixar* points to the importance of certain methodological approaches. First, the corpus-based approach enabled us to describe the *real* uses of the verb. At times, analyses in cognitive semantics run the risk of losing themselves in introspection that is both idealist and uncontrollable (Geeraerts 1999). Second, a lexical-semantic analysis gains with the integration of conceptual and analytical instruments provided by cognitive semantics. The combination of the image-schema approach and the prototype-based model allowed us to describe the coherence of *deixar* and the process of deprototypicalization that led to the homonymic tension of the verb. Third, the analysis of the historical development of *deixar* represents circumstantial proof of our interpretation of the present semasiological complex and shows the inevitable relationship that exists between the synchronic dynamics of a word and its historical evolution. Fourth, the necessarily brief comparisons between *deixar* and alternatives such as *abandonar* and *permitir* reveal the complementarity of the semasiological and onomasiological perspectives. Fifth, the account makes evident the advantages of a polysemic analysis over a homonymic one, as well as the need of an analysis both at a lower level (of psychologically more real readings) and at a higher level (of the schematic contents) of the semasiological structure. A final point concerns the problem of mental representations, brought up in the recent debate between Croft (1998), Sandra (1998), and Tuggy (1999). I hope to have provided some linguistic evidence (particularly of a historical nature) for the polysemy of *deixar* in the language, and, possibly, in the mind.

In conclusion, this analysis suggests that the coherence of a lexical category is an important theoretical issue and that cognitive semantics ought to take upon itself both the task of investigating the different cognitive processes that constitute the basis of categorial coherence and that of clarifying the relation between these processes. It can accomplish this by developing models for the structure of polysemy and by making use of the methodological approaches referred to above. This analysis shows specifically that image schemas and their transformations are important cognitive processes for the coherence of a polysemous category.

References

Beitel, Dinara, Raymond W. Gibbs and Paul Sanders
2001 The embodied approach to the polysemy of the spatial preposition *on*. In: Hubert Cuyckens and Britta Zawada (eds.), *Polysemy in Cognitive Linguistics*, 241–260. Amsterdam: John Benjamins.

Brugman, Claudia
1981 Story of *over*. M.A. thesis, University of California, Berkeley.
Cienki, Alan
1997 Some properties and groupings of image schemas. In: Marjolijn Verspoor, Kee Dong Lee and Eve Sweetser (eds.), *Lexical and Syntactical Constructions and the Construction of Meaning*, 3–15. Amsterdam: John Benjamins.
1998 STRAIGHT: An image schema and its metaphorical extensions. *Cognitive Linguistics* 9: 107–149.
Clausner, Timothy C. and William Croft
1999 Domains and image schemas. *Cognitive Linguistics* 10: 1–31.
Croft, William
1998 Linguistic evidence and mental representations. *Cognitive Linguistics* 9: 151–173.
Dewell, Robert B.
1994 *Over* again: Image-schema transformations in semantic analysis. *Cognitive Linguistics* 5: 351–380.
Edelman, Gerald M.
1992 *Bright Air, Brilliant Fire: On the Matter of the Mind*. New York: Basic Books.
Geeraerts, Dirk
1993 Vagueness's puzzles, polysemy's vagaries. *Cognitive Linguistics* 4: 223–272.
1995 Representational formats in cognitive semantics. *Folia Linguistica* 29: 21–41.
1997 *Diachronic Prototype Semantics. A Contribution to Historical Lexicology*. Oxford: Clarendon Press.
1999 Idealist and empiricist tendencies in cognitive semantics. In: Theo Janssen and Gisela Redeker (eds.), *Cognitive Linguistics: Foundations, Scope, and Methodology*, 163–194. Berlin: Mouton de Gruyter.
Gibbs, Raymond W., Dinara Beitel, Michael Harrington and Paul Sanders
1994 Taking a stand on the meanings of *stand*: Bodily experience as motivation for polysemy. *Journal of Semantics* 11: 231–251.
Gibbs, Raymond W. and Herbert L. Colston
1995 The cognitive psychological reality of image schemas and their transformations. *Cognitive Linguistics* 6: 347–378.
Johnson, Mark
1987 *The Body in the Mind: The Bodily Basis of Meaning, Imagination, and Reason*. Chicago: The University of Chicago Press.
1993 *Moral Imagination: Implications of Cognitive Science for Ethics*. Chicago: The University of Chicago Press.

Lakoff, George
1987 *Women, Fire, and Dangerous Things: What Categories Reveal about the Mind*. Chicago: The University of Chicago Press.
1990 The Invariance Hypothesis: Is abstract reason based on image-schemas? *Cognitive Linguistics* 1: 39–74.
Langacker, Ronald W.
1987 *Foundations of Cognitive Grammar*, Volume 1: *Theoretical Prerequisites*. Stanford: Stanford University Press.
1991 *Foundations of Cognitive Grammar*, Volume 2: *Descriptive Application*. Stanford: Stanford University Press.
1999 *Grammar and Conceptualization*. Berlin: Mouton de Gruyter.
Mandler, Jean
1992 How to build a baby: II Conceptual primitives. *Psychological Review* 99: 587–604.
McNeill, David
1992 *Hand and Mind: What Gestures Reveal about Thought*. Chicago: The University of Chicago Press.
Norvig, Peter and George Lakoff
1987 Taking: A study in lexical network theory. In: Jon Aske, Natasha Beery, Laura Michaelis and Hana Filip (eds.), *Proceedings of the Thirteenth Annual Meeting of the Berkeley Linguistics Society*, 195–206. Berkeley, CA: Berkeley Linguistics Society.
Rice, Sally
this volume Growth of a lexical network: Nine English prepositions in acquisition.
Sandra, Dominiek
1998 What linguists can and can't tell you about the human mind: A reply to Croft. *Cognitive Linguistics* 9: 361–378.
Seiler, Hansjakob
1983 *Possession as an Operational Dimension of Language*. Tübingen: Gunter Narr Verlag.
Soares da Silva, Augusto
1999 *A Semântica de* DEIXAR*: Uma Contribuição para a Abordagem Cognitiva em Semântica Lexical* [The Semantics of the Verb *Deixar*: Towards a Cognitive Approach in Lexical Semantics]. Lisboa: Fundação Calouste Gulbenkian and Fundação para a Ciência e a Tecnologia. (Ph.D. dissertation, Catholic University of Portugal, Braga, 1997)
2000 The "letting" causation: Evidence from Portuguese. Paper presented at the Winter Symposium "Structures of Causal Meaning", Center for Semiotic Research, Aarhus, 27–29 January 2000.

in press a Verbs of letting: Some cognitive and historical aspects. In: Nicole Delbecque and Bert Cornillie (eds.), *On Interpreting Construction Schemas*. Amsterdam: John Benjamins.

in press b La structure sémantique de "laisser" dans les langues romanes. In: Fernando Sánchez Miret (ed.), *Actas del XXIII Congreso Internacional de Lingüística y Filologiia Románica*. Tübingen: Max Niemeyer Verlag.

Sweetser, Eve

1990 *From Etymology to Pragmatics: Metaphorical and Cultural Aspects of Semantic Structure*. Cambridge: Cambridge University Press.

Talmy, Leonard

1988 Force dynamics in language and cognition. *Cognitive Science* 12: 49–100.

1996 The windowing of attention in language. In: Masayoshi Shibatani and Sandra A. Thompson (eds.), *Grammatical Constructions: Their Form and Meaning*, 235–286. Oxford: Oxford University Press.

Taylor, John R.

1995 a *Linguistic Categorization: Prototypes in Linguistic Theory*, 2nd edition. Oxford: Clarendon Press.

1995 b Approaches to word meaning: The network model (Langacker) and the two-level model (Bierwisch) in comparison. In: René Dirven and Johan Vanparys (eds.), *Current Approaches to the Lexicon*, 3–26. Frankfurt am Main: Peter Lang.

Tuggy, David

1999 Linguistic evidence for polysemy in the mind: A response to William Croft and Dominiek Sandra. *Cognitive Linguistics* 10: 343–368.

The Nawatl verb *kīsa*: A case study in polysemy

David Tuggy

Abstract

Even a cursory examination of the meanings of the Orizaba Nawatl verb *kīsa* (perhaps best glossed as 'emerge') illustrates a number of basic principles that are relevant to debates about the status of polysemy. These principles are commonsensical, so ubiquitously evident that it is difficult not to call them "facts" or "truths"; yet they have been denied by some linguists, so it is useful to reaffirm them. Among them are the following: (i) polysemy is rampant; (ii) polysemous meanings are related in multiple, reasonable, even systematic ways; (iii) context is necessary for the establishing and maintenance of these meanings and for choice among them; (iv) nevertheless, all of this does not amount to prediction or allow meanings to be omitted from the theoretical lexicon because of their relation to more basic meanings or to context. Learning a language still involves learning which of these meanings are and which are not established.

Keywords: construal, criteria for polysemy, decontextualization, elaboration, extension, idiosyncrasy, landmark, monosemic bias, monosemy, motivation, multiple homonymy, partial schematicity, polysemy, present context, relatedness of meaning, schema, trajector.

1. Introduction

There are certain propositions about language which bear on much debate about polysemy, and which seem to me to have such ample, even ubiquitous support that they are almost self-evident; for brevity and convenience I propose to refer to them as "facts", even though some theoreticians, including notably Ruhl (1989), have been eager to deny crucial aspects of them. These facts must be accounted for by any adequate theory of meaning. Among them are the following: (i) polysemy is rampant; (ii) polysemous meanings are related in multiple, reasonable, even systematic ways; (iii) context is necessary for the establishing and maintenance of these meanings and for choice among them; (iv) yet this does not warrant a deterministic account of those meanings such as might allow them to be omitted from the theoretical lexicon because of their relation to more basic meanings or to context. The meanings are neither arbitrary nor inevitable with respect to each other and to context; they are only reasonable.

In this chapter, I pursue as a case study a single verb root of Orizaba Nawatl (henceforth Nawatl),[1] comparing it occasionally with the English and Spanish structures that would be used to translate it. These data will repeatedly illustrate the above-mentioned facts and appropriate conclusions will be drawn.

2. The verb *kīsa*: the data

2.1. Sentences illustrating usages of kīsa

Kīsa is the citation form of an intransitive verb root of Nawatl which is probably best glossed in English as 'emerge'. To exemplify its

1. Orizaba Nawatl is spoken in the mountainous area south of the city of Orizaba, Veracruz, Mexico. It has been referred to by a number of other names, perhaps the most common of them being Zongolica Nahuatl or Náhuatl de la Sierra de Zongolica. The data in this paper are from the town of San Juan del Río, also known as Rafael Delgado. (Much of this town's economy depends on floriculture, a concern reflected in some of the examples.) "Nawatl" is used instead of the traditional "Nahuatl" because it reflects the orthography most used in the area (and adopted in this paper). Serendipitously, its most natural English pronunciation is much more nearly correct. (The first of the two syllables is stressed; and the *tl* is a voiceless lateral affricate.) Most of what is said here regarding *kīsa* holds true of its usage in other variants of Nahuatl (Aztecan) as well.

I wish to thank Victor Hernández de Jesús, in particular, for helping me learn Orizaba Nawatl and for providing much of the data used in this paper, including all the example sentences.

usage, I have selected from a database of illustrative sentences a baker's dozen of sentences in which it appears. They had all been composed to illustrate the usage of words other than *kīsa*, and happened to be the first thirteen usages of *kīsa* which were found following a randomly chosen spot. For presentational ease, I have altered their ordering so as to group similar cases together; otherwise they are as they occurred in the database.[2] *Kīsa* is in each case glossed as 'emerge', but the free translations show the inadequacy of that gloss in many cases.[3,4]

---

2. They originally occurred in the order (1) (5) (6) (4) (7) (12) (9) (13) (8) (10) (2) (3).
3. Each Nawatl sentence is followed by a word-for-word translation line, in which a sequence of English words joined by periods corresponds to a single Nawatl word. The orthography is that used by the Decanato de la Sierra de Zongolica for their vernacular publications. It does not show vowel length (which is very elusive); thus, the forms of *kīsa* do not have the long *i* marked. Everything is pronounced essentially as in Spanish, except that *x* is the alveopalatal voiceless fricative [š] or [ʃ], *h* is like English *h*, *tl* is the voiceless lateral affricate [ƛ] or [$t^{ɬ}$], *ll* is a long *l*, and *w* is pronounced [w] or [v] depending on which town a speaker comes from. Almost all words have penultimate stress.
4. As might be expected in an agglutinative language like Nawatl, *kīsa* does not usually occur as a naked stem, and it may be questioned what effect the affixes attached to it have on the meanings here set forth. The reader will have to take my word for it that the answer is, essentially, "nothing significant". Note, however, that (i) as noted in the text, reduplication is involved in the 'wiggle back and forth' sense of sentence (4), (ii) the 'almost' or 'practically' sense of (12) and (13) cannot occur with affixes, but is associated with the naked stem (see footnote 15), and (iii) for obvious reasons, meanings with non-human trajectors (subjects) will not allow first or second person subject markers, those which specify singular trajectors will not allow plurals, and so forth.

   Here are the forms of *kīsa* which occur in this paper, with affix cuts and glosses indicated. ("ø" indicates the third-person zero subject-marking prefix, and "trunc" is a process morpheme of truncation, indicating preterite tense except in *kīstikah*, where it is morphologically mandated): *kīsa* [emerge] or [ø-emerge], *kīsa-h* [ø-emerge-plural], *kīsa-s* [ø-emerge-future], *kīs-tikah* [ø-emerge-trunc-honorific], *ō-kīsa-ko* [past-ø-emerge-came.to], *ō-kīs* [past-ø-emerge-trunc], *ō-kīs-ki* [past-ø-emerge-trunc-preterite.singular], *ō-ti-kīs* [past-you.singular-emerge-trunc], *ti-ki-kīsa* [you.singular-reduplication-emerge], *yi-on-kīsa-s* [already-ø-suddenly/surprisingly-emerge-future].

2.2. *Physical emergence: prototypical* kīsa

If a naïve Nawatl speaker is asked what *kīsa* means (or a naïve English speaker what *emerge* means), he (or she)[5] will probably describe or demonstrate a situation in which one physical entity is enclosed within another, and the first entity moves, through time, out from within the enclosing entity. This sort of process is, intuitively, the central or *prototypical* notion of EMERGE.[6] The following sentences illustrate usages of *kīsa* which fit that notion.

(1) *Mokmotlapokan* *apanmeh,* *walkiawis*
may.they.yet.be.opened ditches it.ups.and.rains
yionkah *kanik* *kisas* *n* *atl.*
there.already.is whereabouts it.will.emerge the water
'Let's first open up the ditches, so that if it should rain there will be a place where the water can get out.'

(2) *Yi* *tetahtzin* *Daniel,* *machok* *keman*
already someone's.father.honorific Daniel not.still when
kistikah *iseltihtzin.*
he.emerges.honorific his.alone.honorific
'Daniel is an old man now, and he does not ever go out by himself any more.'

5. To avoid such awkward parenthetical expressions as this, I will follow in this paper the tradition of using a masculine pronoun to refer to a human being who could perfectly well be of either gender.
6. Prototypicality generally correlates with such things as statistical predominance, early position among examples chosen when speakers are asked to illustrate or explain the meaning, and logical centrality (prototypical meanings are more likely to have extensions in several different directions). Prototypical relations (including verbal concepts) will tend to occur between prototypical participants (e.g., in this case physical objects as trajector and landmark). Assessing these characteristics thus provides a rough (because indirect) measurement of prototypicality which goes beyond intuition (and often confirms it). Other measures, such as comparison of recognition response times, are also useful, but are more difficult to use in a field situation. In text, the most common meanings of *kīsa* are physical emergings (subcases of 1.a), followed by 'result' or 'change of state' readings (subcases of 3.o).

(3) *N Ramón kualli yimomachilihtih;*
the Raymond good already.he.goes.along.feeling.himself
kihtowa kanah sábado koxamo
he.says.it somewhere Saturday whether.not
yionkisas kanah.
already.he.will.up.and.emerge somewhere
'Raymond is feeling better and better now; he says that by about Saturday maybe he can go out somewhere.'

In (1), rainwater is envisioned as emerging from where it is pent up (presumably in a field) through a ditch, and in (2) and (3) a person emerges from his home into the world outside it. Of course, in English we would not use the word *emerge* in normal speech, but rather (depending on a number of factors including the viewpoint we assume in speaking) verb-particle phrases such as *get out*, *come out*, or *go out*.

Following Langacker (1987, 1991), we will refer to the moving entity in this prototypical notion as the *trajector* (tr) and the enclosing entity as *landmark* (lm). This concept is diagrammed in 1.a.[7] The two subcases attested in sentences (1) and (2)–(3), of water emerging from a containing structure, and of a person emerging from his house, are diagrammed in 1.b and 1.c respectively.[8]

7. Labeled subdiagrams of figures are referred to by a number followed by a period and a letter (or two). The same designation is used for the concept which such a subdiagram represents: thus, "1.c" means either "the subdiagram labeled 'c.' in Figure 1" or "the concept (of leaving the house) which is represented in 1.c". The identifying letter of these subdiagrams remains constant: thus, 2.a is a repetition of 1.a, and 5.h of 3.h.
8. Figure 1 illustrates the following diagramming conventions (from Langacker 1987): meanings are represented in boxes whose boldfacing or lack thereof correlates to posited degree of cognitive prominence or *salience*. Categorizing or generalizing structures (*schemas*) such as 1.a are connected by arrows to their subcases or *elaborations* (1.b–c). The schema contains only material common to the elaborations. A dashed arrow such as those in Figure 2 indicates *partial schematicity*: here the categorized concepts contain specifications which conflict with specifications of the categorizing schema. Thus, A ----→ B means "A is schematic for B and B elaborates A; B is unproblematically an example of

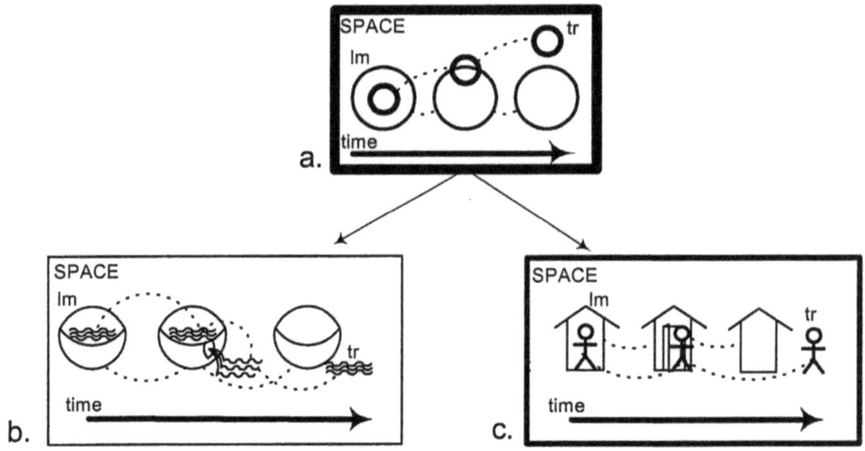

Figure 1. Prototypical *kīsa.*

2.3. *Extensions from the prototypical* kīsa

The other examples diverge from prototypical EMERGE in one way or another.

Actually, the meaning in (2) and (3) is very likely not quite the same as that represented in 1.c. The trajector may be construed not as leaving the interior of the house and moving to the area immediately

---

the kind A; B has all of A's specifications plus some of its own which do not conflict with them". A → B means rather "A is partially schematic for B; B can be seen (with some difficulty) as a kind of A; A and B are similar but they have specifications that conflict".

For representational and mnemonic ease, crude graphic representations are used, such as circles for objects, and stick-men for humans. These are not unsuitable to concepts which have an important spatial-configuration component which is nevertheless not specified in all details. Labels are also utilized, particularly tr to mark the trajector, and lm the landmark. The passage of conceived time (crucial to the verbality of these meanings) is represented by a labeled arrow, and different configurations are aligned along it. Identity of participants in those configurations is indicated by dotted lines.

outside of it (a slightly more precise version of 1.c which is represented in 2.d and is translatable as 'go outside'). Rather, he may be construed as leaving the vicinity of the house – whether he is originally inside the house or not is basically irrelevant – a concept translatable as 'go out' or 'leave the house' (2.e).[9] Here, the landmark is a "virtual" one: there are no clear physical boundaries setting off the enclosing area (the vicinity of the house) from its surroundings. English allows such landmarks with some verbs (e.g., *leave* or *move out of your place/the center of the room*) but not easily with *emerge* (*?*emerge from your place/the center of the room*). Nawatl, in contrast, puts no such restriction on *kīsa*: i.e., 2.f is well-established in Nawatl.

(4)

Amo	*semitzillihtok*	*welitis*
not.question	we.are.telling.you	possibly

tikmomaas	*n*	*tlaketzalli*	*san*
you.will.hit.yourself.against.it	the	stood.up.thing	just

tikikisa	*Leonardo*
you.reduplication.emerge,	Leonard.

'Haven't we been telling you you were liable to bang into that pillar, the way you keep wiggling back and forth, Leonard?'

This notion of emergence from a virtual landmark helps us understand example (4). Here Leonard, who from the way he is addressed is presumably a child, is represented as repeatedly (the repetition being coded by the reduplication) moving out of (and, of course, back into) the area where he is supposed to remain.[10] Both 2.g (the non-repetitive notion from (4)) and 2.e. are subcases of 2.f, in which

9. The greater salience of 2.e vis-à-vis 2.d relates to the fact that 2.e is more likely to be understood in structures like (2) and (3), where context does not specifically favor one over the other.

10. Another (and not incompatible) analysis would take *kīsa* as meaning 'leave' (an established meaning; see below) and the reduplication as indicating insincerity or non-genuineness (as it does elsewhere), yielding something like 'make like you're going to leave', a meaning quite close to that appropriate in the context.

a person leaves a virtual landmark. The arrows connecting 2.a to 2.f, 2.c to 2.e, and 2.d and 2.e to each other are dashed, indicating a relationship of *partial schematicity*, since there is a degree of conflict in the specifications, so that, e.g., 2.e is not a straightforward elaboration of 2.c (leaving home is not a clear example of a kind of emerging from the house) but rather involves some degree of semantic extension from it.

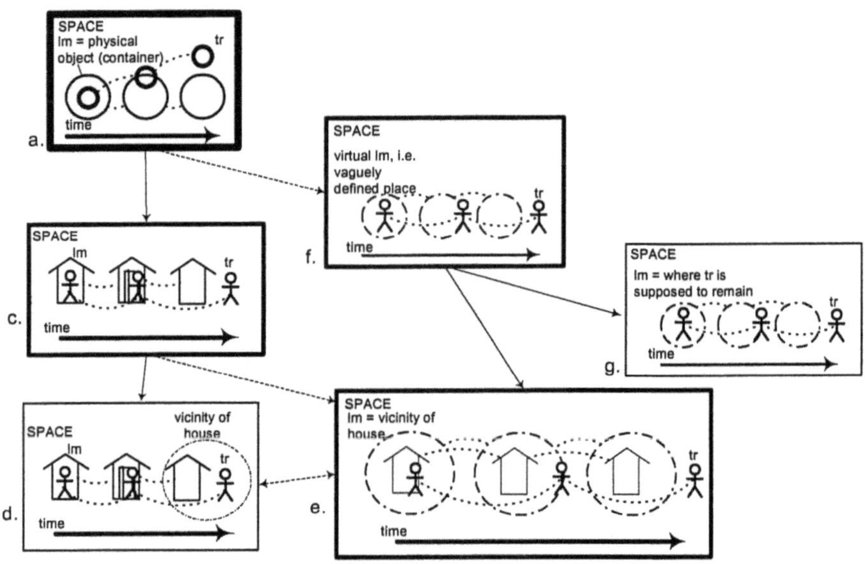

Figure 2. *kīsa* with "virtual" landmarks.

(5) *Kihtowa n* *Tomasa* *tlenoh* *imak* *okis.*
she.says the Thomasina what.is.that on.her.hand it.emerged
'Thomasina wonders what it is that has broken out on her hand.'

In (5), *kīsa* refers to something like a wart or a pimple or a boil appearing on the body, a process which in English is not labeled *emerging* but rather *breaking out* or perhaps *popping up* or *erupting*. Yet it seems clear that there is something closely akin to the idea of emerging here: a trajector that presumably was inside the body (the material that forms the wart or pimple) breaks through the normal boundary of the body, appearing on its outside surface. However, the trajector (the wart) and the landmark (the body) are not as distinct from each other, either before or after the process happens, as one might wish for a clear case of emerging. Note, too, that the trajector has changed form in the process. (Incidentally at this point, but relevantly later, *īmak* in other contexts can mean 'in his power, under his control'.)

(6) *N Rufino no okimaka totonki, yekin yalla*
the Rufino also it.had.hit.him hot barely yesterday
okiski.
it.emerged
'Rufino had also gotten a fever; it did not stop till yesterday.'

For (6), it is relevant to know that in Nawatl illnesses are construed as entities located within a sick person; when a person gets a fever, the fever is often said to enter that person (although alternative expressions such as the HIT metaphor exemplified in (6) are also used). Given such reification and location of the fever, it is not surprising that the cessation of the fever can be construed as a kind of EMERGING. Yet it is not a prototypical EMERGING, and in English we would speak of the fever *stopping*, *ceasing*, or *breaking*,[11] or perhaps (though it sounds a bit archaic) *leaving* the sick person. Here, the fact that the trajector is not a physical object is part of why the concept does not exactly fit the prototype.

(7) *Kexan estatuahtih ken kualli kisah n san*
like statues how good they.emerge the just
kinmachihchiwah.
they.make.them.by.hand

11. For some speakers, including myself, a fever *breaking* refers to a sudden decrease which may not coincide with a complete cessation; similarly, *dropping* need not imply complete cessation. Yet both words are often used to name a process which does include complete cessation as its end point.

'Take statues, now; how do they turn out so good when people make them by hand?'

(8)	*Machno*	*kualli*	*okiski*	*n*	*Elisabet*	*ivestido.*
	not also	good	it.emerged	the	Elizabeth	her.dress

'Elizabeth's dress didn't turn out right either.'

The usages of (7) and (8) are closely parallel: the process of an artifact being made is construed as a process of its emerging from the materials of which it is made. As in (5), the concept combines a change of state of the trajector with a less than sharp separation between the trajector and landmark. In fact, if the landmark is viewed as a distinct physical object rather than as a mass (i.e., in these cases, if the landmark is construed as the particular piece of rock, wood, etc., from which the statue is made or the particular piece of cloth from which the dress is made), it ceases to be itself through the process. But one can see how this also could be a kind of EMERGING. The fact that the particle *out* occurs in the translating English phrase *turn out* is almost certainly no accident.

(9)	*Kualli*	*otikis,*	*Marsiano,*	*tla*	*san*
	good	you.emerged	Marcian	if	just
	otimawiwiontiah.				
	you.went.swinging.arms				

'Things went well with you/You came out all right, Marcian, considering that you went there empty-handed.'

As in the cases of making an artifact, in (7) and (8), we are dealing in (9) with a change of state, but here it is a change of the situation of a human trajector. This trajector was "in" one situation and now has moved from that situation to another. This change can be seen as EMERGING from the former situation into the latter. Note again the *out* in the English translation *come out.*

Note also that in all three of these usages, i.e., (9), (7), and (8), the word *kualli* 'good' appears with *kīsa*. This is no accident; rather, it reflects the fact that in both the 'creation-of-an-artifact' and the 'person-changing-situations' senses of *kīsa*, an evaluation of the new state is a very prominent notion. This ties in closely with the fact that the final state in (9) and (7) is an approximation to a desired or intended state, and the closeness of that approximation is a natural matter for concern. Similarly in (8), it is a difference in quality between the two states that prompts the usage, and again an evaluation of the difference is natural.[12] In fact, if there does not occur an evaluative word or phrase such as *kualli* or *mach kualli* 'not good, bad', or some other adjective indicating the quality of the trajector in the new state, *kīsa* will usually need to be translated 'come/turn out well' rather than just 'come/turn out'.

The construals of *kīsa* in (5), (6), (7), (8), and (9) are represented in 3.h, 3.i, 3.j, 3.k, and 3.n, respectively, together with some of the generalizing concepts which unite them.[13]

(10) *Merino kitta machok miek kisas n*
Merino he.sees.it not.still much it.will.emerge the
xochitl, sa omen tlatekitinweh.
flower just two they.go.to.cut.something
'Merino figures that there won't be much of a flower crop left, so there are just two of them going off to harvest them.'

(11) *Tla okisako ehekatl koxamo*
if it.came.to.emerge wind whether.not
waltlamomachilis tlaseseya.
there.will.likely.begin.to.be.felt it.gets.cold
'If the wind has started blowing, it will probably start to feel like it is cold.'

---

12. Evaluations of different kinds of goodness or badness presumably consist in comparison of the final state of a concept with a desired or desirable state. I did not attempt to represent this in 3.o and its subcases, rather I have simply included an *ad hoc* label stating that that final state is evaluated, in order to simplify the diagrams.

13. In order to help the diagrams fit in a reasonable space, only the initial and final states of the process are represented. To be sure, even the diagrams in Figures 1 and 2, with one medial state represented, underspecify the true complexity of the concepts along this dimension.

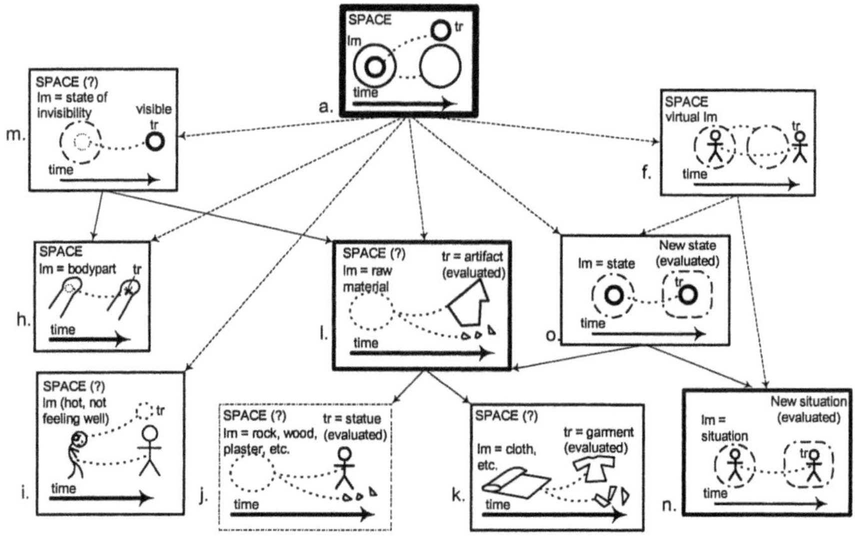

Figure 3. Warts, fevers, and artifacts *kīsah*, people *kīsah* from situations.

Sentences (10) and (11) are, I believe, more closely related than might appear from their English translations; they are also closely related to another type of usage which happened not to be exemplified in our random sampling of thirteen usages. In that usage, represented in 4.p, an event which occurs is said to *kīsa*. (One might say, for instance, *Nochipah ihkon nopan kīsa* [always thus on.me it.emerges] 'That's how it always happens to me'.) A characteristic common to many kinds of prototypical, physical EMERGING, and also to the developmental or artefactual emergings of (5), (7), and (8) (cf. 3.m), is that before the trajector emerges from the landmark it is difficult or impossible for most people to see it or interact with it. One can readily see how the most important part of the emergence, in both speakers' and hearers' minds, can come to be the beginning of accessibility or of knowability (4.q). This idea is probably active in another usage (4.r), in which thoughts which pop up in a person's mind are said to *kīsa*. By a parallel construal, then, an event as it occurs can be seen as coming into being and into knowability, and this is naturally seen as a kind of EMERGING (4.p). Since events which occur *kīsah*, it takes no great stretch of the mind to see a crop becoming ripe as a similar kind of EMERGING (4.s). One could also note that ripeness is analogous to the finished state of an artifact or the final state of a developing situation; thus, achieving any of those states can be seen as undergoing the same sort of process (4.t) and it should not be surprising that it can be called by the same name. Similarly, a wind arising (why do we say *arise*?) can also be seen as an event occurring, thus as a kind of EMERGING, or at any rate the wind's coming into contact with humans, entering their perception and interacting with them, can be seen as EMERGING (4.u).

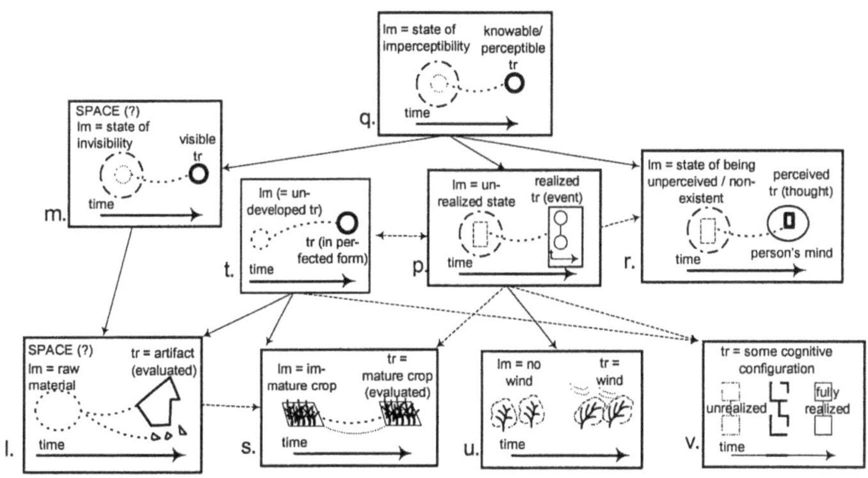

Figure 4. Events and crops *kīsah*, "adverbial" *kīsa*.

(12) *Nikan toaltepeh momatennamikih kisa*
here our.town they.greet.each.other.kissing.hands emerge
san yen itech ilwitl.
just that's.it on.it feast
'Here in our town people greet each other with the hand-kiss practically only at religious feasts.'

(13) *N*	*changohtih*	*mayehkeh*	*kisa*	*kexan*	*tehwan.*
the	monkeys	hand.havers	emerge	like	we

'Monkeys have hands almost like we do.'

This leaves only (12) and (13) from our random sample. In these cases, we are practically forced to translate *kīsa* with an adverb such as *practically* or *almost.* I suggest that this notion is another extension of the idea of EMERGING as coming into existence. A particular semantic configuration – in (12), that of occurring only on feast days; in (13), that of being precisely like us humans – is viewed not as having occurred, as already "there", so to speak, but as in an arrested process of occurring, almost but not quite yet "there".[14] This meaning is diagrammed in 4.v.[15]

14. A reviewer for this article suggests calling this notion "coming up (to a certain degree)"; one might also suggest "approaching". I have no objection, as long as it is clear that these are English ways of expressing the notion, and not Nawatl, in that the Nawatl has no forms particularly tied to meanings 'come', 'up', or 'approach'. An alternative construal might involve a DEPARTURE metaphor: real, definitive occurrence might be viewed as the landmark, the ideal out from which the actual departs. *Kīsa* can, and often does, mean physical departure, and it is not unreasonable to suppose that this notion may be/have been active in some speakers' minds. However, it is less clearly parallel to other usages where the trajector is an event or configuration, and thus would presumably not be as likely or as strong as the construal mentioned in the text. It has not (if my memory serves me) been advanced to me as a possible explanation for this usage by native speakers, whereas that in the text has.
15. The adverbiality versus verbality of *kīsa* in these usages is a difficult call, and, to my mind at least, not a crucial one. If taken verbally (as in 4.v, i.e., as a process, a situation developing or extending through conceived time), the form is naturally (though not by logical necessity) always in third person singular, since the subject is a conceived configuration or situation rather than a (conceived) person. Somewhat less predictably, but still very naturally, it is also always in present tense. It thus winds up with the uninflecting form *kīsa*, without normal overt verbal morphology to establish or authenticate verbal status. Its subject clause or phrase tends to be semantically much "heavier", a more important part of the communication between speaker and hearer; this tends to relegate *kīsa* to modifier (rather than head) status. If verbal, *kīsa* must be construed imperfectively, i.e., one stage in the perfective process of becoming is

2.4. *Further usages of* kīsa*; complexities in cases of physical emergence*

All the usages of *kīsa* which we have examined are commonplace, fully robust patterns;[16] hundreds of examples of most of them would show up from any large corpus of Nawatl data. And they are by no means all of the attested patterns. I would like to single out for additional comment a complex of cases involving physical emerging, subcases of the prototypical 1.a (= 5.a).

Kīsa is used conventionally to describe the rising of the sun; in Nawatl the sun does not rise, it emerges (5.w).[17] Similarly, the moon's rising may be coded by *kīsa* (5.x); the commonality of these concepts is captured by 5.y, which specifies emergence of an astronomical luminary from behind the horizon.[18] The stars' rising is, somewhat surprisingly, not coded by *kīsa* but rather by *mo-tta* [reflexive-see] 'be(come) visible'.

---

singled out and extended through conceived time. The difference between that and a stative (atemporal) construal is so minimal as to be practically negligible in a modifier. I would suppose speakers may construe it either way. If *kīsa* is construed as an atemporal modifier of a relation, whether a verbal relation as in (12), or a stative one as in (13), that makes it, on the Cognitive Grammar definition, an adverb. The fact that adverbs provide the best English translations is unsurprising.

16. The particular notion of a statue "turning out" (well or otherwise) is doubtless an exception to this statement, and it is so represented in 3.j. Thus, 3.j, I claim, is good Nawatl because it straightforwardly elaborates schema 3.1 (it is *sanctioned* by 3.1). Clothing turning out well (3.k), in contrast, is a common topic of conversation at least in many households, so I would claim that it is established in its own right, as well as being sanctioned by 3.1. Similarly, I make no claim that the notions of occurring practically only on feast days (12), or of being nearly like humans (13), are established meanings of *kīsa*, although they are straightforward elaborations of 4.v; I did not even include them in the diagram.
17. The extent to which the sun (*tōnal-tzin*) is personified by Nawatl speakers is debatable and no doubt variable. It/he is rarely mentioned without the honorific *-tzin* suffix attached.
18. The setting of sun, moon, and stars is, in Nawatl, conventionally coded by the stem *pol-iwi* [lose-intransitive] 'be lost, disappear', not by the opposite of *kīsa* (*kalaki* 'enter'). *Kalaki* is used in other dialects, however, e.g., in the Mösiehuali̱ (Nahuatl) of Tetelcingo, Morelos.

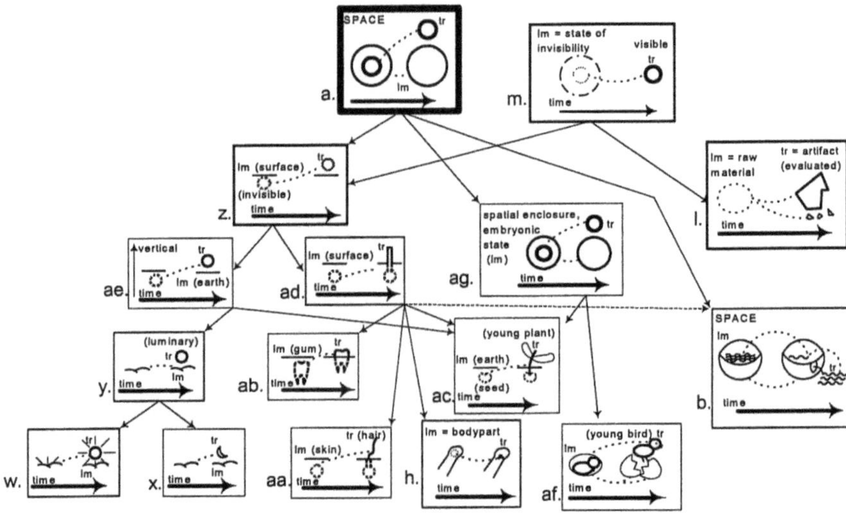

Figure 5. More physical emergings coded by *kīsa*.

These meanings are part of a group of concepts in which the landmark is a physical entity with an extensive surface, and the trajector is at first invisible, as it is either hidden under that surface or hidden behind a fold or bulge of it, and later becomes visible, having penetrated or come out from behind the surface. Schema 5.z characterizes this class; it is, like 3.l, a subcase of the notion of the trajector becoming visible (3.m). Surprisingly, since it would be a straightforward subcase of this schema, *kīsa* is not used of a person or a vehicle coming into sight over the horizon. Other subcases of 5.z which are coded with *kīsa* are hair sprouting from head or chin (5.aa), or a baby's tooth "coming in" (as we say in English – the Nawatl is nearer to "coming out", though it lacks the prominent deixis of *come*) (5.ab),[19] or a seed sprouting from the earth (5.ac), or an eruption breaking out on the body (3.h = 5.h). Subschemas 5.aa–ac and 5.h all

19. *Tlan* 'tooth' is incorporated on *kīsa* to form *tlan-kīsa* 'teethe, cut a tooth, have your teeth come in'. Compare with *tlan-kopīni* [tooth-be.plucked] or *tlan-wetzi* [tooth-fall] 'lose a tooth, have a tooth fall/come out', and *tlan-chapāni* [tooth-fall.multiple.subject] 'lose your teeth'.

share the notion of the trajector not emerging as a whole but rather one part of the trajector becoming visible above the surface while another part remains invisibly anchored beneath it (5.ad).[20] This notion is also close to the concept in (1) (1.b = 5.b) of water emerging from some enclosing or containing object; during and often even at the end of the process, some water will still be in the container and perhaps all along the path of the emerging.

Subschema 5.ac (the sprouting of a seed) is further linked with 5.y (the rising of sun or moon) in that both have the earth as landmark and presume a vertical orientation; this commonality is expressed in schema 5.ae.[21] Schema 5.ac is also complex in that with the spatial emerging there is a concomitant emergence of an organism from an embryonic state into full life. It shares this complexity with 5.af, which represents the conventional use of *kīsa* to describe the hatching of chicks; schema 5.ag represents the commonality of these concepts.

All of this is not even nearly an exhaustive treatment of the meaning of *kīsa*. An hour's run-through of text netted the following additional usages, many of them occurring repeatedly: set out on a journey, (water) come up onto the ground (in a seep or spring), (dye) come out (of cloth),[22] come out (around a corner into view), (part of a fence) stick out, (bile) be secreted (from the liver), be divided (into parts), (a plague of grasshoppers) appear, (flower bulbs) come out (of the ground), be spit out, play a role, leave a field, come to a decision. It should be obvious that these could easily be fitted, in quite com-

---

20. "Above" and "beneath" here do not necessarily imply vertical orientation; a tooth emerging downwards from the upper gums or a hair sprouting from the bottom of the chin are perfectly valid instances.

21. The validity of this schema is reinforced by the fact that these cases more often than not are coded by the complex stem *pan-kīsa* [on-emerge] 'come up on top of the ground/over the horizon' rather than by *kīsa* alone. *Pan-kīsa* may also designate (as *kīsa* alone does not) a person or vehicle's coming into view over the horizon or a hill; it is not used of teeth or hair sprouting, nor of any of the other situations discussed here.

22. In this usage, as in English, the dye or stain is not said to (perfectively) *kīsa* when some comes out but when none remains. This contrasts rather directly with, e.g., 1.b, or especially 5.ad.

plex ways, into the diagrams in Figures 1–5; it should also be clear that some usages (e.g., stick out, be divided, play a role, come to a decision) involve significant extensions from what has so far been presented. In causative forms (based on *kīxtia* 'take out'), many of these usages were repeated; *kīxtia* also denoted (a shaman's) taking a (supposed cause of) sickness out of a person's body (cf. 3.i), picking out good flower bulbs from bad, pulling teeth (contrast 5.ab), taking goods from a truck, gruel from a pot, toys from a box, and a tree out of a brook, and throwing a fiesta (causing it to occur, cf. 4.p).

2.5. *High-level schemas*

In the previous sections, I have presented a number of schemas, that is, generalizing concepts that abstract away from the differences between more specific meanings. (In fact, all the concepts I have described, and probably all concepts used in language, are schematic to one degree or another, generalizing over particular sensory experiences or other cognitive events which may differ slightly from person to person.) Other schemas might be posited which generalize over the highest-level schemas I have described so far.[23] Schema 6.ah generalizes over the cases where spatial movement is involved (the prototypical 1.a, 2.f, and 3.i), 6.ai generalizes over that concept and the not-necessarily-motional change-of-state concepts of 3.o and 4.q, and 6.aj unites that concept with the "almost" concept of 4.v, in which a change of state is incipient but not fully realized. Schema 6.aj, then, is a generalization covering all the meanings examined so far. If there

23. I would not claim that these schemas are necessarily present, much less salient, for all speakers of Nawatl. Langacker is probably right (1987: 372–377) in claiming that any extension of meaning or perception of similarity between meanings involves at least the momentary activation of the specifications common to the compared meanings. Those specifications constitute a schematic concept, and to the degree that that schema becomes routinized and conventionalized, it will become part of the language. Yet subschemas can be accessed on their own and can function independently: higher-level schemas are not necessarily activated and may well be marginal to the system.

is one meaning of *kīsa* which can be said to include all the others, this is it.

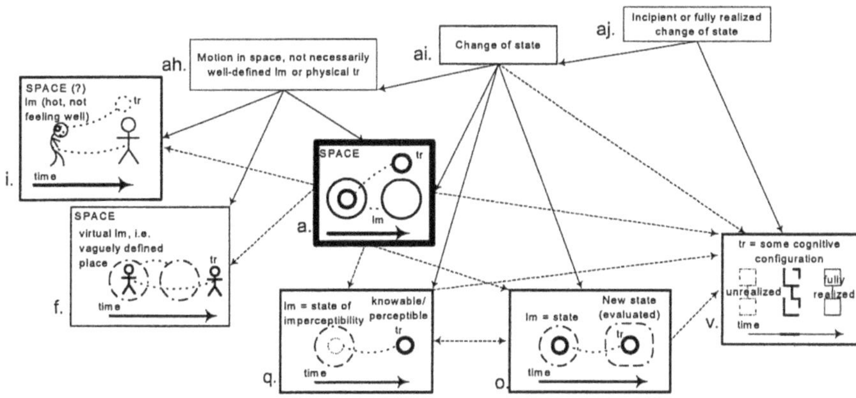

Figure 6. High-level schemas for *kīsa.*

3. Basic facts illustrated by the data

The data we have examined so far conveniently illustrate a number of points which are so well-substantiated that it is difficult for me to see how they can be questioned. Each of these "facts" will be discussed in the sections ahead. They are:

(a) Polysemy is rampant.
(b) Polysemous meanings are separate but intricately related.
(c) The links among the meanings are reasonable.
(d) Not all reasonable links obtain, however. There are holes in the patterns.
(e) The reasonableness of the links helps a person learn the system but does not mean that one can predict it and needn't learn it.
(f) Context is the key to letting the meanings function separately and the means of establishing them in the first place, but …

(g) Context cannot be used to explain the meanings away.
(h) Conclusion: One cannot eliminate these meanings on the basis of their relationships to each other or to context.

3.1. *An alternative view: monosemy*

Crucial aspects of these "facts" are denied by certain linguists, who claim that monosemy rather than polysemy is the norm. Here, I am especially interested in replying to Charles Ruhl (1989). I have singled Ruhl out from among those who espouse or assume monosemy for several reasons: (i) His model incorporates typical features of monosemic models, and offers unusually full justification for them; (ii) He takes seriously the implications of those features and follows them out conscientiously, even when they lead to conclusions others would resist; (iii) Anyone who appreciates Bolinger as palpably as Ruhl does and yet disagrees with him cannot be thinking about these issues superficially and is worth hearing; (iv) Ruhl has offered me the great pleasure of reading one who really has considered the data – time after time he brings up considerations which others ignore but which seem to me of the highest relevance and importance – and with whom I agree at least 90% of the time, but with whose conclusions, arising from all that agreement, I find myself in quite violent disagreement.

Those positing monosemy generally do so in the interest of theoretical simplicity.[24] Accordingly, Ruhl seeks a semantics that is limited to "closed, finite systems" and "rules ... with only a few options" (1989: xi, 36). Undoubtedly, life would be simpler for semanticians if each linguistic form had only one meaning. The question is ultimately empirical, however. Do the data support a model which posits only one meaning? If this particular kind of simplicity can be

24. Although few would state it quite as bluntly as Bouchard (1995), many seem to be motivated by a desire for a semantics which does as little as is necessary to let their syntactic machinery run smoothly.

bought only at the expense of greater, more mysterious, and less probable complexities elsewhere, it may not be worth the price.

The general drift of monosemic analyses is to seek a high-level generalization which covers all of the apparent meanings of the lexical item in question, and to assume *a priori* that that generalization must be the whole meaning (Ruhl's "monosemic bias", 1989: 3–5).[25] This involves acceptance (usually covert) of the dictum that to list particulars is to lose a generalization, and making the generalization entails excising the particulars. Thus, Ruhl (1989: 51) states (atypically, without supporting argument) that "when meanings generalize, … concrete meanings become pragmatic specifications of the abstract meaning, which is *the* meaning of the word" (1989: 51). ("Pragmatic", for Ruhl, is "extralinguistic"; e.g., 1989: 15.) This seems the central point of disagreement between Ruhl's view and mine. As Langacker (1987: 28–29, 41–42) states, we are not faced with a simple "either-or" choice between lists of particulars and general rules; a "both-and" option must also be considered. To assume otherwise is to subscribe to the rule-list fallacy. I argue below that the "facts" indicate that the "both-and" option is in fact the correct one.

On a closely related matter, Ruhl assumes a dichotomy between meanings which are related (and therefore reducible to one meaning) and those which are not. In other words, although he calls it polysemy, what he is really arguing against is multiple homonymy. Having admitted that his highly abstract meaning for the English verb *bear* is not intuitively accessible but reachable only by inference, he asks, "On the other hand, is a polysemic solution warranted? Is it possible, with the previous data, to argue that *bear* breaks into a number of discrete semantic parts? … The challenge is to understand why all the data in this chapter (and of course many more) *seem to be related* [italics his], especially so when *bear* appears to be … a highly idiomatic word" (1989: 63). In presenting those data, he repeatedly demonstrates parallels to particular constructions or usages

---

25. It is tempting to dismiss the "monosemic bias" as pure question-begging; at best it is a fiat declaration that the burden of proof is heavily on those who claim (as I do) that particular meanings are not predictable. Ruhl need not prove a meaning is predictable: we must prove it is not.

and argues that those constructions and usages cannot therefore be idiomatic, which means, on his either-or view, that they must be predictable. Thus, he argues, e.g., that "contrary to Bolinger's claim that *bear the brunt* is an idiom, *burden*, *brunt*, *load*, *impact*, and *strain* fit the general pattern". He notes that "*bear witness* is treated as a separate phrase in some dictionaries, but it relates directly to *bear testimony*; in the light of previous examples, it loses its apparent idiosyncrasy". Elsewhere, he uses the virtually definitional phrase "idiomatic, with no systematic explanation" (1989: 55, 57, 17, cf. 49). We might phrase his criterion as: "if not fully idiosyncratic, then predictable by Ruhl". He is entirely right about the relationships being there, but wrong, I believe, in assuming that this means the forms are fully predictable. In other words, idiomaticity or idiosyncrasy are matters of degree, not plus-or-minus qualities; the truth is that while the forms are reasonable given the system, they still cannot be predicted and must be learned.

Ruhl recognizes that monosemic meanings are of necessity highly abstract. He admits that his premises force him into "claiming that meaning almost universally ceded to be semantic should be considered pragmatic" (1989: ix). Thus, for *bear*, "distinctions such as abstract-concrete, horizontal-vertical, and movement-nonmovement are … determined pragmatically, not semantically … [and similarly] effects of being 'on top', such as control, dominance, and effect … intensity … speed, and the like" (1989: 39). The resulting "general abstract meanings elude consciousness; the interpretations of the conscious mind by necessity are oriented towards reality and thus are not purely semantic" (1989: 51). In other words, native speakers will not be conscious of the linguistic meanings of the words they use, but only of their pragmatically contaminated variants. Ruhl would posit for *kīsa* a meaning like 6.aj, and it would not bother him that native speakers would be unlikely to think of it as even a meaning of *kīsa*, much less as *the* meaning.

Ruhl would certainly agree that (apparent) polysemy is rampant (section 3.2). That people do separate senses in their minds may be true (section 3.2.1), but would be essentially irrelevant, as these are only pragmatic variants, not semantic meanings. The connections among the senses (sections 3.2.2 and 3.3) are certainly there, and are important; in fact, they are the justification for arriving inferentially at the one true meaning (6.aj or its equivalent). And the role of context is definitive for selecting one of these concrete (non-semantic) meanings from among the possibilities, and new contexts can be expected to produce new variants (section 4.2). The major arguments for which I do not believe Ruhl has good answers are in sections 3.4 (holes in the patterns and differing patterns), 3.5 (multiple reasonable solutions, need to account for speakers' as well as hearers' usages), 4.2 (duplication of meaning is allowable, even normal), and 4.3 (context does not supply all the missing information.)

3.2. Polysemy is rampant

I cannot contemplate a lexical item like *kīsa* without being impressed by the sheer number of meanings which are clearly related to each other but just as clearly distinguishable from each other. And *kīsa* is not really unusual in this characteristic. A good many common verb stems in Nawatl are comparably complex, and there are dozens that are an order of magnitude less complex. There are not very many that do not have more than one meaning clearly established. Nouns, adjectives, and postpositions also typically have multiple meanings. And this is true of any other language, at least of those I am at all familiar with; just look up, in any good dictionary, a word like *get*, *pass*, *turn*, *break*, *jack*, *rack*, or *heart*. In this light, then, one comes to expect any commonly used lexical item to have multiple meanings.

3.2.1. Many times a word's meanings should be distinguished from each other

It may not be all that significant theoretically that I can distinguish a word's multiple meanings and that they "feel" like different meanings to me. Monosemists' counter-arguments to the apparent proliferation of meanings generally appeal to a supposed difference between what is in speakers' minds and what may be in analysts', or to a supposed possibility of predicting the multiple meanings from some one central meaning. The second of these two arguments will be dealt with later (section 3.4); here, I address briefly the related questions of whether the meanings are distinguished in native speakers' minds, and whether analysts' intuitions are at all trustworthy.

Doubtless, any analyst is influenced on this matter by intuitions: feelings or convictions – preceding any argumentation – that (for instance) two meanings are different enough that one of them does not automatically entail the other. I confess to such intuitions in the case of *kīsa*. But they are confirmed by indications that native speakers share them to some degree at least. For instance, if native speakers are asked to explain the meaning of *kīsa*, they will tend to indicate the prototypical meaning, either by gesture, by exemplification, by paraphrase, or by translation, and then if presented with a sentence where another meaning is needed, they will say that is another meaning. If invited to state what different things *kīsa* means, they can make a list of several. They can make or enjoy plays on the different meanings: they will at least smile when asked how a goal in soccer *ōkīs* 'emerged', i.e., 'happened, was scored', when the scoring player *ōkikalaktih* 'caused it to enter', i.e., 'put it in' the goal mouth, or if you ask whether the baby's tooth *ōkīs īkamak* 'emerged in/[or conceivably from] his mouth' by itself or whether someone *ōkikīxtih* 'caused it to emerge', i.e., 'took it out, pulled it [as a dentist would]'. The fact that different synonyms are available within the language for certain meanings but not for others makes it clear at least that speakers can make (and are used to making) distinctions between the concepts involved.

Analysts' or native speakers' intuitions are confirmed by the fact that in many cases the meanings are different enough that their truth values can clash. The traditional tests for ambiguity and vagueness (Lakoff 1970; Zwicky & Sadock 1975), involving various forms of conjunction and reduction, rely crucially on such clashes. They can easily be made to yield results indicating separate meanings for many forms. If Martha has 'emerged' from her home in the sense of leaving the building or the premises (2.c–e), and Eliza has 'emerged' in the sense of going away to live elsewhere (a well-established meaning closely related both to 2.e and 3.n), to say *Yalla Marta ōkīs īchān iwan Elisa nō* [yesterday Martha emerged her.dwelling and Eliza also] is quite inappropriate. Many other examples could be given.

I am by no means claiming that all the distinctions I have represented in Figures 1–6 are salient in speakers' minds. On the contrary, some groups of meanings, for instance 3.j–l, or 4.v and its subcases, are quite strongly vague, with distinctions among them quite unlikely to be focused on by speakers and virtually any new instance (e.g., building a computer) likely to be acceptable without question (cf. Tuggy 1993). But I cannot accept, and the evidence seems to me clearly to deny, that this is the case for all the meanings represented, that the only thing speakers have in mind when they say the word *kīsa* is the schematic meaning 6.aj, which "includes" all the others.[26]

A question beyond what is consciously in speakers' minds is what is there subconsciously. This is, naturally, information that cannot in general be directly accessed, although introspection by speakers themselves may be of some use in pushing the borders back. Psychological tests for unconscious knowledge work from indirect evidence, measuring some response which is best explicable by hypothesizing such unconscious knowledge. About such work I have little to say, although I am convinced it is a worthwhile endeavor. However, patterns of language use often give us similar indirect evidence, which does not need a psychology laboratory to measure it. The ambiguity tests mentioned above, or the holes that one finds in patterns (section 3.4), give evidence that, even if speakers are not aware of doing so, they are discriminating among the logically expectable members of a category.

26. Ruhl, of course, would agree, but claim that says nothing about semantics: "the interpretations of the conscious mind [even of native speakers] by necessity are oriented towards reality and thus are not purely semantic" (1989: 51).

3.2.2. A word's multiple meanings are intricately related

Polysemy, to be sure, is not just a matter of there being different meanings attached to a form: the same is true of lexical ambiguity, or homonymy. In polysemy the meanings are not only separable, but related.

There is probably no need to belabor the point that there are multitudinous links of similarity to be recognized among the meanings so far discussed, with many examples of both the strict, non-contradicting similarity of a schematic relationship and the looser similarity of partial schematicity.[27] I cannot prove, and need not presume, that every single one of the relationships I have represented or discussed is active in all speakers' minds, much less that there are no other connections to be discerned. (As with the meaning discriminations mentioned above, we may reasonably expect there to be meaning connections subconsciously active even when speakers are not aware of them.) What I see no reason to deny, and every reason to affirm, is that links of similarity do exist in Nawatl speakers' minds, whether consciously or subconsciously, that they bind the meanings of *kīsa* into a more or less coherent category and subcategories, and that they aid immensely in the establishing of the different meanings in children's and other learners' minds. This is, I believe, completely typical of the meanings of polysemous lexical items.

27. Although I do not discuss it here, what are usually recognized as metaphoric and metonymic (or collectively, figurative) extensions of meaning can be viewed as subclasses of partially-schematic relationships. E.g., the 'fever ceasing' sense (3.i) might be seen as a metaphoric version of the prototype (3.a), and the 'leaving home' sense might be seen as a metonymic extension of 2.e (leaving the physical vicinity of one's house is a part of leaving home). The labels "metaphor" or "metonymy" are more likely to be applied when the degree of semantic strain is greater, but the phenomena are basically the same. These relationships, of course, also help bind concepts together.

3.3. *The links among polysemous meanings are reasonable, even systematic*

These links among polysemous meanings are reasonable. Their very nature makes them so. I know no one who doubts that perception of similarity is at the heart of the human power of reasoning, and these are relationships of similarity. It is no accident that emergence from a physical enclosure (1.a = 2.a) and from a "virtual" physical landmark (2.f) are classified together in Nawatl and coded by the same phonological form; they are linked by a relationship of similarity that is quite certain to occur to anyone who compares the two concepts. Even less closely similar concepts, such as physical emergence and the "emergence" of an artifact from raw materials (3.l), or a person's "emergence" (3.n) from one situation into another, are based on reasonable connections between the concepts.

These connections are reasonable not only for Nawatl speakers. The semantic ranges of *kīsa* and its Spanish counterpart *salir* overlap considerably: *salir* is a standard way to speak of most of the cases involving emergence from a physical object or a virtual landmark (e.g., of a baby's teeth coming in), and also for the cases of an artifact turning out (well or badly), or of a person coming out (well or badly) from a situation. The repeated occurrence of *out* in the English glosses of these concepts (a pimple *breaks out*, a dress *turns out well*, a person *comes out well* from a situation, etc.) is also far from purely accidental. (I assume the semantic similarity of *out* to *emerge* need not be substantiated.) And a historical investigation would certainly indicate that borrowing or contact among the three languages is unlikely to be a factor in any but perhaps a small minority of cases. What is much more likely is that the same reasonable connections among the concepts, the same naturally perceptible similarities, are utilized independently in the different languages to unite the related concepts into categories which are lexically linked to a single phonological structure.

Sometimes the linkages are not only reasonable, but systematic in some degree, i.e., their reasonableness is reflected in the fact that related linkages can be found in numerous other lexical items in the language,[28] to the point where the pattern might even be considered productive. The most widespread case of this is *elaboration*, i.e., the linkage from a well-established schema to a subcase of that schema. Sometimes certain kinds of *extensions* are systematic as well. Much ink has been employed in the exposition of systematic metonymies, for instance, such as the naming of literary works by their authors (*Milton is on the shelf next to Plato*) or restaurant patrons according to the dish they have ordered (*The ham sandwich in the corner needs more coffee*). Other extensions are systematic in being tied into an extended metaphorical system for structuring a domain of knowledge.

Cases of systematic elaborations are not hard to come by. For instance, the 'creation-of-an-artifact sense' (3.l) is linked to its subcase dealing with the creation of a garment (3.k) and to a large number of other such subcases (including subschemas such as one of food in preparation), and it can even apply productively, as in sentence (7) (=3.j). Extensions, in contrast, often fail to be systematic to any great degree, and there are no straightforward examples in the Nawatl data. Still, there are a few marginal cases: (i) the 'achieve perfected form' sense is extended to the 'event be realized' sense (3.t ----→ 3.p) in a manner parallel to a similar meaning extension in *mo-chīwa* [reflexive-do] 'be made, become, happen'; (ii) the (metonymic) extension of prototypical *kīsa* to primarily have to do with visibility (3.a ----→ 3.m) might be seen as cross-linguistically systematic: many languages use words for emergence to refer to becoming perceptible; (iii) the extension to the cessation of a fever (3.a ----→ 3.i) is clearly related to a standard construal of sickness as entering a person, remaining within him while he is sick, perhaps being drawn out by a skilled shaman, etc. But most of the extensions, although reasonable enough, are not systematic even to that degree.

28. And perhaps other languages as well. This would be a many-to-many correspondence across languages, and thus differ from the essentially one-to-one correspondences noted above.

3.4. ... but they are not predictable

The reasonableness of a linkage is not the same as its inevitability. Not all reasonable relationships of similarity, even those that would be systematic, are necessarily perceived (or conceived) by all reasonable people. Much less is it the case that a perception of similarity will necessarily entail people linking both the similar concepts to the same phonological structure. Several lines of reasoning strongly support this contention.

First, there are holes in the patterns. These are obvious at the most abstract levels. For instance, most cases of incipient or actual change of state are not coded by *kīsa* (6.ai–aj), nor are most cases of spatial motion (6.ah). One cannot call falling, or eating, or deteriorating, or running, or any of myriad other processes involving motion or change of state, *kīsa*. Under a monosemic analysis, why should this not be possible? These instances would be reasonable, systematic elaborations of the motion and change-of-state schemas. The answer is that there is no reason, nothing that would allow us to predict it: that these instances are not coded by *kīsa* is just a fact. Either the high-level schemas do not exist as meanings of *kīsa*, or one cannot expect all their subcases to automatically come with them.

Whether the high-level schemas are retained or not, there are holes at much more specific levels as well. If the sun and moon, when they rise, are said to *kīsah* (5.w–y), why aren't the stars? Even though it would be perfectly reasonable, and even systematic, it just happens not to be the case. If plants *kīsah* when they sprout and chicks when they hatch (5.ac, 5.af), why don't humans or animals at birth? Birth is a perfectly reasonable candidate for such coding: like sprouting and hatching, it is a physical emergence marking the beginning of independent life (5.ag). If the sun or moon coming into view over the horizon is considered to be a kind of *kīsa*, why isn't a truck coming into view over the horizon? If there is only one meaning and all the submeanings are inevitable results of it, I see no way to explain such gaps in the patterns.[29]

I mentioned above how striking it is that languages which have no genetic relationship to Nawatl should use their words for prototypical physical emergence to also express some of the same extended senses for which Nawatl uses *kīsa*. It is at least equally striking that they do not use those words for all of *kīsa*'s senses. I can think of no good way using *out* or *emerge* or anything similar to approximate, in English, to the 'almost, practically' sense (4.v), or the '(wind) arise' sense (4.u). We could say *come out* or something similar for a chick hatching (5.af) or the sun rising (5.w), but we generally do not. Similarly, *salir* is not used in Spanish to talk about an event occurring (4.p), and although it could be used for a seed sprouting (5.af) (as it is for a chick hatching), the verb *nacer* 'be born' is usually used instead. *Salir* and *emerge* or *come/go out* are also used in extended senses for which *kīsa* is not. *Emerge*, *come out*, and *salir* are all used to refer to the process of a fact becoming publicly known; I do not believe I have ever heard *kīsa* so used. In the Spanish of the Orizaba area, *sale* (lit. 'it emerges') is often used to mean 'that's fine, OK, agreed'; again, I have not heard *kīsa* used to similar effect.

If *kīsa*, *emerge*, and *salir* each has only one meaning, and all the other supposed meanings are automatic consequences of that meaning, then the three meanings must be subtly different from each other, in order to account for these differences in the ranges of the terms.[30]

29. Ruhl (1989: 55–56) agrees that an abstract, unspecified concept should "exhibit all degrees … (including lack)" of the characteristics it is unspecified for. Thus, any holes in the pattern (ranges of cases which should be included but in fact are not) are problematic.

30. Alternatively, the nature of the pragmatic/combinatorial principles which derive the context-specific meanings must be different for each language. Positing this would be subject to the same objections as given in the text; in addition, it would be difficult to maintain that those principles were "non-linguistic", as they are supposed to be.

If the pragmatic or combinatorial principles must in fact be specified in detail not just for each language but for their application to each lexical item, a very close theoretical equivalent to polysemy will result. I would certainly not deny that some such particular specifications may be involved in many cases,

The precision and delicacy of these subtle differences must be simply amazing. From slight differences in meanings on the order of 6.ah or 6.aj, abstract enough to include wide ranges of both physical and non-physical emergings, the model must specify whether or not, for instance, a chick hatching or a seed sprouting will be included in the meaning. It must guarantee that in English a baby's teeth will *come in*, not *come out*, whereas in Nawatl they *kīsah*, or that in English the stars *come out* but the sun and moon do not, whereas in Nawatl it is the other way around. The nature of this astonishing subtlety seems wholly mysterious, as is the way it would operate through pragmatic or combinatorial principles (non-linguistic, universal, and automatic) to produce the desired results. The whole scenario strikes me as fantastic in both senses of the term. Since the only reason for positing it is to avoid polysemy, it seems obviously preferable to allow the relatively straightforward complexity of polysemy.

This ties in with the experience of second-language learners, who not only need to learn the names of the closest equivalents of the concepts they are used to thinking with, but who also need to learn where the ranges of the terms do not coincide. They have to learn that, reasonable though it might seem, a term does not mean concepts it obviously would fit very well, or surprisingly does mean concepts which one would not have thought of, much less been able to predict.

The same argument can be repeated with dialectal (or even idiolectal) differences. A number of other dialects of Nahuatl do not have the 'almost, practically' meaning of *kīsa* (4.v), and in at least one the sun is said to *tlākati* 'be born' rather than to *kīsa* (5.w). They may also extend the meaning of *kīsa* past that allowed in Orizaba Nawatl; some do use *kīsa* of the stars as well as of the sun and moon. This is perfectly reasonable, but the monosemist claim is that it must be in-

---

enriching the polysemy that would be posited without them, but I do not think all polysemy can be reduced to that. In other words, I believe that sometimes a sense may initially only be accessed from a more basic (more strongly-entrenched) sense via an established semantic (originally pragmatic) pathway, but I believe that such senses easily become established in their own right, outgrowing the need for such an established pathway to the point that the pathway is activated only contingently, rarely, or even not at all.

evitable. If *kīsa* has only one highly abstract meaning, what conceivable change in that meaning accounts for such differences?

3.5. Comprehension vs. production; multiple reasonable solutions

The foregoing argument speaks more strongly to the speaker's knowledge of his language than the hearer's. Possibly it is a legacy of the "interpretive semantics" metaphor, but the arguments Ruhl and others bring to claim that a usage is predictable almost always try to show, and would be satisfied to show, that hearers could understand an attested usage without having to learn it. However, they really should be obliged to show as well that speakers (and hearers) would know that was the proper usage to employ for the concept, again without having to learn it.[31] Hearers understand much that they know better than to say. If I speak as if the stars *kīsah* when they rise, Nawatl hearers understand what I mean. But they are aware that that is not the way to say it, and they do not say it themselves. They can understand the deviant utterance, but it is clearly part of their linguistic knowledge that it is deviant. Similarly, if Nawatl speakers were to say in English, in an appropriate context, *I wonder when the chicks will emerge/come out*, we might well understand that they were talking about them hatching, but we would know that was not the way to say it in English.

When production is considered as well as comprehension, the problem of multiple solutions becomes acute. Other Nawatl verbs, e.g. *patla* 'change', *wetzi* 'fall', *mo-chīwa* [reflexive-do] 'become', or *mo-kuapa* [reflexive-turn] 'turn over/around, change, become', would under a monosemic theory wind up with meanings very close if not identical to that of *kīsa*: something like 'change of state'. It would be perfectly reasonable for them to be used as easily as *kīsa* for most if not all of the cases *kīsa* is used for. The ranges of usage do in fact overlap, but they do so surprisingly little. This is to be ex-

31. As Geeraerts (1991) would phrase it, our semantics must be not only semasiologically but onomasiologically adequate.

pected if the most abstract schemas are not predictive and the occurring ranges are reflected in the polysemic structures under those schemas. It is not explainable under standard monosemic assumptions.

Ruhl acknowledges the force of this argument. After showing that expressions such as *the facts bear me out* fit under his abstract characterizations of *bear* and *out*, he says, "But why *bear* and *out*? If we need an 'abstract sense of movement' …, why use *bear* here rather than *run*, *go*, *move*, which are more obviously motional? Further, *off*, *down*, and *up* … have 'goal' meanings too, so why is *out* the choice? These questions are telling, and I have no answers" (1989: 49).

(14) *Mottas* *kox* *kualli* *kisas* *n*
it.will.be.seen whether good it.will.emerge the
kamohtli *kan* *poxtik* *n* *tlalli.*
flower.bulb where powdery the earth
'We'll see how well the bulbs in the powdery soil will _________.'

(15) *Exkan* *ma* *kisa* *n* *mopehpena* *n*
Three.places may it.emerge the it.is.picked.out the
kamohtli.
flower.bulb
'The flower bulbs which are being picked over should _________ in three places.'

Yet even if just comprehension is considered, the arguments are strong. To drive these points home, I include two more sample usages of *kīsa*. In both cases, the meaning is an ordinary one for Nawatl speakers, a subcase of 6.aj (in fact of 6.ai). I have left the translation for *kīsa* blank, and I challenge the reader to guess what exactly is meant (check the answers in the footnote![32]) and to ask

32. In (14), the meaning is 'produce a crop' (cf. 4.s). In (15), it is 'be divided'; in this case, the combination *exkān kīsa* is better translated 'be separated into three grades'.

himself the following sets of questions: (i) If I guessed incorrectly, what possible change in 6.ai or 6.aj would have enabled me to guess correctly? Would it have made me sure I had done so? (ii) If I guessed correctly, did I really start from 6.ai or was it some more concrete meaning that helped me? Was I absolutely sure this had to be the meaning (as it had to have been if it really was predictable)? In either case, (iii) If I had been given the intended meaning and context and the choice from the whole lexicon of what verb to use, would I have known, starting from 6.aj, that *kīsa* was the correct choice?

4. Meanings cannot generally be reduced to one per lexical entry

It should have become obvious: it is not enough to specify that *kīsa* means something like 6.ai or 6.aj, a kind of abstract emerging. One cannot predict on universal or even on language-wide grounds which reasonable usages will be established and which will not. One has to learn which of the myriad kinds of processes that could reasonably be construed as emergings in fact are named by *kīsa*. *Kīsa*'s meanings are all reasonable in some degree, but they are not predictable. They themselves must be admitted as meanings of the word.

And, as I have stressed repeatedly, *kīsa* is by no means an unusual case. The same arguments could be made from any of a multitude of other cases.

4.1. The role of context

Monosemists generally look to both linguistic and non-linguistic context to fill in the meaning specifications necessary for communication which their abstract semantic meanings allow but do not specify. Thus, Ruhl states: "The important point is that *diversity is provided by context*. What often happens in polysemic analyses is that contextual contributions to meaning are duplicated into the word; the original monosemic sense vanishes" (1989: xii). Reference to context is one of the major ideas which cluster around the notoriously-difficult-to-define concept of "pragmatics".[33] What is the role of context in polysemy?

Unfortunately, space constraints do not permit a thorough discussion of this important topic, so what follows is a summary of what I am convinced is true rather than an argument that it must in fact be so. Only those areas in which I differ with Ruhl are considered at any length.

4.2. Context helps establish and maintain polysemic meanings, and enables choice among them

Monosemists are right, I believe, in assigning great importance to context in the matter. (i) Context makes possible the initial learning of different senses and reinforces them in continuing usage. (ii) Context makes it possible for creative speakers and cooperative hearers to expand meanings to include new senses. (iii) It is "the insulating power of the context" (Lewis 1967: 11–12) that keeps the polysemic senses from colliding and, so to speak, short-circuiting each other. They "do not interfere with one another because they are unlikely to occur in the same context. They live happily by keeping out of each other's way". (iv) Part of the insulation function is that context clues hearers in to which of the established senses is intended. Both linguistic and non-linguistic contexts function in all these ways.

As Langacker reminds us, "all linguistic units are context-dependent ... Rather than context-dependency, it is the process of partial *decontextualization* that requires explication" (1987: 401). All

33. Along with: going beyond truth-values, going beyond strict compositionality, being functionally motivated rather than arbitrary, being calculated on-the-fly rather than established, being implicit rather than overt, having to do with belief and intention rather than reference, being part of extra-linguistic "performance" rather than linguistic "competence", and other things. Schneider's (1995: 636–637) perception of pragmatics as "the wastebasket of linguistics" is accurate, I believe, as is his statement that "it was in fact the precise definition of truth-conditional semantics that created pragmatics by leaving to it the study of all non-truth-conditional aspects of meaning". (The quote may be due to Bertuccelli Papi.)

meanings, not just polysemic meanings, are derived by observation of context and abstraction away from differing contexts.

This is true of the establishment of two kinds of "new" meanings: those that are established in the linguistic system but are new to the learner, and those that are "new" to the linguistic system itself. In either case, the means by which new meanings are established is context. The learner hears a phonological form and must figure out, from the situation (both linguistic and extralinguistic) in which the form is heard, what the speaker intends. As the same form recurs in similar situations, the commonality of the form's contexts becomes more and more strongly associated with it, and that constitutes its meaning.

From this perspective, Ruhl's is a rather odd complaint, that in polysemic analyses "contextual contributions to meaning are duplicated into the word". That, in effect, is what meanings are: duplications from context. The seeming fallacy is mitigated, however, insofar as Ruhl is referring only to the *present context*, i.e., the context in which each particular usage occurs, for spoken language the "context of utterance", while establishing meanings involves the distillation of "duplications" from many past contexts.

Ruhl's objection also seems a little less unreasonable when another fact is considered. I admit (and even insist) that for polysemous meanings the present context must be active enough to enable the correct choice among the meanings. In what other conceivable manner could hearers know, for instance, that in (3) *kīsa* means '[person] go out (from the house)' (2.c–e), in (9) it means 'it go well with [person]' (3.n), and in (8) it means '[artifact] turn out' (3.l–k), rather than some other pattern of meanings in these sentences? By definition the phonology of *kīsa* itself will not be clueing them in to the differences in meaning: context is the only possibility. And context does so by providing overlapping pieces of meaning.

Note, however, that this is equally true of homonymous meanings. Ruhl agrees that "the noun *bank* is homonymic" (1989: 5), presumably between the classic 'river edge' and 'financial institution' senses. How can speakers clue their hearers in to their intent to use one rather than the other of these meanings? It can only be by present context. As far as I know, Ruhl would not object to the duplication of meaning between *bank* and its contexts, or claim that any meaning in the contexts cannot be part of what distinguishes between the meanings of the form.

What's sauce for homonymy ought to be sauce for polysemy: if duplication of meaning between the form and its context is allowable and necessary for proper use of homonymous meanings, it should be allowed for proper use of polysemous meanings as well.[34]

4.3. Context underdetermines meanings

Even more difficult for the monosemic position, however, is the fact that often, even typically, the present context simply does not supply anything like all the information that speakers intend to convey and that hearers in fact understand.

I will discuss a couple of cases, but the argument could be made from any of our example sentences, with a strength inversely proportional to the degree of semantic overlap between *kīsa* and its context in each case. For a Nawatl speaker, (5), or any similar structure in which something unspecified is said to *kīsa* on or at a (skin-covered) bodypart, provides enough context to make it virtually certain that something like a wart is in mind. (Often the extralinguistic context or further linguistic context will reinforce this in some degree, but it is not necessary.) I do not see any way in which this much context, combined only with a monosemic meaning on the order of 6.aj, could produce anything nearly that specific. Why could it not mean that the hair had been singed off, that a thorn or sticker had gotten stuck in, that a blister had healed, that part of the skin had changed color, that a callus had come close to forming, that the skin had gotten wrinkled or cold, that a finger had nearly been cut off, or that any other change of state had occurred or nearly occurred with respect to Thomasina's

34. The argumentation that claims "If a piece of meaning in construction A+B can be shown to come from A, then it must not come from B" is flawed. Semantic overlap between components is not only typical, it (along with phonological overlap) is the very means by which constructions are formed and cohere.

hand? Why should *kīsa* in (12) and (13) not mean 'as it turns out' or 'entirely', instead of 'practically, almost' (4.v)? Those meanings would fit those contexts (and very many others) just fine, and would be just as reasonable specializations of 6.aj as is 4.v.

This problem is exacerbated by the fact that, under thoroughgoing monosemy, the linguistic context itself is far less informative than one might suppose, since often the lexemes forming that context must also be highly schematic. For instance, I mentioned above *kīsa*'s combination with a bodypart term such as *īmak* in (5). But for a monosemist *īmak* is not a bodypart term: its meaning must be abstract enough to include not only 'in/on his hand' but also 'in his power, under his control'; the bodypart sense would only be a pragmatic specialization. Yet nothing in the context provided by (5) would prompt that specialization. The abstract meaning will have to be on the order of a non-spatial 'near him' or 'associated with him'. So the meaning 'potential change of state' (6.aj) is combining in (5) with this abstract 'near him'. The chances of predicting, from this combination, the meaning 'a wart or similar eruption break out' seem to me to be nil.

The only answer I can come up with is that in fact the more specific meanings are established as well as (perhaps even "instead of", quite certainly "more strongly than") the highly abstract schema(s).

5. Conclusions

I have argued that the proliferation of meanings in *kīsa* and most other linguistic forms is not just apparent. *Kīsa* has multiple meanings, separable but related by multiple relationships of similarity.

Monosemists' efforts to establish the contrary position, that each form has only one meaning, founder on the following facts: The indications are that native speakers can and do distinguish among the meanings (3.2.1). Truth value differences can show up among the meanings (3.2.1). There are holes in the pattern, in that not all reasonably expected meanings obtain (3.4). Near-synonyms, translation equivalents, and dialectal variants exhibit differing ranges of meaning that cannot be predicted from a single meaning (3.4). This is especially clear when one considers what speakers must know, not just hearers (3.5). Overlap of meaning with the context cannot be used to prove absence of that meaning from a form (4.2). And finally, context often does not provide enough information to account for what speakers intend and hearers understand (4.3).

In short, polysemy is not just obvious, it is real.

References

Bouchard, Denis
1995 *The Semantics of Syntax*. Chicago: The University of Chicago Press.

Geeraerts, Dirk
1990 The lexicographical treatment of prototypical polysemy. In: Savas L. Tzohatsidis (ed.), *Meanings and Prototypes: Studies in Linguistic Categorization*, 195–210. London: Routledge.

Langacker, Ronald W.
1987 *Foundations of Cognitive Grammar*, Volume 1: *Theoretical Prerequisites*. Stanford: Stanford University Press.
1991 *Foundations of Cognitive Grammar*, Volume 2, *Descriptive Application*. Stanford: Stanford University Press.

Lakoff, George
1970 A note on vagueness and ambiguity. *Linguistic Inquiry* 1: 357–359.

Lewis, C.S.
1967 *Studies in Words*, 2nd edition. New York: Cambridge University Press.

Ruhl, Charles
1989 *On Monosemy: A Study in Linguistic Semantics*. Albany, NY: State University of New York Press.

Schneider, Stefan
1995 Review of Marcella Bertuccelli Papi (1993), *Che cos'è la pragmatica* [What is pragmatics]. Milano: Bompiani. *Language* 71: 637–638.

Tuggy, David
1993 Ambiguity, polysemy, and vagueness. *Cognitive Linguistics* 4: 273–290.

Zwicky, Arnold M. and Jerrold M. Sadock
1975 Identity tests and how to fail them. In: John P. Kimball (ed.), *Syntax and Semantics*, Volume 4, 1–36. New York: Academic Press.

A diachronic perspective on prototypicality: The case of nominal adjectives in Japanese

Satoshi Uehara

Abstract

Along with Nouns, Verbs and Adjectives, Japanese possesses another major lexical category, Nominal Adjectives. This paper examines the structure of the Nominal Adjective category, and shows that the category constitutes a prime example of a prototype category, exhibiting prototype effects in the syntactic behavior of its members. After demonstrating that the semantic factor of gradability motivates the syntactic behavior of Nominal Adjectives, the paper takes a diachronic perspective and examines how the category's prototype structure came about. Drawing on supporting historical evidence, the paper argues that Nominal Adjectives first emerged as a result of the metaphorical interpretation of container-based locational expressions. It also contends that a gradual semantic shift in the semantic structure of the category's members, from designating "things" to designating "properties", and their corresponding occurrence in the modifying function, are responsible for the current prototype structure of the category.

Keywords: adjective, cross-linguistic, diachrony, gradability, grammaticalization; Japanese, lexical category, major syntactic categories, metaphor, metaphorical extension, modification, modifying function, nominal adjectives, noun, pragmatic functions, prototype effects, prototypicality, semantic functions, semantic motivation, verb.

1. Introduction[1]

In addition to the three major syntactic categories, Nouns, Verbs and Adjectives, Japanese has another major category called Nominal Adjectives (Kuno 1973). Some instances of the Noun, Nominal Adjective (henceforth, NA), and Adjective categories are given in (1):

(1)	<u>Noun</u>	*gakusei* 'student'	*mati* 'town'	*misigan* 'Michigan'
	<u>NA</u>	*kirei* 'pretty'	*sizuka* 'quiet'	*seiketu* 'clean'
	<u>Adjective</u>	*ii* 'good'	*ookii* 'big'	*takai* 'expensive'

NAs bear certain semantic similarities to Adjectives, as suggested by the fact that NAs are mostly translated into English as adjectives. In terms of their grammatical behavior, however, NAs pattern with Nouns in that both take the Copula *da* in predication and need a Linker in nominal modification:[2]

(2)		<u>Predication</u>	<u>Nominal modification</u>
	<u>Noun</u>	*Kare wa gakusei da.* he TOP student COP 'He is a student.'	*gakusei no mati* student LINK town 'student town(s)'

---

1. The author would like to thank the editors of this volume, John Taylor, René Dirven, and Hubert Cuyckens, for their valuable comments on the earlier version of this paper. My thanks also go to Bill Croft, Andrew Barke, and especially to anonymous reviewers for critical and helpful comments. Needless to say, all remaining errors are my own.
2. The following abbreviations have been used: ABL (ablative), ACC (accusative), ATTR (attributive), COP (Copula), LINK (Nominal Linker), LOC (locative), NOM (nominative), TOP (topic), and <= (derived from).

NA	*Kare wa*	*sizuka*	*da.*		*sizuka*	*na*	*mati*
	he TOP	quiet	COP		quiet	LINK	town
	'He is quiet.'				'quiet town(s)'		
Adjective	*Kare wa*	*ii*	*(*da*).		*ii*	*(*no/na*)	*mati*
	he TOP	good	COP		good	LINK	town
	'He is good.'				'good town(s)		

Their dual nature is the reason for the label "Nominal Adjective". As will be pointed out later, Nouns, NAs, and Adjectives constitute a continuum, with NAs being situated between Nouns and Adjectives.[3]

It should be noted at the outset that NAs in Japanese do not constitute a minor category exhibiting some idiosyncratic behavior; instead, they make up a major category with a large membership in the language. A survey (Uehara 1998) applying the above structural criteria to the word frequency list of the Japan National Language Research Institute (Kokuritsu1964) showed that the NA category is almost twice the size of the Adjective category, with 257 NAs in contrast to only 142 Adjectives.[4]

This paper is organized as follows. The following section examines syntactic aspects of NAs and concludes that NAs constitute a *bona fide* case of lexical categories exhibiting prototype effects. Section 3 discusses semantic motivations for the grammatical behavior of NAs. The remainder of the paper takes a historical perspective, and argues that historical processes of metaphorical extension and the cross-linguistic correlation of semantic and pragmatic functions are responsible for the prototype structure of the category in Modern Japanese.

---

3. In his Radical Construction Grammar, Croft (2001) refers to the Japanese data cited here and in Uehara (1998) and analyzes Nouns, NAs, and Adjectives in Japanese in terms of a "semantic map", where the three categories form a continuum.
4. The survey took in its scope the most frequently used words in Part 3 "Adjectives and the like" of the List, and found 406 Adjectives and/or NAs. Seven ambivalent words (e.g., *atataka da/atataka-i* 'warm') are excluded from both the NA and Adjective counts; see Uehara (1998: chap. 5) for more details.

2. Grammatical aspects of nominal adjectives

We have seen that Nouns and NAs show similarities in syntactic behavior. Now let us look at the differences between these two categories. The basic differences concern the use of the Linker in adnominal modification, and NAs' (in)ability to take case particles (Table 1). When functioning as modifiers, Nouns take the Linker (the so-called genitive particle) *no,* while NAs take *na*; in addition, Nouns can take case particles such as *ga* NOMINATIVE, *o* ACCUSATIVE, and so on, while NAs cannot. These are, in fact, the tests usually employed in order to formally differentiate the two categories, as illustrated in (3).

Table 1. Grammatical differences between Nouns and NAs.

	Linker in modification	with case particles
Nouns	*no*	OK
NAs	*na*	*

(3) in modification / with case particles

	in modification	with case particles
Noun	*Misigan* 'Michigan'	
	Misigan no mati	*Misigan ga ii.*
	town	NOM be-good
	'Michigan town(s)'	'Michigan is good.'
NA	*kirei* 'pretty'	
	kirei na mati	**Kirei ga ii.*
	town	NOM be-good.
	'pretty town(s)'	'?'

Although the above-mentioned criteria successfully identify lexical items as NAs, they do not by themselves establish the status of NAs as a separate category. In fact, there is some evidence that the grammatical distinction between NAs and Nouns is unclear and gradient, rather than clear-cut. The evidence is surveyed below.

2.1. *Use of the Linkers* na *vs.* no

With respect to the use of *na/no*, some NAs can take either Linker, with no noticeable difference in meaning.

(4) *kenmei* *na/no* *doryoku*
wholehearted effort
'a wholehearted effort'

(5) *iroiro* *na/no* *gyoozi*
various event
'various events'

For other NAs, however (which I call double-function cases), the use of *na* or *no* is associated with a difference, for example, with respect to an NA's collocational pattern with a following Noun.

(6) a. *heiwa* ***na*** *kuni*
country
'a *peaceful* country'

b. *heiwa* ***no*** *sisya*
messenger
'a messenger of *peace*'

(7) a. *kenkoo* ***na*** *hito*
person
'a *healthy* person'

b. *kenkoo* ***no*** *zyootai*
condition
'*health* condition'

2.2. *Case-marking particles*

Further evidence for the fuzziness of the NA category comes from the behavior of NAs with respect to case-marking particles. In fact, one notable characteristic of the double-function words mentioned above is that they often take case particles, which is a characteristic of Nouns, not of NAs:

(8) *Kenkoo ga itiban taisetu da.*
healthy NOM first important COP
'Health is most important.'

(9) *Detarame o yuu na!*
nonsensical ACC say don't
'Don't talk nonsense!'

The 'nouniness' of an NA, i.e., whether an NA can behave as a Noun with respect to case particles, is a matter of degree. Teramura (1982: 67) tested NAs according to whether they occur with case-marking particles, and found gradience in how many particles a word can occur with and how many restrictions there are in its usage with a certain particle. His examples (along with his grammatical judgments) are reproduced in (10)–(13):

(10) *genki* 'vigorous'

Genki ga nai.
NOM exist.not
'(He) is low-spirited.'

Genki o das-e.
ACC put.forth-IMP
'Cheer up!'

?*genki kara* ....
ABL

(11) *sinsetu* 'kind'

Sinsetu ga adu to-naru.
NOM evil become
'The kindness turned out to be an evil.'

Sinsetu kara sitakoto desu.
ABL deed COP-polite
'That's what one did out of kindness.'

(12) *yukai* ?*yukai* *ga/o/kara* ....
'pleasant' NOM/ACC/ABL

(13) *sizuka* **sizuka* *ga* *kini itta*
'quiet' NOM pleased (me)
**sizuka* o *urimono ni site*....
ACC trading on ....

In (10), *genki* behaves like a Noun in that it can take both the nominative particle *ga* and the accusative particle *o* while its awkwardness in occurring with the ablative marker *kara* distinguishes it from a full-fledged Noun. *Sinsetu* 'kind' in (11) resembles *genki* 'vigorous' in terms of nouniness by being able to take two case particles, nominative and ablative. (However, since ablative is an oblique case, its ability to take this case may be less heavily weighted in terms of nouniness judgements.) *Yukai* 'pleasant' in (12) is much less noun-like in that it is infelicitous (though not completely ungrammatical) with any of the three particles, while *sizuka* 'quiet' in (13) is a full-fledged NA, unable to occur with any of the case particles.

Thus, the nouniness of these NAs varies from word to word, as represented in Table 2:

Table 2. Nouniness of NA words exhibited in case particles.

NA	case particles					Nouniness
	ga	*o*	*kara*	--	-----	
genki	ok	ok	?	--	-----	
sinsetu	ok	--	ok	--	-----	
yukai	?	?	?	--	-----	
sizuka	*	*	--	--	-----	
---	--	--	--	--	-----	

Other criteria of nounhood could be taken into consideration, for example, the ability to take the allative case marker *e*, which would fill in the columns on the right side of *kara* in Table 2. However, in order to arrive at a precise calculation of nouniness, we would also have to be able to attach a weighting to each of the criteria. (Since there is no objective way to calculate this, the "nouniness" column has been left blank.) Still, on the basis of data cited so far (and in the absence of weighted criteria), Teramura suggests that Japanese categories are situated along a continuum, whereby they are not strictly distinguished from each other, and individual lexical items displaying variable or ambiguous behavior are located in a boundary region between categories. The closer to the Noun boundary NA words are located, the more they exhibit Noun-like behavior. Teramura (1982: 74) offers a chart to illustrate the situation, the relevant part of which is reproduced in Figure 1.

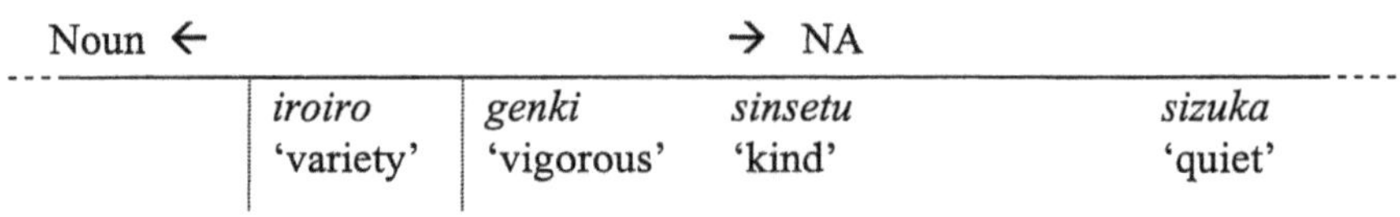

Figure 1. Noun and NA continuum.

2.3. *Lexical survey*

In the previous sections, we have looked at the syntactic behavior of NAs with respect to the form of the Linker and the use of case particles. It has become clear (i) that members of the NA category are not at all homogeneous in terms of their syntactic behavior and (ii) that the boundaries of the category are not clearly drawn. The category, in other words, displays prototype effects (Rosch 1978; Lakoff 1987; Taylor 1989).

Let us consider to what extent the fuzziness of the boundaries between NAs and Nouns is manifested by the individual members of the NA category. To that purpose, I did a lexical survey of the syntactic behavior of NAs, making use of the frequency-based Japanese word list which is compiled by the National Language Research Institute of Japan (Kokuritsu 1964) and which lists 264 *na*-taking lexical items. In particular, I checked the syntactic behavior of each of these items with the Iwanami Japanese Dictionary (1986). The results are shown in Table 3:

Table 3. Most frequently used *na*-taking lexical items.

	Does not take case particles	Does take case particles	Total
Does not take *no*	76 (28.8%)	75 (28.4%)	151 (57.2%)
Takes *no*	37 (14.0%)	76 (28.8%)	113 (42.8%)
Total	113 (42.8%)	151 (57.2%)	264 (100.0%)

Of the 264 *na*-taking lexical items, only 28.8% are clear instances of the NA category, meeting the two criteria mentioned earlier (use of the Linker *na* and no case-marking particles), while more than 70% show some degree of fuzziness. The 14.0% that take *no* and no case-marking particle, and the 28.4% that do not take *no* but do take at least one case-marking particle (the number of case particles introducing further degrees of fuzziness), constitute less clear cases of NAs. The 28.8% that take *no* and take case-marking particles are the least clear cases of the NA category. It is evident, then, that instances of the NA category show varying degrees of category membership, from clear instances of the category through instances with a lower degree of membership, to instances whose membership status is no longer clear. This is the kind of situation which the notion of prototype refers to. The clearest NA instances (*na* only and no case-marking particles) can be regarded as the most prototypical members of the category in that they meet the criteria for NA-membership to the fullest degree, and instances with a decreasing degree of category membership exhibit a decreasing degree of prototypicality.

The syntactic differences between Nouns and NAs do not therefore divide the relevant portion of the lexicon into two separate classes. The situation is depicted schematically in Figure 2.

In Figure 2, "Nominals" refers to the superordinate category of Nouns and NAs, both of which are characterized by taking the Copula *da* in predicative expressions. NAs form a subcategory at one end, with 28.8% being the most prototypical (full-fledged) members, as shown by the use of the Linker *na* and the inability to take case particles, and with the others exhibiting varying degrees of nouniness.

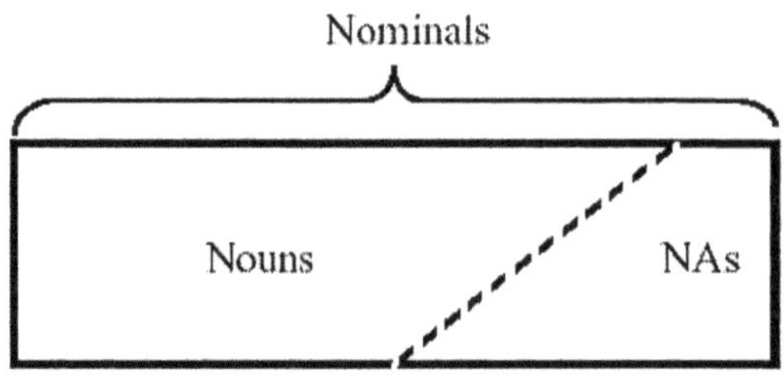

Figure 2. Noun and NA map in Japanese.

3. The semantics of NAs

So far, we have observed that the NA category in Japanese shows a prototype structure. The observations were made on the basis of category members' syntactic behavior. Now let us examine the semantic aspects of the category to find out if there is any semantic motivation for the syntactic behavior.

As has been noted earlier (cf. Introduction), an NA lexical item takes *na* if it is translated as an adjective in English. In other words, the use of *na* is motivated by the "adjectivity" of the lexical items. To see this point more clearly, consider again the double-function cases (6) and (7), which have been repeated here as (14) and (15).

(14) a. *heiwa* ***na*** *kuni*
country
'a *peaceful* country'

b. *heiwa* ***no*** *sisya*
messenger
'a messenger of *peace*'

(15) a. *kenkoo* ***na*** *hito*
person
'a *healthy* person'

b. *kenkoo* ***no*** *zyootai*
condition
'*health* condition'

As we see from the English translations, an NA lexical item takes *na* when it is interpreted as an adjective in English and it takes *no* when it is interpreted as a noun in English.

While this observation seems to be pertinent, there are some obvious problems associated with characterizing semantic factors in Japanese (or in any language, for that matter) by reference to the category status of translation equivalents in another language (English, in this case). In fact, there are a number of instances where adjectives in English translate into Japanese words with *no*, not with *na*, as can be seen in (16)–(20):

(16) E. sick => a sick person
J. *byooki* => *byooki *na/no hito*
person

(17) E. eternal => eternal peace
J. *eien* => *eien *na/no heiwa*
peace

(18) E. professional => a professional player
J. *puro*[5] => *puro *na/no sensyu*
Player

(19) E. ordinary => an ordinary person
J. *hutuu* => *hutuu ?na/no hito*
person

(20) E. true => a true story
J. *hontoo* => *hontoo *na/no hanasi*
story

What, then, is the factor determining the use of *na*? It is significant that, cross-linguistically, adjectives tend to be compatible with comparison. Wierzbicka (1986: 377), in her attempt at a semantic defini-

5 *Puro* 'professional' is a loanword from English.

tion of nouns and verbs, points out that “on the whole, ... adjectives tend to have a category of degree, related to their static and ‘unidimensional’ character”. Croft (1991) also lists “gradability” as one of the parameters associated with his universal definition of the category (in this respect, see also Bolinger 1967).

Now let us reconsider the English/Japanese mismatches discussed above and see how they fare with a word like *motto* ‘more’ in (16')–(20'):[6]

(16')	*byooki *na/no hito* ‘a sick person’	=>	*??motto byooki no hito* ‘a sicker person’
(17')	*eien *na/no heiwa* ‘eternal peace’	=>	**motto eien no heiwa* ‘*more eternal peace’
(18')	*puro *na/no sensyu* ‘a professional player’	=>	**motto puro no sensyu* ‘*a more professional player’, or ‘a more professional player’
(19')	*hutuu ?na/no hito* ‘an ordinary person’	=>	*??motto hutuu no hito* ‘a more ordinary person’
(20')	*hontoo *na/no hanasi* ‘a true story’	=>	**motto hontoo no hanasi* ‘a truer story’

It can be observed that the adjectives in the English glosses and their Japanese (pseudo-)equivalents show differences in gradability. In

6. Grammaticality judgments of the English glosses are by Grant Shafer, a linguistically naïve native speaker of American English. It is worth noting that even the okayed expressions required some effort on the part of the informant to imagine an appropriate context for their use, in contrast to readily accepted sequences with *clever* (*a clever/more clever person*). The informant also mentioned that *professional* can have two meanings: in the sense of ‘paid’ as opposed to ‘amateur’, *professional* is not gradable, while in the sense ‘businesslike’ it is. Even in the latter case, he preferred its collocation with a word like *businessman*, as in *a more professional businessman*.

particular, while the English adjectives are more amenable to gradation (albeit with some effort), the Japanese words are not compatible with comparison. As such, the Japanese examples show that the *na/no* distinction in the language is very much motivated by the gradability of the concept denoted by the lexical item to which the particles are attached.

Differences in the gradability of individual items in the two languages account for most, if not all, cases of English/Japanese mismatches. For example, those concepts which designate points on a scale, rather than the scale itself, take *no* rather than *na* even if such concepts are adjective-like in the English translation, as can be seen in (21).[7]

(21)	*heikin no/*na,* 'average'	*nami no/?na* 'average'
	*tugi no/*na* 'next'	*mata no/*na* 'next time'
	*itiban(me) no/*na* 'the first'	*tasyoo no/*na* 'some amount of'
	syoosyoo no/?na 'somewhat'	*daitai no/*na* 'almost, most of'
	*ganrai no/*na* 'original, by nature'	*motomoto no/*na* 'original'

It appears, then, that the occurrence of the Linker *na* (instead of *no*) – the characteristic syntactic behavior of NAs – is motivated by the semantic factor of gradability. I have employed Cognitive Grammar style pictorial representations (Langacker 1987, 1991) to illustrate the difference in the semantic structures of Nouns and NAs. A Noun typically designates a "thing", defined as "a region in some domain" of conceptual space (Langacker 1987: 189). An Adjective typically

7. For an extensive discussion of these and other marginal cases in terms of semantic gradability, see Uehara (1998).

designates a gradable "property" (cf. Wierzbicka 1986).[8] "Thing" and "property" can be represented schematically as in Figure 3.

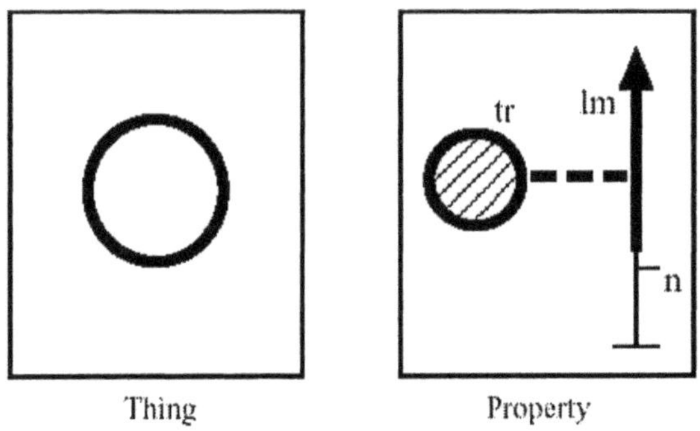

Figure 3. Schematic representations of a prototypical thing and a prototypical property.

Cognitive Grammar characterizes meaning in terms of the relation between a profile (the focal point within the immediate scope of a conception) and the base (the rest of the structure which is less prominent but still evoked by the expression). This makes it possible to describe the meanings of expressions in a precise and detailed manner and to distinguish meanings in terms of differences in their semantic structure. In Figure 3, the enclosing boxes delimit the base, and heavy lines identify the profile. A circle is used to indicate a thing. A property evokes the conception of a scale of comparison and specifies that a thing falls somewhere with respect to the norm (*n*) on the scale. Property predications are therefore inherently relational, and profile the interconnection (the relation of inclusion) between a

8. The term "atemporal relations", used for the semantic structure of adjectives in Langacker (1987), is not used here since the term does not only denote the adjectival concepts in question; adjectives, adverbs, and adpositions all designate atemporal relations.

schematically characterized thing (the trajector, *tr*) and the scalar region (the landmark, *lm*).

Most of the words with ambivalent behavior between prototypical NAs and Nouns discussed above can be described as having the semantic structures of Properties when used with *na*, but may be construed as (non-prototypical) things when used with *no*. An example of a non-prototypical thing is given by a "nominalized property" (e.g., *heiwa* 'peace' and *baka-sa* 'foolishness'); another example is given by a "thing with only one property" (e.g., *baka* 'a fool'). Both contain the notion of property in the base, as shown in Figure 4:

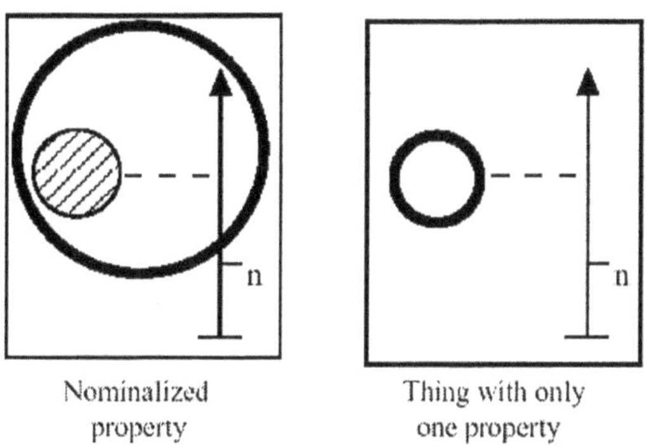

Figure 4. Non-prototypical things.

Seen from the opposite direction, those Nouns with (varying degrees of) NA-like syntactic behavior profile non-prototypical things, and their conceptual closeness to property concepts motivates the (sometimes seemingly sporadic) occurrence of the particle *na* in present-day Japanese. In the following section, I take a diachronic perspective, and argue that the conceptual closeness of non-prototypical things and properties may have motivated the semantic shift from the former to the latter.

4. Diachronic aspect of Nominal Adjectives

An investigation into the history of the NA category leads us to suppose that older stages of the language had only a very small number of NAs. There are two reasons for this assumption. First, as has often been noted (e.g., Uehara 1998: chap. 5), the NA category is an open class, unlike the Adjective category, and loanwords constitute a large part of NA words in present-day Japanese. It is therefore reasonable to assume that the number of NA words used to be much smaller before the borrowing took place. My survey of the 264 most frequent NA words in Table 3 above revealed that about 200 are in fact words of Chinese origin. Second, an examination of the histories of NA words in the *Nihon Kokugo Daijiten* [Japanese Language Encyclopedia] reveals that a majority of NAs, whether native or foreign, can be traced back to regular Nouns, and that their modern uses testify to a semantic shift from a thing to a gradable property concept. Most originate from non-prototypical things as represented in Figure 4, and their subsequent development instantiates a profile shift towards NAs. The present-day NA *zyoozu* 'skillful', for example, used to have the meaning 'expert/person with an excellent skill in something'; it was a Noun with a semantic structure roughly equivalent to that shown on the right in Figure 4. Subsequently, its nominal 'person' sense seems to have bleached to such an extent that its property sense 'skillfulness', the next most salient substructure, came to the fore, as depicted on the right in Figure 3.[9]

Some NAs did not originate from words designating non-prototypical things, but underwent a more radical reconfiguration of their semantic structure. I will mention here only one such example, *sinken* 'serious, earnest' in (22). *Sinken* (*sin* 'true, real' and *ken* 'sword') meant, and still does when it takes *no*, 'real sword' as opposed to 'fake sword made of bamboo', for practice in *kendoo*, one of

9. *Zyoozu* 'skillful' is a Sino-loanword. Among native NAs with a similar history is *keti* 'stingy', which derived its property sense from a regular Noun meaning 'fault(-finding)', 'misfortune', as seen in idiomatic expressions like *keti o tukeru* [fault ACC attach/put] 'find fault with', *keti ga tuku* [fault NOM fall] 'be unfortunate'.

Japan's traditional martial arts. Originally, the word only designated the sword itself, with some properties, such as lethal, expensive, etc., on the encyclopedic margins of the concept. However, when used in a compound as in *sinken-syoobu* 'real sword-fight', or with *no* as in *sinken no syoobu* 'fight with real swords', the seriousness with which the fighters use the lethal sword, in contrast to bamboo swords, is highlighted. Perspectivizing this "seriousness" aspect, the compound, *sinken-syoobu* 'real sword-match' can be used to refer to games which do not involve swords at all (e.g., judo games, or even card games), and *sinken* takes *na* as in *sinken* ***na*** *taido* 'serious attitude, earnestness' (22).[10]

(22)	*sinken*	'real sword', 'serious, earnest'
	sinken-syoobu	'real sword-fight', 'play in real earnest'
	sinken ***no*** *syoobu*	'fight with real swords'
	sinken ***na*** *taido*	'serious attitude, earnestness'

As we go down the list of NAs in this manner, we are left with only a small handful of words of uncertain origin in the NA category of early Japanese, a situation schematically depicted in Figure 5.

These very old NAs include NAs with the no longer productive NA-forming suffix *-ka,* such as *sizu-ka* 'quiet' and *atata-ka* 'warm', which, according to Backhouse (1984: 181), historically "constitute the earliest recorded type" of NAs. Sixteen such NAs in our word frequency list have no Noun-like behavior at all (such as use with case particles and/or use of *no* as a Linker in modification), and seem to support their status as the oldest NAs which have not derived from Nouns.

10. It is interesting in this regard that Chinese students of Japanese have to acquire the property sense of this word, as it has developed in Japanese. Among native NAs with a similar history of radical semantic shift is *dame* 'no good', which derived from the regular noun compounding of *da* 'foolish/useless' and *me* 'a cross/mesh/stitch', and which has the meaning 'a cross that does not constitute a territory in the board game of Go'.

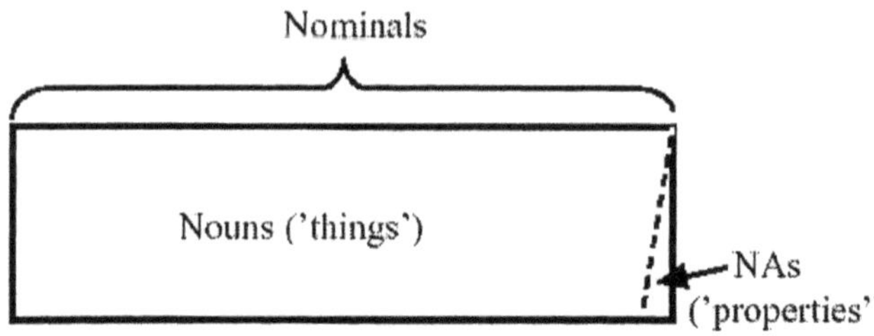

Figure 5. Noun and NA map for early Japanese.

5. The rise and development of NAs

We have examined the diachronic aspect of NAs, and observed that the category of NAs with its prototype structure did not exist in earlier stages of the language; rather, the prototype structure emerged as the category acquired new members over the course of time. Now, let us consider in more detail how the NA category in modern Japanese arose (sections 5.1 and 5.2) and acquired its current prototype structure (section 5.3).

5.1. How the category of NAs arose

We have seen that most of the present-day NAs have derived from Nouns and that in early Japanese there existed only a limited number of NAs, which included those with the *-ka* suffix, the earliest recorded type of NAs. In our search for the origin of the NA category, therefore, it is interesting to take note of Sakakura's (1966: 323) observation that this NA forming morpheme *-ka*, like some other stative forming suffixes, was derived from its homonymous bound morpheme (*-ka*, in this case), which meant 'place' in Old Japanese (e.g., *sumi-ka* 'live-place' [i.e., 'house/residence'], and *ari-ka* 'exist-place' [i.e. 'location/hiding place']).

Spatial concepts are often taken to be the source domain for many semantic extensions, and Sakakura's finding suggests that some spatial conceptualizations were responsible for the rise of the NA category. In the following, I will argue that NAs first emerged from Nouns designating states (like *health* in English) and from the metaphorical interpretation of container-based locational expressions.

For ease of illustration of this metaphorical extension process, let us first take some examples from English, since the homonymy between locational and stative constructions, relevant to our discussion of the rise of NAs, is missing in Modern Japanese, but well documented in English. There exist phrasal expressions using abstract nouns for some adjectival concepts in English, such as *in good health* for *healthy,* and *in luck* for *lucky*. Some other abstract nouns do not have adjectival lexical counterparts, but have the same phrasal pattern, e.g., *in love,* as in *Bill is in love*. These phrasal expressions are patterned on locational expressions (e.g., *Bill is in Tokyo*), a fact which illustrates how "we typically conceptualize the nonphysical *in terms of* the physical" (Lakoff & Johnson 1980: 59). Figure 6 schematically depicts this metaphorical extension. Notice that in this construction, abstract nouns (e.g., *health*) lexically denote things (albeit non-prototypical things), while the phrasal expressions as a whole (e.g., *in good health*) function as stative adjectives.

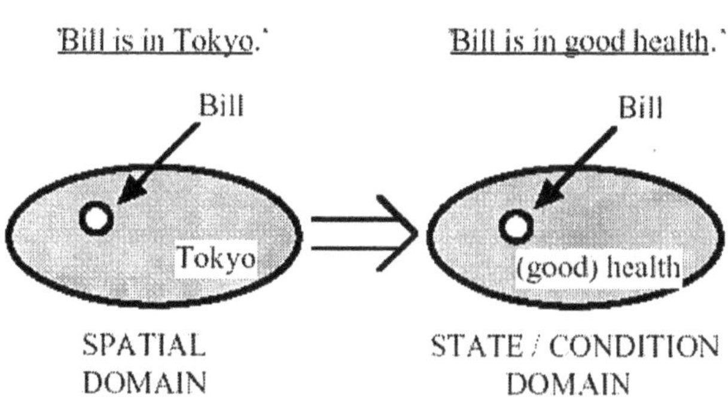

Figure 6. Metaphorical interpretation of location expression.

Japanese NAs, in their inception, seem to have been parasitic on locational expressions with abstract Nouns, and exploited the metaphorical extension to denote adjectival concepts. Unlike their English counterparts, however, abstract Nouns in Old Japanese later underwent a profile shift, and acquired property senses (as NAs) along with their original thing profiles (as Nouns), without any attendant morphological change, as exemplified by *genki* 'vigor, energy' => *genki* 'vigor, energy; vigorous, energetic, healthy'. As their use as property concepts became more routinized and entrenched, they occurred less and less frequently with case particles, and in their reference function deadjectival nominalizers such as *-sa* '-ness' gradually began to accompany them (e.g., *genki* 'vigorous, energetic' => *genki-sa* 'vigorousness, energeticness'). As the number of abstract Nouns undergoing the same semantic shift towards property concepts increased, the NAs became associated with a full-fledged semantico-grammatical paradigm (23), a pattern which was to become typical of the NA category.[11]

(23)	[property concept] + COPULA	in predication function
	[property concept]-*sa* '-ness'	in reference function
	[property concept] + *na*	in modification function

At this stage, property concepts new to the language (e.g., recent loanwords from English, such as *ereganto* 'elegant') directly fitted into the NA paradigm of the language (24). They did not need to go through the process of utilizing the parasitic locational construction with their abstract Noun forms (viz., *eregansu* 'elegance') to yield the NA paradigm in present-day Japanese.

(24) Predication: *Ereganto da.*
Elegant COP
'(He) is elegant.'

11. To put it in "usage-based" terms, the schematic pattern for NAs emerged gradually as their type frequency increased. Cognitive Grammar contends that syntax can largely be understood in terms of the schemas abstracted from linguistic expressions (Langacker 1991).

Reference: *ereganto-sa*
elegant-ness
'elegantness/elegance'

Modification: *ereganto na*
Elegant LINK
'elegant', as in: *ereganto na hito*
elegant *na* person
'an elegant person'

The above scenario for the rise of the NA category is a speculative one, but is consonant with the facts that we have observed in the previous sections concerning Japanese NAs. Sakakura's finding about the development of the oldest NA-forming suffix *-ka* from a morpheme meaning 'place' gives support particularly to the idea that the initial rise of the NA category was triggered by a metaphorical interpretation of the container-based locational expressions.

Furthermore, two historical facts on the development of the NA inflectional paradigm, one concerning Copula formation and the other the Linker *na* formation, lend strong support to, and at the same time offer reasonable accounts for, the scenario as a whole as well as its initial stage. The next two sections discuss the two historical processes.

5.2. *Copula formation and the NAs*

One important fact about the use of the Copula with NAs in predication function is that the Copula *da* in present-day Japanese can be traced back to *nari* in Old Japanese, where the Copula *nari* had itself derived from, and was used interchangeably with, *ni ari*, a sequence consisting of the locative particle *ni* 'in/at' + the existential verb *ari* 'be/exist'.[12] This is summarized in (25).

---

12. To be more precise, *da* can be traced back to *de aru*, which, in turn, had derived from *nite ari*, a more marked variant of *ni ari* (and *nari*, for that matter), the Copula in Old Japanese (Saeki 1956). *De aru* is still used as a stylistic vari-

(25) *da* <= *nari* <= *ni ari*
COP COP LOC exist
in Mod. Jap. in Old Jap.

To understand the significance of this fact, let us illustrate the above scenario of the rise of NAs along with the concurrent process of Copula formation, by using a place Noun *Kyoo* 'capital city' and an ambivalent Noun/NA word *kenkoo* '(good) health/healthy':

(26) Old Japanese — Literal English gloss

Existential: *Kare kyoo ni ari.* 'He exists in the capital.'
he capital LOC exist

⇓ [METAPHORICAL EXTENSION]

Copular: (parasitic) *Kare kenkoo* ***ni ari***. 'He *exists in* (good) health.'
health

↓ [COPULA FORMATION] ↓

Noun: ("thing") *Kare* ***kenkoo*** *nari.* *'He is *(good) health.*'
COP

↓ [SEMANTIC SHIFT] ↓

NA: ("property") *Kare kenkoo nari.* 'He is healthy.'
healthy

The diachronic development of NAs and the Copula illustrated in (26) supports our scenario above in the following two ways. First, the existence of the intermediate stage between the Copula and the loca-

ant of the Copula *da* in present-day Japanese. However, *da* is more grammaticalized than *de aru* in that the former, unlike the latter, can be used only in predication and not in nominal modification. Furthermore, the particle *de* in *de aru* can be used independently in present-day Japanese as a locative particle to mark the location of events, but not of objects. Hence, *de aru* differs from Old Japanese *ni ari* in that only the latter has the (typical) existential function (concerning the location of objects), although the two resemble each other in having the copulative function.

tive expression, where the two were used interchangeably, endorses our position that the metaphorical interpretation of spatial expressions is responsible for the rise of NAs. Initially, not only were the earliest members of the category associated with a spatial meaning lexically, but they were used with the copulative construction involving the locative particle and abstract Nouns, which thus formally paralleled the (spatial) existential construction. In other words, a situation similar to that in English existed in Old Japanese, where the locative and the stative adjectival expressions employed an identical construction.

Furthermore, the formation of the Copula meant the loss of structural identity between the two expressions in Old Japanese. The following three aspects of its structural development offer a reasonable account of why those abstract Nouns in the parasitic construction in the initial stage of NAs developed property senses without any accompanying morphological change (resulting in Modern Japanese possessing a large number of lexical items which are polysemous between a thing (Noun) and a property (NA) meaning, very much like the double-function items discussed earlier[13]). Firstly, when the Copula construction arose from the existential construction by absorbing the locative particle *ni*, the property sense, which had been expressed by the combination of the abstract Noun and the locative particle, was left for the remaining structure (the Noun alone) to carry. Secondly, it should be noted that Nouns in Japanese do not inflect for case, number, or gender, and are not accompanied by articles, but that they take case particles to indicate grammatical relations. Therefore, when the (locative) case particle was lost in the Copula formation, it meant the loss of the sole structural indicator of its nominality (thing profile) in the predication function. Lastly, it is reasonable to assume that the more frequently those (originally

13. This forms an interesting contrast with languages such as English, where outside of color terms – *My folder is red* [adjective] vs. *Red* [noun] *is my favorite color* – it is extremely rare for lexical items to be listed both as nouns and adjectives, that is, to be polysemous between a thing and a property reading. On the other hand, English abounds with words which are listed as both noun and verb (*paint, run, walk*, etc.).

nominal) lexical items were used to designate property concepts rather than things, the less they were used with case particles. By integrating the locative case particle, the Copula *nari* served to initiate the process of reducing the contexts where the abstract Nouns in question originally occurred with case particles. Therefore, as illustrated in (26), Copula formation was consonant with, and possibly facilitated, the semantic shift from abstract Noun to relational (property) NA.

The diachronic process from the existential construction to the Copula in Old Japanese thus gives strong support to our hypothesized scenario, specifically with respect to the cognitive process of metaphorical extension in the rise of the NA category. We have also observed that the Copula formation process offers an account for the development of the NA category after its inception (i.e., the semantic shift and the (non-)use with case particles).

It should be noted here that this diachronic process involving the Copula in Japanese itself represents an interesting case of grammaticalization, with grammatical functions resulting from the cognitive operation of metaphor. Recent cross-linguistic studies in grammaticalization (Heine, Claudi & Hünnemeyer 1991; Hopper & Traugott 1993) have found that the development of grammatical meaning typically results from cognitive operations such as metaphor, inference, perspectivization, and prototype extension. The Japanese Copula presents itself as one example of this cross-linguistic pattern.

The topic of cross-linguistic patterns in the development of grammatical meanings brings us to the other historical fact supporting our NA scenario, which we address in the next section.

5.3. Linker na *formation and NAs' prototypical structure*

We have examined the initial part of our NA scenario, in particular how the NA category emerged. Now let us look at the rest of the scenario, that is, how the NA situation in early Japanese (Figure 5) developed into the present situation with its prototypicality effects (Figure 2).

Interesting in this regard is the historical relation between the NA Linker and the Copula: the Linker *na* for NAs in adnominal modification can be traced back to the same origin as the Copula. The Linker *na* – reflecting the NA's characteristic syntactic behavior which distinguishes the category from Nouns – came into being in Middle Japanese (it did not exist in Old Japanese) and historically originated from *naru*, the adnominal (i.e., attributive) form of the Copula *nari*, which as we have seen was derived from the existential expression. This is summarized in (27):

(27)	*na*	<=	*naru*	<=	*ni*	*aru*
	NA Linker		COP:ATTR		LOC	exist:ATTR
	in Mod. Jap.		in Old Jap.			

Before the NA Linker in Modern Japanese took its present form, its predecessor *naru* had been used for both Nouns and (the emerging category of) NAs in their modifying function, as illustrated in (28):

(28)	<u>Noun</u>	*Komoro*	*Komoro*	*naru*	*yama*
		'Komoro'	Komoro		mountain
			'the mountain (which exists) in Komoro'		
	<u>NA</u>	*sizuka*	*sizuka*	*naru*	*yama*
		'quiet'	quiet		mountain
			'the mountain which is quiet'		
			or 'the quiet mountain'		

The fact that the NA Linker has its origin in the existential construction offers further support for our hypothesis that the NA category arose through metaphorical extension from the spatial domain. In addition, the fact that the Linker *na* – the now salient structural feature distinguishing NAs from Nouns – developed only later, suggests that the status of NAs as a category independent of Nouns was largely obscured formally (and probably conceptually as well).

The historical development of the Linker *na* also sheds light on the development of the NA category after its emergence, since the

Linker took its present form only after the Copula *nari* was formed (and NAs emerged). Consider the examples in (28) again. They depict the situation before the emergence of the Linker *na* and its exclusive use with NAs, when *naru*, the predecessor of *na*, was used for both NAs and Nouns (including locational Nouns). Here, one might wonder why *naru* was subsequently lost for locations (and things) in the modifying function, while only *naru* survived for use with property concepts and got shortened to *na* in Modern Japanese.

Studies of linguistic typology suggest an answer to this question. In his cross-linguistic study of syntactic categories, Croft (1991: 87) found that prototypical adjectival roots designating properties are most frequently attested in the modification function, while prototypical nominal roots denoting what he calls objects are most frequently attested in the reference function. This correlation between the semantics of lexical items and their syntactic function sheds light on the historical development from the use of the Linker *naru* for both Nouns and NAs, as in (28), to the exclusive use of the Linker *na* for NAs in present-day Japanese.

The Nouns in (28) designate nominal concepts (specifically, a "place"), whose semantic structure is very different from that of property concepts. The use of *naru* for (locational) Nouns in the modification function can be assumed to have been infrequent, thus leading to the loss of the form in that function in favor of the Linker *no*, which was used for Nouns in general.[14] On the other hand, NAs (i.e., those words which gradually underwent a semantic shift from things to property concepts) have semantic structures closer to those of property concepts. The use of *naru* for NAs in modification function was much more frequent, which not only lead to the retention of the form *naru* for the function, but also to the reduction of *naru* to *na*.

The same correlation between the semantics of NAs and their sentential function can offer an answer to our question as to why the

14. Readers might wonder about the origin of the Noun Linker *no*. Unlike the NA Linker *na*, *no* is found in the oldest written document of Japanese, and existed long before *na* developed from the Copula *nari*.

NA category has a prototype structure in present-day Japanese. Let us recall the paradigm for prototypical Nouns and NAs (see Table 1):

prototypical Noun paradigm
  use with case-marking particles in reference
  use with the Linker *no* in adnominal modification
prototypical NA paradigm
  use with the Linker *na* in adnominal modification
  no use of case-marking particles in reference

Most NAs used to be Nouns and used to follow the Noun paradigm. However, they underwent a gradual semantic shift, from designating things to designating properties, and the closer their semantic structures came to those of typical property concepts, the more frequently they were used in the modification function, and thus the more thoroughly they conformed with the NA paradigm.

This usage-based frequency model can explain why some prototypical property words like *kirei* 'pretty' are well-entrenched in the NA paradigm, while non-property words such as *nami* 'average' and *tugi* 'next' in (21) are still resistant to the NA paradigm. The syntactic prototypicality of the NA category thus reflects the conceptual prototypicality of its members, with property concepts being the most prototypical.

6. Conclusion

NAs in modern Japanese constitute a prime example of a prototype category with respect to the syntactic behavior of its members. In this paper, I have drawn on diachronic data to argue that NAs first emerged as a result of the metaphorical interpretation of container-based locational expressions, and that the prototype structure of the NA category is the formal reflection of a process of semantic shift from Nouns (designating "things") to prototypical NAs (designating "properties"), associated with the frequent use of NAs in a modifying function.

References

Backhouse, A.E.
1984 Have all the adjectives gone? *Lingua* 62: 169–186.
Bolinger, Dwight
1967 Adjectives in English: Attribution and predication. *Lingua* 18: 1–34.
Comrie, Bernard
1975 Polite plurals and predicate agreement. *Language* 51: 406–418.
Croft, William
1991 *Syntactic Categories and Grammatical Relations: The Cognitive Organization of Information*. Chicago: The University of Chicago Press.
2001 *Radical Construction Grammar: Syntactic Theory in Typological Perspective*. Oxford: Oxford University Press.
Dixon, R.M.W.
1977 Where have all the adjectives gone? *Studies in Language* 1: 19–80.
Haiman, John
1980 Dictionaries and encyclopedias. *Lingua* 50: 329–57.
Heine, Bernd, Ulrike Claudi and Friederike Hünnemeyer
1991 *Grammaticalization: A Conceptual Framework.* Chicago: The University of Chicago Press.
Hopper, Paul J. and Elizabeth C. Traugott
1993 *Grammaticalization.* Cambridge: Cambridge University Press.
Kokuritsu Kokugo Kenkyûjo
1964 *Bunrui Goihyô* [*Word List by Semantic Principles*]. Tokyo: Shûei Shuppan.
Kuno, Susumu
1973 *The Structure of the Japanese Language.* Cambridge, MA: The MIT Press.
Lakoff, George
1987 *Women, Fire, and Dangerous Things: What Categories Reveal about the Mind.* Chicago: The University of Chicago Press.
Lakoff, George and Mark Johnson
1980 *Metaphors We Live By.* Chicago: The University of Chicago Press.
Langacker, Ronald W.
1987 *Foundations of Cognitive Grammar*, Volume 1: *Theoretical Prerequisites*. Stanford: Stanford University Press.
1991 *Foundations of Cognitive Grammar*, Volume 2: *Descriptive Application*. Stanford: Stanford University Press.

Nihon Daijiten Kankôkai (ed.)
1972 *Nihon Kokugo Daijiten* [*Japanese Language Encyclopedia*]. Tokyo: Shôgakkan.
Nishio, Minoru, Etsutaro Iwabuchi and Shizuo Mizutani (eds.)
1986 *Iwanami Kokugo Jiten* [*Iwanami Japanese Dictionary*]. Tokyo: Iwanami Shoten.
Rosch, Eleanor
1978 Principles of categorization. In: Eleanor Rosch and Barbara Lloyd (eds.), *Cognition and Categorization*, 27–48. Hillsdale, NJ: Lawrence Erlbaum.
Saeki, Umetomo
1956 "Ni aru" kara "de aru" e [From "ni aru" to "de aru"]. *Kokugogaku* 26: 1–6.
Sakakura, Atsuyoshi
1966 *Gokôsei no Kenkyû* [*A Study on Lexical Composition*]. Tokyo: Kadokawa Shoten.
Taylor, John R.
1989 *Linguistic Categorization: Prototypes in Linguistic Theory*. Oxford: Clarendon Press.
Teramura, Hideo
1982 *Nihongo no Shintakusu to Imi* [*Japanese Syntax and Meaning*], Volume 1. Tokyo: Kurosio Publishers
Uehara, Satoshi
1998 *Syntactic Categories in Japanese: A Cognitive and Typological Introduction*. (Studies in Japanese Linguistics 9). Tokyo: Kurosio Publishers.
Wetzer, Harrie
1992 "Nouny" and "verby" adjectivals: A typology of predicative adjectival constructions. In: Michel Kefer and Johan van der Auwera (eds.), *Meaning and Grammar: Cross-linguistic Perspectives,* 223–262. Berlin: Mouton de Gruyter.
Wierzbicka, Anna
1986 What's in a noun? (or: how do nouns differ in meaning from adjectives?). *Studies in Language* 10: 353–389.

Containment, support, and linguistic relativity

Claude Vandeloise

Abstract

Bowerman (1996a, 1996b) emphasizes important differences in the way the notions of support and containment are linguistically expressed in Dutch, English, Spanish, and Korean. She takes this diversity as evidence againt the prelinguistic image schemas of containment and support advocated by Mandler (1992, 1994, 1996). In this article, I claim that linguistic diversity is not incompatible with prelinguistic concepts having a role in the acquisition of language. First, I propose a hierarchy of concepts going from the more general level of control to the intermediate level of containment and support and to more specific concepts such as attachment and tight fit. The Spanish preposition *en* is anchored in the more abstract level, *in* in the intermediate level, and *kkita* is mapped to tight fit, at the more specific level. Support and containment are not presented as image schemas but as complex primitives, described by a list of features that behave like traits in a family resemblance. To conclude this article, I propose a hypothesis on the acquisition of words conveying support and containment based on the development of complex primitives that accounts for further linguistic diversity.

Keywords: abstract level, complex primitives, containment, control, *en*, family resemblance, hierarchy of concepts, image schema, intermediate level, *in*, *kkita*, language acquisition, linguistic relativity, specific level, support, tight fit.

1. Introduction[1]

In recent years, an interesting debate has developed concerning the acquisition of spatial relational words. Mandler (1992, 1994, 1996) claims that before these words are acquired, a set of prelinguistic concepts is available. Among these concepts are *support* and *containment*, which I will focus on in this paper. According to Mandler's hypothesis, then, one might expect language acquisition of spatial words to be universal. However, Choi and Bowerman (1991) and Bowerman (1996a, 1996b) emphasize important differences across languages in the way support and containment are linguistically expressed. In English, these concepts are conveyed by the prepositions *in* and *on*; in Spanish, they are expressed by a single preposition *en*; in Dutch, containment is expressed by *in*, but a distinction is made between support (lexicalized by *op*) and *attachment* (lexicalized by *aan*). Korean, on the other hand, uses a verb *kkita* to convey *tight containment* and different words for *loose containment* and *loose support*. (The notion *tight support* will be discussed and rejected later on.) In this article, I will investigate the extent to which universality and relativity play a role in the linguistic description of support and containment.

My explanation relies on previous analyses of the preposition *sur* describing support in French (Vandeloise 1991), and of the preposition *dans* describing containment (Vandeloise 1991, 1994). These analyses introduce two *complex primitives*, the relationship *Container/content* (C/c) and the relationship *Bearer/burden* (B/b). I call them "primitives" because, like Mandler, I believe that they are prelinguistic concepts. I call them "complex" because, in contrast to

1. This paper was presented in April 1998 at the Linguistics Department of the University of California at San Diego. I thank the participants, in particular Laraine McDonough, Gilles Fauconnier, and Ronald Langacker for their comments. Soonja Choi, Jean Mandler, and Laraine McDonough kindly sent me articles which were not accessible in print at the time I was writing this paper. Jean Mandler's comments on earlier versions of this article were particularly helpful. I benefited as well from the comments by Bob Dewell and anonymous readers.

the atomic semantic features advocated by Bierwisch (1967), they are described by a list of properties which behave like common *traits* in a *family resemblance*. In section 2 of this article, I will briefly present my analysis of the preposition *dans*. The difference between *dans* and the Korean verb *kkita* meaning 'tight fit' becomes especially striking if *dans* is analyzed in terms of topological inclusion. My analysis of this preposition, however, demonstrates the importance of dynamic factors in its distribution; it will be seen that the factor force, for instance, makes the similarity between *kkita* and *dans* more apparent.

In section 3, I demonstrate that the existence of a set of spatial prelinguistic concepts is not incompatible with linguistic relativity. In the first part of this section, hierarchical connections proposed between some prelinguistic concepts explain some amount of interlinguistic diversity. At the more general level, the notion *control* reflects what is common between containment and support. Tight containment and loose containment as well as attachment are more specific concepts that result from further elaboration. The preposition *en* in Spanish conveys the more general concept, *dans* in French or *in* in Dutch, English, and German are associated with containment at the intermediate level, and *kkita* in Korean or *aan* in Dutch are anchored in the more elaborate prelinguistic concepts tight fit and attachment, respectively. In the second part of section 3, I discuss some prelinguistic concepts proposed by Mandler (1992), in particular the *image schemas* corresponding to support and containment. I will also address the differences between image schemas and complex primitives such as the relationships C/c and B/b proposed in section 2. To conclude this article, I propose a hypothesis on the acquisition of spatial words conveying support and containment, which is based on the development of complex primitives. From the first step postulating a set of prelinguistic concepts, four further steps explain how linguistic diversity can occur in the acquisition of spatial words.

2. The preposition *in* and the relationship C/c

The preposition *dans* 'in' has been studied in detail in Vandeloise (1991, 1994). In this section, I will first consider the role of force in the distribution of this preposition; afterwards, I will introduce the relationship C/c as an example of a complex primitive.

2.1. The role of force in the distribution of the preposition in

It seems to me that the dynamic factors determining the use of the preposition *dans* (or *in* in Dutch, English, and German) have often been overlooked or downplayed (see Garrod & Sanford 1988, for an exception). However, as is evident from Figure 1, which may be described by sentence (1) but not by sentence (2), this factor may play a crucial role:

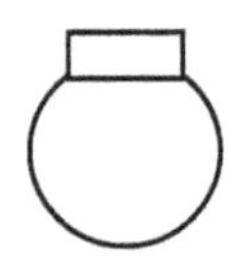

Figure 1. Ambiguous shape.

(1) *The bulb is in the socket.*
(2) **The bottle is in the cap.*

It can be seen that the bulb/the bottle and the socket/the cap correspond to the same shapes; still, these entities enter into different relationships, as can be seen from the fact that the relationship between the bulb and the socket is lexicalized by *in*, whereas that between the bottle and the cap is not. It is neither a *geometric* factor such as three-dimensionality (Hawkins 1988; Hottenroth 1991; Cuyckens 1994) nor a *topological* factor such as inclusion (Miller & Johnson-Laird 1976; Wunderlich 1985; Herweg 1989) which can explain the contrast in acceptability between sentences (1) and (2). Instead, the contrast is motivated by the different ways in which force is exercised between the container entity and the content. Indeed, in (1) the socket determines the position of the bulb whereas in (2) the bottle controls the position of the cap; this makes the socket and the bottle the dominating objects and the bulb and the cap the dominated objects. In order for *in* to successfully lexicalize the relationship between a container and a content, the figure/content must correspond to the dominated object and the landmark/container must correspond to the dominating object. The preposition *in* does not admit the inversion of its arguments.

The role of force in the use of the preposition *in* is confirmed by the acquisition of this word: children use the preposition *in* as easily when the content is partially included in the container as when it is totally included. These two situations, configurationally different, are dynamically equivalent. Indeed, whether flowers are totally or partially included in the vase, the latter will determine the position of the flowers and not the reverse. Children use the preposition *in* as easily for partial inclusion as for total inclusion because, despite the topological difference, the dynamic similarity is more important for them than the configurational difference. Sentences (1) and (2) show that, in a similar spatial configuration, the acceptability of the preposition *in* may vary for dynamic considerations. It thus becomes evident that, if the dynamic relations between entities are equivalent, important topological changes are disregarded in the choice of the preposition *in*. In section 3, the role of force in the distributions of prepositions *in* and *dans* will make their connection with the Korean verb *kkita* conveying tight fit easier to see.

2.2. *The relationship C/c (Container/content) and the family resemblance C/c*

This section is based on previous analyses of the distribution of the French preposition *dans* (Vandeloise 1991, 1994). The data are consistent with the behavior of the English preposition *in*.[2] For ease of cxposition, I present my analysis for the English preposition. The circumstances in which *a is in b* is used can be characterized as follows:

(a) *b* controls the position of *a*;
(b) if there is movement, *a* moves toward *b* rather than the reverse;
(c) *b* surrounds *a*;[3]
(d) *b* protects *a*.

None of these properties is a necessary or sufficient condition. For example, condition (c) is not met by sentence (1) and condition (b) is not met by sentence (3) since the container (the ladle) moves toward the content (the soup):

(3) *The soup is in the ladle.*

These properties, then, are not necessary. Neither is condition (a) sufficient since a locomotive, for instance, may control its wagons but the wagons are not *in* the locomotive. However, each situation in which *in* is used shares at least one property with the other situations allowing for the use of this preposition. The properties describing the use of the preposition *in*, then, are structured like *traits* in a *family resemblance*, which I call the *family resemblance C/c*. The structure of lexical categories defined by family resemblance features is represented in Figure 2 in which the circles represent the configurations satisfying features (a), (b), and (c) respectively. This structure would be extremely loose (Vandeloise 1992) without the important core of prototypical configurations that satisfy all the features and warrant the cohesion of the category.

2. This is not to say, however, that, outside the data presented in this section, there are no differences between the two prepositions.
3. In Vandeloise (1991: 225), this property is presented more technically as follows: The content is included, at least partially, in the convex closure of the containing part of the container.

Figure 2. The extension of a family resemblance category.

Indeed, these configurations, like those described by sentence (4), satisfy all the traits (a)–(d):

(4) *The jewels are in the box.*

The jewels, in this case, are clearly a content and the box a container. This suggests that properties (a)–(d) determining the use of the preposition *in* are not abstract and isolated properties. They are all aspects of a single relation of containment which I will call *relationship C/c.*[4] In this relationship, dynamic properties play an important role; as such, it cannot be completely determined by perceptual information alone. Consider, for instance, the C/c relation lexicalized in *The water is in the glass*. An important aspect of the function of containment in this particular relationship is to keep the water from escaping from the glass, even though this fact cannot be perceived as such.

In Vandeloise (1991), I propose a monosemic definition of the preposition *dans* in terms of the functional relationship C/c. This relationship is a *complex primitive.* It is complex because it is described by the traits (a)–(d) of family resemblance C/c. It remains to be explained why this complex concept is a primitive. The evidence does not come from linguistic analysis but from developmental psychology. In experiments testing the acquisition of the prepositions *in* and *on* by young children, Clark (1973) noticed that her subjects did not pay attention to her instructions but were adopting non-linguistic

4. This technical term is needed because containment belongs to natural language and is often used very loosely. In some cases, this term is even chosen as a synonym for topological inclusion.

strategies. They preferred to put the objects they handled in a container any time a container was available. When a container was not available, a heightened bearer was their choice. These preferences demonstrate that the prelinguistic child is interested in the function of bearers and containers and can recognize them under their different guises. Knowledge of the prelinguistic concepts of support and containment by infants will also be documented in section 3. Therefore, the relationships C/c and B/b may be considered as primitives relative to the conceptualization of space.

In establishing a connection between the properties (a)–(d) describing the preposition *in* and the primitive concept C/c, I am jumping from a linguistic analysis of the distribution of this preposition to a hypothesis about its mental representation. Figure 3 illustrates this process:

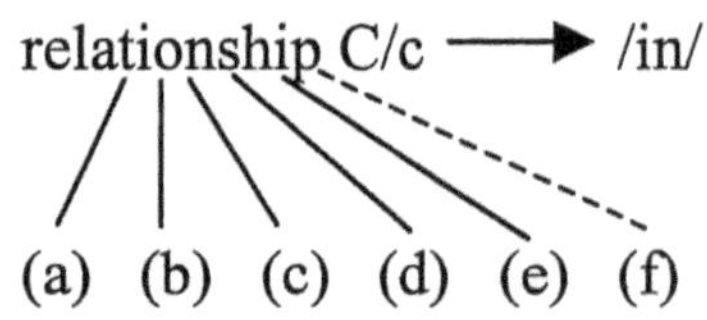

Figure 3. Prototypical and marginal uses of *in*.

Traits (a)–(d) may be rewritten as follows:

(a) the container controls the position of the content;
(b) the content moves toward the container;
(c) the container surrounds the content;
(d) the container protects the content.

The relationship C/c has further properties such as:

(e) the container hides the content;
(f) ....

The indeterminate property (f) shows that the list might need to be extended. This extended list (a)–(f) is the complete family resemblance C/c describing the set of spatial configurations C/c out there in the world. In this array of properties, however, each language chooses different traits by which it extends the use of the word it associates with the prototypical relationship C/c to marginal manifestations of this relation. Among the traits of the family resemblance C/c, then, the linguist must recognize the *pertinent* traits for the language (s)he is describing, that is, the traits which are necessary to motivate at least one member in the lexical category which would not be motivated by the other traits. To the best of my knowledge, French and English do not rely on the trait (e) to extend the use of the prepositions *dans* or *in*. Cora, in contrast, an Indian language of the South-East of Mexico, takes advantage of this property to develop the use of the particle *u*, used to describe the prototypical situations represented by the preposition *in* in English (Casad & Langacker 1985). Indeed, besides these uses, the particule *u* can also describe an entity going out of the visual field of the speaker. While it is pertinent for Cora, trait (e) is irrelevant for English and French and should be discarded from the family resemblances C/c which describe the prepositions *in* and *dans* in these languages.

As illustrated in Figure 3, important prototypical effects appear in the set of spatial configurations exemplifying complex primitives such as the relationship C/c or B/b. The notion *prototype*, however, must be used carefully since linguists sometimes employ it to designate category examplars, and sometimes to designate mental representations (propositional or analog).[5] Focal colors, for example, are prototypical exemplars of colors, while mental representations have been proposed as prototypes for natural categories such as "dog" or "cat". Because they are very likely to play a role in the mental representations of color categories, I call focal colors *physiological* prototypes. As for the alleged prototypes of the categories "dog" or "cat", it is unclear whether they play a role in the organization of the category or whether they are rather a secondary by-product of their structure.

---

5. For more details on the notion "prototype", see Kleiber (1990) and Vandeloise (1995).

Because the conceptualization of containment and support by prelinguistic infants has been demonstrated, I believe that the core of the categories C/c and B/b acts rather like a physiological prototype and is an important factor in the organization of the category. However, prototypical spatial configurations differ both from focal colors and from the alleged prototypes of natural categories in an important respect. Indeed, while these prototypes are essentially *perceptual*, prototypical spatial configurations in the category C/c and B/b are mainly *functional*. Even though some of the traits involved in the characterization of relationships C/c and B/b, such as surrounding, contact, or order on the vertical axis, are registered perceptually, the fundamental trait of control involved in containment and in support can only be noticed when it fails to work. In other words, while kinetic mechanics is always noticeable, static mechanics involved in support and containment escapes one's notice as long as the balance is respected. This is not to say that balance is not important in the relationships C/c and B/b. On the contrary, their function is to keep all the liquid content under control and all the utensils we are using in our life world easily available.

3. Compatibility of linguistic diversity and prelinguistic concepts

While Mandler (1992, 1994, 1996) insists on the importance of prelinguistic spatial concepts such as support and containment in the organization of the spatial lexicon, Bowerman posits that a universal influence of spatial conceptualization is difficult to conciliate with the diversity and relativity in the acquisition of words like *en* (Spanish), *in* and *on* (English), *op* and *aan* (Dutch), and *kkita* (Korean). All these words may convey some kind of containment and/or support but their distributions are very different. In section 2.1, I have already shown that diversity depends partially on the linguistic analysis of spatial words. Indeed, the connection between the preposition *in* and the Korean verb *kkita* is difficult to establish if, with Bowerman (1996b), one considers containment as a topological concept. However, once the dynamic nature of containment is taken into consideration, the link between the two words becomes evident. In the first part of this section, I will show that the discrepancies between the prepositions *en* in Spanish, *in* and *on* in English, and *op* and *aan* in Dutch can be motivated by hierarchical connections between the concept of control and the concepts of containment, support, and attachment. In the second part of this section, I will present Mandler's prelinguistic concepts and show the difference between the *image schemas* she proposes for support and containment on the one hand and complex primitives such as the relationships C/c and B/b on the other hand.

3.1. A hierarchy of prelinguistic concepts

The hierarchical connections between containment and support are reflected by the Spanish preposition *en*, which can be used to cover the domains of the prepositions *in* and *on* in English. This preposition *en* suggests the existence of a concept of control, which captures what is shared by containment and support. Tight fit and attachment, on the other hand, may be considered as elaborations of containment and support respectively. The hierarchical connections between these concepts are illustrated in Figure 4 below.

At the highest level of generality, *b* controls *a* if *b* prevents *a* from moving in at least one direction. At the second level of elaboration, containment and support can be defined as "control in more than one direction" and "control in the vertical axis", respectively. Finally, at the third level of elaboration, we find tight fit and attachment, and containment' and support'. Tight fit and containment' are elaborations of containment, and attachment and support' are elaborations of support. They are complementary sets, negatively defined; in other words, containment' and support' signal those properties of containment and support that are not captured by tight fit and attachment. Indeed, for containment, control may be either effective or potential. For example, a fly may be *in* the middle of a glass or a prisoner *in* the middle of his cell, even though there is no contact between the content and the container and the prisoner is free to walk inside the limits of his/her cell. Tight fit, in contrast, implies contact *and* direct control. Similarly, for support, control may be direct or through an intermediary. As such, attachment may be roughly defined as support with an intermediary between a non-horizontal bearer and the burden.

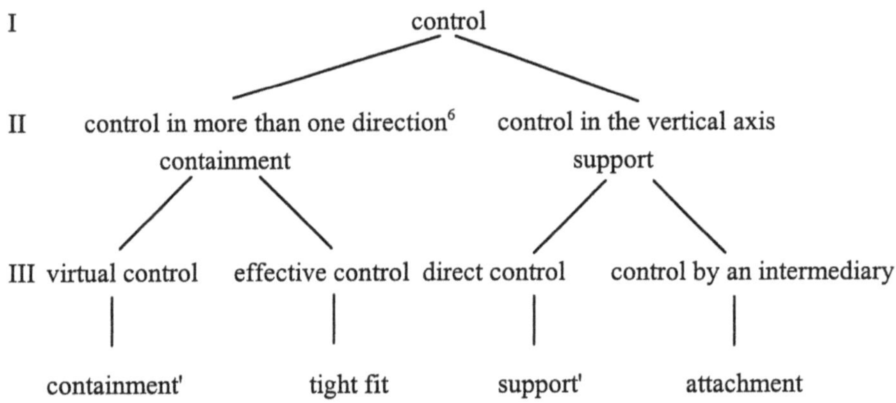

Figure 4. A hierarchy of concepts.

There remain intriguing questions concerning the relationship between the second and the third level of elaboration. As far as the relationships support and attachment are concerned, Bowerman (1993) notices that Dutch children are more likely to overgeneralize the preposition *op*, corresponding to support, to cases in which adults use the preposition *aan*, related to attachment, rather than the other way around. This observation is consistent with my hierarchy since one expects a more elaborate concept to be more difficult to learn. In the case of tight fit, however, direct control might be a prototypical type of containment, easier to learn than the virtual control involved in the case of *the fly in the glass*. Indeed, the dynamic relation involved in containment is particularly salient in tight fit. English infants, then, might use *in* for tight fit before extending this preposition to loose

6. This partitioning does not cover configurations for which there is control in one non-vertical direction only. On the basis of French examples such as *La voiture est entrée dans le mur* 'The car bumped into the wall', they might be considered as marginal cases of containment.

containment. In other words, while attachment is clearly an extension of support, loose containment might be a development from a prototypical core corresponding to tight fit. The linguist who tries to answer this question reaches his/her limits and can only peruse journals on language acquisition in the hope of finding relevant information. As a matter of fact, Choi et al. (1999) and McDonough et al. (to appear) investigate the comprehension of *in* and *kkita* by English and Korean young children who have not reached the stage of production.[7]

In the hierarchy proposed in Figure 4, there is no direct relationship between support and tight fit. However, *kkita* may be used for circumstances in which the preposition *on* is used in English.[8] It would be a problem for my hierarchy if this partial overlap between the distributions of *on* and *kkita* implied that this Korean verb signals tight support. From the data available to me, however, this might not be the case. First, at the conceptual level, if one accepts my definition of support, tight support is very difficult to imagine. Indeed, tightness normally involves control in many directions whereas support involves the bearer controlling the burden in the vertical axis only. Furthermore, tightness usually requires an energy superior to the force of gravity, which is the only force active in the case of support. It is no wonder then that Laraine McDonough (personal communication) had a very hard time finding objects representing tight support for her experiments. One way of introducing tightness in support without involving a further direction of control is when using a magnet: in this case, the pressure between the bearer and the burden can be stronger than the weight of the burden. Now, from the data of Choi and Bowerman (1991), it appears that Korean children use *kkita* in these types of situation. However, they constitute an overextension of the word as adults use *pwuchita* instead of *kkita*. The situations in which *on* coincides with *kkita* in adult language are very marginal. The examples proposed by Bowerman (1996b: 413) are *small ring on*

7. I would like to thank Laraine McDonough, who was kind enough to show me the labatory and the material used in the experiments.
8. This fact was brought to my attention by an anonymous reader.

pole, *pillowcase on pillow*, and *top on pen*. All these examples involve control in many directions and would necessitate extension from the prototypical use of *on*.[9] On the other hand, conceptually, each of the situations where *kkita* coincides with *on* are very clear cases of tight fit in many directions. Therefore, I do not believe that, from a partial overlapping of the distribution of *kkita* with the distribution of *on*, one should draw the conclusion that *kkita* describes tight support, a very rare configuration in the world we are living in.

According to Choi and Bowerman (1991: 113), if there is a set of prelinguistic concepts used in all the languages of the world, any time a conceptual distinction is missing in a language, children would be using the word covering this distinction in a homonymous way. For example, English children using *in* for entering the bathtub (when Korean children would use *tule*), for loose containment (when Korean children would use *nehta*), or for tight fit (when Korean children would use *kkita*) would use three homonymous *in*s. But, the authors wonder, "Do we feel comfortable with homonymous *in*s for putting a book in a tight-fitting box versus a looser box (*kkita* vs *nehta* for Korean children)?" Even though the answer is certainly negative, the argument does not make the existence of a prelinguistic concept of tight fit in the mind of Korean and English children implausible. First, in order to be homonyms, the *in*s describing containment and tight fit should be completely unrelated. Since tight fit is unambiguously a dynamic concept, this would be the case if *in* was a topological preposition. If, following section 2.1, one allows containment as an essentially dynamic concept, however, one should speak of polysemy between the two *in*s instead of homonymy. But it is clear from Figure 4 that even polysemy would not properly characterize the connection between *in* describing containment and *in* describing tight fit. Indeed, tight fit may be considered as an elaboration of containment: while the latter concept involves effective *or* potential control in many directions, the former involves only effec-

9. The preposition *sur*, the equivalent of *on* in French, could not be used to translate *pillowcase on pillow* or *small ring on pole* when the pole is vertical. The translations would be *un coussin dans une taie* or *des petits anneaux autour d'une tige* respectively.

tive control. The two *in*s corresponding to containment and to tight fit, then, would be neither homonymous nor polysemic, but the latter would be an elaboration of the former (or the former an extension of the latter). This certainly does not prevent English children from having a prelinguistic concept of tight fit. Thus, the interesting linguistic diversity brought up by Bowerman (1996a, 1996b) may be compatible with the existence of prelinguistic concepts postulated by Mandler (1992, 1996). In section 3.2, I will compare the image schemas proposed by Mandler for the prelinguistic concepts of containment and support with the relationships C/c and B/b presented in section 2.2.

3.2. Prelinguistic concepts as image schemas and as complex primitives

The acquisition of prelinguistic concepts by the child, according to Mandler, must not be confused with the recognition of perceptual similarities among the members of a category. Indeed, there is a big difference between *perceptual categories* and *conceptual categories* on which language is grounded. The latter categories

> involve analysis of what is being perceived into simplified and more abstract representations (...) *Perceptual analysis* picks out selected aspects of a highly complex perceptual event and puts them into simpler and more abstract form (...) As a result, perceptual information takes an *image-schematic* format which is discrete, simpler, more abstract, less context-bound and well-suited to serve a symbolic function. (Mandler 1998: 273–274; emphasis mine)

Thus, the prelinguistic concepts necessary for the linguistic description of space are understood as image schemas, abstracted by perceptual analysis. They are "dynamic analog representations of spatial relations and movements in space"[10] (Mandler 1992: 591). Even

---

10. However, Mandler (2000) expresses reservations on the role of force in the mental architecture of infants because of their limited ability to analyze kinesthetic information.

though image schemas have been abundantly used in Cognitive Linguistics, I have the feeling that their definition in this domain has never been very carefully spelled out. Despite Mandler's efforts to make image schemas more explicit, there remains space for further specification of their definition. True, they are schematic, but schematicity is not their exclusive privilege. Furthermore, as Mandler (1998: 263) rightly emphasizes, they are not images. Their name, then, is not very well chosen and is likely to entertain confusion. In this section, I will review the prelinguistic concepts proposed by Mandler.

A first group of image schemas in the infant's conceptualization of space is related to movement. They include SELF-MOTION, ANIMATE MOTION, SELF-MOVING-ANIMATE, and CAUSED MOTION.[11] These concepts are, in keeping with Mandler's characterization of image schemas, highly schematic and, admittedly, analog. A second group of prelinguistic concepts like CONTAINMENT and SUPPORT, however, seems different to me. Following Lakoff (1987), Mandler characterizes CONTAINMENT by three structural elements: interior, boundary, and exterior.[12] SUPPORT, on the other hand, requires only a representation of contact between two objects in the vertical domain. Figure 5 shows the schemas proposed by Mandler (1992) to illustrate CAUSED MOTION, SUPPORT, and CONTAINMENT as well as a reproduction of the last schema by Bowerman (1996b: 420):

11. SELF-MOVING-ANIMATE is the image schema associated with the word *animal.* Since the concept "animal" is learned before basic categories such as "dog", "cat", etc., Mandler emphasizes that "the kind of concept of animal I have been describing is a far cry from a true superordinate class. Since babies initially understand animals as a relatively undifferentiated category, we call it a global concept rather than a superordinate one" (Mandler 1994: 66). Therefore, even though the concept "animal" discovered by Mandler, Bauer and McDonough (1991) reveals important facts about infants' categorization, it might have no direct connection with the English word *animal* (see Carey 1985 for an extensive study of the concept "animal" as it is used by older children).

12. There is no reason to believe that "interior" or "exterior" are more primitive concepts than containment; for a study of the concept "interior", see Vandeloise (1999).

Figure 5. CAUSED MOTION, SUPPORT, CONTAINMENT, CONTAINMENT reproduced from Mandler by Bowerman.

An obvious difficulty for pictorial representations is that they are doomed to represent properties which are irrelevant for the relationship.[13] For example, containment is indifferent to contact between the container and the content but a graphic representation must commit itself either to contact or to separation. Mandler's schema chooses the latter solution. Pictorial representations also impose a choice between open containers (as in Mandler's schema) or closed containers (as in Bowerman's reproduction of Mandler's schema).[14] My feeling is that the drawings proposed by Mandler to represent support and containment hide the functional complexity of these concepts, which is difficult to reconcile with the high degree of abstraction required from image schemas. This remains the case even when she makes clear that image schemas are primitive not in the sense of being unitary and indivisible symbols but in the sense of being "foundational" (Mandler 1992: 591), i.e., in the sense that they are the most basic meanings on which language is grounded. The family resemblances C/c and B/b, describing the relationships C/c and B/b in section 2, are an attempt to go beyond the very summary characterization proposed in the pictorial representations for the image schemas of containment and support.[15]

13. For further shortcomings of pictorial representations, see criticism of Lakoff's analysis of the preposition *over* in Vandeloise (1990).
14. Vieu (1991) treats *dans*-total and *dans*-partial as two different meanings of the polysemous preposition *dans*. Without going this far, I believe that the distinction between closed and open containers plays an important role in the analysis of the prepositions *dans* and *in*. Image schemas, then, should not overlook this contrast so lightly.
15. As noted by an anonymous reader, Mandler says as well that image schemas are "at the same time providing some of the desirable characteristics of propositional representations" (Mandler 1996: 373).

The common point between prelinguistic concepts such as self-motion, animate motion, self-moving-animate on the one hand and containment and support on the other hand is not so much their structure as their utmost importance in the interaction of the child with her/his environment. The interest of new-borns in self-moving objects may be directly related to their survival, and the attention they bestow on self-moving entities might be quite germane to the behavior of ducklings which follow faithfully the first self-moving object they see in the two hours after their birth. Containment and support are equally pervasive in young children's behavior (violations of support, for instance, may provoke the falling of the infant or of his/her belongings). These concepts are determined by their "high level of usual utility" (Brown 1958) and need not be simple abstract schemas. As far as schematicity is concerned, prelinguistic concepts like self-motion and animate motion may meet Mandler's description of image schemas. I do not believe, however, that the schematic representations of containment and support proposed by Lakoff (1987) and Mandler (1992) capture the complexity of these concepts. The family resemblances C/c and B/b proposed in section 2.2 are needed for this purpose. Therefore, support and containment, or the relationships B/b and C/c, as they are called in this paper, belong to complex primitives, a second group of prelinguistic concepts.

The acquisition of concepts in these two groups does not require the same type of information. While image schemas only need perceptual information, support and containment require the handling of objects in order to be completely assimilated. Now, because of the limitations on infants' manual abilities, Mandler (2000) suggests that early analyses are more spatial than force-related. Force, however, plays an essential role in the acquisition of the relationships C/c and B/b. This constraint is respected if functional complex primitives which require interaction with the objects are acquired after kinesthetic prelinguistic concepts, when children begin to handle objects. Mandler herself (2000) suggests this two-step development when she comments on Nelson's (1985) emphasis on function. Whereas Mandler is talking about processes that begin earlier in infancy, she agrees with Nelson that "analysis of motion may underlie the later development of understanding of function". Because it requires only perceptual information, the concept of control belongs to the kinesthetic concepts. Containment and support are the functional elaboration of control, itself a result of perceptual analysis.

The prelinguistic conceptual ability of infants is well-documented. Baillargeon, Needham and DeVos (1991) describe the elaboration of the concept of support by infants of three months for a period of a few months. By six months, their subjects had begun to differentiate between partial but inadequate support (15% overlap between the object and the supporting surface) and adequate support (70% overlap). These experiments are challenging for functional prelinguistic concepts such as the relationship C/c and the relationship B/b because subjects in these experiments are too young to have an active functional experience of support or containment. However, if containment and support are developments of control, these data might be interpreted in a slightly different way. According to this interpretation, instead of observing support or containment, the subjects in these experiments are only aware of control, that is, obstruction of the movement of an object likely to move otherwise. Indeed, the rules of movement may be observed perceptually only. A complete command of containment occurs only later: as Caron, Caron and Allen (1988: 626) point out in this respect, "at 14 months and possibly older, infants have not yet differentiated the precise combination of properties that affords containment and genuine understanding of the causal basis of that function does not begin to emerge until 17 months of age".

4. Complex primitives and acquisition of spatial relational words

The description of the prepositions *in* and *on* in terms of complex primitives suggests a number of hypotheses concerning the acquisition of words describing spatial relations. Five steps are proposed in this section. Steps 1 and 2 assess the role of prelinguistic concepts advocated by Mandler (1992). Step 2 allows for linguistic diversity as well since each language can assign its words to different levels in the hierarchy proposed in section 3.1. Steps 3 and 4 account largely for further diversity of the linguistic descriptions of space.

- *Step 1.* Some prelinguistic concepts such as the relationship C/c, the relationship B/b, or general orientation (Levine & Carey 1982; Vandeloise 1987) are prelinguistically available and facilitate the anchoring of basic linguistic expressions in the conceptualization of the world.
- *Step 2.* Children associate words in their language to the prototypical manifestations of (some of) these prelinguistic concepts, globally understood. The preposition *in*, then, is correctly used for the prototypical relationship C/c and the preposition *on* for the prototypical relationship B/b.
- *Step 3.* In each language, children passively notice exceptions to the word–concept associations they have established. Thanks to their memory, they are able to associate the use of a word to the marginal situations which triggered it.[16]
- *Step 4.* Children analyze the complex primitives which, at this juncture, they only know globally.
- *Step 5.* At the final step, they actively extend the use of spatial words to appropriate novel marginal situations, and only to those situations.[17]

These five steps will be elaborated in turn. Evidence for the existence of prelinguistic concepts postulated in Step 1 has been discussed sufficiently in section 3.2. At Step 2, all these prelinguistic concepts – control, containment, support, attachment, and tight fit – are connected with spatial words: *en* in Spanish, *in* and *on* in English, *kkita* in Korean, and *op* and *aan* in Dutch. As demonstrated by the experi-

16. I am essentially thinking here of marginal *spatial* situations. It is not clear whether temporal uses of *in* are extensions from the spatial *in* or rather have independent representations (for Sandra and Rice 1995, the latter hypothesis is more likely).
17. In order to do that, they may use the properties of the relationship they have analyzed, they may build further subprototypes associated to the word, or they may combine both strategies.

ments of Choi et al. (1999) and McDonough et al. (to appear), production of these words may stay behind long after comprehension begins.

Step 2 accounts for language diversity in two ways:

(a) The child may associate a prelinguistic concept with a word only if the word exists in her/his language. If there is no such word, it will be difficult to assess the existence of this concept through the first words of the child. This does not mean that this concept does not exist. As such, all infants might have the same set of prelinguistic concepts but their manifestations might be dependent on the availability of a word in the language. While Dutch represents attachment by the preposition *aan* and Korean describes tight fit by *kkita*, there are no words available in the early spatial vocabulary of English children enabling them to demonstrate linguistically their knowledge of these prelinguistic concepts.

(b) Different languages may associate a word with prelinguistic concepts at different levels of generality. For example, Spanish associates the preposition *en* with control at the most abstract level in Figure 4 (level I). English and French map the prepositions *on* and *sur* to the concept support at level II, while Dutch attaches the preposition *op* at a more fine-grained level (level III). Indeed, this language makes a difference between support and attachment, which is lexicalized by the prepositions *op* and *aan*.

Step 2 postulates a connection between spatial words and prelinguistic concepts *globally* understood. The idea that concepts develop from a global or holistic level of organization to an articulated, analyzed one can be attributed to Vygotsky (1934 [1962]). The preference of young children for global understanding rather than analytic comprehension has been amply demonstrated (cf. Smith 1979).[18] While the notion of analytical categorization relative to one or several features is clear enough, *global* conceptualization is not as explicit as one might wish. Global conceptualization is often understood as "overall similarity" between the members of the category. This type of organization can certainly account for the formation of perceptual categories, but it is of little avail for conceptual categories like self-moving or support, where perceptual similarity may be lacking. Indeed, there is no overall similarity between a mouse and an elephant walking or between a pumpkin *on* a table and a hat *on* a head. When Mandler (1992: 591) writes that "early conceptual understanding is of a *globally* analyzed character", she means that it is "shallowly analyzed". *Animal*, in this sense, is more globally analyzed than *sparrow.* If Mandler's claim is correct, young children would first associate spatial words for support and containment at the more general level, i.e., control. How functional concepts may be *globally* understood is best suggested by Olson and Bialystok (1983), who state that children access the conceptualization of space through the understanding of objects and events: infants recognize objects in their environment because they have a *meaning*, namely an important function in the plans and intentions of the child. Meanings, according to Olson and Bialystok (1983: 24), have four properties:

> First, they mark the significance of objects and events; they are the articulated constituents of goal directed intentional actions, and they serve as the criteria for the construction of recognition routines ... called *structural descriptions*. Finally, ... they provide a level of structure, commensurate with the structure of language, indicating, for example, the ways in which words are related.

Structural descriptions, by which the infant recognizes the object or the event, are implicit. They are *holistic* because even though they are complex, the child is incapable of disentangling their features.

---

18. The debate between Ward, Vela and Duffin Hass (1990) and Kemler Nelson (1990), however, shows that this hypothesis is not unchallenged.

Therefore, the association between a spatial word and a meaning described by a structural description is *global.*

A correlation between Olson and Bialystok's analysis and complex primitives such as containment and support may be easily established. In this system, the meaning of containment or of support is their function and the structural description includes all the criteria through which the infant recognizes the spatial configurations fulfilling these conditions. Thus, their structural description corresponds to the list of traits of the family resemblances C/c and B/b characterizing the relationships C/c and B/b, *before* the pertinent features are determined by the language the child is learning. Indeed, the recognition of pertinent features occurs only at Step 4 of the process of acquisition. The development of complex primitives is also in keeping with Barrett's (1986: 60) description of prototypes:

> The prototypes for these new words [acquired by the child] may also be analyzed into their constituent features by the child, these words similarly being extended to label novel objects or actions on the basis that these objects or actions share one or more of these features with the prototype.

Step 3 of the above hypothesis paves the way for further variation in the acquisition of spatial terms in different languages. Indeed, at this stage, the child notices when a spatial word (s)he is learning is used by adults for circumstances which do not fit her/his knowledge of the word. Temporal and abstract usages may look so far apart from the spatial usages that they are treated as homonyms rather than as extensions of the spatial usages.[19] The child, then, constitutes a repertory of spatial situations (s)he will analyze at Step 4 of the acquisition. If the prototypical meaning associated by the child with the word covers most of its usages, the exceptions (s)he will notice need not to be many. Choi and Bowerman (1991) mention the case in Korean of children using *kkita* for hanging objects or magnets on a two-dimensional surface, circumstances for which adults would use different words. Empirically, this type of mistake is essential to sustain the hypotheses put forward in this article.

19. See Sandra and Rice (1995) for experimental confirmation.

The repertory of configurations associated with a word depends on the choices made in each single language. Let us take Korean as a first example. Because of the structure of their language, Korean children can only associate *kkita* with tight fit. Since loose fit is lexicalized by *nehta* or *nohta*, their repertory of spatial configurations associated with *kkita* will not be infected by situations involving potential control or loose fit. Should English children associate *in* exclusively with tight fit, however, adult language would immediately provide them with a repertory of situations where direct control is absent, and *in* would be rapidly extended to loose containment. Thus, even if English children have the prelinguistic concept of "tight fit" available, its linguistic expression will be quickly diluted in English. Awareness of the concept of tight fit appears more easily in a language such as Korean. This is not to say that children never reveal awareness of prelinguistic concepts which are not linguistically conveyed by their language. This is illustrated by a further discrepancy between English and Korean and data provided by Bowerman on the acquisition of English by her two daughters. Unlike English, Korean makes a difference in the description of spontaneous movements of the body and movements caused by the body. Even though English does not use different words for "entering in a bathtub" (self-motion) and "putting something in a bathtub" (cause-to-move-inanimate), Bowerman's data, in Choi and Bowerman (1991: 99), show that English children are conceptually ready to make this distinction. Indeed, Bowerman notices that in the age period 14–16 months, all Path particles used by her daughters C. and E.,

> were applied to either spontaneous motion or caused motion, but not both. In some cases this reflected the child's initial restriction of the form to specific contexts; for example, at first C. said *out* only for going outdoors (spontaneous) and E. said *off* only for removing clothes and other objects from the body (caused). In other cases, however, the child used the form quite productively within the limits of spontaneous or caused motions. (Choi & Bowerman 1991: 99)

From these data, one may infer that at Step 2, like the Korean children, C. was ready to map spontaneous movements to *out* and E. was ready to map caused movements to *off*.[20] In contrast to Korean children, however, E. and C. were confronted with many examples of *out* used by adults for caused movements and many examples of *off* used for spontaneous movements. Therefore, at Step 3, their repertory of marginal uses of these words was different from the repertory of Korean children. This may be the reason why, according to Bowerman, by 19–20 months of age, C. and E. used *in* for a wide variety of spontaneous and caused motion events.

Children learning the words conveying support in English, Dutch, and Spanish are also confronted with different repertories of uses. In English, the child learning *on* will deal with situations corresponding to *attachment*. Such will not be the case for a child learning *op* in Dutch since for attachment, adults use the preposition *aan*. In addition to the variation across languages in children's acquisition of spatial terms, it should also be kept in mind that children speaking the same language may not necessarily follow the same path of acquisition either. Indeed, the level at which a child connects spatial words with prelinguistic concepts may account for individual variation in one language. By way of example, imagine a Spanish child learning the preposition *en*. (S)he might first associate the preposition with the concept of control or, at a different level of granularity, with containment or support. Each of these two concepts has good reasons to emerge first.[21] Indeed, containment has the advantage of control in several directions while support puts the vertical axis to the fore, a direction to which three-month-old infants already pay special attention (Quinn 1994). Suppose this Spanish child chooses support first. Then, (s)he might be expected to underextend the preposition *en* to the circumstances in which an English child would use the preposition *on*. For that child, all the circumstances for which *en* is used to

20. This observation is consistent with data quoted by Stockman and Vaughn-Cooke (1992: 1106), according to which even when both members of a pair of spatial prepositions (e.g., *off/on*) emerged at the same time, children used one member (e.g., *off*) to code movement and the other one (e.g., *on*) to code static events.

21. See Correa-Beningfield (1991) for a comparison between the acquisition of *in* in English and *en* in Spanish

describe containment will sound as marginal usages for which (s)he has to make adjustments. The reverse would be true for a Spanish child that first associates *en* to containment, in that the Spanish child will underextend *en* to circumstances in which the English child uses *in*. This situation of English children acquiring *in* compared to Spanish children acquiring *en* is similar to English children learning the preposition *on* compared to Dutch children learning the preposition *op*. Indeed, Dutch children will never get linguistic clues tempting them to associate *op* to attachment since this does not occur in their language.[22] The situation is different however because, in contrast to containment and support which are functionally equally important, the function of attachment may be less pervasive than support (cf. infra).

At Step 4, the child must analyze the global structural descriptions (s)he has associated with the repertory of marginal situations her/his language has provided her/his for the usage of each spatial word. In this process, the recognition of the specific features of a complex primitive deserves attention. Even though structural descriptions are complex, their perceptual features remain at first implicit and unperceived as such. Actually, the analysis of the complex primitive might be close to the model proposed by Olson and Bialystok (1983), who argue that the development of one of the features of a complex structural description, for example *form representation*, requires explicit attention to parts of the structural descriptions that were employed implicitly in the recognition of objects. When the child recognizes that a lollipop and a stop sign are composed of a circle and a straight line standing in a certain relation, "she is not constructing new spatial images, but is becoming aware of aspects of the structural description that she was already automatically (implicitly) using for object recognition" (Olson & Bialystok 1983: 37). Thus, the per-

22. I believe that attachment involves an intermediary between the bearer and a passive burden. Therefore, I do not believe that *op* is used for attachment in *De vlieg zit op de zoldering* 'The fly is on the ceiling', an example brought to my attention by an anonymous reader. I rather consider this example as a case of marginal support. *De poster zit op/tegen/aan de muur* 'The poster is on the wall' (cf. Cuyckens 1994) might give more trouble to the Dutch children.

ception of forms is embedded in the perception of objects and events. Prepositions like *in* and *on*, then, may be associated globally to the relationships C/c and B/b before the role of dimensionality or topological configurations in these relations is explicitly recognized.

The explicit recognition of the features of the relationship C/c (Step 4) is helped by the array of marginal situations gathered at Step 3. Indeed, in the same way that the similarity between a lollipop and a stop sign may draw attention to forms per se, the comparison between prototypical containment and marginal containment may bring the features they have in common to the fore. Such may be the case when a child wonders what "an apple *in* a cup" and a marginal situation in her/his repertory described by sentence (5) may have in common:

(5) *John is in England.*

Since dynamic interaction between John and England does not justify the use of the preposition *in* in sentence (5) (except maybe if John is in an airport), the comparison brings the configurational aspect of surrounding, trait (c) of the family resemblance C/c, to the fore. In the same way, the comparison of "a pear *in* a bowl" with "a gift *in* the wrapping" may draw the attention of the child to protection (trait [d] of the family resemblance C/c). In this way, the child will recognize all the features of containment *pertinent* to her/his language. In the case of the entities *England* and *wrapping*, one may wonder if the child considers her-/himself confronted with marginal containers or with objects which are not containers at all. Whatever the answer, *England* can be described by a combination of the features characterizing canonical containers. The family resemblance C/c relevant for English, then, describes adequately the use of *in* in sentence (5). Some combinations of the pertinent features of the relationship C/c and B/b, however, do not sanction the use of the preposition *sur* in French (Vandeloise 1992). Some of these gaps may be explained by the whole prepositional system of French and the interactions between the different complex primitives competing to absorb borderline situations.

Step 5 is the final task of the child acquiring spatial prepositions; at this juncture, (s)he must be able to extend the use of the preposition to *novel marginal situations*. At Step 4, the child has analyzed prelinguistic concepts and made their structural description explicit. Her/his strategy might therefore be *propositional*, in which case, (s)he registers the combinations of features characterizing the situations which allow the use of each preposition and discards the unacceptable combinations. Her/his strategy might also be *analog*, in which case, (s)he might use some representation of marginal situations in her/his repertory as subprototypes and extend the preposition to situations that are similar in a relevant way. At this point, I believe that a decision about which strategy is more likely lies beyond the province of linguistics.

5. Conclusions

Data proposed by Levinson (1996) on the description of space in non-Indo-European languages and by Bowerman (1996a, 1996b) on the acquisition of spatial words in languages such as Dutch, Finnish, and Korean are a tremendous challenge to the proponents of a universal prelinguistic basis for the anchoring of spatial terms in human experience. Even though Bowerman recognizes the influence of the conceptualization of space on the acquisition of spatial vocabulary, her papers are devoted to emphasizing the importance of linguistic relativity. As she points out, the role of prelinguistic concepts in language acquisition would be dubious if, each time we get new data on the acquisition of spatial terms in a new language, the list of alleged prelinguistic concepts had to be extended (Bowerman 1996b: 421). Nevertheless, I believe that, in order to cover the data provided by Choi and Bowerman (1991), the additions need not be unrealistically numerous.

The role of dynamic factors in the use of the preposition *in* has been established in section 1. Taking account of these factors makes the difference between *in* and the Korean verb *kkita* less dramatic than if *in* is associated with topological inclusion. In addition, the distribution of this preposition is determined by the properties of prototypical containment organized like the *traits* of a *family resemblance*. In section 3.1, I have demonstrated that the indisputable role of language in the acquisition of spatial terms does not preclude the existence of a universal set of prelinguistic concepts. Hierarchical connections between the prelinguistic concepts of control, containment, support, attachment, and tight fit strongly reduce the linguistic relativity exemplified by the Spanish preposition *en*, the English prepositions *in* and *on*, the Dutch preposition *aan*, and the Korean verb *kkita*. Prelinguistic concepts, however, do not need to be *semantic primitives* in the sense of Bierwisch (1967; quoted by Bowerman 1996b: 424). Section 3.2 has shown that prelinguistic concepts do not need to be treated on a par. While SELF-MOTION and CONTROL may have the characteristics attributed by Mandler (1992) to image schemas, the nature of support and containment is different. In my analysis, they are *primitive* because they are prelinguistic and *complex* because they are described by the traits of the family resemblances B/b and C/c respectively. The spatial words *on* and *in* associated with these concepts may be considered monosemic at the level of their functional meaning. In the last section of this article, I have shown how complex primitives can motivate the acquisition of spatial words like *in* and *on*. According to Olson and Bialystok (1983), the functional knowledge of complex concepts precedes their analysis in simple features. Therefore, the functions of support and containment are globally understood before their perceptual characteristics such as form or dimensionality are singled out. At an early stage of acquisition, spatial words are associated with the prototypical manifestations of the concepts they convey. Later, the core of the corresponding category is analyzed and unfolds itself to include marginal configurations. Because many configurations are in the scope of several complex concepts, the semantics of each language must conventionally make a choice among the candidates. These choices introduce further relativity in the linguistic description of space.

References

Baillargeon, Renée, Amy Needham and J. DeVos
1991 The development of young infants' intuitions about support. Urbana, IL: Unpublished manuscript, University of Illinois.

Barrett, Martyn D.
1986 Early semantic representations and early word-usage. In: Stan A. Kuczaj II and Martyn D. Barrett (eds.), *The Development of Word Meaning: Progress in Cognitive Development Research*, 39–68. New York and Berlin: Springer Verlag.

Bierwisch, Manfred
1967 Some semantics universals of German adjectivals. *Foundations of Language* 3: 1-36.

Bowerman, Melissa
1993 Typological perspectives in language acquisition: Do crosslinguistic patterns predict development? In: Eve Clark (ed.), *Proceedings of the Twenty-fifth Annual Child Language Research Forum,* 7–15. Stanford: CSLI Publications.

1996 a The origins of children's spatial semantic categories: Cognitive versus linguistic determinants. In: John J. Gumperz and Stephen C. Levinson (eds.), *Rethinking Linguistic Relativity,* 145–176. Cambridge: Cambridge University Press.

1996 b Learning how to structure space for language. In: Paul Bloom, Mary A. Peterson, Lynn Nadel and Merill F. Garrett (eds.), *Language and Space*, 383–435. Cambridge, MA: The MIT Press.

Brown, Roger
1958 How shall a thing be called. *Psychological Review* 65: 14–21.

Carey, Suzan
1985 *Conceptual Change in Childhood.* Cambridge, MA: The MIT Press.

Caron, J. Albert, Rose F. Caron and Sue E. Allen
1988 Infant understanding of containment: An affordance perceived or a relationship conceived? *Developmental Psychology* 24: 620–627.

Casad, Eugene H. and Ronald W. Langacker
1985 'Inside' and 'outside' in Cora grammar. *International Journal of American Linguistics* 51: 247–281.

Choi, Soonja and Melissa Bowerman
1991 Learning to express motion events in English and Korean: The influence of language-specific lexicalization patterns. *Cognition* 41: 83–121.

Choi, Soonja, Laraine McDonough, Melissa Bowerman and Jean M. Mandler
1999 Early sensitivity to language-specific spatial categories in English and Korean. *Cognitive Development* 14: 241–268.
Clark, Eve
1973 Non-linguistic strategies and the acquisition of word meanings. *Cognition* 2: 161–182.
Correa-Beningfield, Margarita
1991 *Prototypes and Language Transfer*. Ann Arbor, MI: University Microfilm International.
Cuyckens, Hubert
1994 Family resemblance in the Dutch spatial preposition *op*. In: Monika Schwarze (ed.), *Kognitive Semantik/Cognitive Semantics*, 180–195. Tübingen: Gunter Narr.
Garrod, Simon C. and A.J. Sanford
1988 Discourse models as interfaces between language and the spatial world. *Journal of Semantics* 6: 147–160.
Hawkins, Bruce
1988 The category MEDIUM. In: Brygyda Rudzka-Ostyn (ed.), *Topics in Cognitive Linguistics*,. 231–270. Amsterdam: John Benjamins.
Herweg, Michael
1989 Ansätze zu einer semantischen Beschreibung topologischer Präpositionen. In: Christopher Habel, Michael Herweg and Klaus Rehkamper (eds.), *Raumkonzepte in Verstehenprozessen,* 99–127. Tübingen: Max Niemeyer.
Hottenroth, Priska M.
1991 Präpositionen und Objektkonzepte: Ein kognitiv orientiertes, zweistufiges Modell für die Semantik lokaler Präpositionen. In: Gisa Rauh (ed.), *Approaches to Prepositions*, 77–107. Tübingen: Gunter Narr.
Kemler Nelson, G. Deborah
1990 When experimental findings conflict with everyday observations: Reflections on children's category learning. *Child Development* 61: 606–610
Kleiber, Georges
1990 *La Sémantique des Prototypes.* Paris: Presses Universitaires de France.
Lakoff, George
1987 *Women, Fire, and Dangerous Things: What Categories Reveal about the Mind*. Chicago: The University of Chicago Press
Levine, Suzan and Suzan Carey
1982 Up front: The acquisition of a concept and a word. *Journal of Child Language* 9: 645–657.

Levinson, Stephen C.
1996 Relativity in spatial conception and description. In: John J. Gumperz and Stephen C. Levinson (eds.), *Rethinking Linguistic Relativity,* 177–202. Cambridge: Cambridge University Press.

Mandler, Jean M.
1992 How to build a baby: II Conceptual primitives. *Psychological Review* 99: 587–604.
1994 Precursors of linguistic knowledge. *Transactions of the Royal Philological Society* 346: 63–69.
1996 Preverbal representation of language. In: Paul Bloom, Mary A. Peterson, Lynn Nadel and Merill F. Garrett (eds.), *Language and Space*, 365–382. Cambridge, MA: The MIT Press.
1998 Representation. In: Deanna Kuhn and Robert Siegler (eds.), *Cognition, Perception and Language.* 225–308. New York: Wiley.
2000 Perceptual and conceptual processes in infancy. *Journal of Cognition and Development* 1: 3–36.

Mandler, Jean M., Patricia J. Bauer and Laraine McDonough
1991 Separating the sheep from the goats: Differentiating global categories. *Cognitive Psychology* 23: 263–298.

McDonough, Laraine, Sooja Choi, Melissa Bowerman and Jean M. Mandler
to appear The use of preferential looking as a measure of semantic development. In: Edith L. Bavin and D. Burnham (eds.), *Advances in Infancy Research.* Norwood: Ablex Publishing.

Miller, George and Philip Johnson-Laird
1976 *Language and Perception.* Cambridge, MA: Harvard University Press.

Nelson, Katherin
1985 *Making Sense: The Acquisition of Shared Meaning.* Orlando: Academic Press.

Olson, R. David and Ellen Bialystok
1983 *Spatial Cognition: The Structure and Development of the Mental Representation of Spatial Relations.* Hillsdale, NJ: Lawrence Erlbaum.

Quinn, Paul C.
1994 The categorization of 'above' and 'below' spatial relations by young infants. *Child Development* 65: 58–69.

Sandra, Dominiek and Sally Rice
1995 Network analyses of prepositional meaning: Mirroring whose mind – the linguist's or the language user's? *Cognitive Linguistics* 6: 89–130.

Smith, Linda
1979 Perceptual development and category generalization. *Child Development* 50: 705–715

Stockman, J. Ida and Fay Vaughn-Cooke
1992 Lexical elaboration in children's locative action expressions. *Child Development* 63: 1104–1125.

Vandeloise, Claude
1987 Complex primitives in language acquisition. *Belgian Journal of Linguistics* 2: 11–36.
1990 Representation, prototypes and centrality. In: Savas Tsohatzidis (ed.), *Meanings and Prototypes: Studies in Linguistic Categorization*, 403–437. London: Routledge.
1991 *Spatial Prepositions: A Case Study in French*. Chicago: The University of Chicago Press.
1992 Structure of lexical categories and family resemblances. Duisburg: LAUD (Series A; 325).
1994 Methodology and analyses of the preposition *in*. *Cognitive Linguistics* 5: 157–185.
1995 Cognitive linguistics and prototypes. In: Thomas A. Sebeok and Jean Umiker-Sebeok (eds.), *Advances in Visual Semiotics: The Semiotic Web 1992–1993*, 423–442. Berlin: Mouton de Gruyter.
1999 Une place pour chaque chose et chaque chose à sa place [One place for each thing and each thing at its place]. In: Marc Plénat (ed.), *L'emprise du sens: Hommages à Andrée Borillo,* 303–322. Amsterdam: Rodopi.

Vieu, Laure
1991 *Sémantique des relations spatiales et inférences spatio-temporelles* [The semantics of spatial relations and spatio-temporal inferences]. Ph.D dissertation, Université Paul Sabatier, Toulouse.

Vygotsky, L.S.
1934 [1962] *Thought and Language*. Cambridge, MA: The MIT Press.

Ward, B. Thomas, Edward Vela and Sally Duffin Hass
1990 Children and adults learn family-resemblance categories analytically. *Child Development* 61: 593–605.

Wunderlich, Dietrich
1985 Raum, Zeit und das Lexicon. In: H. Schweitzer (ed.), *Sprache und Raum: Psychologische und linguistische Aspekte der Aneignung und Verarbeitung von Raumlichkeit,* 66–90. Stuttgart: Metzle.

The Dutch hedges *echt* and *gewoon*: Markers of prototypicality?

Christof Vanden Eynde[1]

Abstract

The use of hedges such as *real* and *par excellence* are often thought to reflect the prototype structure of lexical categories. In this paper, it is argued that the Dutch hedges *echt* 'real, true' and *gewoon* 'ordinary, common' effectuate a temporary, context-dependent restructuring of categories. *Echt* serves to narrow the category down to its "real" members; the hedge, in other words, exploits a classical view of categories, whereby each category is clearly distinct from each other. *Gewoon*, on the other hand, sets up a contrast between "ordinary", or unmarked members of a category, in contrast to more marked members; the hedge exploits a cognitive-functional view of categories. The hedges *echt* and *gewoon*, therefore, are metalinguistic devices which speakers use for rhetorical effects; their use cannot throw light on the stored representations of lexical categories.

Keywords: category membership, folk theories, gradable adjectives, hedges, implicatures, lexical category, monosemy, polysemy, prototype structure, prototypical core, rhetorical devices.

---

1. I would like to thank Johan De Caluwe, Dominique Lebbe, and the organizers and the participants of the "Workshop on Cognitive Approaches to Lexical Semantics" (held at the University of Turku, Finland, 15 November 1996) for their comments on previous versions of this paper; thanks are also due to two anonymous reviewers, whose remarks have been very helpful.

1. Introduction

The internal structuring of categories manifests itself in a number of well-known ways, such as degree of category membership, vagueness at the edges of categories, etc. (Geeraerts, Grondelaers & Bakema 1994: 45–56). These effects are indirect reflexes of the prototypical organization of categories. Given the prominence of that organization, one would also expect to find *direct* reflexes, such as words and expressions in everyday language which refer to the prototypical organization of lexical categories.

In his (1972) article on hedges, Lakoff claimed that this expectation is borne out. Citing sentences like those in (1),

(1) a. *A robin is a bird par excellence.* (true)
b. *A chicken is a bird par excellence.* (false)
c. *A penguin is a bird par excellence.* (false)

he concludes that "people do make the full range of distinctions in the birdiness hierarchy. Though these distinctions may be subtle, they can be thrown into clear relief by hedges" (Lakoff 1972: 197). The use of hedges is thus seen as evidence of the way in which individual lexical categories are organized. A similar view can be found in Taylor (1989), who concludes that "hedges both confirm and complement the psycholinguistic evidence [i.e. for the prototypical organization of categories]" (1989: 80).

There is, however, reason to believe that this view of hedges is naive, and that it is an example of what Lakoff (1987) has called the "EFFECTS=STRUCTURE interpretation". Kay (1983) draws attention to the fact that hedges are essentially metalinguistic devices that are used by speakers to manipulate language. As such, hedges should not be seen as direct reflections of the organization of lexical categories; in other words, the claim that hedges constitute direct evidence for the prototypical structuring of categories cannot be sustained.

In this chapter; I will look at two Dutch hedges which, at first sight, seem to function as vernacular equivalents of the linguistic term *prototypical*, viz., *echt* 'real, true' and *gewoon* 'ordinary, common'. In section 2, I show why one might initially be led to think that speakers of Dutch use both hedges to refer to the prototypical core of a lexical category. Section 3 shows that this assumption is incorrect: not only are *echt* and *gewoon* not interchangeable in many contexts, they are even mutually exclusive when combined with gradable adjectives. Section 4 illustrates the claim that these hedges do not reflect the prototypical structuring of a lexical category, but are used as rhetorical devices to impose a certain structure on a category. Section 5 examines the effects that the use of these two hedges has on the interpretation of an utterance. It is also suggested that two different folk theories of lexical meaning and category membership underlie the use of *echt* and *gewoon*.

2. *Echt* and *gewoon*: markers of prototypicality (?)

At first sight, the Dutch hedges *echt* and *gewoon* appear to be straightforward markers of the prototypical core of a lexical category. A simple example may illustrate their use. Take the Dutch word *thee* 'tea'. Like many of its cognates in other European languages, this word has undergone semantic extension. Referring originally to a hot infusion of tea leaves, it later came to be used for infusions of other plants and herbs (known, in French, as *tisanes*). Hence, we have *kamillethee* 'camomile tea', *lindethee* 'linden blossom tea', etc. Tea made from tea leaves, however, remains central within the extended TEA category: there is no compound or lexicalized phrase which uniquely refers to this central subcategory. There are, to be sure, words to refer to different types of tea made from tea leaves, but Dutch lacks a word which unambiguously refers to the central subcategory as a whole. This is clearly a consequence of the category's prototypical status within the larger TEA category: *thee* refers to the central subcategory by default. But what if speakers of Dutch want to contrast tea made from tea leaves with other infusions? In such cases, they will use either *gewone thee* 'common/ordinary tea' or *echte thee* 'real tea'.[2]

Similarly, if Dutch speakers wish to refer to a normal-sized horse as opposed to a pony, they could again use *echt/gewoon*:

(2) *Ik wil een echt/gewoon paard, geen pony.*
'I want a real/normal horse, not a pony.'

Color words (which, incidentally, have played an important role in the development of the notion of prototypicality) behave similarly. If I had to refer to prototypical red, I would probably use *echt rood* 'real red'. But *gewoon rood* 'common red' also sounds acceptable, and in a neutral context I can only interpret it as referring to prototypical red.

The use of *echt* and *gewoon* to refer to central subcategories within a larger category is even found in Dutch biological names. Thus, within the family of *zeehonden* 'seals' (Phocidae), we find the *gewone zeehond* (Phoca vitulina) alongside the *kleine zeehond* and the *Baikalzeehond*. Similarly, a particular subfamily of *spechten* 'woodpeckers' is called *echte spechten*. An interesting case is also the word *kamille* 'camomile', which refers to the genus Matricaria. This genus has several species, the best-known of which is Matricaria camomilla, known in Dutch as either *gewone kamille* or *echte kamille*.

In all these examples, the extensions of the expressions with *echt* and *gewoon* seem to be the same. Intuitively, it would seem appropriate to say that the extensions correspond to the prototypical cores of thc respective categories.

2. These and other judgments are based on my own observations, intuitions, and on informal questioning of eight of my colleagues. I am aware of the limited value of this method, but would like to point out that the examples given in this chapter have not been contested by other speakers of Dutch.

3. Non-interchangeability of *echt* and *gewoon*

The examples cited in the previous section suggest that the hedges *echt* and *gewoon* single out the prototypical cores. It would be premature, however, to conclude that *echt* and *gewoon* are used as straightforward markers of prototypicality.

A first problem is that, although *echt* and *gewoon* can be substituted without changing the extension in, e.g., *echt/gewoon rood*, this is not the case in several other examples. Take the following example:

(3) *...dat die verhoogde afzet van karnemelk (...) ten koste gaat van de verkoop van gewone melk.* (INL)[3]
'...that the increased sale of buttermilk (...) is at the expense of the sale of ordinary milk.'

Here, *gewone melk* contrasts with *karnemelk* 'buttermilk'. Again, a peripheral subcategory which has a name of its own contrasts with the central subcategory for which no specific name exists. This is very much like our previous examples, but it is unlike them in that we would not contrast *karnemelk* with *echte melk* 'real milk'. This does not necessarily imply that the phrase *echte melk* is unacceptable, as it might very well contrast with synthetic milk. However, in the contrast between prototypical milk and buttermilk, the phrase *echte melk* is less appropriate than *gewone melk.* A similar observation can be made about the following example, where traditional roller skates are compared with so-called in-line skates:

(4) *De gewone rolschaatsen met de wielen twee aan twee of de "in-line-skates" met de wieltjes achter ekaar.* (INL)
'The common roller skates with the wheels two by two, or the "in-line skates", with the wheels one behind the other.'

---

3. Examples followed by *INL* are taken from the 27 million word newspaper corpus of the "Instituut voor Nederlandse Lexicografie" (Institute for Dutch Lexicography). I would like to thank the INL for allowing me to make use of this corpus.

Conversely, it is not difficult to find examples in which *echt* seems to be used to refer to the prototypical core, but where it cannot be replaced by *gewoon*. Take the following sentence:

(5) *Ik wil een echte hond, geen poedel.*
'I want a real dog, not a poodle.'

The speaker in (5) obviously wants a dog that is fierce and strong, characteristics which we may consider to be typical of dogs. Here, we could not replace *echt* with *gewoon* without also changing the extension of the expression. If *gewone hond* is contrasted with *poedel*, we would be inclined to interpret *gewone hond* as referring to a dog of a non-descript breed or to a dog whose breed is of no relevance.

While the extensions of *echte hond* and *gewone hond* in the above case are not identical, they might still overlap. But there are also cases in which *echt* and *gewoon* are clearly incompatible. Consider a word like *succes* 'success'. Whether something counts as a success is obviously a matter of degree. When someone says that some event is *een echt success* 'a real success', they imply that they are using the word *succes* in an appropriate and sincere way. In the case of a gradable word like *succes*, this leads to an interpretation in which *echt* functions as an intensifying word. *Een echt succes* is, like its English counterpart, synonymous with *a great success*. Likewise, when used to modify gradable adjectives, *echt* in Dutch is synonymous (at least, extensionally) with *zeer* 'very':[4]

(6) *Jan is echt rijk.*
'John is really/very rich.'

On the other hand, when *gewoon* is used to modify gradable words, it explicitly signals the inappropriateness of an intensifying meaning.

4. The use of equivalents of *echt* and *real* as intensifiers is a phenomenon which can be observed in languages around the world (Bolinger 1972: 94; Lindström 1996). Indeed, English *really* and *truly* are often used as intensifiers. Note also that the English intensifier *very* is cognate with French *vrai* 'true'.

Usually, the absence of intensification need not be signaled since it is conveyed by a Gricean quantity implicature. Thus, if someone describes a person as *tall*, it will be implicated that the use of *very tall* is inappropriate. Describing someone as *tall* when they are in fact *very tall* (e.g., 2.10m) is similar to saying that someone has two children when they have three: in neither case could it be claimed that the utterance is, technically speaking, false, but in both cases the utterance is pragmatically inappropriate. To be sure, given that implicatures are subject to cancellation, speakers will sometimes feel the need to make implicatures explicit. *Gewoon* is used in just this manner:[5]

(7) *... iemand "die altijd buitengewoon goed" is, maar soms ook maar "gewoon goed"*. (INL)[6]
'... someone who is always "extraordinarily good", but sometimes just "plain good"'

We seem to have reached the rather awkward conclusion that, when combined with a color adjective like *rood* 'red', *gewoon* and *echt* are (extensionally) synonymous, whereas when they are combined with gradable adjectives, *gewoon* and *echt* are mutually exclusive; someone who is *GEWOON groot* 'plain tall' is definitely not *echt groot* 'really tall'.

One possible reason why *echt* and *gewoon* might not always be interchangeable is that there may be two distinct meanings of the word *echt*. Certainly, Dutch dictionaries suggest that we should distinguish at least between a meaning having to do with truth and one having to do with (proto)typicality. These two distinct meanings are illustrated by the following two sentences:

---

5. Similarly, a word like *exactly* can be used to make explicit the quantity implicature in *He has two children.*
6. Note that in *gewoon goed*, the stress will be on *gewoon*. If the stress were on *goed*, a different meaning would be conveyed: *Hij is gewoon GOED* means something like 'Frankly, he is good'. In the latter case, *gewoon* seems to function more like a discourse particle (De Vriendt & Van De Craen 1995).

(8) *Ik wil een echte hond, geen speelgoedhond.*
'I want a real dog, not a toy dog.'

(5) *Ik wil een echte hond, geen poedel.*
'I want a real dog, not a poodle.'

It could be claimed that in (8) *echt* is used to distinguish members of the category DOG from non-members of the category, whereas in (5) it is used to distinguish central, prototypical members from more peripheral members.

It is, however, not at all obvious that there actually are two distinct meanings of *echt*. The question depends on whether *hond* 'dog', in *speelgoedhond* 'toy dog', has a meaning – something like 'dog-shaped object' – distinct from its normal meaning. If *hond* has just a single meaning in these sentences, in other words, if it refers to a single category, then we could no longer argue that *echt* has two distinct meanings. We would have to say that in both sentences *echt* has to do with centrality/prototypicality.

Unfortunately, the question of whether *hond* is ambiguous between the meanings 'canis familiaris' and 'object representing a specimen of canis familiaris' is not at all easy to decide. Indeed, answering this question involves some of the central problems of Cognitive Semantics: the notion of *degree of membership* and its relation to *centrality* (Croft & Cruse, 1996); the fact that, from a theoretical point of view, it is impossible to strictly distinguish between polysemy and generality (Geeraerts 1993; Tuggy 1993);[7] and the fact that, on an operational level, the tests which are used to test polysemy turn out to be inadequate (Geeraerts 1993).

Rather than trying to prove that *hond* (and hence also *echt*) has a single meaning in the above examples, I will try to show why it would be improbable that there are two distinct meanings involved.

7. *Generality* is used here in the sense of underdetermination. The word *uncle* is underdetermined with regard to whether it refers to a brother of one's father or of one's mother. There is, however, no reason to suppose that *uncle* is ambiguous between the two readings. This phenomenon is sometimes referred to as *vagueness*, which is a somewhat unfortunate term, given that *vagueness* is also often used to describe the absence of clear boundaries.

First, it should be noted that the use of *echt* in (8) would be inappropriate if there were no doubt about the non-membership of toy dogs in the DOG category. The following sentence would be at best awkward, because there is no reason to doubt that cats do not belong to the DOG category. In order for *echt* to be used appropriately, the category boundaries should at least be under dispute.

(9) *?Ik wil een echte hond, geen kat.*
'I want a real dog, not a cat.'

Secondly, if we look at the actual use of sentences with *echt*, it becomes clear that the distinction between "truth meaning" and "prototypicality meaning" is not at all easy to make. Suppose we were to encounter the following example:

(10) ... *want wie ziet (...) het verschil tussen een echt pistool en een alarmpistool?* (INL)
'... because who sees the difference between a real gun and an alarm gun?'

Conceivably, many people would claim that *echt* is used here in the truth meaning, i.e., to distinguish members from non-members: an alarm gun is to a real gun as a toy dog is to a real dog. However, example (10) is not the sentence that was actually attested in the INL corpus. Instead of *echt pistool*, *gewoon pistool* was used. This indicates that, at least for some people, alarm guns definitely belong to the GUN category, since a contrast like *een gewoon X not a Y* implies that Y is an X. Thus, by contrasting *pony* with *gewoon paard* 'normal horse', one implies that ponies are horses. From the example as it originally occurred in the INL corpus, it becomes evident that alarm guns might be seen as belonging to the GUN category. Consequently, it is not at all evident that in (10) *echt* has to do with truth and category membership. While it may not be easy to distinguish between the truth meaning and the prototypicality meaning of *echt*, I obviously do not wish to claim that no difference can be detected between the uses of *echt* in examples such as (5) and (8), or that *echt* has a single monolithic meaning.[8] My point, however, is that it would be mistaken to identify two discrete meanings.

My initial hypothesis about the use of *echt* and *gewoon* as markers of prototypicality cannot be maintained for the simple reason that *echt* and *gewoon* are not as interchangeable as the examples in section 2 might suggest. What is more, there are cases where *echt* and *gewoon* are mutually exclusive. One way in which these counterexamples could be explained is by invoking polysemy in the case of *echt*. However, it was shown that there is little reason to assume distinct meanings for *echt*, one having to do with truth, the other with prototypicality, and still another with sterotypes.

4. Imposing a structure on categories through the use of hedges

The main mistake in my initial hypothesis lies in the assumption that hedges in general, and *gewoon* and *echt* in particular, reflect the organization of a category. This section shows that *echt* and *gewoon* are not used to passively reflect the structure of a category, but rather to restructure the category.

In our initial hypothesis, it was assumed that a speaker uses the hedges *echt* and *gewoon* to refer to the prototypical core of a category, and that the prototypical organization of the category is not an idiosyncratic or contextual matter. Although there is much controversy about the exact nature of the notion of prototype, there seems to be agreement about the fact that prototypes are more or less stable; generally speaking, speakers in the same speech community tend to agree about what belongs to the prototypical core of a category and what belongs to the periphery. If it is indeed the case that the use of *echt* and *gewoon* faithfully reflects the internal structure of a category, we would expect the interpretation of *gewoon X* and *echt X* to be quite stable across contexts.

8. Indeed, as was pointed out by one reviewer, one could argue that the meaning of *echt* itself is prototypically organized.

This, however, is not the case. Take, for example, the phrase *iemands echte moeder* 'someone's real mother'. The default interpretation refers to the birthgiver. However, as Lakoff (1987: 75) has pointed out, it is perfectly acceptable for someone to say *My adoptive mother is my real mother, because she has always taken care of me.* In this example, the speaker highlights caregiving as the central defining feature of the motherhood concept. In using the hedge *real*, the speaker does not reflect the (given) internal structure of the category, but imposes a structure on it, and is thus redefining the concept.

Among the sentences from the INL corpus in which *echt* occurs before a noun, quite a number can be found in which *echt* is used to redefine a concept. Here is just one example:

(11) *Jungle-haters beweren dat een jungle-party pas een echt feest is als er genoeg cocaïne, crack en geweren voor handen zijn.* (INL)
'People who hate jungle [a type of dance music, CVE] say that a jungle party is only a real party if enough cocaine, crack, and guns are available.'

Like *echt*, *gewoon* can also be used to impose a certain structure on a category, rather than just reflecting its given structure. To illustrate this, let us return to one of our initial examples: *gewone thee.* In a neutral context (i.e., a context in which there is no explicit contrast to something else), people tend to interpret this phrase as referring to tea made from tea leaves. However, it is perfectly acceptable to speak of *geen gewone thee maar Orange Pecoe* 'not ordinary tea but Orange Pecoe'. In this case, *gewone thee* does not contrast tea made of tea leaves with a herbal tea, but a tea of a non-descript brand or flavor with tea of a specific brand or flavor.

Centrality within the category to which *gewoon* refers is not an absolute matter, but something which is relative to context. The use of the hedges allows the speaker to present an alternative construal of a lexical category, thereby restructuring the concept. This claim does not imply that the restructuring takes place at the level of the mental representation of the concept involved. It should be seen, rather, as a rhetorical operation. For instance, when someone utters sentence (5),

(5) *Ik wil een echte hond, geen poedel.*
'I want a real dog, not a poodle.'

they make clear that in their view, poodles are not good examples of dogs. The strongest way to get this view across is simply by implying that poodles are not dogs at all. It should be obvious, however, that even for someone who utters (5), poodles will almost certainly be part of the mental DOG category. It is unlikely that there are speakers for whom poodles actually do not belong to the category DOG.

We see, then, that very little remains of the initial hypothesis that *echt* and *gewoon* are everyday language equivalents of the linguistic term *prototypical*. Instead of stating this strong hypothesis, we have retreated to a vaguer hypothesis: *echt* and *gewoon* are used to indicate centrality within a category. This notion of centrality cannot be equated with the traditional linguistic notion of prototypicality, since it is a context-dependent, relative notion. Furthermore, the centrality to which *echt* refers is not the same as the centrality to which *gewoon* refers, since *echt* and *gewoon* are not always interchangeable and sometimes even incompatible.

5. What do *echt* and *gewoon* mean?

It has become clear that it is mistaken to equate the everyday language hedges *echt* and *gewoon* with the linguistic notion *prototypical*. In this section, I will discuss the effect of *echt* and *gewoon* on the interpretation of an utterance, claiming that the two hedges reflect two distinct folk theories of linguistic meaning.

To see how *gewoon* and *echt* differ, we need to return to cases where *echt* and *gewoon* are incompatible, i.e., where they modify gradable adjectives. As we saw earlier, *gewoon groot* 'plain tall' implies *niet zeer groot* 'not very tall', whereas *echt groot* is synonymous with *zeer groot* 'very tall'. Here, prominence is given to a contrast within a category. In uttering *gewoon groot* the speaker opposes *gewoon groot* to *zeer groot*.

As pointed out earlier, the effect of *gewoon* on the interpretation of the utterance is similar to that of a Gricean quantity implicature. Such an implicature arises in the following way: given two linguistic expressions *X1* and *X2*, of which *X2* is the more informative or stronger because it implies *X1*, the use of *X*1 will implicate that the use of *X2* is inappropriate; hence implicatures such as *some* → *not all* or *cool* → *not cold.* Similarly, the use of *tall* implicates *not very tall.* An implicature, however, is always subject to cancellation, so if a speaker wants to make absolutely sure that the meaning *tall but not very tall* is conveyed, he/she can make use of the hedge *gewoon.*

Now, the similarity between the Gricean quantity implicature and the use of *gewoon* is not absolute. For instance, a sentence such as (12),

(12) *Jan is groot.*
'Jan is tall.'

implicates that Jan is not very tall, but it does not primarily focus on the contrast between *groot* and *zeer groot.* In uttering (12), the speaker focuses on the implicit contrast between "tall" and "non-tall". By adding the hedge *gewoon,* however, the implicature is not only made explicit, there is also a shift of focus:[9] the speaker now focuses on the contrast between normally tall and very tall. The hedge *gewoon* draws attention to an *intracategorial contrast.*

We can extend this analysis to cases where *gewoon* is used to modify nouns. With *gewoon*, there is a contrast (be it implicit or explicit) between a subcategory which is marked, because it is perceived as being defined by some extra feature, and for which a separate name exists, and a subcategory which is unmarked and which does not have a name of its own. In the case of *paard* 'horse', there is

9. Other hedges seem to have a similar function. Compare:
(a) *Some passengers survived the crash.* (as opposed to *no passengers*)
(b) *Only some passengers survived the crash.* (as opposed to *all passengers*)
In (b), an implicature of (a) is made explicit and brought into focus.

a subcategory of small horses for which there is a separate name, viz., *pony*. There is no such separate name for the unmarked subcategory of normal-sized horses (which is simply the complement of the category HORSE with respect to the subcategory PONY, or to put it less technically, what remains of the category HORSE if the subcategory PONY is subtracted). By using the word *paard*, a speaker will, via quantity implicature, implicate that *pony* is not an appropriate lexicalization. In this case as well, it is possible to make the implicature explicit by using the hedge *gewoon.*[10] We can claim, then, that the meaning of the hedge *gewoon* is something like 'no more than'. In fact, we also find this meaning in *gewoon*'s use as an adverbial modifying a verb phrase:[11]

(13) *Je moet gewoon op de knop duwen.*
'You simply have to push the button.' = 'You have to do nothing more than push the button.'

To recapitulate, when we use, e.g., *gewoon rood* to refer to prototypical red, the underlying assumptions about the category RED are the following:

(a) Different kinds of red can be distinguished within the category RED.

---

10. It could be claimed that in the case of *paard* the implicature has been semanticized, in that it is possible to contrast *paard* and *pony* without a hedge: *Ik wil een paard, geen pony* 'I want a horse, not a pony'. This would indicate that *paard* has become autohyponymous. It is similar to a word like *rectangle*, which may refer to all rectangles, or only to those rectangles which are not squares (Kempson 1980; Horn 1984). However, given the complexity of autohyponymous words, a speaker might still feel the need to make use of the hedge *gewoon*.

11. It is likely that the meaning of *gewoon* as a discourse particle can be derived from this basic meaning. An utterance such as *Hij is gewoon GEK* 'Frankly, he is mad' seems to convey the following: "I could give all kinds of fancy explanations for his behavior, but in fact the statement 'He is mad' suffices." *Gewoon* as a discourse particle thus indicates that the predication to which it is added is sufficient, and that nothing needs to be added to it.

(b) It is possible to name those types of red which are in some way special or peripheral. These special types are marked, and specific names like *bordeaux* or *dark red* are available to refer to these marked subcategories.
(c) When a more specific name is not used, it is normally implicated via quantity implicature that the more specific name cannot be used.
(d) By using the hedge *gewoon* the speaker reinforces the implicature in (c), and also brings into focus the contrast between "unmarked" red and "special" red.

The use of *echt rood* on the other hand corresponds to a different view of the category RED. In using the hedge *echt*, the speaker focuses not on an intracategorial, but on an intercategorial contrast. The speaker, in effect, narrows down the category under consideration.

(a) Only *echt rood* belongs to the category RED.
(b) There are other colors like bordeaux or dark red which are sometimes called *rood*. When *rood* is used to refer to these colors it is used in an "incorrect" or loose way.

Let us return, then, to our initial example (*echte thee* vs. *gewone thee*, which refer to tea made from tea leaves). While the expressions *echte thee* and *gewone thee* may be synonymous on the extensional level, they do not have the same meaning, since they rest on different views of the meaning of the word *thee*. In the case of *gewone thee*, the speaker acknowledges that infusions[12] also belong to the category TEA, whereas in using *echte thee* the speaker is taking a strict view of the category TEA, which does not include infusions. (In fact, Belgian

12. Note that *infusion* can be used to refer to all infusions except those made from tea leaves, although obviously tea itself is an infusion. *Infusion* thus seems to have undergone a narrowing of its meaning. Again, this can be explained by Gricean quantity implicature.

and Dutch legislations seem to agree with the latter view, since it is apparently not allowed to sell infusions as *thee.*[13])

It follows that it would be a mistake to see *echt groot* 'really tall' and *zeer groot* 'very tall' as synonyms. When a person X is said to be *echt groot*, it is implied that someone shorter than X cannot adequately be called *groot.* The use of *zeer groot* to describe X, on the other hand, leaves open the possibility that someone shorter than X is still tall. This explains why there is a difference in acceptability between the following two sentences:

(14) ?*Jan is groot maar Piet is echt groot.*[14]
'Jan is tall, but Piet is really tall.'

(15) *Jan is groot maar Piet is zeer groot.*
'Jan is tall, but Piet is very tall.'

This difference in acceptability becomes even more evident if we try to use *echt groot* in a sentence involving metalinguistic negation (Horn 1985), as in the following (capitals indicate emphasis):

(16) *Jan is niet* GROOT, *hij is* ZEER *groot.*
'Jan is not tall, he's very tall.'

Unlike ordinary negation, the negation in (16) is not used to deny the truth of a proposition. What it does deny is the implicature of *Jan is groot* 'John is tall', namely that Jan is not very tall. In (16), it is not possible to replace *zeer groot* by *echt groot.* This follows from the

13. I have never come across a packet of, e.g., camomile infusion on which the word *thee* could be found. In bars and cafés, however, infusions are almost always sold as *thee.* Advertisers appear to be aware of this ambiguity: in a recent advertisement for Pickwick, infusions were referred to as *thee zonder thee* 'tea without tea'.

14. As pointed out by a reviewer, the acceptability of (14) improves considerably if particles are added: *Jan is wel groot, maar Piet, die is pas echt groot* 'Jan may be tall, but Piet, now he is really tall'. I cannot readily explain this difference in acceptability.

fact that the use of *echt groot* implies that anything shorter than *echt groot* cannot be called *groot.*

The meaning expressed by (16) could also be expressed by the use of *gewoon*.

(17) *Jan is niet GEWOON groot, hij is zeer groot.*
'Jan is not just tall, he is very tall.'

Just as in (16), *zeer groot* cannot here be replaced by *echt groot*. Again, this follows from the fact that *gewoon groot* and *echt groot* invoke two different models of tallness.

A final argument which indicates that *echt* and *zeer* with a gradable adjective cannot be synonyms concerns the difference in acceptability between the following two sentences. If *echt* and *zeer* were synonyms, both sentences would be equally acceptable.

(17) *Jan is echt zeer groot.*
'Jan is really very tall.'
(18) **Jan is zeer echt groot.*
'Jan is very really tall.'

I conclude then that intensification of *groot* by *echt* differs from intensification by *zeer*: whereas *zeer* singles out a subcategory within a larger category, the use of *echt* moves the boundary between "tall" and "not tall" upwards. I have tried to represent this in Figure 1.

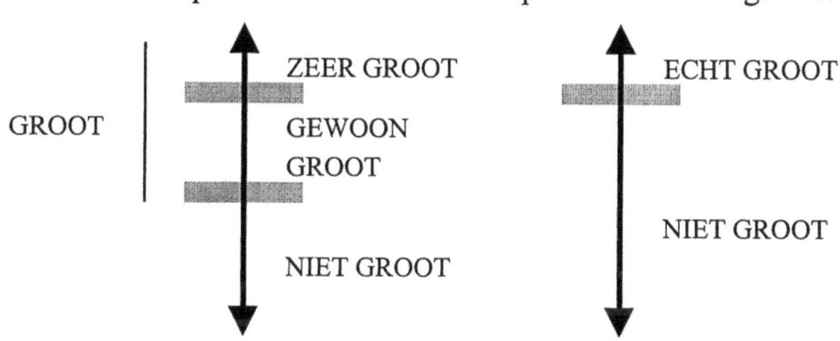

Figure 1. Intensification of *groot* by *zeer* and *echt.*

The hedges *echt* and *gewoon* invoke two different folk theories of lexical meaning and category membership (cf. Kay's 1983 study of the hedges *technically* and *strictly speaking*). The hedge *gewoon* invokes a theory of linguistic meaning with a cognitive-pragmatic orientation; the speaker (temporarily, and for rhetorical effect) redefines the internal structure of a category. By using *gewoon*, the speaker primarily draws the attention to relations within a category. The use of *echt*, on the other hand, presupposes a view of linguistic meaning as being strict and rigid, where category membership is not a matter of degree. The focus, therefore, is on intercategorial contrast (members versus non-members). Hence, the use of *echt* can be related to what is generally referred to as the classical view of meaning. In this respect, it is interesting to note that the meaning of *echt* in Middle Dutch was 'legal (with regard to marriages)'; *een echt kind* was a child born in wedlock. The legal origin of the word can still be seen in the strict view about categories which the hedge *echt* assumes.

5. Conclusion

The fact that speakers of Dutch can either use *echte thee* or *gewone thee* to refer to tea made from tea leaves shows that there are two different views of the meaning of *thee*. It does not follow, however, that the use of the hedges directly reflects the internal structure of categories, as represented in the mental lexicon. Rather, speakers use the hedges to "manipulate" categories, by imposing a structure on them.

As noted in introductory section 1, the idea that hedges reflect category structure was endorsed by Taylor. However, to be fair, it should be pointed out that Taylor also emphasizes that hedges can be used to restructure a category. For instance, he writes: "One could say that the hedge [*par excellence*] restructures BIRD in such a way that the category consists only of prototypical, or close to prototypical birds" (1989: 77). However, he goes on to write, "That *par excellence* functions in this way at all, of course, presupposes that BIRD is a category with different degrees of membership." I do not see why the use of the hedge should presuppose the internal structuring of a category. Suppose I introduce someone to a new ad hoc category X and refer to one of the members of that category as *an X par excellence*. This very utterance establishes the member in question as a central member, irrespective of whether the category is indeed prototypically structured. The adequate use of hedges does not depend on the way in which a given category is structured.

The fact that there is no direct relationship between hedges and the structure of lexical categories does not imply that the hedges *echt* and *gewoon* are of no interest in the study of lexical semantics. On the contrary, they indicate that language users are operating with different folk theories about lexical meaning. And while it may be the case that the use of these hedges bears no direct relationship to the actual internal organization of lexical categories, it may still be true that on a more abstract level they do tell us something about the organization of categories. These hedges are used to indicate centrality. As such, they reveal an awareness on the part of language users about the structured, flexible nature of lexical categories.

References

Bolinger, Dwight
1972 *Degree Words*. The Hague: Mouton.

Croft, William and D. Alan Cruse
1996 Resolving the prototype controversy. Paper presented at the XVIth Scandinavian Conference of Linguistics, Turku, Finland.

De Vriend, Sera and Piet Van de Craen
1995 Hoe gewoon is *gewoon*? In: José Cajot, Ludger Cremer and Hermann Niebaum (eds.), *Lingua Theodisca: Beiträge zur Sprach- und Literaturwisenschaft; Jan Goossens zum 65. Geburtstag*, 831–838. Münster: Lit.

Geeraerts, Dirk
1993 Vagueness's puzzles, polysemy's vagaries. *Cognitive Linguistics* 4: 223–272.

Geeraerts, Dirk, Stefan Grondelaers and Peter Bakema
1994 *The Structure of Lexical Variation: Meaning, Naming and Context*. (Cognitive Linguistics Research 5). Berlin: Mouton de Gruyter.

Horn, Laurence Robert
1984 Toward a new taxonomy for pragmatic inference: Q-based and R-based implicature. In: Deborah Schiffrin (ed.), *Meaning, Form and Use in Context: Linguistic Applications*, 11–42. Washington, DC: Georgetown University Press.
1985 Metalinguistic negation and pragmatic ambiguity. *Language* 61: 121–174.

Kay, Paul
1983 Linguistic competence and folk theories of language. In: Amy Dahlstrom, Claudia Brugman, Monica Macaulay, Inese Civkulis, Michele Emanatian, Donna Sakima, and Raquel Teixeira (eds.), *Proceedings of the Ninth Annual Meeting of the Berkeley Linguistics Society,* 128–137. Berkeley: Berkeley Linguistics Society.

Kempson, Ruth M.
1980 Ambiguity and word meaning. In: Sidney Greenbaum, Geoffrey Leech and Jan Svartvik (eds.), *Studies in English Linguistics: For Randolph Quirk*, 7–16. London: Longman.

Lakoff, George
1972 Hedges: A study in meaning criteria and the logic of fuzzy concepts. In: Paul Peranteau, Judith Levi, and Gloria Phares (eds.), *Papers from the Eighth Regional Meeting of the Chicago Linguistic Society*, 183–228. Chicago: Chicago Linguistic Society.
1987 *Women, Fire, and Dangerous Things: What Categories Reveal about the Mind.* Chicago: The University of Chicago Press.

Lindström, Jan
1996 Intensification and authenticity: On the relation between intensifier adverbs and reduplication. Paper presented at the XVIth Scandinavian Conference of Linguistics, Turku, Finland.

Taylor, John
1989 *Linguistic Categorization: Prototypes in Linguistic Theory*. Oxford: Clarendon Press

Tuggy, David
1993 Ambiguity, polysemy, and vagueness. *Cognitive Linguistics* 4: 273–290.

Polysemy or generality? Mu.

Jordan Zlatev

"Mu" becomes appropriate when the context of the question is too small for the truth of the answer.
Robert Pirsig, *Zen and the Art of Motorcycle Maintenance*

Abstract

This chapter proposes a conception of lexical meaning as use-potential, in contrast to prevailing atomistic and reificational views. The issues are illustrated on the example of spatial expressions, pre-eminently prepositions. It is argued that the dichotomy between polysemy and semantic generality is a false one, with expressions occupying points on a continuum from full homonymy to full monosemy, and with typical cases of polysemy falling in between. The notion of use-potential is explored in connectionist models of spatial categorization. Some possible objections to the use-potential approach are also addressed.

Keywords: connectionist modeling, creativity, epigenesis, hermeneutics, meaning-holism, monosemy, polysemy, semantic generality, situatedness, spatial expressions, use-potential.

1. Introduction[1]

It is well-known that prepositions and other types of grammatical morphemes like verb-particles and case markers have a wide variety of different meanings, according to their context of use. Johnson

1. This chapter is a thoroughly revised version of Chapter 4 in Zlatev (1997).

(1987: 31) illustrates such semantic variation in the following paragraph:

> You wake *out* of a deep sleep and peer *out* from beneath the covers *into* your room. You gradually emerge *out* of your stupor, pull yourself *out* from under the covers, climb *into* your robe, stretch *out* your limbs, and walk *in* a daze *out* of the bedroom and *into* the bathroom. You look *in* the mirror and see your face staring *out* at you. ... Once you are more awake you may even get lost *in* the newspaper, might enter *into* a conversation, which leads to your speaking *out* on some topic.

While there may be agreement on the phenomenon itself, its analysis has proved to be amazingly elusive and controversial, even if only the explicitly *spatial* uses of these expressions are considered.[2] A central question is: Does semantic variation involve a number of different *lexical senses*, or is it rather a matter of different contextual interpretations? Cognitive linguistic analyses have generally opted for the first answer, maximizing polysemy at the expense of semantic generality, in contrast to more traditional approaches, which maximize generality.

The solution to the question of "polysemy or generality" proposed in the title of this chapter is different from either of these alternatives. The question presupposes a conception of lexical meaning which is both atomistic and reificational and which is at odds with the conceptual framework and the evidence to be presented. Hence, the answer to the question is "Mu".

The argument comprises three steps. Section 3 outlines an approach to lexical meaning as use-potential. This approach is holistic and non-reificational and effectively dissolves the opposition "lexical sense" vs. "contextual interpretation". Second, in order to explicate the concept of meaning as use-potential, along with the concept of non-reificational polysemy ensuing from it, section 4 applies a hermeneutic/normative interpretation along the lines of Itkonen (1978) and of Regier's (1996) connectionist model of spatial categorization

2. Throughout this chapter, I will be concerned mainly with *spatial* meanings, where the expressions in question are involved in the specification of the (trans)location of an entity, the trajector.

and describes a series of experiments performed with it. Third, section 5 observes that not only spatial morphemes, but lexical items in general can be seen as occupying points on a continuum from full homonymy to full monosemy, with typical cases of polysemy falling in between, and, furthermore, that the position of a particular item on the continuum is susceptible to contextual influence (cf. Geeraerts 1993). Such variation is shown to be predicted by the concept of use-potential.

Section 6 briefly considers two possible objections to the argument: the systematic character of polysemy and speakers' ability to create novel utterances. Section 7 summarizes the major points of the investigation.

2. The dilemma: polysemous or general?

The best-known example of polysemy within Cognitive Linguistics is probably the Brugman/Lakoff analysis of *over* (Brugman 1981; Lakoff 1987). Since the connectionist experiments described in Section 4 also concern this lexical item, it is worth recapitulating the analysis one more time. In Lakoff's version, a radial structure of twenty-two separate senses is required to capture the spatial meaning of the word. The central schema (or sense) is expressed in (1): the trajector (tr) (in this example, the plane) crosses the region above some implicit landmark (lm). The senses in (2)–(7), where the lm is spelled out, are regarded as separate instances of this central schema.

(1) *The plane flew over.* (CENTRAL SCHEMA)
(2) *The bird flew over the yard.*
(3) *The plane flew over the hill.*
(4) *The bird flew over the wall.*
(5) *Sam drove over the bridge.*
(6) *Sam walked over the hill.*
(7) *Sam climbed over the wall.*

Lakoff briefly considers the possibility that these senses may be contextual variants of the central schema – the "minimal specification interpretation". This is rejected in favor of a "full specification" model in which each sense is a separate (sub)schema in the mental lexicon. Only in this way, Lakoff claims, can the senses in (5) and (6) function as links to senses such as those in (8) and (9), respectively. Since an END-POINT FOCUS interpretation requires an extended lm, such as a bridge or a hill, the senses in (8) and (9) cannot be derived from the central schema directly.[3]

(8) *Sausalito is over the bridge.* (by END-POINT FOCUS from 5)
(9) *Sam lives over the hill.* (by END-POINT FOCUS from 6)

Another group of senses, exemplified in (10) and (11), are static and require NON-CONTACT. Lakoff describes the sense in (11) as being derived through an image-schema transformation between an extended PATH and a 1DIM TR (one-dimensional tr), in this case, the powerline.

(10) *Hang the painting over the table.* (ABOVE SCHEMA, from 1)
(11) *The powerline stretches over the yard.* (by PATH => 1DIM TR from 2)

The senses in (12)–(19), with (12) as local center, are another subgroup based on the notion of COVERING. Since the "vertical" senses in (12)–(15) are (claimed to be) neutral with respect to CONTACT, while the "rotated" senses in (16)–(19) require CONTACT, the two sets need to be distinguished, the latter set being derived through a ROTATION transformation.

(12) *The board is over the hole.* (COVERING SCHEMA, from 1)
(13) *The city clouded over.* (from 12)

3. Cf. "On the full specification interpretation, the schemas in Figures 2–7 are part of that chain. Some of those schemas form links to other senses. The existence of such links suggests that the full specification view is correct." (Lakoff 1987: 422)

(14) *The guards were posted all over the hill.* (from 12)
(15) *I walked all over the hill.* (from 14)
(16) *There was a veil over her face.* (by ROTATION from 12)
(17) *The ice spread all over the windshield.* (by ROTATION from 13)
(18) *There were flies all over the ceiling.* (by ROTATION from 14)
(19) *The spider had crawled all over the ceiling.* (by ROTATION from 15)

Finally, there are two sense-types where *over* is not a preposition, but an adverb or verb-particle (20, 21) and a verb-prefix (22). The adverb use can be connected to the central schema by describing the tr as REFLEXIVE, i.e., the log (in 20) and the fence (in 21) are, in a way, falling over themselves.

(20) *Roll the log over.* (REFLEXIVE SCHEMA, from 1)
(21) *The fence fell over.* (from 20)
(22) *The bathtub overflowed.* (EXCESS SCHEMA, from 1)

According to Lakoff, the radial structure is psychologically real and motivates the spatial polysemy of the lexical item independently of the context in which the word appears. An advantage of such an analysis compared to traditional approaches is that it can capture generalizations over whole patterns of polysemy (cf. Taylor 1993), albeit at the expense of introducing a proliferation of lexical senses. Traditionally, the non-prepositional uses of *over* in (13) and (20)–(22) would not be regarded as being senses of the same item as the prepositional senses. The latter would perhaps be grouped in three or at most four types, roughly corresponding to the CENTRAL SCHEMA (1), the ABOVE SCHEMA (10), the COVERING SCHEMA (12), and the END-POINT FOCUS SCHEMA (8). The other uses would most likely be regarded as contextual variants of these – a far more economical account. With respect to (2)–(7), the minimal specification interpretation would be quite straightforward, while the constraints on END-POINT FOCUS uses invoked by Lakoff may be independently motivated (cf. Ekberg 1993, 2001) without having to rely on intervening linking senses.

An approach to minimizing polysemy in favor of semantic generality is evident in the spatial analyses of Miller and Johnson-Laird (1976). They propose a single general schema as the meaning of *in*, designed to cover examples such as those in (23), observing that "the schema leaves uncertain how much of the referent must be inside the relatum before one is willing to say it is *in* it, but such uncertainty is not inappropriate" (1976: 385).

(23) a. *a city in Sweden*
  b. *the coffee in the cup*
  c. *the spoon in the cup*
  d. *the scratch in the surface*
  e. *the bone in the leg*

To summarize, the time-honored dilemma of "polysemy or generality" in spatial semantics involves the following questions: Do referential differences of spatial expressions (a) correspond to many different senses? Or (b) can some if not all differences be accounted for by assuming a single general sense, which is specified in particular contexts? And if some cases involve (a) and others (b), how do we decide which is which? The last question constitutes a methodological problem for so-called network analyses of prepositional (and other) meanings, such as that of Lakoff/Brugman, a problem which has been identified and characterized by Sandra and Rice (1995: 125) as one "of determining whether the fine distinctions are part of the mental representation (as predicted by the prepositional network approach) or the result of an interaction between monosemous mental representations and a process of contextual specification". I argue that there is a radical way of answering such questions: not "Either-or" but "Mu".

3. Theoretical framework

If the contrast between an analysis in terms of polysemy ("full specification") vs. generality ("minimal specification") is to make sense, there must be a difference in kind between the notions of *lexical sense* and contextual interpretation. These are illustrated in Figure 1. In (a), a distinct (in this case, non-prototypical) sense of lexical item *W* is being *selected* in a particular context (represented by the oval including the boxes [A] and [B]); in (b), this same context *specifies* an aspect of the semantically general meaning of *W*. As pointed out in section 2, Brugman and Lakoff analyze *over* according to (a), while Miller and Johnson-Laird's analyze *in* according to (b).

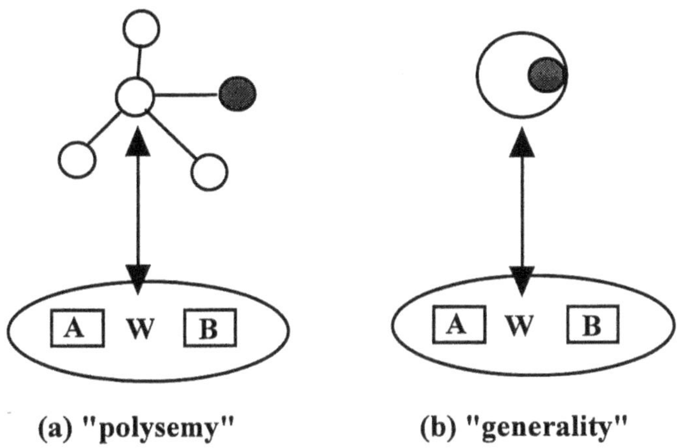

Figure 1. An illustration of the allegedly different phenomena of polysemy and semantic generality: Selection of a pre-established sense (a) vs. contextual specification of an interpretation (b).

The representations in Figure 1 not only clarify the opposition between polysemy and generality, they show that the opposition rests on the implicit acceptance of the following two interrelated assumptions:

- *The atomist assumption.* The relationship between word forms and word meanings (whether polysemous or not) is predominantly one-to-one, making word meanings (largely) context-independent.
- *The reificational assumption.* Word meanings, including separate senses, have the status of (mental) objects.

These assumptions have been taken for granted in most varieties of lexical semantics. Indeed, the atomist assumption is more or less axiomatic; if word meanings could not be analyzed in isolation, the rationale for distinguishing lexical from sentence/utterance semantics would evaporate (cf. Geeraerts 1993). Suppose, however, that these assumptions could be shown to be unnecessary, and even inadequate, for an account of lexical meaning in general and of spatial meaning in particular. In that case, one would expect the polysemy/generality dichotomy to evaporate also.

3.1. Situated embodiment and MDLGs

The conceptual framework for the present study (Zlatev 1997, 2003) complements the cognitive semantic notion of *embodiment* (e.g., Johnson 1987) with Wittgenstein's (1953) view of language as constituting "forms of life", embedded or *situated* within sociocultural practices. One of the motivations for such a synthesis is that without the balance of a social, use-oriented, "language-dominant" (Forrester 1996) perspective, Cognitive Semantics is bound to remain individualistic, trapped in solipsism or neural reductionism, and incapable of accounting for cross-linguistic variation other than through parameter-fixing of a pre-given (innate) potential, as within Chomskyan linguistics (Zlatev 1997: chap. 2).

The major theoretical notion of the proposed framework is that of a minimal, differentiated language game (MDLG). It is "minimal" since it involves only a single utterance, i.e., the smallest independently meaningful unit of language, and the smallest move in discourse. It is "differentiated" because both utterance form and utterance meaning are not unitary entities, but analyzable into component elements, while at the same time preserving their holistic character. Finally, it is called a "language game" to emphasize that the relationship between (elements of) form and (elements of) meaning is a matter of social convention, whereby the latter – rather than "truth conditions" or "conceptualizations" of individual minds – constitute conditions (criteria) of appropriate use of the former. The illustration of a MDLG in Figure 2 shows that it may be analyzed as consisting of six interrelated aspects:

- a situation type [shown as the upper white oval];
- epigenetically constructed semantic categories [shown as the black geometric figures within the upper white oval];
- an utterance type [shown as the lower white oval];
- form-classes (e.g., noun, verb, preposition, case suffix) which categorize elements of the utterance [shown as the small rectangles, labeled A, B...];
- a many-to-many mapping relationship between (classes of) elements of the utterance and the situation [shown as black arrows];
- a set of relevant background practices.

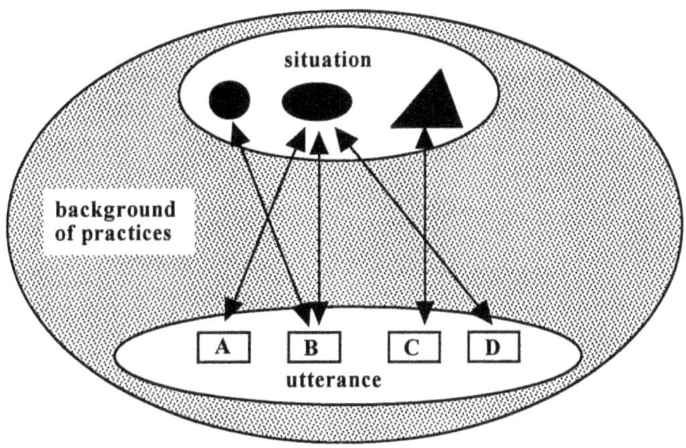

Figure 2. A schematic illustration of a minimal, differentiated language game (MDLG).

As in Cognitive Grammar (Langacker 1987), situated embodiment assumes that linguistic knowledge can be characterized as a mapping between a "phonological pole" and a "semantic pole". However, the semantic pole does not consist of a "conceptualization", but of a situation (type), which can be either real or virtual, and constitutes *a humanly significant, in part linguistically construed aspect of reality,* not an objective, language-independent state of affairs. Situations can be partially analyzed into semantic categories, which are epigenetic in the sense that they are primed by language-independent, sensorimotor categories, but are developmentally shaped into language-*specific* categories. These categories are assumed to be mutually dependent, forming aspects of meaningful wholes as in *frame semantics* (Fillmore 1982). On the utterance level, a similar partial analyzability is assumed. In addition to linearly separable morphemes, which fall into form classes and which are determined both semantically and distributionally, there are also "suprasegmental" components, such as intonation and various collocational structures (Pawley & Syder 1983).

The mapping between semantic categories and utterance units is not required to be one-to-one, but rather is expected to be many-to-many. Talmy's (1985) lexicalization patterns document the mapping of more than one semantic unit into a single lexical item ("conflation"), while distributed spatial semantics (Sinha & Kuteva 1995) illustrate the reverse relationship of one semantic unit to several utterance units. Such cases are expected to be the rule rather than the exception.

Finally and importantly, the notion of a MDLG intends to capture the fact that the meaning of an utterance is fixed only relative to a socially shared background. In this connection, Dreyfus (1991, 1993) refers to a "background of shared practices", while Searle (1992: 179) characterizes the background in terms of "human capacities", that is "abilities to engage in certain practices, know-how, ways of doing things, etc" (see also Searle 1985). What these notions have in common, and what separates them from the conception of the background adopted in, e.g., Lakoff's (1987) ICMs, is that according to Dreyfus and Searle the background is non-representational and, on pain of infinite regress, *cannot* be fully represented. This is the conception of the background adopted within situated embodiment and is "represented" in Figure 2 by the fact that the smaller utterance and situation ovals – gestalt-like in themselves – require the larger oval of background practices to be connected appropriately.

What does all this imply for word meaning? Consider Figure 3, in which a lexical item *W* has taken the place of form class [B] of Figure 2. If we compare Figures 1 and 3, we see that the atomist and reificational assumptions with respect to lexical meaning would be invalidated within the framework of situated embodiment.

First, due to the many-to-many mapping between expressions and semantic categories, *W* will not express a particular semantic category independently from other elements of the utterance. In Figure 3, the same category which *W* expresses is also expressed overtly by a member of [A], and covertly by a member of [C], the latter being signified by the dashed arrow. This implies that the meaning of *W* cannot be specified without considering the context in which it appears. Its meaning will be "a function of the meaning of the whole", which is the classical definition of meaning holism. All this obviously contradicts the atomist assumption.

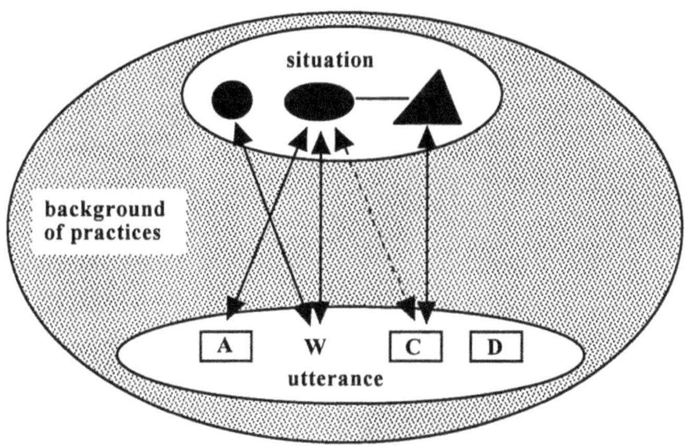

Figure 3. A schematic MDLG with form class [B] instantiated as the word form *W*.

What about the reificational assumption? In Figures 2 and 3, the semantic pole does not consist of conceptualizations, but rather of actual or virtual situations, and the semantic categories into which they may be (partially) analyzed are not mental pictures or even image schemas, but rather *criteria of appropriateness*. The meaning of an utterance (type) is thus the set of all MDLGs in which it could be appropriately used. Included in its meaning are so-called speech-act, or illocutionary aspects: A declarative utterance would fit a language game in which a statement is appropriate; a question, one where asking is appropriate, etc. Thus, *to know the meaning of an utterance is to know the MDLGs in which it would be appropriately used,* or, less technically, *to be able to use it appropriately*. This notion of meaning can be referred to as use-potential, and exhibits both similarities and differences to the notion of "meaning potential", which according to Halliday (1976: 9) "presupposes speaker, hearer and situation – in terms of the language system, a set of options and the ability to select appropriately within them, to say 'four hearts' at the right place".

The same notion could be applied straightforwardly to word meaning: *to know the meaning of a lexical item* W *is to know its use-potential*, i.e., the set of MDLGs in which *W* can participate. This proposal is similar to, but more general than that of frame semantics: lexical meaning is not only relative to scenes, but to MLDGs, consisting of (i) situations, (ii) other words of the utterance, and (iii) backgrounds. Given the non-representational character of the background, it follows that a word's use-potential cannot be explicated in complete detail – dictionaries of any kind must remain approximate. However, a complete explication is not necessary either, since as described so far the notion of use-potential is more akin to a practical ability than to any kind of object, mental or otherwise. In other words, the reificational assumption is sidestepped.

At first glance, the notion of lexical meaning as use-potential may seem to make polysemy impossible, since there are no distinct senses to arrange in polysemy networks as in Figure 1a. However, the use-potential of a word *W* may very well be analyzable in terms of distinguishable subtypes. In this case, *W* may be regarded as polysemous, even though this polysemy is a matter of clusters of contextual interpretations. These clusters need not necessarily have a common core, so the idea of a single general meaning, illustrated in Figure 1b, is inappropriate as well. This conception of polysemy is referred to as non-reificational polysemy.

It should be pointed out that the framework of situated embodiment and the approach to lexical meaning outlined above do not constitute empirical theories, in the sense of involving falsifiable predictions. Their role is much more conceptual in that they provide a means to think about linguistic meaning, and to suggest what kind of questions it makes sense to investigate (and what kind do not). The following subsection and section 4 may be seen as such particular investigations, which come a few steps closer to empirical science. Following Itkonen (1978, 1983), I assume that like philosophy, linguistics is primarily a hermeneutic rather than a natural science, its major method being one of explication rather than causal explanation, since "causal descriptions answering the *what-and-how*-question logically presuppose non-causal descriptions answering the *what*-question, but not vice versa" (Itkonen 1983: 6).

This epistemological standpoint implies a non-orthodox interpretation of connectionist modeling of language – not as an implementation of the actual causal mechanisms involved in language learning and language use (i.e., as implementing a "neural theory of language"), but primarily as a model explicating normative concepts such as conditions of appropriateness, as will be elaborated in section 4.

3.2. *Holistic spatial semantics*

Holistic spatial semantics is a theory of the linguistic expression of spatial meaning within the framework of situated embodiment. The basic object of analysis is the *spatial utterance*, defined as an utterance (type) through which the speaker gives the hearer information concerning the location or motion of a given entity (person or thing), or asks for such information. The following spatial concepts are assumed to be universal, i.e., involved in all human languages: Trajector, Landmark, Motion, Path, Region, Frame-of-Reference, and Direction (cf. Zlatev 1997, 2003). However, the values of the categories may differ from language to language, sometimes drastically (cf.

Bowerman 1996).[4] Languages also differ in the way the categories are expressed, though always through some combination of overt expression, covert expression, and background specification.

3.2.1. Overt expression

A semantic category is expressed overtly only if its values vary systematically with different expressions belonging to a particular form class. There are three general patterns of overt expression: *conflation*, when more than one semantic category is expressed by the members of a single form class; *distributedness,* when the same category is expressed by a set of different form classes; and *complementarity,* when different form classes typically express different categories. The Japanese example (24) illustrates all three patterns:

– conflation	Path-V (*deru*) ↔ Path + Region
– distributedness	Path-V (*deru*) + Post (*ni*) ↔ Path
– complementarity	Region-N (*soto*) ↔ Region, Postposition (*ni*) ↔ Path

(24) *Sensei ga dojo no soto ni*
teacher SUBJ dojo GEN outside to
Region:EXTERIOR Path:END
deta
go+PAST
Path:BEGIN–Region:INTERIOR
Path:END–Region:EXTERIOR
'The karate instructor left the dojo and went out.'

4. The theory has been applied to the analysis of six Indo-European languages, English, Swedish, Spanish, Italian, Serbo-Croatian, and Bulgarian, and four non-Indo-European languages, Finnish, Estonian, Japanese, and Thai, supplemented with analysis of secondary data from languages whose spatial systems are reputedly difficult for universalist accounts: Archi (Dagestanian), Ewe (West African), and Tzeltal (Mayan).

3.2.2. Covert expression

Covert expression implies that a word that primarily expresses one semantic category participates in the expression of another. For example, the semantic category Region is usually not overtly expressed by English verbs; verbs of locomotion (e.g., *go, run, fly, float*) will typically express Manner-of-motion rather than information pertaining to the Path and/or Region of the motion event. However, the use of particular verbs will constrain the value of Region, as shown by the contrast between (25a) and (25b) below. This covert expression of Region by certain verbs in English (the broken line between [C] and the ellipse in Figure 3) may be seen as an effect of the holistic relationship between concepts within situations.

(25) a. *John flew over the bridge.*
Region: SUPERIOR
b. *John walked over the bridge.*
Region: SURFACE

3.2.3. Background specification

Background specification is involved in (24), albeit not in the domain of spatial semantics. Consider the translation of *sensei* 'teacher' as 'karate instructor'; it is the word *dojo* 'place for practicing karate' which strongly predisposes a background context of karate training, which in turn constrains the interpretation of *sensei.* This also shows that covert expression and background specification are closely related, and it may not be determinate whether a word co-expresses a certain category or triggers a more general context for its interpretation. On the other hand, both may be said to correspond to *pragmatic,* as opposed to semantic meaning (cf. Levinson 1983). Thus, holistic spatial semantics maintains a weak form of the distinction between semantics and pragmatics, as opposed to, e.g., Cognitive Grammar, which openly denies it.

3.2.4. Implications

The theory sketched out above has the following important implications concerning the meaning of spatial expressions. Firstly, the spatial prepositions of the familiar Indo-European languages, far from expressing conceptually basic spatial relations as often assumed, appear from a cross-linguistic perspective as clear cases of conflators, expressing at the same time the semantic categories Path and Region.[5] Secondly, and more relevant to the central topic of this chapter, the analysis of prepositional meaning implied by the theory of holistic spatial semantics *rejects the meaningfulness of the distinction between polysemy and generality*. Looking back at the meaning of English *over*, we can see that if we identify it with *W* in Figure 3, there will be no need to postulate two separate lexical senses in order to account for the difference in meaning between (25a) and (25b), since the difference can be attributed to covert expression from the verb. In other words, we may reject a polysemy analysis as in Figure 1a. At the same time, there is no requirement that the "basic meaning" of *over* should remain constant across all contexts of use; hence, the generality analysis of Figure 1b may be rejected as well.

4. Connectionist modeling of polysemy

I now show how the theoretical framework outlined in section 3 may be explicated and, to some extent, validated through a series of experiments carried out on Regier's connectionist model. I also propose an interpretation of the model which differs in important ways from that given by Regier himself. As suggested earlier, my claim is that the model should be primarily seen as a representation of the *ability to apply appropriate descriptions to situations*, rather than of the underlying neural processes and structures.

---

5. The same observation has been made by Heine, Claudi and Hünnemeyer (1991) and Sinha and Kuteva (1995).

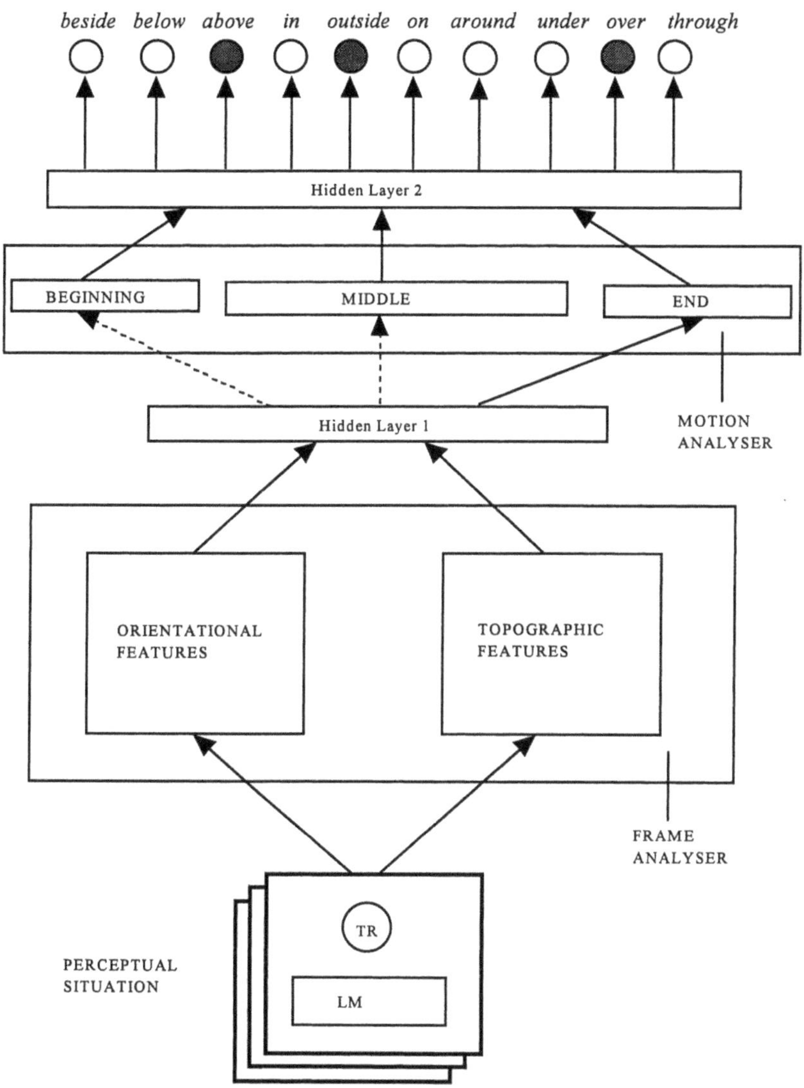

Figure 4. Regier's model of spatial categorization. A situation with a trajector (TR) in the region above the landmark (LM) is presented as input, and three output nodes, corresponding to the English prepositions *above*, *outside*, and *over* are activated as output.

4.1. Regier's model of spatial categorization

The model developed by Regier (1992, 1995, 1996) represents a form of constrained connectionism that emphasizes the importance of learning while at the same time imposing architectural constraints which do not emerge as a result of the interactions of simpler factors, but are hand-coded directly. In Figure 4, the model is presented graphically in a simplified and slightly modified form compared to Regier's diagrams.

Technically, the model is a structured, feed-forward connectionist network, using the error backpropagation learning rule (Rumelhart, Hinton & Williams 1986). A set of input patterns is to be associated with a corresponding set of output patterns. This is achieved by comparing the actual output pattern produced for every input pattern with the desired output pattern and calculating the error, i.e. the discrepancy between the two. The error is "backpropagated" down the network so that all the connection weights of the network are adjusted in such a way that the next time the input pattern is presented the actual output will be closer to the correct output, i.e., the error will be smaller. This process is iterated until the net converges, i.e., the combined error for the whole pattern set approaches zero. This is a (very informal) characterization of all "supervised" connectionist nets.[6] What is characteristic about Regier's model is (i) the nature of the input patterns, (ii) the nature of the output patterns, and (iii) the internal structure of the model.

4.1.1. Input patterns: situations

The input patterns consist of what Regier calls "movies". Each movie is a series of frames, each being a two-dimensional picture of two geometrical objects. In dynamic situations, the frames differ in the

6. "Supervised learning" implies the availability of a "teacher signal" and the adaptation of the weights based on minimizing the calculated error. "Unsupervised" nets are more self-organizing in managing without this signal. (cf. Hertz, Krogh & Palmer 1991)

relative position of the trajector. For purposes of illustration, Regier shows the frames overlapped on top of each other with a dashed line connecting the center of the trajector, frame-by-frame, and a little circle within the trajector in the final frame, as shown in Figure 5.

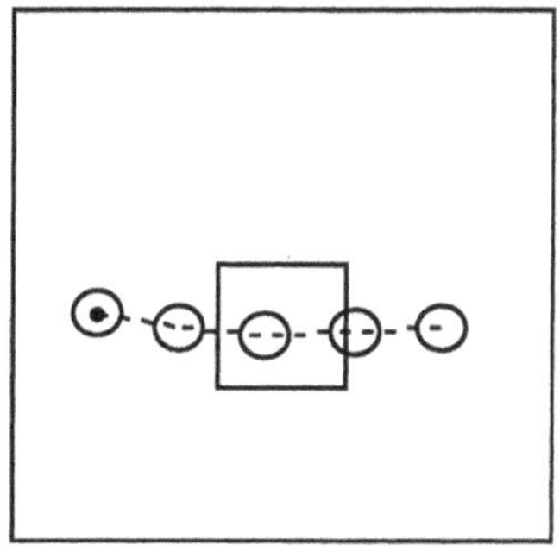

Figure 5. A dynamic situation, where the trajector moves through the landmark from left to right, the small black circle signifying the last position.

Regier interprets these representations as deriving more or less directly from sensory input, and therefore regards his model as being based in "perceptual grounding". However, it is clear that the representations are more abstract than that, consisting as they do of only two two-dimentional geometric "objects", where it is pre-determined which is the trajector and which is the landmark. In line with the framework presented in section 2, it is thus possible to regard the input patterns as schematic representations of real or virtual situations.

4.1.2. Output pattern: a paradigm of (closed-class) items

The output associated with a single situation during training is always a single output node, interpreted by Regier as a closed class element expressing the given spatial relation between trajector and landmark.[7] After training, however, when the net is tested on novel situations, several items standing in a paradigmatic relationship may be activated simultaneously by a given input situation, as illustrated in Figure 4.

4.1.3. Internal structure: adaptive parametric analysis

How does the net manage to perform this image-to-expression mapping (or transduction)? The built-in structure here is crucial. First, the information from each frame passes through what in Figure 4 is designated as the FRAME ANALYSER, which has two components. The ORIENTATIONAL component compares certain relational orientations such as the imaginary line that connects the centers of mass of the two objects (Center-of-Mass Orientation) with certain reference orientations such as Upright Vertical. The closer their overlap, the stronger will be the output signal of a certain connectionist unit. While the types of relational orientations are fixed in advance, the reference orientations are allowed to fluctuate during training, so that they will tend to take on a value most appropriate for the given language (training set). The result is that this component "learns" to detect relevant orientational features during training. The TOPOGRAPHIC component consists of a few "topographic maps" of the landmark and trajector objects. These are superimposed upon each other in such a way that the output will be a function of the relative overlap between the maps. Thus, this component has the potential to distinguish (at least) between no overlap, contact, partial overlap, and total overlap. Again, this potential will be utilized only if these distinctions are linguistically relevant.

The HIDDEN LAYER of units above the frame analyser (Hidden Layer 1) will contain the relevant information for a single frame. If

7. Cf. " ... a system which takes a set of such movies, each labeled as a positive example of some natural language spatial term ... and learns the association between the words and the events or relations which they describe" (Regier 1992: 1) and "these movies, each one labeled as an instance of some English spatial term, make up the training set for English" (Regier 1996: 123).

all the frames are identical, i.e., the situation is static, this layer could be mapped directly to the output layer. But stasis may be regarded as a special case of motion, with zero variation in the position of the trajector. The model therefore maintains a copy of the output of the feature detector for the first frame in a buffer, which in Figure 4 is called BEGINNING. Information from all but the last frame is kept in a condensed form in the buffer called MIDDLE, while the activation from the last frame is sent directly to Hidden Layer 2 – though for the sake of perspicuity, it is presented in Figure 4 as passing through a buffer called END.[8]

Notice that only the line from Hidden Layer 1 to END is not dashed in Figure 4; the dashed lines to BEGINNING and MIDDLE indicate connections whose weights are not modified. This signifies that only for the final frame of the motion sequence is the error signal allowed to be backpropagated down the network and reach the frame analyser, which implies that the model will be strongly biased toward the perceptual features present in END. As Regier (1996: 132) points out, "This means that the network learns to detect those static features that appear at the end of movies and is much less likely to detect those that do not. I shall refer to this as the *endpoint configuration constraint*." This constraint, deriving from considerations of simplicity, has some implications regarding polysemy, and we will return to it in section 6.1.

Regier attempts to motivate some of the inbuilt structures neurobiologically (e.g., the existence of orientation-sensitive cells in the visual cortex), but it is also possible, and more reasonable, considering the interpretation of the input patterns as situations, to see them as a *parametric analysis* of the relevant appropriateness conditions. This is especially evident in the use of the different "buffers" which is not based on any known neural structures, but on the results of *linguistic* analysis.

---

8. The terminology used here is my own, in line with that used in section 3 – the semantic category Path, having BEGINNING, MIDDLE, and END as values – rather than that of Regier, who uses the Fillmorian trio *Source–Path–Goal*.

As a whole, in the interpretation adopted here, Regier's model does not correspond to neural/causal processes that link perceptual input and linguistic output in a mechanical, behavioristic fashion, but to *the ability of a conscious language user to perceive that certain linguistic descriptions are appropriate for certain situations, while others are not*. A simulation with a particular converging set of input and output patterns has settled on a consistent set of appropriateness conditions. On the other hand, one which fails to converge during a large number of trials indicates that such set is missing, at least according to the adopted parametrization.

4.2. *Regier's model and holistic spatial semantics*

Adopting the hermeneutic/normative interpretation suggested above, Regier's model of the linguistic categorization of space can be regarded as an explication of the framework of situated embodiment, and the theory of holistic spatial semantics. However, if we compare Figure 4 with an upside-down version of the diagram in Figure 2, we notice directly that Regier's model incorporates a crucial limitation – *a single output unit* is associated with a given perceptual situation during training. Since Regier interprets each output unit as a single spatial term, this is clearly a reflection of the atomist assumption with respect to spatial semantics. The inadequacy of this assumption for a model of the expression of spatial meaning is perhaps clearest when Regier (1996: 25) discusses the Japanese examples in (26) and observes that "the Japanese spatial term *ue ni* ... seems to subsume English *above* and *on*".

(26)	a. *Kappu*	*wa*	*teeburu*	*no*	*ue*	*ni*	*aru.*
	cup	TOP	table	GEN	on		exist
	'The cup is on the table.'						
	b. *Ranpu*	*wa*	*teeburu*	*no*	*ue*	*ni*	*sagatte-iru.*
	lamp	TOP	table	GEN	above		hang
	'The lamp is hanging above the table.'						

However, *ue ni* should not be regarded as a *single* term in Japanese. As shown in section 3, Japanese displays a complementarity pattern where locative nouns such as *ue* express the category Region. On the other hand, *ni* is a postposition expressing the PLACE value of the category Path. In other words, what is clearly a composite expression is treated as a single entity.

This discrepancy between Regier's original model and holistic spatial semantics may be capitalized on and used for connectionist experimentation. The idea is to compare the performance of Regier's original atomistic model with a slightly more holistic extension of it with respect to its acquisition of polysemous spatial terms, and in this way to formulate a kind of adequacy test: If the atomistic model succeeds in associating a variety of perceptual situations corresponding to the different senses of a preposition with a single output unit (= spatial term), this would support the atomist assumption and the full specification model of polysemy. However, if an adequate association can *only be achieved in the context of other syntagmatic elements*, then this may be regarded as support for the theory of holistic spatial semantics.

Considering the representational limitations of the model (only two dimensions, no gravity, no role for perspective and goal-directedness, etc.), it should come as no surprise that only a limited amount of polysemy can be handled. In the case of *over*, only some of the twenty-two different senses of the Brugman/Lakoff analysis reviewed in section 2 can be simulated. Those that have to do with END-POINT FOCUS (8)–(9), COVERING (12)–(19), and REFLEXIVE trajectors (20)–(21) are unavailable.

But even the remaining ones contain some non-trivial variation. Consider the set of situations displayed in Figure 6, which may be given as input to the model when it is being taught the preposition *over*.

In examples 0, 1, 2, 3, 4, and 5 (see the upper left corner of each movie) the trajector is static and located *above*/*over* the landmark. In the next six examples (6–11), the trajector is moving around, but without leaving the region above the landmark. In examples 12 and 13, the trajector is in contact with the landmark while it moves from one side to the other. The case in examples 22, 23, and 24 is similar, but in these examples the landmark is extended vertically. Finally, in movies 14–21, the trajector is moving from one side of the landmark to the other, without ever touching it.

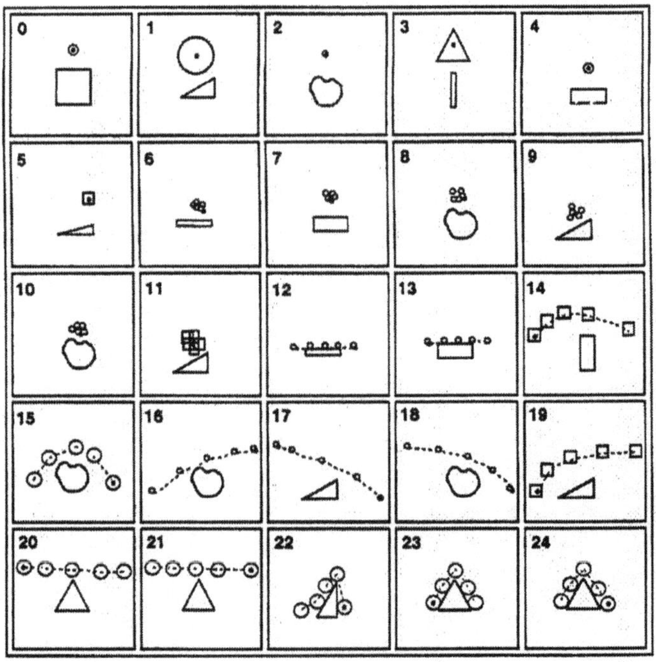

Figure 6. Example situations ("movies"), describable in part with the preposition *over* (the small circle in each movies signifies the final position of the trajector).

All of these situations can indeed be described by English spatial utterances including the preposition *over*: e.g., the descriptions *The circle is over the square* (1), *The circle is hovering over the rectangle* (7), *The circle is flying over the triangle* (17), etc. The point, however, is that while from the holistic spatial semantics perspective, it is these whole utterance-types which should be associated with the respective situations, according to the atomist assumption adopted by Regier, *over* is considered as the single "label" for each of these situations, or, rather, for the spatial relation involved in each, since the identity of the trajector and landmark objects is established in advance. Is there a way to test which of these interpretations is more appropriate?

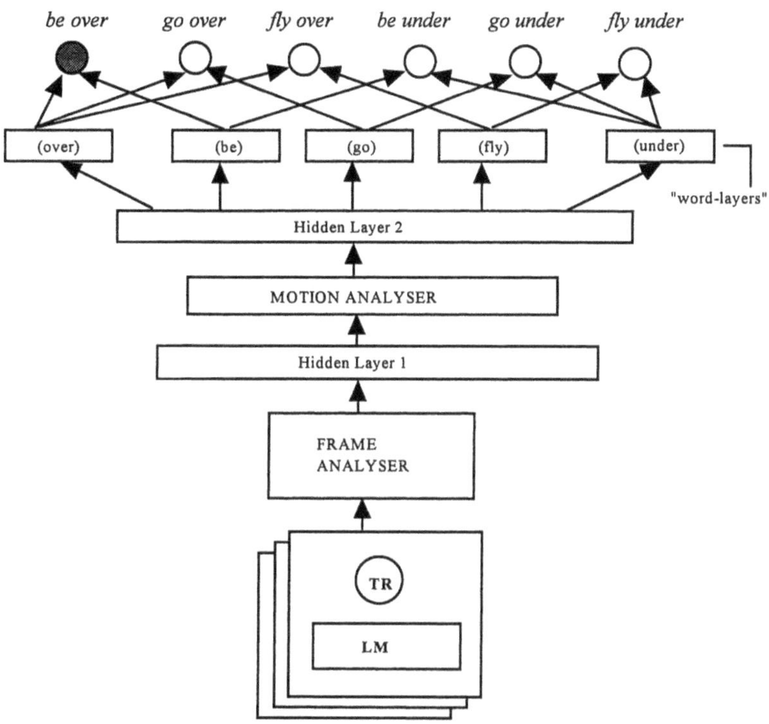

Figure 7. One of the extended versions of Regier's model, in which five "word layers" (of five nodes each) corresponding to the individual words are connected to the output nodes, interpreted as verb-preposition pairs

4.3. *Procedure*

In one set of experiments, training was performed with Regier's original model (cf. Figure 4). In another set, the same type of data was presented to modified versions of the model such as those described in Zlatev (1992) and Zlatev (1999). In the extended model shown in Figure 7, the output nodes are interpreted as verb-preposition pairs. This interpretation was enforced by the architecture of the network as well as by the way the input situations were presented – preceding the output nodes there were small hidden layers of five nodes each, one for each word in the lexicon, whose purpose was to make generalizations over the semantic contributions of the individual lexical items. I will refer to these as *word layers*. Each output node received input from exactly two word layers – one for the verb and one for the preposition.

The experiments focused on the English preposition *over*, and to a lesser extent on the preposition *in*. As in the standard training procedure, training sets consisting of situations such as those in Figure 6 were given as positive examples of the given expression. Simultaneously, a standard set of eighty movies exemplifying other types of spatial relations, e.g., those that could be described by *on* and *through*, were presented to the network as negative evidence.[9] The network was trained with the backpropagation algorithm until the error fell below a certain low level, i.e., until the net converged, and was subsequently tested on novel examples. The performance of the two models was compared with respect to the following criteria:

- *Convergence.* Could the network converge on the training set at all, given a set of input situations which vary considerably?
- *Generalization.* How well could the network generalize to novel situations?
- *Clustering.* It is well-known that feed-forward networks with hidden layers of units – of which Regier's original model has two and the extended model three – utilize these layers in order to re-structure the input space in a way that enhances categorization. By analyzing the activation patterns within these layers

9. The negative examples are necessary in order to save the model from excessive overgeneralization, when it is *not* being trained simultaneously on a set of terms standing in paradigmatic opposition. In this latter case, Regier shows how overgeneralization can be avoided by letting every positive example of a term provide *weak negative evidence* for all the others (cf. Regier 1996: chap. 4).

with statistical techniques such as hierarchical clustering analysis, it is possible to visualize this re-structuring (cf. Elman 1990). The question may be posed: How well does the net's restructuring of the input situations reflect the polysemous structure of words such as *over*?

4.4. Results

Before turning to the more complex polysemy of *over*, let us first look at a more modest kind of semantic variation. All the situations in Figure 8 may be described using the English word *in*. Examples 1, 3, 5, and 7 are static, 2 is dynamic, though in all these examples the trajector's location is entirely within the confines of the landmark. Examples 0, 4, 6, 8, and 9, on the other hand, depict situations in which the path begins outside, but ends inside the landmark. These latter examples may be (and from the perspective of normative grammar should be) described with the preposition *into*. Following the analysis suggested in Section 3, I will refer to these as Path:END uses of *in*.

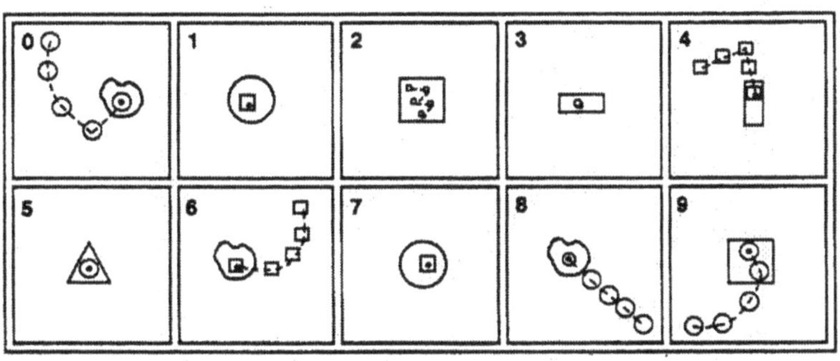

Figure 8. Situations that can be described (in part) with the preposition *in*.

How does Regier's model deal with such polysemy? The original model converged very rapidly – after approximately thirty *epochs*, i.e., iterations through the training set – when trained on examples such as those in Figure 8. Generalization to other examples describable as instances of *in* was also satisfactory. This result is not surprising since (i) all the examples share the same Region characteristics in the final frame, and (ii) Regier's model is biased towards features present in the final frame (cf. the endpoint configuration constraint mentioned earlier).

The next question to ask, however, is whether the difference between the subgroups is reflected in the representations of the relevant hidden layer. The answer to this question is negative. When the model is tested on the movies in Figure 8, the activation patterns in Hidden Layer 2 (cf. Figure 4) are almost completely identical. This is also not difficult to explain. In training the net to associate such situations with a *single* output node (interpreted as *in*), there is no reason for the situations to be treated as falling into different subcategories if a common basis for solving the categorization task can be found, in this case, inclusion in the final time-step.

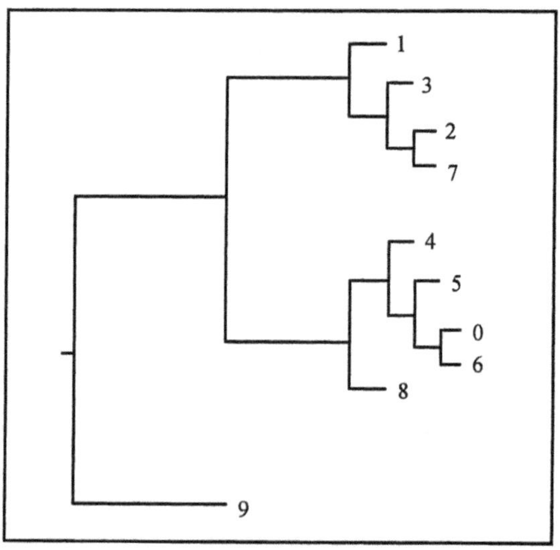

Figure 9. Hierarchical clustering analysis of the activation patterns in the top hidden layer of Regier's original model in response to the input situations for *in* displayed in Figure 8.

This conclusion was confirmed by hierarchical clustering analysis of the activation patterns, whose results are displayed as a binary-tree graph in Figure 9. This graph should be interpreted in the following way: The number appearing as a node in the tree is the same as the number of the example situation. Its place in the tree is determined by how close the corresponding activation pattern is to all the other patterns – the closer two patterns are (in terms of Euclidean distance), the closer they are on the horizontal axis of the graph. The distance between two clusters is the distance between their nearest two points.

Figure 9 shows that the minimal differences in the activation patterns cannot be reliably correlated with the two (or more) sub categories of situations. Admittedly, neither of the examples in the top branch involve Path:END uses, but the last member of this subclass (example 5) is placed in the other cluster for unknown reasons. Example 9, on the other hand, is regarded as the most distant from all the other examples.

Turning again to the polysemy of *over*, experiments were run where training sets similar to that shown in Figure 6 were presented to the two models. This time, unlike the training set for *in*, there is no obvious common abstraction to be found. That the trajector is at some point of time within the region above the landmark is a necessary but not a sufficient feature. In particular, if the situation is dynamic, *over* is appropriate either if the trajector remains in this region (as in examples 6 to 11) or if it starts on one side and moves to the other (12–24) – but not in intermediary cases, for example if the path of the trajector starts on one side of the landmark and ends above it as in the example in Figure 10. (Such examples were actually given as explicit negatives in the training set.) A similar problem involves the feature CONTACT: *over* is appropriate when CONTACT is present in the "side-to-side" type of situation (examples 12–13 in Figure 6), but not in situations of the "above" type.

These complexities appeared to be detrimental to the performance of the original model. When presented with a training set including examples such as those in Figure 6, *it failed to converge at all*. After a large number of trials, described in some detail in Zlatev (1992), it became clear that the model could learn to associate no more than two subcategories of *over*-examples with a single output node. For example, it could converge given a set consisting of examples such as 0–5 together with 6–11, in which case the net seemed to form an abstraction as with *in*. Or it could learn examples such as 6–11 together with 14–21 and then, with some difficulty, the network seemed to develop a disjunctive category. But irrespective of changes in the values in the different adjustable parameters, such as learning rate and size of the hidden layers, the original model failed in the categorization task with a training set of greater complexity.

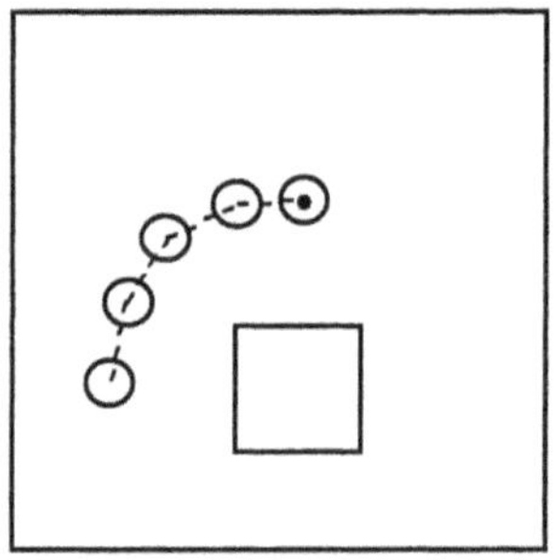

Figure 10. A negative example of *over*, which was problematic for the original model.

The performance of the extended model was considerably more successful. Given six separate training sets, corresponding to the six verb-preposition output nodes, the network converged (on approximately every second trial) in less than 100 epochs. Generalization was satisfactory and analysis of the activation patterns in the (*over*) word-layer using the hierarchical clustering technique provided the graph shown in Figure 11. Unlike the graph for *in* (Figure 9), this structure shows an intuitive clustering of the different sub categories of *over* situations. All the ABOVE region uses are clustered together and there is a tendency to separate the static ("be over") from the dynamic uses ("hover over"), even though this distinction was not reflected in the training sets – no "hover over" examples were presented during training – or in the output nodes. Similarly, the major division between CONTACT ("go over") and NON-CONTACT cases (the other examples) is captured, though again not in an absolutely hierarchical manner. This is hardly something to be deplored, considering that contact is largely irrelevant in the "crossing" uses of *over*. As a whole, the clustering may be said to reflect a kind of family-resemblance structure, derived by plotting the different uses of *over* in a use space that is defined by the parameters of the situations in which the word is appropriate and the linguistic context.

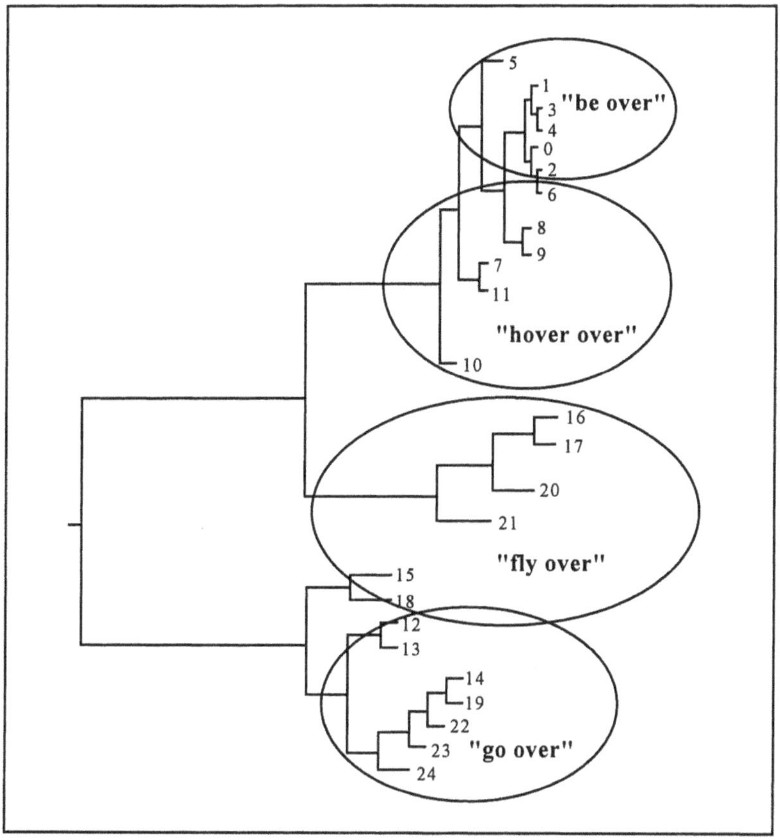

Figure 11. Hierarchical clustering analysis of the activation patterns in the (*over*) word-layer (cf. Figure 7) in response to the situations in Figure 6. (The labeling is performed after the fact and does not affect the categorization performed by the net.)

The results were similar to the activation patterns of other word layers, for example, when the extended model was exposed (after convergence on the training set described above) to a test set consisting of situations where the trajector (i) moves over-and-across the landmark, (ii) moves under-and-across the landmark, and (iii) moves to a place under the landmark. These three types of situation correspond to different clusters of activation patterns in the word layer for the verb *go*. The major division was between (i) on the one hand, and (ii) and (iii) on the other, with (ii) and (iii) separated as subclusters.

This can be interpreted in the following way: the modified model is not making any qualitative distinction between the polysemy of *over* (as reflected in Figure 11) and the semantic differences that can be attributed to a verb such as *go*. For those who believe that there should be such a distinction, this would be a deficiency of the model. But from the theoretical perspective presented in section 3, according to which polysemy is an "emergent" phenomenon involving contextual interpretations and not reified senses, this overlap is only to be expected.

4.5. *Regier's experiments concerning the role of "paradigmatic context"*

Similarly to the experiments described above, Regier compared the performance of his connectionist model with respect to polysemy in two types of learning conditions. However, he compared the atomist, a-contextual version of the model not with a model which takes into account the role of other elements in the syntagmatic sequence, but with a training arrangement in which several spatial terms are being learned simultaneously. In Regier's words, he modeled the influence of thc "paradigmatic context" on polysemy.

When Regier trained the net on *in* alone, he obtained practically identical results to the ones described above – the net converged easily, but there was no indication of polysemy in the hidden layer. However, when the model was trained on *in* and *through* at the same time, the PLACE and Path:END examples of *in* gave rise to separate clusters. Regier explains this result as follows:

> Although it might not be obvious ahead of time that this might be the case, it makes perfect sense: learning *through* forces the system to bring information concerning inclusion (or lack thereof) from earlier parts of the movie into its top-hidden-layer representation, since inclusion occurs in midmovie for *through*. That would serve to differentiate the two senses of *in*. ... It suggests that the basis of our intuition that the two senses of *in* are distinct may be found in the nature of the representations that are formed when we learn *in* together with other words. (Regier 1996: 165)

Here, Regier is acknowledging an aspect of meaning-holism – one very much emphasized in structuralism (e.g., Saussure 1916) – namely, that the semantic *value* of a lexical item can only be determined by considering its relationships to other items in the language.

But when Regier trained the model on a more extensive contrast set – *in* was taught together with *above*, *below*, *left*, *right*, *around*, *on*, *out of*, *through*, and *over* – the clear separation of the two senses of *in* reflected in the hidden layer disappeared. The reason was that in the same way that *through* had made "inclusion in midmovie" relevant, the other items had brought their own relevant features to the activation patterns (superiority, inferiority, etc.) and the patterns that formed in response to *in* had become rather opaque. What could save the paradigmatic context motivation account for *in*, Regier points out, would be some "as yet unspecified mechanism" that could ensure that only spatial terms such as *through* and *out of* would exert an influence on *in* and each other – though Regier admits to being agnostic as to what such a mechanism would be.

Holistic spatial semantics could be of some help here as well. Recall that the atomistic notion of "spatial relation" is deconstructed into seven general spatial semantic categories, two of which are Path and Region. It was suggested in section 3 that these are conflated by the prepositions in the Indo-European languages, but morphosyntactically distinguished in Japanese. Given this analysis, it becomes clear that *in*, *out of*, *through*, and *into* would constitute a *subclass*: all four expressions express the INTERIOR value of the category Region, while they differ with respect to Path. Similarly *off*, *on*, *across*, and *onto* would be associated by the Region value SURFACE, while expressing different Paths (cf. Table 1 in section 6). Considering this, it is not unreasonable to suppose that a learning mechanism of somewhat different character than Regier's would partition the use space in a way which would reflect the fact that expressions from a subclass exercise a stronger syntagmatic context effect *within* the class, than outside it.

With respect to modeling the polysemy of *over*, Regier reports somewhat better performance when the preposition is being learned by itself than what my experiments showed. In particular, the original model converged on a training set consisting of three types of *over*-situations: static *over*, across-*over* with contact, and across-*over* without contact. However, one notices that the shape of the path of the trajector is much more uniform in Regier's test set (Regier 1996: Figure 7.7) than in the one in Figure 6, and I would also suspect that the set of negatives did not include examples such as that in (this chapter's) Figure 10. In any case, visualization of the activation patterns in the hidden layer as well as hierarchical clustering analysis show no sign of polysemy. The network seemed to have found an abstraction over the three subtypes, as was the case with *in*, though the nature of this abstraction is less obvious because of the problematic role of CONTACT, which is disallowed in the static case but allowed in the crossing case. Again, however, when *over* was trained with the full contrast set, i.e., together with *above*, *below*, *left*, *right*, *around*, *on*, *out of*, *through*, and *in*, the three different subtypes of situations clustered very clearly. Regier (1996: 171) summarizes the results of both my and his experiments as follows: "This set of experiments as a whole then illustrates the importance of both syntagmatic and paradigmatic context in the development of polysemous representations."

5. The continuum from generality to homonymy

5.1. Implications of the experiments

As described in the previous section, Regier's model failed to converge when attempting to associate a more extensive training set with a single node, interpreted as a single spatial term. Even when it could converge on a given polysemous training set, it tended to neutralize the differences between the examples, unless it was presented with a syntagmatic or, as in Regier's experiments, paradigmatic context. These results may, therefore, be seen as providing some evidence against the full specification interpretation of polysemy. Their major purpose has been, however, to explicate the alternative view of the phenomenon suggested in section 3, i.e. polysemy as clusters of contextual interpretations (that is, non-reificational polysemy), as illustrated in Figure 11.

From this perspective, polysemy and generality differ only in the degree to which the particular uses of the expression cluster in distinguishable types. *Over* is properly regarded as more polysemous than *go* not because it is associated with a larger network of senses in the mental lexicon than *go* which – at least with respect to *going over* and *going under* – has a single, general sense, but because the uses of *go* are more closely related and normally perceived as indistinguishable. This implies that there should be a *continuum* between polysemy and generality, with total homonymy – where the uses of an expression are normally not perceived as being related at all – and total monosemy constituting limiting cases. This continuum is illustrated in Figure 12.

We are now in a position to see why the question expressed in the title of this chapter presents a context which, in the words of Pirsig, "is too small for the truth of the answer". As pointed out, behind this question lies the presumption that a given expression is either monosemous and that any semantic variation is the result of contextual modulation, or that it is truly polysemous (these are the alternatives illustrated in Figure 1). But as the discussion in this chapter has tried to show, the contextual view of polysemy presented in sections 3 and 4 makes the distinction between "mentally represented senses" and "contextual interpretations" nonsensical. This distinction is meaningful only on the assumption of meaning-atomism and reification, which are rejected on conceptual as well as empirical grounds within the framework of situated embodiment. In their place, the non-reificational and holistic conception of lexical meaning as use-potential has been proposed; according to this view, words are learned in particular linguistic and situational contexts (language games) whose parts co-determine each other's meaning.

The basic argument in this chapter can thus be summarized by means of the following implicational relation: *no reification of meaning => no polysemy/generality dichotomy.*

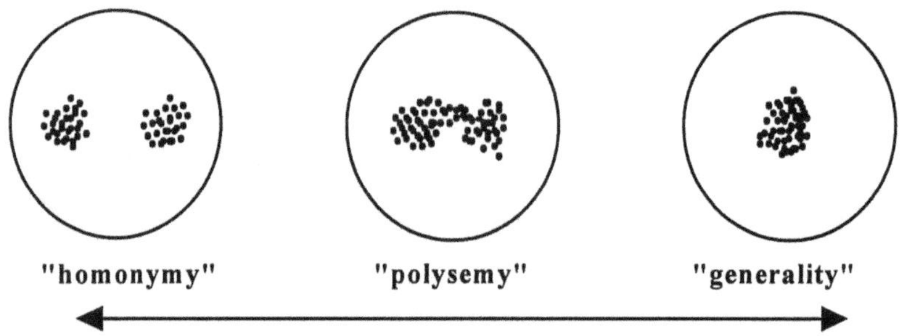

Figure 12. The continuum from generality to homonymy. Each dot is a particular contextual interpretation of a given expression in a multidimensional use-space (inadequately presented as a 2-dimensional circle).

5.2. Complementary evidence: methodological indeterminacy

The implicational statement can also be turned around: *No polysemy/generality dichotomy => no reification of meaning.* This way of framing the argument has been presented in an important paper by Geeraerts (1993), who convincingly shows that there is an instability in the distinction between polysemy and homonymy on the one hand, and generality on the other.[10]

10. Geeraerts refers to semantic generality as "vagueness", but this terminology easily leads to confusion, since one tends to think of vagueness in terms of the referential vagueness associated with an expression such as *tall*, and this is rather different from the generality of, e.g., *grandmother* with respect to 'mother's mother' and 'father's mother'.

The major thrust of Geeraerts' argument is that there is a methodological indeterminacy involved in attempting to separate polysemy and generality. He reviews a number of tests traditionally used to separate one from the other. One is the "logical test": if a statement of the type "This is X, but not X" can be true, then X must be ambiguous and not general, as in (27). Another group of tests pertain to semantic constraints on the use of anaphoric expressions: if an anaphoric interpretation is possible, then the two uses have the same sense; if not, the expression must be polysemous; see Geeraerts' example (28).

(27) *This is a bank* (i.e., financial institution) *but not a bank* (i.e., river bed).
(28) **At midnight the ship passed the port* (i.e., the harbor) *and so did the bartender* (i.e., pass the wine).

The indeterminacy between polysemy and generality is reflected in two ways. On the one hand, different tests may yield contradictory results with respect to a particular expression. For example, by the logical test the word *door* is polysemous, since (29) may be asserted. At the same time, (30) is felicitous, even though anaphoric *it* refers to the second sense of *door*, and hence *door* should be general.

(29) *This is a door* (i.e., a door-frame), *but not a door.*
(30) *He went through the door and shut it.*

On the other hand, one and the same test may yield different results depending on variations in context. In (31) – an example borrowed from Deane (1988) – the homonymous word *bank* may appear as semantically general in a context of explicit comparison according to the "identity-of-sense" anaphora test.

(31) *Financial banks resemble those that you find by rivers: they control, respectively, the flow of money and water.*

Thus, not only is there a continuum between homonymy and generality – also pointed out by Tuggy (1993) on the basis of the Cognitive Grammar notion of *entrenchment* – but a given expression is not fixed to a particular point on this continuum, yet may shift in either direction depending on the context it appears in. This conclusion has implications that go beyond the question of the proper analysis of polysemy, since, as Geeraerts (1993: 228) writes, "The distinction between vagueness and polysemy involves the question whether a particular piece of semantic information is part of the underlying semantic structure of the item, or is the result of a contextual (and hence pragmatic) specification."

By undermining the distinction between polysemy and generality, the distinction between "underlying semantic structure" and "contextual interpretation" are undermined simultaneously, and more generally, the reificational view of lexical meaning, according to which "meanings" are objects of some kind (in the mental lexicon). The convergence between this argument and the thesis presented in this chapter should be obvious.

6. Possible objections

Before concluding this chapter, I wish to briefly address two possible objections to the argument denying a stable distinction between polysemy and generality, and reificational meaning in general. In truth, the objections would require more space for a proper answer, but since that is not available in the present chapter, the reader is referred to Zlatev (1997) for a more complete discussion.

6.1. The systematicity of polysemy

The first objection goes as follows: "In blurring the distinction between polysemy and generality you sacrifice the ability to account for the systematicity of polysemy, as captured by cognitive linguistic analyses in terms of networks of senses, such as the Brugman/Lakoff analysis of *over*." The systematic and motivated character of polysemy, reflected in the existence of what Taylor (1993) calls "patterns of polysemization" across different lexical items – and across different languages – is a phenomenon which calls for an explanation. However, an explanation need not necessarily be couched in terms of a full specification model of polysemy and involving something akin to Lakoff's image-schema transformations.

First, we may observe that separating the two semantic categories Region and Path allows a number of generalizations concerning polysemy. If we provisionally assume that each of the English prepositions in Table 1 has as its basic spatial sense the one shown in the table, then much of the prepositions' spatial polysemy can be generalized to three basic patterns:

- Path:PLACE → Path:END ("Resulting state")
- Path:MIDDLE → Path:PLACE ("Virtual motion")
- Path:MIDDLE → Path:END ("End-point focus")

Table 1. English prepositions classified according to the categories Path and Region

Region	Path			
	PLACE	BEGINNING	MIDDLE	END
INTERIOR	*in*	*out-of*	*through*	*into*
SURFACE	*on*	*off*	*across*	*onto*
PROXIMATE	*at*	*from*	*past*	*to*
LATERAL	*beside*		*along*	
SUPERIOR	*above*		*over*	
INFERIOR	*below*		*under*	

The first pattern states that a preposition with Path-value PLACE may be used to express Path-value END – in the appropriate context – while maintaining its value for the category Region. Examples of the application of the first two patterns are provided in (32) and (33); the third has already been illustrated in examples (8) and (9).

(32) *John fell on the ground.*
Region:SURFACE, Path:PLACE → Path:END

(33) *The path goes along the river.*
Region:LATERAL, Path:MIDDLE → Path:PLACE

Using the terminology of "patterns" implies that the analysis is purely descriptive. To provide an *explanation* for these patterns, we would need to answer the question: What is the source of their motivation? The answer to this question in the present framework is still tentative, but it is illustrative to see how it differs substantially from that of "main-line" (Lakovian) cognitive semantics.

In the analysis of Lakoff (1987) and Ekberg (1993, 2001), polysemy patterns are explained through image-schema transformations, whose naturalness is due to general cognitive processes such as the (mental) scanning of "the path of a moving object until it comes to rest, and then to focus on where it is" (Lakoff 1987: 442). The motivation is therefore entirely cognitive and language-independent. Transformations such as End-point focus would be equally present in the minds of all people, but only for some expressions and in some languages would they be utilized for language, as stated by Lakoff:

> In each of these cases, the metaphorical and metonymic models exist in the conceptual system independently of the given expression. [...] Similarly, the schemas for *over* exist for expressions in the spatial domain independent of the existence of *oversee*, *overlook*, and *look over*. What one learns when one learns these words is which of the independently existing components of their meaning are actually utilized. (Lakoff 1987: 438)

Apart from the fact that this view is strongly ethnocentric – English and other European languages appear as the clearest reflections of the human conceptual system – it faces problems such as the following:

- *Methodological*. The evidence for the linguistic relevance of such language-independent processes is (so far) purely linguistic. No psycholinguistic results of mental scanning during the interpretation of, e.g., *Sam lives over the hill* – unlike the results of the scanning of true mental images obtained by

Shepard and Cooper (1982) – have been reported, nor are such results likely.

- *Empirical.* The view of language acquisition that this conception implies is grossly conceptualist while, as mentioned earlier, the facts of language acquisition point towards a much more epigenetic model in which semantic structures emerge as a product of the interaction between language-independent experience and linguistic convention (Bowerman 1996).
- *Conceptual.* The notion of "image-schema transformation" suggests the existence of explicitly represented senses – a transformation needs an input and an output – which is in line with Lakoff's full specification view of polysemy (cf. section 2), but as argued in this chapter, this creates a false dichotomy between polysemy and generality.

What from the present perspective appears to be the motivation (or "naturalness") behind the phenomenon of motivated polysemy is mutually enhancing factors such as the following:

- *Pragmatic.* Practical knowledge of the type that when an object reaches the END of a path, this leads to a state which is similar to the one which would have obtained if the object had already been located in the respective PLACE.
- *Functional-communicative.* Given the availability of such knowledge – and suitable principles of linguistic interpretation – languages will tend to economize on formal distinctions.
- *Learning.* Certain patterns of polysemy may be easier to learn than more "unnatural" ones.

This last set of factors may be illustrated on the workings of Regier's model (cf. Section 4.1). While Regier never addresses the issue in these terms, the "Resulting state" polysemy pattern is motivated by the endpoint configuration constraint. Recall that independently of considerations of polysemy, the model incorporates the principle that a dynamic situation is provided with the correct linguistic description only at the last-time step of the motion event. Only then is the error calculated and backpropagated. This constraint turns out to have a number of ramifications, one of which is that the model learns much easier and generalizes more adequately when trained on a term corresponding simultaneously to Path:PLACE and Path:END situations, than a hypothetical term expressing Path:PLACE and Path:BEGINNING situations. This leads Regier (1992) to make a generalization, which he formulates as a hypothetical universal prediction: "The use of a single word to denote either static location in some configuration or motion into that configuration will be more likely to appear in a language than the use of a single word to denote either static location in some configuration or motion out of that configuration" (1992: 149).

Thus, Regier's model suggests a way of approaching the "cognitive reality" of patterns of polysemization. Instantiations of such patterns are simply *more likely* than other kinds of polysemy. The two sides of the image-schema transformations may be regarded as co-attractors for the distribution of uses of a single linguistic form. This means that it is not necessarily the case that one use type has cognitive priority with respect to the other, i.e., that one is the "prototype" and the other the "extension" in any psychologically real way. Furthermore, these "extended senses" need not be regarded as independently existing mental entities, but rather as part of the word's use-potential which a certain context may utilize. The question whether the extended senses exist (in the mental lexicon) independently of this context is a meaningless question.

6.2. *The creativity of language use*

The second objection runs as follows: "If lexical meaning is as context-sensitive as you claim, it would be virtually impossible to produce and understand a word in a totally novel context. You would face the same predicament as the behaviorists, who could not explain 'the creativity of language use', i.e., the ability to produce and understand novel utterances, as pointed out already by Chomsky (1959). Creativity requires semantic compositionality, based on stable, context-independent meanings."

It is indeed indisputable that all normal language users – including children from about the age of two – are able to understand and produce novel utterances. What *is* disputable is that this ability requires the postulation of context-independent meanings and a compositional mechanism for their combination.

Consider again the schematic presentation of a minimal, differentiated language game (MDLG) displayed in Figure 2. After having proposed that linguistic knowledge may be characterized in terms of such structures, it is only natural to suggest that linguistic creativity may be viewed as the ability to extrapolate (analogize) from the repertoire of MDLGs to novel utterances and/or situations. This is not at all as unrealistic as it might seem at first. The MDLG analysis does not imply that all aspects of linguistic knowledge are equally context-dependent. This, again, is something which may be described as a continuum. Least dependent are cases where one-to-one mappings are fairly adequate, as in the relationship between many nouns and their referents. Then, there are cases with systematic many-to-many mappings, involving whole classes of lexical (and grammatical) items, for which spatial expressions provide ample illustration. Next come item-specific dependencies involving covert expression, and finally the pervasive though almost invisible dependence on the background of practices. Viewing linguistic knowledge in this way – rather than imposing an arbitrary dividing line separating "semantics" and "grammar" on the one hand and "pragmatics" on the other – resonates much better with the *robustness* of the process of linguistic creativity. Furthermore, the (implicit) systematicity inherent in such mappings – combined with a powerful analogizing capacity – is not to be underestimated when it comes to the ability to deal with novelty (cf. Zlatev 1997: chap. 7; Zlatev 2000).

The common denominator in the replies to both objections is that *systematicity does not require reification*. With its ability to deal with analogue "emergent" structures and non-linear processes, connectionism offers an important conceptual tool for the study of semantics, in a way which avoids the reificational trap that language itself tends to lead us into (Wittgenstein 1953).

7. Summary

The rather long argument presented in this chapter may briefly be summarized by the following seven statements:

1. The question whether spatial expressions are polysemous or semantically general arises from an inadequate *reificational* and *atomistic* conception of lexical meaning; the question should therefore be "unasked".
2. The general framework of *situated embodiment* and the theory of *holistic spatial semantics* may serve as a basis for an alternative conception of lexical meaning in terms of use-potential, a notion which is non-reificational and holistic.
3. Analyzing the meaning of spatial prepositions in terms of use-potential predicts the existence of a continuum ranging from typical cases of homonymy to typical cases of generality, with typical cases of polysemy falling in between.
4. A general account of lexical meaning as use-potential predicts the instability between polysemy and generality observed by, e.g., Geeraerts (1993).
5. This perspective on lexical meaning is not incompatible with the systematicity of (spatial) polysemy, though it suggests an explanation of the phenomenon in terms of functionally motivated co-attractors rather than in terms of image-schema transformations.
6. The ability to understand and produce novel utterances does not constitute a counterexample to an analysis according to statements (1)–(5), since it may be seen as the ability to extrapolate and/or analogize from existing minimal, differentiated language games.
7. In providing a tool for conceptualizing non-reificational structures and processes, as well as some empirical validation for their adequacy, connectionism can play an important role in the

study of linguistic meaning. An important requirement is, however, that connectionist models are interpreted as *explications of linguistic knowledge,* implying normative notions such as conditions of appropriateness, rather than as implementations of neural/causal processes, as is most often the case.

References

Bowerman, Melissa
1996 Learning how to structure space for language: A cross-linguistic perspective. In: Paul Bloom, Mary A. Peterson, Lynn Nadel and Merill F. Garret (eds.), *Language and Space*. Cambridge, MA: MIT Press.

Brugman, Claudia
1981 Story of *over*. M.A. thesis, University of California, Berkeley.

Chomsky, Noam
1959 Review of B.F. Skinner (1957), *Verbal Behavior*, New York; Appleton-Century-Crofts. *Language* 35: 26–58.
1965 *Aspects of a Theory of Syntax.* Cambridge, MA: The MIT Press.

Deane, Paul
1988 Polysemy and cognition. *Lingua* 75: 325–361.

Dreyfus, Hubert
1991 *Being-in-the-World: A Commentary on Heidegger's "Being and Time, Division I"*. Cambridge, MA: The MIT Press.
1993 [1972] *What Computers (Still) Can't Do: A Critique of Artificial Reason*, 3rd revised edition. Cambridge, MA: The MIT Press.

Ekberg, Lena
1993 Slutpunktfokus i svenskan [End point focus in Swedish]. In: Anders Holmberg and Kent Larsson (eds.), *Svenskans beskrivning 20*, 118–130. Lund: Lund University Press.
2001 Transformations on the Path-schema, and a minimal lexicon. *Studia Linguistica* 53: 301–323.

Elman, Jeffrey
1990 Finding structure in time. *Journal of Cognitive Science* 14: 179–211.

Fillmore, Charles
1982 Frame semantics. In: Linguistic Society of Korea (ed.), *Linguistics in the morning calm*, 111–138. Seoul: Hanshin.

Forrester, Michael
1996 *Psychology of Language: A Critical Introduction*. London: Sage Publications.

Geeraerts, Dirk
1993 Vagueness's puzzles, polysemy's vagaries. *Cognitive Linguistics* 4: 223–272.

Halliday, M.A.K.
1976 The form of a functional grammar. In: Günther Kress (ed.), *Halliday: System and Function in Language*, 7–25. Oxford: Oxford University Press.

Heine, Bernd, Ulrike Claudi and Friederike Hünnemeyer
1991 *Grammaticalization: A Conceptual Framework.* Chicago: The University of Chicago Press.

Hertz, John, Anders Krogh and Richard G. Palmer
1991 *Introduction to the Theory of Neural Computation*. Redwood City: Addison-Wesley.

Itkonen, Esa
1978 *Grammatical Theory and Metascience: A Critical Investigation into the Methodological and Philosophical Foundations of 'Autonomous' Linguistics*. Amsterdam: John Benjamins.
1983 *Causality in Linguistic Theory: A Critical Investigation into the Philosophical and Methodological Foundations of 'Non-autonomous' Linguistics*. Bloomington: Indiana University Press.

Johnson, Mark
1987 *The Body in the Mind.* Chicago: The University of Chicago Press.

Lakoff, George
1987 *Women, Fire, and Dangerous Things: What Categories Reveal about the Mind.* Chicago: The University of Chicago Press.

Langacker, Ronald
1987 *Foundations of Cognitive Grammar*, Volume 1: *Theoretical Prerequisites*. Stanford: Stanford University Press.

Levinson, Steven
1983 *Pragmatics*. Cambridge: Cambridge University Press.

Miller, George A. and Philip N. Johnson-Laird
1976 *Language and Perception.* Cambridge, MA: Harvard University Press.

Pawley, Andrew and Frances H. Syder
1983 Two puzzles for linguistic theory: Nativelike selection and nativelike fluency. In: J.C. Richards and R.W. Schmidt (eds.), *Language and Communication*, 191–227. London: Longman.

Regier, Terry
1992 *The Acquisition of Lexical Semantics for Spatial Terms: A Connectionist Model of Perceptual Categorisation*. Ph.D. dissertation. TR–92–062. International Computer Science Institute, University of California, Berkeley.
1995 A model of the human capacity for categorizing spatial relations. *Cognitive Linguistics* 6: 63–88.
1996 *The Human Semantic Potential: Spatial Language and Constrained Connectionism*. Cambridge, MA: The MIT Press.

Rumelhart, David, Geoffrey Hinton and Ronald Williams
1986 Learning internal representations by error propagation. In: David Rumelhart and James McClelland (eds.), *Parallel Distributed-Processing: Explorations in the Microstructure of Cognition,* Volume 1, 318–362. Cambridge, MA: The MIT Press

Sandra, Dominiek and Sally Rice
1995 Network analyses of prepositional meaning: Mirroring whose mind – the linguist's or the language user's? *Cognitive Linguistics* 6: 89–130.

Saussure, Ferdinand de
1916 *Cours de Linguistique Générale*. Paris: Payot.

Searle, John
1983 *Intentionality: An Essay in the Philosophy of Mind*. Cambridge: Cambridge University Press.
1992 *The Rediscovery of Mind*. Cambridge, MA: The MIT Press.

Shepard, Roger N. and Lynn A. Cooper
1982 *Mental Images and their Transformations*. Cambridge, MA: The MIT Press.

Sinha, Chris and Tanya Kuteva
1995 Distributed spatial semantics. *Nordic Journal of Linguistics* 18: 167–199.

Talmy, Leonard
1985 Lexicalization patterns: Semantic structure in lexical forms. In: Timothy Shopen (ed.), *Language Typology and Syntactic Description,* Volume 3: *Grammatical Categories and the Lexicon*, 57–149. Cambridge: Cambridge University Press.

Taylor, John R.
1993 Prepositions: Patterns of polysemization and strategies of disambiguation. In: Cornelia Zelinsky-Wibbelt (ed.), *The Semantics of Prepositions*, 151–175. Berlin: Mouton de Gruyter.

Tuggy, David
1993 Ambiguity, polysemy, and vagueness. *Cognitive Linguistics* 4: 273–290.

Wittgenstein, Ludwig
1953 *Philosophical Investigations.* Oxford: Basil Blackwell.

Zlatev, Jordan
1992 A study of perceptually grounded polysemy in a spatial micro-domain. TR–92–048, International Computer Science Institute, University of California, Berkeley.
1997 *Situated Embodiment: Studies in the Emergence of Spatial Meaning*. Stockholm: Gotab.
1999 Situated embodied semantics and connectionist modelling. In: Jens Allwood and Peter Gärdenfors (eds.), *Cognitive Semantics*, 175–194. Amsterdam: John Benjamins,.
2000 Connectionism and language understanding. In: Denis Burnham, Sudaporn Luksaneeyanawin, Chris Davis and Mathieu Lafourcade (eds.), *Interdisciplinary Approaches to Language Processing*, 166–192. Bangkok: NECTEC.
2003 Holistic spatial semantics of Thai. In: Eugene Casad and Gary Palmer (eds.), *Cognitive Linguistics and Non-Indo European Languages*, 305–336. Berlin: Mouton de Gruyter.

List of contributors

Jens Allwood
Dept. of Linguistics
University of Göteborg
Box 200
SE 405 30 Göteborg
Sweden
e-mail: <jens@ling.gu.se>

Hubert Cuyckens
Department of Linguistics
University of Leuven
Blijde-Inkomststraat 21
3000 Leuven
Belgium
e-mail: <hubert.cuyckens@arts.kuleuven.ac.be>

René Dirven
Beekstraat 39
2800 Mechelen
Belgium
e-mail: <rene.dirven@pandora.be>

Dirk Geeraerts
Department of Linguistics
University of Leuven
Blijde-Inkomststraat 21
3000 Leuven
Belgium
e-mail: <dirk.geeraerts@arts.kuleuven.ac.be>

Stefan Grondelaers
Department of Linguistics
University of Leuven
Blijde-Inkomststraat 21
3000 Leuven
Belgium
e-mail: <stefan.grondelaers@arts.kuleuven.ac.be>

Theo A.J.M. Janssen
Faculteit der Letteren
Vrije Universiteit
De Boelelaan 1105
1081 HV Amsterdam
The Netherlands
e-mail: <thajm.janssen@let.vu.nl>

Hanna Lehti-Eklund
Nordiska språk och nordisk litteratur
University of Helsinki
PB 24
00014 Helsinki
Finland
e-mail: <Hanna.Lehti-Eklund@Helsinki.fi>

Laura Michaelis
Department of Linguistics
295 UCB
University of Colorado
Boulder, CO 80309
USA
e-mail: <michaeli@spot.Colorado.EDU>

Kurt Queller
Department of English
University of Idaho
P.O. Box 441102
Moscow, ID 83844-1102
USA
e-mail: <kqueller@uidaho.edu>

Sally Rice
Dept. of Linguistics
Faculty of Arts
4-60 Assiniboia Hall
University of Alberta
Edmonton, T6G 2E7
Canada
e-mail: <sally.rice@ualberta.ca>

Augusto Soares da Silva
Universidade Catolica Portuguesa
Faculdade de Filosofia de Braga
Largo da Faculdade, 1
4710-297 Braga
Portugal
e-mail: <assilva@facfil.ucp.pt>

John Taylor
Linguistics Section
School of Languages, University of Otago
P.O. Box 56
Dunedin
New Zealand
e-mail: <john.taylor@stonebow.otago.ac.nz>

David Tuggy
Camino Nacional 809 #12
Fraccionamiento Orquídeas
CP 68010 Oaxaca, Oax.
México
e-mail: <david_tuggy@sil.org>

Satoshi Uehara
Graduate School of International Cultural Studies
Tohoku University
Kawauchi, Aoba-ku, Sendai, 980-8576
Japan
e-mail: <uehara@intcul.tohoku.ac.jp>

Claude Vandeloise
Louisiana State University, Department of French
Baton Rouge, Louisiana 70803
USA
e-mail: <Vdllsu@aol.com>

Christof Vanden Eynde
Visserij 136
9000 Gent
Belgium
e-mail: <christof.vandeneynde@pandora.be>

Jordan Zlatev
Department of Linguistics and Phonetics
Helgonabacken 12
Lund University
223 62 Lund
Sweden
e-mail: <Jordan.Zlatev@ling.lu.se>

Index

abduction 215f, 218, 229f, 232, 249
abstract level 351, 393, 413, 445
adjective 2, 20, 35, 52f, 142, 200, 202f, 333, 345, 363–365, 372–375, 378, 381, 433
argument structure 166, 168f, 171, 174, 176, 180, 185, 190, 197, 203
aspect 24f, 163, 165, 179, 181, 184, 187, 190–192, 194, 197f, 204, 254, 259, 366, 372, 378, 453, 456, 489
category membership 72, 371f, 428f, 435, 444
cognitive mechanisms 243, 248
compatibility principle 100, 107
complex primitives 393–396, 399, 401, 403, 410–412, 415, 418f, 421
comprehension and production 212, 216, 354f, 405, 413f
concord construction 172–175, 178, 182, 184, 187, 189, 190, 194, 203f
conjuncts 123–126, 130, 132f, 135f, 138, 140
connectionist modeling 447–449, 459, 462, 464, 466, 469, 478, 491
construal 8, 47, 172, 174, 184f, 189, 191, 193, 204, 211, 228–232, 237, 244, 272, 286, 288, 293, 303, 316, 333f, 350, 437
construction grammar 23f, 163, 365
constructional meaning 3, 25, 54, 163, 165f, 179, 181f, 204
containment 20, 188, 393–395, 399f, 402–412, 414–419, 421
control 20, 146, 287, 299, 344, 393, 395, 397f, 400, 402–407, 411–414, 416f, 421
creativity 15, 224, 488f
criteria for polysemy 36, 323, 345, 348
cross-linguistic 247, 249, 264, 274f, 350, 365, 373, 386, 388, 454, 462
decontextualization 6, 357
dehomonymization 281, 315
deprototypicalization 309, 311f, 315, 319
determination of meaning 40, 43, 46, 52, 58, 61f
diachrony 363, 377f, 380, 384, 386, 389
discourse
– markers 20f, 128–130, 132f, 135, 139, 143–146, 149, 153–157
– particles 128, 132, 150, 153–155, 433, 440
elaboration 19, 45, 67, 90, 166, 173f, 179, 181f, 213, 218, 233, 235, 295f, 302, 316, 330, 350f, 395, 403f, 406f, 411
emergence 223, 230, 233, 236, 250, 252, 257, 259–270, 272–274, 326, 329, 334, 337, 339, 349–352, 387f
en 393–395, 402f, 412f, 417f, 421
epigenesis 447, 455f, 487
extension 30, 40–42, 75f, 108, 182, 212, 217–220, 225, 232, 243, 251, 267, 271, 273, 275, 293, 295, 297, 301, 305f, 311, 317, 328, 330, 336, 340, 350, 363, 386, 399, 405–407, 415, 430–432, 469, 488
family resemblance 1f, 42, 217, 393, 395, 398–401, 409f, 415, 419, 421
fixed expression 243, 254f, 259–261, 263, 265–267, 271f

folk theories 14, 429, 438, 444f
force dynamics 20, 286–288, 297, 299, 316
frequency 2, 72, 74–77, 81–83, 85–87, 134f, 156, 188f, 204, 243, 249, 252, 254, 256f, 259, 260–263, 265–272, 274–276, 301–303, 312f, 365, 370, 379, 389
genitive 93, 108–111, 113, 115, 124, 366
Gesamtbedeutung 'common meaning' 29–31, 33, 36, 38–43, 46, 62
gradability 104, 363, 374f, 378
gradable adjectives 429, 432f, 438, 443
grammatical function 130, 163, 165, 167, 177, 243, 386
grammaticalization 21, 123, 125, 128–130, 132, 138, 144f, 152–154, 156, 247, 249f, 253, 260, 264, 269, 274, 293, 303, 305, 363, 386
Grundbedeutung 'basic meaning' 29, 31–33, 36, 38–43, 46, 62
hedges 21, 427–429, 431, 436–441, 444f
hermeneutics 448, 459, 468
heterosemy 94, 103
hierarchy of concepts 393, 403f
homonymy 29, 35–38, 40f, 55–62, 248, 315f, 348, 359, 381, 406, 447, 449, 480f, 482, 484, 490
idealized cognitive model 212–216, 223
idiosyncrasy 55, 165, 170, 256f, 344, 365, 436
image schema 204, 281f, 289f, 293–296, 301f, 309, 311, 315–317, 319, 393, 395, 403, 407–410, 421, 457
image-schema transformation 2, 238, 293, 309f, 314–316, 318, 450, 485–488, 490
implicatures 102, 188, 304, 433, 439–442
implicit/explicit type-shifting 163, 175, 204
in 20, 36, 100, 188, 243, 252, 256f, 260–262, 353, 381, 393–407, 411f, 416–421, 448, 452f, 472–476, 478–480, 485
intermediate level 393, 395
Japanese 2, 20, 363–365, 370–375, 377–389, 460, 468f, 479
kkita 393–395, 397, 402, 405f, 412f, 415f, 420f
landmark 98f, 101f, 257, 286, 327, 329–332, 334, 338f, 349, 377, 397, 449, 459, 463, 465f, 469–471, 473, 475, 478
language acquisition 204, 248, 250f, 262, 273, 394, 405, 420, 487
lexical
– acquisition 243–245, 250, 273
– category 21, 70–72, 75–78, 82, 243, 260, 263f, 267, 272, 274f, 289, 314, 319, 363, 365, 398, 401, 427–429, 437, 445
– meaning 30, 93, 117, 211, 228, 243, 356, 444, 447f, 488f
– projection 166, 168, 170, 197, 200f
– selection 67f, 71, 78, 80, 89f
– semantics 1–3, 6, 67, 163, 216, 218, 223, 243, 256, 276, 314, 427, 445, 454
– variation 78–80
lexicology 68, 70–72, 78, 80, 89f
linguistic relativity 393, 395, 420f
linguistically motivated extension 245, 248, 274f

locative meaning 243f, 249f, 255, 260f, 264, 269, 274
major syntactic categories 364
meaning activation 29, 53, 58
meaning
– potential 21, 24, 29, 42–62, 97, 244, 458
– reification 29, 51, 53, 56f
– variation 29, 31, 40f, 56, 58–60
meaning-holism 479
metaphor 2, 7–17, 20f, 23–25, 37, 40–42, 47, 70f, 117, 170, 217, 235, 243f, 249, 272, 276, 295, 301, 331, 336, 348, 354, 365, 381f, 384–387, 389
metaphorical extension 40–42, 108, 238, 276, 297, 301, 305f, 365, 381f, 384, 386f
metonymy 2, 21, 70f, 94, 116, 211f, 215, 217, 225, 227, 232, 243f, 249, 304, 306, 348
modification 151, 364, 366, 379, 382f, 387–389
modifying function 363, 387–389
monosemic bias 342–344, 351, 354–356, 359, 399, 421
monosemy 18f, 36, 38, 40, 93, 342, 360, 427, 447, 449, 481
monosyllabic 243, 253
motivation 90, 94, 131, 178, 247, 323, 454, 479, 486f
multiple homonymy 343
network model 4, 22, 243–246, 305, 307
nominal adjectives 2, 20, 363–366, 378
non-basic sense 244
noun 20f, 35, 37f, 50, 52f, 106, 108, 171–175, 180f, 200, 232–234, 264, 345, 358, 363–375, 377–382, 384–389, 437, 439, 455, 469, 489
onomasiology 67–71, 79, 90, 216, 303, 312, 318f
partial schematicity 327, 330, 348
part-whole relationship 101–103, 108f, 114, 317
polysemy 2, 16, 18–20, 22, 29, 35–38, 40f, 43, 46–48, 55–62, 70, 93, 109, 113, 169, 182, 248–250, 264, 311, 314–317, 319, 323f, 341–345, 348, 353, 357, 359, 361, 406, 434, 436, 447–449, 451–454, 458, 462, 467, 469, 473, 475, 478, 480–488, 490
possessive pronoun 93, 108–111, 113, 115
posture verb 100–102
pragmatic
– functions 155, 168, 365
– relevance 243, 249, 256, 269
pragmatics 52, 67–71, 79, 87, 107, 125, 128, 131, 145, 155, 168f, 197, 202f, 216, 243, 256, 260, 269, 276, 343f, 353, 357, 360, 461, 484, 487, 489
preposition(s) 22, 36, 49, 52–54, 98–102, 108, 171, 243–276, 393–406, 411–413, 417–421, 447, 451f, 455, 462f, 469–473, 476, 479f, 485, 490
present context 147, 358f
prototype
– effects 275, 363, 365, 370
– structure 1f, 20, 363, 365, 372, 380, 389, 427
prototypical core 405, 429–432, 436
prototypicality 2, 22, 39, 67, 70, 72, 74f, 78, 88–90, 180, 295, 301, 303, 305, 315, 318, 326, 363, 371, 386, 389, 427, 429–431, 434–436, 438
reference-point relationship 93, 108, 115

relatedness of meaning 97, 323, 343, 345, 348, 360
rhetorical devices 429
salience 68, 71f, 76, 89, 112, 272, 276, 301, 303, 305, 312
schema 96, 213, 216f, 219–221, 223–225, 228–230, 232–237, 251, 286, 295, 308, 316, 338–341, 350f, 355, 360, 382, 408–410, 449–452
schematization 106, 243–245, 249, 251, 275, 305, 318
semantic
– backformation 211, 218, 232–234, 237
– change 21, 81, 125f, 131, 157, 211, 218, 225, 232, 235–238
– extension 182, 243–245, 248f, 272, 274–276, 311, 330, 381, 429
– functions 363, 365, 372, 388
– generality 447f, 452f, 482
– motivation 363, 365, 372
– transparency 243, 256
semantic-functional change 123, 131, 138, 145
semasiology 69–71, 293, 295, 301–303, 305, 307, 309, 312, 314–319
sense types 243f, 250, 252, 256f, 259–261, 263–271, 274
sentence types 163, 165, 176, 196f, 199–204
shift construction 173–175, 182f, 187, 192, 194f, 204
situatedness 454–457, 459, 468, 481, 490
sociolexicology 68, 78, 80f, 89
sociolinguistics 22, 67f, 72, 78, 80f, 88–90, 229f
spatial expressions 385, 447, 452, 462, 489f
specific level 351, 393
subjectification 131, 138, 145, 155
support 20, 82, 301, 393–395, 400, 402–415, 417f, 421
tight fit 393, 395, 397, 403–407, 412f, 416, 421
trajector 98, 101f, 295, 305, 327f, 330–334, 338f, 377, 449, 459, 463, 465–467, 469–471, 475, 478, 480
uni-/directionality 243, 249
usage-based model 211, 218, 230, 232, 238, 251, 382, 389
use-potential 447–449, 458, 481, 488, 490
variation 29, 31, 35, 37, 40f, 56, 58–60, 62, 67–69, 78–82, 84f, 88f, 168, 271, 316, 415, 417, 448f, 454, 467, 469, 473, 481, 483
verb 19f, 32f, 35, 38, 48–50, 52–54, 94, 100–102, 106, 125f, 130, 132, 139, 141, 144, 154, 163, 165f, 168–171, 176–184, 187, 189–191, 201f, 205, 222f, 233, 253, 260, 262, 264f, 269, 272, 281f, 286, 288, 299, 301–303, 307, 315f, 318f, 323f, 329, 343, 345, 352, 354, 356, 363f, 374, 383, 394f, 397, 402, 405, 420f, 440, 455, 461f, 471f, 478

Cognitive Linguistics Research

Edited by René Dirven, Ronald W. Langacker and John R. Taylor

Mouton de Gruyter · Berlin · New York

---

1 Ronald W. Langacker, *Concept, Image, and Symbol. The Cognitive Basis of Grammar.* 1990.
2 Paul D. Deane, *Grammar in Mind and Brain. Explorations in Cognitive Syntax.* 1992.
3 *Conceptualizations and Mental Processing in Language.* Edited by Richard A. Geiger and Brygida Rudzka-Ostyn. 1993.
4 Laura A. Janda, *A Geography of Case Semantics. The Czech Dative and the Russian Instrumental.* 1993.
5 Dirk Geeraerts, Stefan Grondelaers and Peter Bakema, *The Structure of Lexical Variation. Meaning, Naming, and Context.* 1994.
6 *Cognitive Linguistics in the Redwoods. The Expansion of a New Paradigm in Linguistics.* Edited by Eugene H. Casad. 1996.
7 John Newman, *Give. A Cognitive Linguistic Study.* 1996.
8 *The Construal of Space in Language and Thought.* Edited by Martin Pütz and René Dirven. 1996.
9 Ewa Dąbrowska, *Cognitive Semantics and the Polish Dative.* 1997.
10 *Speaking of Emotions: Conceptualisation and Expression.* Edited by Angeliki Athanasiadou and Elżbieta Tabakowska. 1998.
11 Michel Achard, *Representation of Cognitive Structures.* 1998.
12 *Issues in Cognitive Linguistics. 1993 Proceedings of the International Cognitive Linguistics Conference.* Edited by Leon de Stadler and Christoph Eyrich. 1999.
13 *Historical Semantics and Cognition.* Edited by Andreas Blank and Peter Koch. 1999.
14 Ronald W. Langacker, *Grammar and Conceptualization.* 1999.
15 *Cognitive Linguistics: Foundations, Scope, and Methodology.* Edited by Theo Janssen and Gisela Redeker. 1999.
16 *A Cognitive Approach to the Verb. Morphological and Constructional Perspectives.* Edited by Hanne Gram Simonsen and Rolf Theil Endresen. 2001.

17 *Emotions in Crosslinguistic Perspective.* Edited by Jean Harkins and Anna Wierzbicka. 2001.

18 *Cognitive Linguistics and Non-Indo-European Languages.* Edited by Eugene Casad and Gary B. Palmer. 2003.

19.1 *Applied Cognitive Linguistics I: Theory and Language Acquisition.* Edited by Martin Pütz, Susanne Niemeier and René Dirven. 2001.

19.2 *Applied Cognitive Linguistics II: Language Pedagogy.* Edited by Martin Pütz, Susanne Niemeier and René Dirven. 2001.

20 *Metaphor and Metonymy in Comparison and Contrast.* Edited by René Dirven and Ralf Pörings. 2002.

21 *Grounding. The Epistemic Footing of Deixis and Reference.* Edited by Frank Brisard. 2002.

22 Cristiano Broccias, *The English Change Network.* 2003.

23 *Cognitive Approaches to Lexical Semantics.* Edited by Hubert Cuyckens, René Dirven and John Taylor. 2003.

24 *Cognitive Models in Language and Thought. Ideology, Metaphors, and Meanings.* Edited by René Dirven, Roslyn Frank and Martin Pütz. 2003.

25 Rong Chen, *English Inversion. A Ground-before-Figure Construction.* 2003.

26 Liesbet Heyvaert, *A Cognitive-Functional Approach to Nominalization in English.* 2003.

Bei Fragen zur Produktsicherheit wenden Sie sich bitte an:
If you have any questions regarding product safety,
please contact:

Walter de Gruyter GmbH
Genthiner Straße 13
10785 Berlin
productsafety@degruyterbrill.com